T0179880

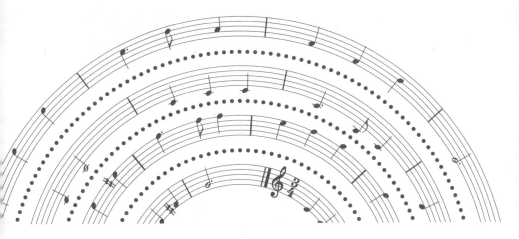

THE ONE YEAR ®

BOOK *of* HYMNS

· ·

365 DEVOTIONS BASED ON POPULAR HYMNS

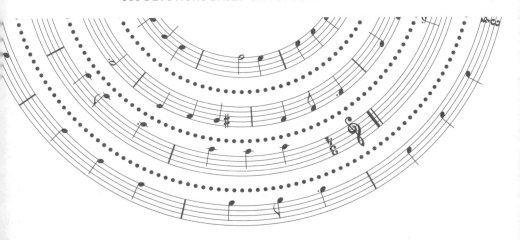

TYNDALE
MOMENTUM®

A Tyndale nonfiction imprint

Visit Tyndale Momentum online at tyndalemomentum.com.

Tyndale, Tyndale's quill logo, *Tyndale Momentum*, and the Tyndale Momentum logo are registered trademarks of Tyndale House Ministries. Tyndale Momentum is a nonfiction imprint of Tyndale House Publishers, Carol Stream, Illinois.

The One Year is a registered trademark of Tyndale House Ministries.

The One Year Book of Hymns: 365 Devotions Based on Popular Hymns

Copyright © 2024 by Robert K. Brown and Mark R. Norton. All rights reserved.

Previously published in 1995 under ISBN 978-0-8423-5072-3, in 2005 as *The One Year Great Songs of Faith* under ISBN 978-1-4143-0699-5, and in 2017 under ISBN 978-1-4964-2826-4.

Cover illustrations are the property of their respective copyright holders from TheNounProject.com, and all rights are reserved. Treble clef, sharp, and natural © Elizabeth Lopez; bass clef, eighth, quarter, and half notes © Rhys de Dezsery.

Cover designed by Sarah Susan Richardson

Edited by Kathryn S. Olson

Unless otherwise indicated, all Scripture quotations are taken from the *Holy Bible*, New Living Translation, copyright © 1996, 2004, 2015 by Tyndale House Foundation. Used by permission of Tyndale House Ministries, Carol Stream, Illinois 60188. All rights reserved.

Scripture quotations marked NKJV are taken from the New King James Version,® copyright © 1982 by Thomas Nelson, Inc. Used by permission. All rights reserved.

Scripture quotations marked NIV are taken from the Holy Bible, *New International Version*,® *NIV*.® Copyright © 1973, 1978, 1984, 2011 by Biblica, Inc.® Used by permission. All rights reserved worldwide.

Scripture quotations marked KJV are taken from the *Holy Bible*, King James Version.

For information about special discounts for bulk purchases, please contact Tyndale House Publishers at csresponse@tyndale.com, or call 1-855-277-9400.

ISBN 978-1-4964-8114-6

Printed in China

30   29   28   27   26   25   24
7   6   5   4   3   2   1

PREFACE

*Shout with joy to the LORD, all the earth! Worship the LORD
with gladness. Come before him, singing with joy.*
PSALM 100:1-2

From the earliest days of the church, the singing of hymns has been an integral part of Christian worship. In the book of Acts we find Paul and Silas "praying and singing hymns to God" (Acts 16:25) while chained in the Philippian jail. It was also the apostle Paul who admonished believers with these words: "Be filled with the Holy Spirit, singing psalms and hymns and spiritual songs among yourselves, and making music to the Lord in your hearts. And give thanks for everything to God the Father in the name of our Lord Jesus Christ" (Ephesians 5:18-20).

But the tradition of singing in worship is far older than even Paul and the early Christians. Many centuries earlier, Moses and his sister, Miriam, led the nation of Israel in song after their miraculous escape through the Red Sea. And who can forget King David, Israel's beloved singer, who composed numerous psalms expressing both personal and corporate praise. Centuries later, translations of the psalms would provide the nurturing cradle for English hymnody.

In centuries past, singing hymns was an important means for teaching Christian truth in a church that was largely illiterate. Even so, hymn singing was and is far more than just a way of disseminating knowledge. It is a means for all believers, educated or uneducated, great or lowly, to express praise to their Creator and Savior. It is a way for all of us to communicate with God using more than just words. It allows us to pour out the grateful feelings of the heart—feelings awakened by the experience of forgiveness and the gracious work of the Holy Spirit.

As you come each day to this devotional, lift your heart and voice in praise to the Lord of all peoples and centuries—Jesus Christ. Join the chorus of believers throughout history and throughout the earth as you express praise and commitment to God through their words. Meet the hymnwriters and discover how God's work in their lives has left this legacy of hymns for us to share. And as you worship through this treasury of hymns, look forward to the day when all believers—past, present, and future—will join in one great chorus around God's throne. For as the great hymnwriter Isaac Watts once recognized, "The singing of God's praise is the part of worship most closely related to heaven."

Another Year Is Dawning

Frances Ridley Havergal enjoyed New Year's Day. It was a day of promise, looking forward in faith to God's blessing in the coming twelve months. She had such a positive spirit that when she entered a room, it was said she brought a "burst of sunshine." New Year's Day was the source for today's hymn, "Another Year Is Dawning," which she wrote on a card she was sending to a friend.

Frances Havergal died when she was only forty-three. Even at the end of her life she remained steadfast in reminding Christians that "fresh glory" is just as important as fresh air and fresh water. We need to celebrate God's glorious mercies each new day as well as each new year.

• • • •

May the Lord bless you and protect you. May the Lord smile on you and be gracious to you. May the Lord show you his favor and give you his peace.

NUMBERS 6:24-26

Another year is dawning:
 Dear Father, let it be,
In working or in waiting,
 Another year with Thee;
Another year of progress,
 Another year of praise,
Another year of proving
 Thy presence all the days.

Another year of mercies,
Of faithfulness and grace;
Another year of gladness
In the shining of Thy face;
Another year of leaning
Upon Thy loving breast;
Another year of trusting,
 Of quiet, happy rest.

Another year of service,
 Of witness for Thy love;
Another year of training
 For holier work above.
Another year is dawning:
 Dear Father, let it be,
On earth or else in heaven,
 Another year for Thee.

Frances Ridley Havergal (1836–1879)

May the Mind of Christ, My Savior

May the mind of Christ, my Savior,
Live in me from day to day,
By His love and pow'r controlling
All I do and say.

May the word of God dwell richly
In my heart from hour to hour,
So that all may see I triumph
Only through His pow'r.

May the peace of God my Father
Rule my life in ev'rything,
That I may be calm to comfort
Sick and sorrowing.

May the love of Jesus fill me
As the waters fill the sea;
Him exalting, self abasing—
This is victory.

May I run the race before me,
Strong and brave to face the foe,
Looking only unto Jesus
As I onward go.

May His beauty rest upon me
As I seek the lost to win,
And may they forget the channel,
Seeing only Him.

Kate B. Wilkinson (1859–1928)

Many Christians have made the New Year's resolution to be more like Jesus—but where do you start? The apostle Paul told the Philippian believers, "You must have the same attitude that Christ Jesus had" (Philippians 2:5). But how do we develop the attitude of Christ? Kate Wilkinson directs us to Colossians 3:16 for the answer: "Let the message about Christ, in all its richness, fill your lives." In the third stanza Wilkinson returns to Philippians for this promise: "God's peace . . . will guard your hearts and minds as you live in Christ Jesus" (Philippians 4:7). And so the song builds.

Christian growth is not instantaneous but gradual. It flows naturally from obeying God's Word. Thomas à Kempis, who wrote the Christian classic *The Imitation of Christ*, said, "One thing that draws back many from spiritual progress is the fear of the difficulty of the labor of the combat." Don't give up what you have started.

• • • •

Let the message about Christ, in all its richness, fill your lives. Teach and counsel each other with all the wisdom he gives. Sing psalms and hymns and spiritual songs to God with thankful hearts. And whatever you do or say, do it as a representative of the Lord Jesus.

COLOSSIANS 3:16-17

Great God, We Sing That Mighty Hand

In Scripture the "hand of God" often refers to judgment. But for the Christian it is also an image of providential care. We can see this throughout the book of Ezra, where Ezra attributed his success to the fact that the gracious hand of God was upon him.

Philip Doddridge felt the same way. The youngest of twenty children, Doddridge was considered too sickly to live, but the gracious hand of God was upon him. His parents died when he was only a teenager, but he was taken in by a minister who nurtured him in spiritual matters. Doddridge became a pastor, an educator, a hymnwriter, and an author. One theme remained uppermost in his mind—the providence of God. He wrote his hymns to illustrate his sermons and taught them to his congregation after he finished preaching. "Great God, We Sing That Mighty Hand" apparently illustrated a New Year's sermon.

• • • •

The Lord is a shelter for the oppressed, a refuge in times of trouble. Those who know your name trust in you, for you, O Lord, do not abandon those who search for you.

PSALM 9:9-10

Great God, we sing that mighty hand
By which supported still we stand;
The opening year Thy mercy shows;
That mercy crowns it till it close.

By day, by night, at home, abroad,
Still are we guarded by our God;
By His incessant bounty fed,
By His unerring counsel led.

With grateful hearts the past we own;
The future, all to us unknown,
We to Thy guardian care commit,
And peaceful leave before Thy feet.

In scenes exalted or depressed,
Thou art our Joy, and Thou our Rest;
Thy goodness all our hopes shall raise,
Adored through all our changing days.

Philip Doddridge (1702-1751)

Lead, Kindly Light!

Lead, kindly Light! amid th'encircling gloom,
Lead Thou me on;
The night is dark, and I am far from home,
Lead Thou me on;
Keep Thou my feet: I do not ask to see
The distant scene; one step enough for me.

I was not ever thus, nor prayed that Thou
Shouldst lead me on;
I loved to choose and see my path; but now
Lead Thou me on;
I loved the garish day, and, spite of fears,
Pride ruled my will. Remember not past years.

So long Thy pow'r has blessed me, sure it still
Will lead me on
O'er moor and fen, o'er crag and torrent, till
The night is gone;
And with the morn those angel faces smile
Which I have loved long since, and lost awhile!

John Henry Newman (1801-1890)

In 1833 John Henry Newman, a leader in the Church of England, went to visit Catholic leaders in Italy. There he contracted Sicilian fever and boarded a ship back to England. But a lack of wind kept the ship motionless in the Mediterranean, and a dense fog left them unable to navigate. Restless and sick, Newman penned the words of this hymn. Along with his desire for physical health, he wanted to see spiritual recovery in the Church of England. And he wanted the ship to get moving!

Finally, the ship's captain pointed heavenward and said, "The star is shining tonight. If a wind rises, we can chart our course. At night one little star is sufficient." Newman took that as a divine assurance. He later wrote that he had been looking for dazzling sunlight to guide him through his life, "but He sent me the kindly light of a star to show me the way one step at a time."

• • • •

Your own ears will hear him. Right behind you a voice will say, "This is the way you should go," whether to the right or to the left.
ISAIAH 30:21

The Lord's My Shepherd, I'll Not Want

Scottish Bibles in the seventeenth century often had psalms in meter printed after the book of Revelation. The metrical psalms were sung twice a day in most of the humble cottages of Scotland and so became more familiar to the people than the Bible text itself.

This text of the familiar Twenty-third Psalm comes from a metrical version by Francis Rous, a member of the British Parliament. He was dissatisfied with the accuracy of other psalm translations being used by the Puritans, some of which took liberties with the meaning to make the words rhyme. As you can see, this version is a faithful paraphrase of David's original. Rous's Psalter was widely used and was authorized by the Westminster Assembly, which also created the Westminster Confession of Faith.

• • • •

The Lord is my shepherd; I have all that
I need. He lets me rest in green meadows;
he leads me beside peaceful streams. He
renews my strength. He guides me along
right paths, bringing honor to his name.

PSALM 23:1-3

The Lord's my Shepherd, I'll not want;
He makes me down to lie
In pastures green; He leadeth me
The quiet waters by.

My soul He doth restore again;
And me to walk doth make
Within the paths of righteousness,
E'en for His own name's sake.

Yea, though I walk through death's dark vale,
Yet will I fear no ill;
For Thou art with me, and Thy rod
And staff me comfort still.

My table Thou hast furnished
In presence of my foes;
My head Thou dost with oil anoint,
And my cup overflows.

Goodness and mercy all my life
Shall surely follow me;
And in God's house forevermore
My dwelling place shall be.

Scottish Psalter, 1650

We Three Kings of Orient Are

We three kings of Orient are;
Bearing gifts we traverse afar,
Field and fountain, moor and mountain,
Following yonder star.

**O star of wonder, star of night,
Star with royal beauty bright,
Westward leading, still proceeding,
Guide us to thy perfect light.**

Born a King on Bethlehem's plain,
Gold I bring to crown Him again,
King forever, ceasing never
Over us all to reign.

Frankincense to offer have I;
Incense owns a Deity nigh;
Prayer and praising all men raising,
Worship Him, God on high.

Myrrh is mine: its bitter perfume
Breathes a life of gathering gloom:
Sorrowing, sighing, bleeding, dying,
Sealed in the stone-cold tomb.

Glorious now behold Him arise,
King and God and sacrifice;
Alleluia, Alleluia!
Sounds through the earth and skies.

John Henry Hopkins, Jr. (1820-1891)

Unfortunately, we tend to sing only the first stanza of most Christmas carols, even though the depth of meaning is often found in later stanzas. Everyone knows that the wise men brought gifts, but what was their significance? John Henry Hopkins, an Episcopalian minister (as well as a news reporter and stained-glass artist), pondered this question in hymn form in 1857.

Gold was a gift for a king. Frankincense was brought by priests in their worship of God. Myrrh was a spice used in burial. Thus Jesus was honored by these sages as King, God, and Sacrifice.

How then shall we approach the King of kings? What gold shall we bring? What incense can we offer as priests of our God? How can we honor our crucified Lord? It makes sense to consider these questions today, the traditional date of Epiphany, celebrating the magi's worship of our Lord.

• • • •

Now after Jesus was born in Bethlehem of Judea in the days of Herod the king, behold, wise men from the East came to Jerusalem, saying, "Where is He who has been born King of the Jews? For we have seen His star in the East and have come to worship Him."
MATTHEW 2:1-2, NKJV

As with Gladness, Men of Old

The church has traditionally celebrated the coming of the wise men two weeks after Christmas. But on Epiphany Sunday in 1860, William Dix was too sick to attend church. At home in bed, he read the story of the wise men and tried to apply the lesson to his own heart. The result was a new Christmas hymn that celebrated while it instructed, one that applied not only to the author, but to future generations of Christians as well. The pattern is obvious: As the wise men did—following, adoring, giving—so should we.

Dix was a brilliant linguist and poet, but he made his living as the manager of a maritime insurance company in Glasgow, Scotland. He knew the rigors of travel and the joy of bringing gifts from afar. Yet rather than focusing on the costliness of the magi's gifts, Dix emphasized the magi's finding of what they sought and their worship of the Christ child.

• • • •

When they saw the star, they were filled with joy! They entered the house and saw the child with his mother, Mary, and they bowed down and worshiped him. Then they opened their treasure chests and gave him gifts of gold, frankincense, and myrrh.

MATTHEW 2:10-11

As with gladness men of old
Did the guiding star behold;
As with joy they hailed its light,
Leading onward, beaming bright;
So, most gracious Lord, may we
Evermore be led to Thee.

As with joyous steps they sped
To that lowly manger bed,
There to bend the knee before
Him whom heaven and earth adore;
So may we with willing feet
Ever seek Thy mercy seat.

As they offered gifts most rare
At the manger rude and bare,
So may we with holy joy,
Pure and free from sin's alloy,
All our costliest treasures bring,
Christ, to Thee, our heavenly King.

Holy Jesus, every day
Keep us in the narrow way;
And, when earthly things are past,
Bring our ransomed souls at last
Where they need no star to guide,
Where no clouds Thy glory hide.

In the heavenly country bright
Need they no created light;
Thou its light, its joy, its crown,
Thou its sun which goes not down,
There forever may we sing
Hallelujah to our King.

William Chatterton Dix (1837-1898)

Like a River Glorious

Like a river glorious
Is God's perfect peace,
Over all victorious
In its bright increase;
Perfect, yet it floweth
Fuller ev'ry day,
Perfect, yet it groweth
Deeper all the way.

**Stayed upon Jehovah,
Hearts are fully blest—
Finding as He promised
Perfect peace and rest.**

Hidden in the hollow
Of His blessed hand,
Never foe can follow,
Never traitor stand;
Not a surge of worry,
Not a shade of care,
Not a blast of hurry
Touch the spirit there.

Ev'ry joy or trial
Falleth from above,
Traced upon our dial
By the sun of love;
We may trust Him fully
All for us to do—
They who trust Him wholly
Find Him wholly true.

Frances Ridley Havergal (1836–1879)

It is difficult to remain calm while reading the daily paper or watching the TV news. The world is filled with violence and senseless crime. But Frances Ridley Havergal, a devout Bible scholar as well as a poet, drew upon two passages from the prophet Isaiah to give fresh understanding to Christian peace in difficult circumstances. More than once in Isaiah, God promises "peace like a river." And in Isaiah 26:3 the prophet says, "You will keep in perfect peace all who trust in you, all whose thoughts are fixed on you!" These verses have served as the basis of many hymns over the last two centuries, but none is as picturesque as this one.

It is not only peace that God promises, but perfect peace—perfected, completed in Christ.

• • • •

Oh, that you had listened to my commands! Then you would have had peace flowing like a gentle river and righteousness rolling over you like waves in the sea.
ISAIAH 48:18

Jesus, Lead Thou On

The writer of this hymn, Count Nicolaus von Zinzendorf, knew all about problems. One biographer comments, "Although one of the worthiest of men, Zinzendorf had to bear the misrepresentation of friends as well as the opposition of enemies. He was continually spoken against."

As a German count, he was a man of wealth and position. But as a Christian, he opened his estate to persecuted Moravian believers. While visiting the king of Denmark, he met a slave from the West Indies who told him of the bitter conditions there. Soon Zinzendorf organized a mission to the West Indies, one of the earliest European missionary endeavors. Even in this, he was criticized and misunderstood by religious and secular authorities. Zinzendorf knew well that the way was "often cheerless," yet he followed "calm and fearless" in the footsteps of Christ.

• • • •

And through your faith, God is protecting you by his power until you receive this salvation, which is ready to be revealed on the last day for all to see. So be truly glad. There is wonderful joy ahead, even though you have to endure many trials for a little while.

I PETER 1:5-6

Jesus, lead Thou on
Till our rest is won;
And although the way be cheerless,
We will follow calm and fearless:
Guide us by Thy hand
To our fatherland.

If the way be drear,
If the foe be near,
Let not faithless fears o'ertake us;
Let not faith and hope forsake us;
For through many a woe
To our home we go.

When we seek relief
From a long-felt grief;
When temptations come alluring,
Make us patient and enduring;
Show us that bright shore
Where we weep no more.

Jesus, lead Thou on
Till our rest is won.
Heav'nly Leader, still direct us,
Still support, control, protect us,
Till we safely stand
In our fatherland.

Nicolaus von Zinzendorf (1700-1760)

Collected and arranged by Christian Gregor (1723-1801)
Translated by Jane Laurie Borthwick (1813-1897)

Be Still, My Soul

Be still, my soul! the Lord is on thy side;
Bear patiently the cross of grief or pain;
Leave to thy God to order and provide;
In every change He faithful will remain.
Be still, my soul! thy best, thy heavenly Friend
Through thorny ways leads to a joyful end.

Be still, my soul! thy God doth undertake
To guide the future as He has the past.
Thy hope, thy confidence let nothing shake;
All now mysterious shall be bright at last.
Be still, my soul! the waves and winds still know
His voice who ruled them while He dwelt below.

Be still, my soul! the hour is hastening on
When we shall be forever with the Lord,
When disappointment, grief, and fear are gone,
Sorrow forgot, love's purest joys restored.
Be still, my soul! when change and tears are past,
All safe and blessed we shall meet at last.

Katharina Amalia von Schlegel (1697–?)

Translated by Jane Laurie Borthwick (1813–1897)

In the midst of the psalmist's troubles, the Lord said, "Be still, and know that I am God." These words spoke to Katharina von Schlegel in the turbulent times of post-Reformation Germany. A century after Luther's reforms, central Europe was racked by the Thirty Years' War, which pitted Catholics against Protestants. The Lutheran church lapsed into formalism and dead orthodoxy. In the darkness of that time, God raised up the Pietist movement, which stressed personal holiness, charity, missions, and music.

The songs of the Pietists were largely unknown outside of Germany until three British women—Jane and Sarah Borthwick and Catherine Winkworth—began to translate them into English a hundred years later. Today's hymn, penned by the leading woman of the Pietist movement, a canoness of a women's seminary, was among those forgotten songs.

• • • •

"Be still, and know that I am God! I will be honored by every nation. I will be honored throughout the world." The Lord of Heaven's Armies is here among us; the God of Israel is our fortress.
PSALM 46:10-11

Fear Not, O Little Flock

As Martin Luther's great hymn "A Mighty Fortress Is Our God" (October 31) was the battle cry of the Protestant Reformation, this hymn by Lutheran pastor Johann Altenberg became the battle cry of the Protestant cause during the Thirty Years' War (1618–1648). While the conflict began as a quarrel over the throne of Bohemia, it was primarily a religious battle. The Catholic emperor of the Holy Roman Empire sought to install Catholic leadership in Bohemia but was resisted by the Protestant princes in Germany and Scandinavia. The result was thirty years of suffering for millions of innocent people throughout Europe.

King Gustavus of Sweden, possibly the greatest of the Protestant military leaders, had his army sing this hymn before fighting the Battle of Lützen. The roused army of Gustavus was victorious, but their king died in the battle. Ever since, this hymn has been associated with this pious Swedish king.

· · · ·

Can anything ever separate us from Christ's love? Does it mean he no longer loves us if we have trouble or calamity, or are persecuted, or hungry, or destitute, or in danger, or threatened with death? . . . No, despite all these things, overwhelming victory is ours through Christ, who loved us.

ROMANS 8:35, 37

Fear not, O little flock, the foe
Who madly seeks your overthrow;
Dread not his rage and pow'r:
What though your courage sometimes faints,
His seeming triumph o'er God's saints
Lasts but a little hour.

Be of good cheer; your cause belongs
To Him who can avenge your wrongs;
Leave it to Him, our Lord:
Though hidden yet from all our eyes,
He sees the Gideon who shall rise
To save us and His Word.

As true as God's own Word is true,
Nor earth nor hell with all their crew
Against us shall prevail.
A jest and byword are they grown;
God is with us, we are His own;
Our vict'ry cannot fail.

Amen, Lord Jesus, grant our pray'r;
Great Captain, now Thine arm make bare,
Fight for us once again;
So shall Thy saints and martyrs raise
A mighty chorus to Thy praise,
World without end.

Johann Michael Altenberg (1590–1650)

Translated by Catherine Winkworth (1827–1878)

Guide Me, O Thou Great Jehovah

Guide me, O Thou great Jehovah,
Pilgrim through this barren land;
I am weak, but Thou art mighty;
Hold me with Thy powerful hand;
Bread of heaven, Bread of heaven,
Feed me till I want no more,
Feed me till I want no more.

Open now the crystal fountain,
Whence the healing stream doth flow;
Let the fire and cloudy pillar
Lead me all my journey through;
Strong deliverer, strong deliverer,
Be Thou still my strength and shield,
Be Thou still my strength and shield.

When I tread the verge of Jordan,
Bid my anxious fears subside;
Death of death and hell's destruction,
Land me safe on Canaan's side;
Songs of praises, songs of praises
I will ever give to Thee,
I will ever give to Thee.

William Williams (1717–1791)

Stanza 1 translated from Welsh by Peter Williams (1722–1796)
Stanzas 2 and 3 probably translated by the author

Wouldn't you like to know what next December holds in store for you? But it's still January! God leads us a day at a time, a step at a time. No need to worry about distant events. The Welsh hymnwriter William Williams compared the Christian life to the Israelites' trek through the wilderness. We may not know the route by which God is leading us, but we humbly count on His guidance.

As a college student, Williams prepared for a career in medicine. But one Sunday morning he heard a man preaching in a Welsh churchyard. Williams responded in faith, and his life was radically changed. For forty-three years he preached and sang throughout Wales. "He sang Wales into piety," said one writer. He was the poet laureate of the Welsh revival. Soon all of Wales was singing their way to the coal mines and soccer matches. And their favorite hymn was this marching song by one of their own.

• • • •

The Lord will guide you continually, giving you water when you are dry and restoring your strength. You will be like a well-watered garden, like an ever-flowing spring.
ISAIAH 58:11

I Need Thee Every Hour

You don't often think of hymns being written by thirty-seven-year-old homemakers from Brooklyn, but that's the story of this hymn. Annie Hawks was busy with her household chores when the words came to her. She later wrote, "I was so filled with a sense of nearness to my Master that, wondering how one could live without Him in either joy or pain, these words, 'I need thee every hour,' were flashed into my mind. Seating myself by the open window in the balmy air of the bright June day, I caught up my pencil and the words were soon committed to paper."

Hawks reflected, "It was not until years later, when the shadow fell over my way, the shadow of a great loss, that I understood something of the comforting power in the words." God often allows us to learn in the sunshine what we will need to lean on in the darkness.

• • • •

*Bend down, O Lord, and hear my prayer;
answer me, for I need your help. Protect
me, for I am devoted to you. Save me, for I
serve you and trust you. You are my God. Be
merciful to me, O Lord, for I am calling on
you constantly. Give me happiness, O Lord,
for I give myself to you.*

PSALM 86:1-4

I need Thee ev'ry hour,
Most gracious Lord;
No tender voice like Thine
Can peace afford.

I need Thee, O I need Thee;
Ev'ry hour I need Thee!
O bless me now, my Savior,
I come to Thee.

I need Thee ev'ry hour,
Stay Thou nearby;
Temptations lose their pow'r
When Thou art nigh.

I need Thee ev'ry hour,
In joy or pain;
Come quickly, and abide,
Or life is vain.

I need Thee ev'ry hour,
Teach me Thy will,
And Thy rich promises
In me fulfill.

Annie Sherwood Hawks (1835–1918)

Robert Lowry (1826–1899), refrain

13

It Is Good to Sing Thy Praises

It is good to sing Thy praises
And to thank Thee, O Most High,
Showing forth Thy loving-kindness
When the morning lights the sky.
It is good when night is falling
Of Thy faithfulness to tell,
While with sweet, melodious praises
Songs of adoration swell.

Thou hast filled my heart with gladness
Thro' the works Thy hands have wrought;
Thou hast made my life victorious,
Great Thy works and deep Thy thought.
Thou, O Lord, on high exalted,
Reignest evermore in might;
All Thy enemies shall perish,
Sin be banished from Thy sight.

But the good shall live before Thee,
Planted in Thy dwelling place,
Fruitful trees and ever verdant,
Nourished by Thy boundless grace.
In His goodness to the righteous
God His righteousness displays;
God my Rock, my Strength, my Refuge,
Just and true are all His ways.

The Psalter, 1912

Commenting on Psalm 92, Charles Haddon Spurgeon said, "Silent worship is sweet, but vocal worship is sweeter." Maybe you are a "silent worshiper." Certainly Scripture affirms the importance of quiet meditation. But it also urges us to sing out in praise to God. The psalmists often fretted about their enemies, but when they launched out in praise, they were no longer alarmed. As Martin Luther said, "Come, let us sing a psalm and drive away the devil." There is power in a song of thanksgiving. As Isaac Watts paraphrased this psalm: "Sweet is the work, my God and King, to praise Thy name, give thanks, and sing."

Upon their return from exile in Babylon, the Jews began their Sabbath services in the Temple with this psalm. In fact, it is the only psalm with an inscription indicating Sabbath use. What a great way to begin any day!

• • • •

It is good to give thanks to the Lord, to sing praises to the Most High. It is good to proclaim your unfailing love in the morning, your faithfulness in the evening. . . . You thrill me, Lord, with all you have done for me! I sing for joy because of what you have done.

PSALM 92:1-2, 4

Lead On, O King Eternal

In 1887 Ernest Shurtleff was about to graduate from Andover Seminary. Because he had already had four books of poetry published, his classmates asked him to write the class poem. Instead of writing a poem, Ernest wrote a hymn for the entire graduating class to sing. He told his fellow seminarians, "We've been spending days of preparation here at seminary. Now the day of march has come, and we must go out to follow the leadership of the King of kings, to conquer the world under His banner."

Thus, "Lead On, O King Eternal" was written for a seminary graduating class. Our commencements are not always so dramatic, but there is no reason our eternal King cannot open a new door for us today. We can step out and march forward under His banner, "not with fears, for gladness breaks like morning where'er [His] face appears."

• • • •

Attending [the Lord] were mighty seraphim, each having six wings. With two wings they covered their faces, with two they covered their feet, and with two they flew. They were calling out to each other, "Holy, holy, holy is the Lord of Heaven's Armies! The whole earth is filled with his glory!"
ISAIAH 6:2-3

Lead on, O King eternal,
The day of march has come;
Henceforth in fields of conquest
Thy tents shall be our home.
Through days of preparation
Thy grace has made us strong,
And now, O King eternal,
We lift our battle song.

Lead on, O King eternal,
Till sin's fierce war shall cease,
And holiness shall whisper
The sweet amen of peace.
For not with swords' loud clashing,
Nor roll of stirring drums,
With deeds of love and mercy
The heavenly kingdom comes.

Lead on, O King eternal,
We follow, not with fears,
For gladness breaks like morning
Where'er Thy face appears.
Thy cross is lifted o'er us;
We journey in its light;
The crown awaits the conquest;
Lead on, O God of might.

Ernest Warburton Shurtleff (1862–1917)

All the Way My Savior Leads Me

All the way my Savior leads me;
   What have I to ask beside?
   Can I doubt His tender mercy,
Who through life has been my guide?
Heav'nly peace, divinest comfort,
   Here by faith in Him to dwell!
For I know whate'er befall me,
   Jesus doeth all things well;
For I know whate'er befall me,
   Jesus doeth all things well.

All the way my Savior leads me;
Cheers each winding path I tread,
   Gives me grace for ev'ry trial,
   Feeds me with the living bread:
Though my weary steps may falter,
   And my soul athirst may be,
Gushing from the Rock before me,
   Lo! a spring of joy I see;
Gushing from the Rock before me,
   Lo! a spring of joy I see.

All the way my Savior leads me;
   Oh, the fullness of His love!
Perfect rest to me is promised
   In my Father's house above:
When my spirit, cloth'd immortal,
   Wings its flight to realms of day,
This my song through endless ages:
   Jesus led me all the way;
This my song through endless ages:
   Jesus led me all the way.

Fanny Jane Crosby (1820–1915)

"Jesus doeth all things well." It probably wasn't always easy for Fanny Crosby to believe that. When she was only six weeks old, she lost her sight because of a doctor's error. "I have always believed," she said, "that the good Lord, in His infinite mercy, by this means consecrated me to the work that I am still permitted to do." And generations of hymn singers have been blessed by Crosby's thoughtful and praise-filled hymn texts.

This particular hymn was written on a day when Crosby needed five dollars and didn't know where she would get it. She prayed about it, and a few minutes later a stranger came to her door and handed her that exact amount.

She was amazed at the Lord's marvelous answer to her simple prayer. She wrote, "My first thought was, 'It is so wonderful the way the Lord leads me.'"

• • • •

O God, we meditate on your unfailing love as we worship in your Temple. As your name deserves, O God, you will be praised to the ends of the earth. Your strong right hand is filled with victory. . . . He is our God forever and ever, and he will guide us until we die.
PSALM 48:9-10, 14

Begin, My Tongue, Some Heavenly Theme

In his original hymnal, Isaac Watts put this hymn under the heading "The Faithfulness of God." At that point there were six stanzas, one of which was "Proclaim 'Salvation from the Lord for wretched dying men!' His hand has writ the sacred Word with an immortal pen."

A Yorkshire preacher, speaking of the sure promises of God, told of seeing a young lad rubbing at the engraved letters on a brass plate, trying to rub them out. The harder he rubbed, the brighter the letters shone. "Ah," said the preacher, "that is what Satan is trying to do. But the harder he rubs, the more it shines, because God's hand has writ the sacred Word with an immortal pen."

Your faith in God's promises may be under attack, but you can rest in the assurance that God's Word stands firm. The harshest opposition only serves to enhance the brilliance of His care for you.

Begin, my tongue, some heav'nly theme
And speak some boundless thing:
The mighty works or mightier name
Of our eternal King.

Tell of His wondrous faithfulness
And sound His pow'r abroad;
Sing the sweet promise of His grace,
The love and truth of God.

His very word of grace is strong
As that which built the skies;
The voice that rolls the stars along
Speaks all the promises.

O might I hear Thy heav'nly tongue
But whisper, "Thou art mine!"
Those gentle words shall raise my song
To notes almost divine.

Isaac Watts (1674–1748)

• • • •

Then I will praise you with music on the harp, because you are faithful to your promises, O my God. I will sing praises to you with a lyre, O Holy One of Israel. I will shout for joy and sing your praises, for you have ransomed me.
PSALM 71:22-23

Lamp of Our Feet

Lamp of our feet, whereby we trace
Our path when wont to stray,
Stream from the fount of heavenly grace,
Brook by the traveler's way.

Bread of our souls, whereon we feed,
True manna from on high,
Our guide and chart, wherein we read
Of realms beyond the sky.

Word of the everliving God,
Will of His glorious Son:
Without Thee how could earth be trod,
Or heaven itself be won?

Lord, grant us all aright to learn
The wisdom it imparts,
And to its heavenly teaching turn,
With simple, childlike hearts.

Bernard Barton (1784-1849)

Psalm 119 is a marvelous and ingenious poem, praising God for His Word in verse after verse. In the Hebrew, it is a cleverly constructed acrostic, going through the entire alphabet in eight-verse stanzas. That is, each line in the first stanza begins with *aleph*, the first Hebrew letter; with *beth* (the second letter) in the second stanza; and so on.

Throughout the psalm, God's Word is described in many ways, but the picture in verse 105 stands out: "Your Word is a lamp to my feet and a light for my path."

Early in the last century, as Bernard Barton wrote this hymn, he incorporated several biblical images to describe God's Word: a lamp, a stream, bread, and a chart or map. Scripture describes itself as being an indispensable source of life, as many, many believers have found to be true.

• • • •

Your word is a lamp to guide my feet and a light for my path. . . . Your laws are wonderful. No wonder I obey them! The teaching of your word gives light, so even the simple can understand.
PSALM 119:105, 129-130

He Leadeth Me!

The Civil War was being waged, and the outcome was still uncertain. Joseph Gilmore, pastor of Philadelphia's First Baptist Church, wanted to turn his people's attention to the security of God's guidance. The important thing, he said, is to know that God is leading—no matter *how* or *where* He leads us. After the service, Gilmore went to a deacon's home, and the conversation continued to revolve around the blessedness of God's leading. As others went on talking, he took out a pencil and wrote the words of this hymn, gave it to his wife, and forgot about it.

Three years later he was a pastoral candidate for a church in Rochester, New York. Since he was unfamiliar with the church's hymnal, he began leafing through it and spotted the hymn "He Leadeth Me"—his own hymn! Without his knowledge, Mrs. Gilmore had sent the words to a Christian periodical, which had them set to music.

He leadeth me! O blessed thought!
O words with heav'nly comfort fraught!
Whate'er I do, where'er I be,
Still 'tis God's hand that leadeth me!

He leadeth me, He leadeth me,
By His own hand He leadeth me:
His faithful follower I would be,
For by His hand He leadeth me.

Lord, I would clasp Thy hand in mine,
Nor ever murmur nor repine,
Content, whatever lot I see,
Since 'tis Thy hand that leadeth me!

And when my task on earth is done,
When, by Thy grace, the vict'ry's won,
E'en death's cold wave I will not flee,
Since God through Jordan leadeth me!

Joseph Henry Gilmore (1834–1918)

• • • •

You are my rock and my fortress. For the honor of your name, lead me out of this danger.

PSALM 31:3

Come, Sound His Praise Abroad

Come, sound His praise abroad
And hymns of glory sing:
Jehovah is the sovereign God,
The universal King.

He formed the deeps unknown;
He gave the seas their bound;
The watery worlds are all His own,
And all the solid ground.

Come, worship at His throne;
Come, bow before the Lord:
We are His works and not our own;
He formed us by His Word.

Today attend His voice,
Nor dare provoke His rod;
Come, like the people of His choice,
And own your gracious God.

Isaac Watts (1674-1748)

Even as a child, Isaac Watts liked to make rhymes. Once when he was scolded by his father for making rhymes in ordinary conversation, he responded, "Oh, Father, do some pity take, and I will no more verses make." But Isaac Watts continued to write poems. As an older teenager, he complained about the ponderous psalms the church was singing. His exasperated father told Isaac that if he was dissatisfied he should write something better. So he did. For the next two years the young Watts wrote a new hymn every week.

Many of the hymns, like "Come, Sound His Praise Abroad," were paraphrases of the psalms. Later in life, Watts said, "My design was not to exalt myself to the rank and glory of poets, but I was ambitious to be a servant to the churches, and a helper to the joy of the [lowliest] Christian."

• • • •

Come, let us sing to the Lord! Let us shout joyfully to the Rock of our salvation. Let us come to him with thanksgiving. Let us sing psalms of praise to him. For the Lord is a great God, a great King above all gods.
PSALM 95:1-3

In Heavenly Love Abiding

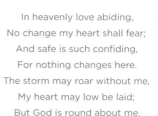

Anna Laetitia Waring was a shy, retiring woman who lived in south Wales. If her best-known hymns are any indication, she was also concerned about the changes that she might have to face in the future. In another hymn she prayed, "So I ask Thee for the daily strength to none that ask denied, and a mind to blend with outward life while keeping at Thy side, content to fill a little space if Thou be glorified."

A brilliant woman, Waring taught herself Hebrew so she could read the Old Testament in the original language. Despite her shyness, she spent much of her later years visiting prisons, yet she always avoided publicity. She was "content to fill a little space." And despite the changes in society—and there were plenty during her long life—she learned the truth of this hymn. When God is round about us, how can we be dismayed?

• • • •

Yes, the Sovereign Lord is coming in power. He will rule with a powerful arm. See, he brings his reward with him as he comes. He will feed his flock like a shepherd. He will carry the lambs in his arms, holding them close to his heart. He will gently lead the mother sheep with their young.

ISAIAH 40:10-11

In heavenly love abiding,
No change my heart shall fear;
And safe is such confiding,
For nothing changes here.
The storm may roar without me,
My heart may low be laid;
But God is round about me,
And can I be dismayed?

Wherever He may guide me,
No want shall turn me back;
My Shepherd is beside me,
And nothing can I lack.
His wisdom ever waketh,
His sight is never dim;
He knows the way He taketh,
And I will walk with Him.

Green pastures are before me,
Which yet I have not seen;
Bright skies will soon be o'er me,
Where darkest clouds have been.
My hope I cannot measure,
My path to life is free;
My Savior has my treasure,
And He will walk with me.

Anna Laetitia Waring (1823-1910)

God Moves in a Mysterious Way

God moves in a mysterious way
His wonders to perform;
He plants His footsteps in the sea,
And rides upon the storm.

Deep in unfathomable mines
Of never-failing skill,
He treasures up His bright designs,
And works His sovereign will.

Ye fearful saints, fresh courage take;
The clouds ye so much dread
Are big with mercy, and shall break
With blessing on your head.

Judge not the Lord by feeble sense,
But trust Him for His grace;
Behind a frowning providence
He hides a smiling face.

His purposes will ripen fast,
Unfolding every hour;
The bud may have a bitter taste,
But sweet will be the flower.

Blind unbelief is sure to err,
And scan His work in vain;
God is His own interpreter,
And He will make it plain.

William Cowper (1731–1800)

William Cowper, whose poems appear in most collections of great English literature, was beset with emotional problems throughout his life. His mother died when he was six, at school he was teased and ridiculed, and his father prevented him from marrying the girl he loved. Forced to study law, he panicked when he learned he would have his bar exam before the House of Lords—and tried to commit suicide. After a year in an insane asylum, he was released into the care of a Christian couple.

It seemed that hymnwriting was the best therapy Cowper could get. But mental illness continued to plague the poet, and he frequently lapsed into deep depression. You can almost see his self-portrait in the "fearful saints" who need to take "fresh courage" in the future blessings of God. Intellectually he knew the truth of these lines, but emotionally he was still trying to grasp it.

• • • •

The Lord passed in front of Moses, calling out, "Yahweh! The Lord! The God of compassion and mercy! I am slow to anger and filled with unfailing love and faithfulness."
EXODUS 34:6

Great God of Wonders

Samuel Davies was the first American-born hymnwriter whose hymns had broad acceptance. A Presbyterian evangelist in colonial Virginia, he helped to raise funds for what is now Princeton University. At the age of thirty-four he was named president of Princeton, succeeding Jonathan Edwards.

This hymn was published in a book of poems by Davies with the subtitle "For the religious entertainment of Christians in general," and soon it was being sung in some unusual places.

England had a penal colony in the South Seas, called Van Diemen's Land, to which incorrigible prisoners were sent. One writer commented, "With no companions but other convicts like themselves, they grew to be almost fiends." But some of the men were reached by the mercy of God and were converted. And the favorite hymn on that island was this one.

Great God of wonders! all Thy ways
Are matchless, Godlike, and divine;
But the fair glories of Thy grace
More Godlike and unrivaled shine,
More Godlike and unrivaled shine.

Who is a pard'ning God like Thee?
Or who has grace so rich and free?
Or who has grace so rich and free?

In wonder lost, with trembling joy
We take the pardon of our God;
Pardon for crimes of deepest dye,
A pardon bought with Jesus' blood;
A pardon bought with Jesus' blood.

O may this strange, this matchless grace,
This Godlike miracle of love,
Fill the whole earth with grateful praise,
And all th'angelic choirs above,
And all th'angelic choirs above.

Samuel Davies (1723-1761)

• • • •

Where is another God like you, who pardons the guilt of the remnant, overlooking the sins of his special people? You will not stay angry with your people forever, because you delight in showing unfailing love.
MICAH 7:18

Jesus, I Am Resting, Resting

Jesus, I am resting, resting
In the joy of what Thou art;
I am finding out the greatness
Of Thy loving heart.
Thou hast bid me gaze upon Thee,
And Thy beauty fills my soul,
For by Thy transforming power,
Thou hast made me whole.

O, how great Thy loving-kindness,
Vaster, broader than the sea!
O, how marvelous Thy goodness,
Lavished all on me!
Yes, I rest in Thee, Beloved,
Know what wealth of grace is Thine,
Know Thy certainty of promise,
And have made it mine.

Simply trusting Thee, Lord Jesus,
I behold Thee as Thou art,
And Thy love, so pure, so changeless,
Satisfies my heart;
Satisfies its deepest longings,
Meets, supplies its every need,
Compasseth me round with blessings:
Thine is love indeed!

Ever lift Thy face upon me
As I work and wait for Thee;
Resting 'neath Thy smile, Lord Jesus,
Earth's dark shadows flee.
Brightness of my Father's glory,
Sunshine of my Father's face,
Keep me ever trusting, resting,
Fill me with Thy grace.

Jean Sophia Pigott (1845–1882)

We find it difficult to be at rest—to be still—in a society that is always on the move. We live in a world of ten-second sound bites and short attention spans. We are taught to be dissatisfied with what we have and to strive for more.

In one of Christ's grandest invitations, He offered rest to the weary: "Come to me, all you who are weary and burdened, and I will give you rest" (Matthew 11:28, NIV). "In repentance and rest is your salvation, in quietness and trust is your strength," God told the Israelites in Isaiah 30:15 (NIV).

If we focus on God, as this nineteenth-century British author did, we can rest, finding that He will satisfy our heart and its deepest longings, meet and supply our every need, and compass us around with blessings.

• • • •

So there is a special rest still waiting for the people of God. For all who have entered into God's rest have rested from their labors, just as God did after creating the world.
HEBREWS 4:9-10

O God of Bethel

On January 16, 1737, Philip Doddridge preached a sermon about Jacob at Bethel. After the message, he taught the congregation this hymn, which he had just written.

Born in a humble London home, Doddridge always remembered the Bible stories that his parents had taught him. Scenes of Bible history were pictured on the blue-and-white delft tiles lining the fireplace. One depicted the Garden of Eden with Eve and the forbidden fruit; another, Noah at the window of the ark; another, Jonah and the whale; and another, Peter crossing the sea of Galilee (in a Dutch three-decker).

Doddridge always liked songs and pictures and stories more than systematic theology. It was a controversial age when theologians were arguing about fine points of doctrine. But Doddridge preferred to seize the simple truths of Scripture and to present them in ways that everyone could understand.

• • • •

I look up to the mountains— does my help come from there? My help comes from the Lord, who made heaven and earth! He will not let you stumble; the one who watches over you will not slumber. Indeed, he who watches over Israel never slumbers or sleeps.

PSALM 121:1-4

O God of Bethel, by whose hand
Thy people still are fed,
Who through this earthly pilgrimage
Hast all our fathers led.

Our vows, our prayers, we now present
Before Thy throne of grace;
God of our fathers, be the God
Of their succeeding race.

Through each perplexing path of life
Our wand'ring footsteps guide;
Give us each day our daily bread,
And raiment fit provide.

O spread Thy cov'ring wings around,
Till all our wand'rings cease,
And at our Father's loved abode
Our souls arrive in peace.

Philip Doddridge (1702–1751)

Be Not Dismayed

Be not dismayed whate'er betide,
God will take care of you;
Beneath His wings of love abide,
God will take care of you.

God will take care of you,
Through every day, o'er all the way;
He will take care of you,
God will take care of you.

Through days of toil when heart doth fail,
God will take care of you;
When dangers fierce your path assail,
God will take care of you.

All you may need He will provide,
God will take care of you;
Nothing you ask will be denied,
God will take care of you.

No matter what may be the test,
God will take care of you;
Lean, weary one, upon His breast,
God will take care of you.

Civilla Durfee Martin (1866-1948)

A child's comment prompted this gospel song. W. Stillman Martin had been invited to preach at a church a few hours away from his home. But his wife became ill that Sunday morning, and he was about to cancel his speaking engagement. Then his young son spoke up. "Father, don't you think that if God wants you to preach today, He will take care of Mother while you are away?" Martin made the trip, and when he returned home later that day he found that his wife had written this hymn in his absence. That evening, he composed the music.

Perhaps Civilla Martin was thinking of Philippians 4 as she wrote the words to this hymn. Paul had counseled, "Don't worry about anything"; and later he said, "this same God who takes care of me will supply all your needs." Or perhaps it was 1 Peter 5:7, "Give all your worries and cares to God, for he cares about you."

• • • •

Those who live in the shelter of the Most High will find rest in the shadow of the Almighty. This I declare about the Lord: He alone is my refuge, my place of safety; he is my God, and I trust him.
PSALM 91:1-2

Abide with Me

Henry Lyte coined the phrase "It is better to wear out than to rust out." And Henry Lyte wore out when he was fifty-four years old, an obscure pastor who labored for twenty-three years in a poor church in a fishing village in Devonshire, England. This hymn, written shortly before his death, was inspired by the words of the two disciples met by Jesus on the road to Emmaus: "Stay the night with us, since it is getting late" (Luke 24:29).

Note the fourth stanza, which carries such hope for the Christian. As Lyte wrote this, he knew he was dying of tuberculosis and asthma. It was "eventide" for him, darkness was deepening, and he felt very much alone. But he was not alone, and we are not alone even in our darkest times. Our Lord is with us, "the help of the helpless," the One who never changes, our guide and security. He will never leave us nor forsake us.

• • • •

The one thing I ask of the Lord—the thing I seek most—is to live in the house of the Lord all the days of my life, delighting in the Lord's perfections and meditating in his Temple.

PSALM 27:4

Abide with me; fast falls the eventide;
The darkness deepens; Lord, with me abide!
When other helpers fail and comforts flee,
Help of the helpless, O abide with me.

Swift to its close ebbs out life's little day;
Earth's joys grow dim; its glories pass away;
Change and decay in all around I see;
O Thou who changest not, abide with me.

I need Thy presence every passing hour;
What but Thy grace can foil the tempter's power?
Who, like Thyself, my guide and stay can be?
Through cloud and sunshine, Lord, abide with me.

I fear no foe, with Thee at hand to bless;
Ills have no weight, and tears no bitterness.
Where is death's sting? Where, grave, thy victory?
I triumph still, if Thou abide with me.

Hold Thou Thy cross before my closing eyes;
Shine through the gloom and point me to the skies;
Heaven's morning breaks, and earth's vain
shadows flee;
In life, in death, O Lord, abide with me.

Henry Francis Lyte (1793-1847)

If Thou but Suffer God to Guide Thee

If thou but suffer God to guide thee,
And hope in Him through all thy ways,
He'll give thee strength, whate'er betide thee,
And bear thee through the evil days;
Who trusts in God's unchanging love
Builds on the Rock that nought can move.

Only be still, and wait His leisure
In cheerful hope, with heart content
To take whate'er thy Father's pleasure
And all discerning love hath sent;
Nor doubt our inmost wants are known
To Him who chose us for His own.

Sing, pray, and swerve not from His ways,
But do thine own part faithfully;
Trust His rich promises of grace,
So shall they be fulfilled in thee;
God never yet forsook at need
The soul that trusted Him indeed.

Georg Neumark (1621–1681)

Translated by Catherine Winkworth (1827–1878)

Through the centuries, Christians have waited for the end of persecution. "How long, O Lord?" they pray. We sit and watch the rise of evil around us, and we wonder why God doesn't pull the plug. Why is He waiting?

Georg Neumark wrote this hymn amid the tremendous upheaval of seventeenth-century Germany. Through Catherine Winkworth's translation, the words have spoken to many subsequent generations, teaching us that by trusting in God's "unchanging love," we will find the only true security for our lives.

Catherine Winkworth began translating German hymns into English as a personal devotional enterprise. After numerous trips to the continent, she eventually found and translated four hundred new hymns. One writer said, "She faithfully transplanted Germany's best hymns and made them bloom with fresh beauty in their new gardens."

• • • •

But I will call on God, and the Lord will rescue me. Morning, noon, and night I cry out in my distress, and the Lord hears my voice. . . . Give your burdens to the Lord, and he will take care of you. He will not permit the godly to slip and fall.
PSALM 55:16-17, 22

O God, Our Help in Ages Past

In 1714, the people of England were anxious. Queen Anne lay dying, and she had no son or daughter to succeed her. Who would be the new monarch, and what changes would that make? Isaac Watts had reason to worry. His father had been imprisoned under the previous regime because his views did not please the ruling family. As a young child, Isaac had been carried by his mother to visit his father in jail. But Queen Anne had brought a new tolerance, and freedom for the elder Watts. Now that she was dying, what would happen?

Isaac Watts turned to Psalm 90 on this occasion and penned what may be the greatest of his more than six hundred hymns. The greatness of our eternal God was a favorite theme for Watts. When the events of the day bring worry, the God of the ages remains our eternal home.

• • • •

Lord, through all the generations you have been our home! Before the mountains were born, before you gave birth to the earth and the world, from beginning to end, you are God. . . . For you, a thousand years are as a passing day, as brief as a few night hours.

PSALM 90:1-2, 4

O God, our help in ages past,
Our hope for years to come,
Our shelter from the stormy blast,
And our eternal home!

Under the shadow of Thy throne
Still may we dwell secure;
Sufficient is Thine arm alone,
And our defense is sure.

Before the hills in order stood,
Or earth received her frame,
From everlasting Thou art God,
To endless years the same.

A thousand ages in Thy sight
Are like an evening gone;
Short as the watch that ends the night,
Before the rising sun.

Time, like an ever-rolling stream,
Bears all its sons away;
They fly, forgotten, as a dream
Dies at the opening day.

O God, our help in ages past,
Our hope for years to come;
Be Thou our guide while life shall last,
And our eternal home.

Isaac Watts (1674-1748)

Leaning on the Everlasting Arms

What a fellowship, what a joy divine,
Leaning on the everlasting arms;
What a blessedness, what a peace is mine,
Leaning on the everlasting arms.

Leaning, leaning,
Safe and secure from all alarms;
Leaning, leaning,
Leaning on the everlasting arms.

O, how sweet to walk in this pilgrim way,
Leaning on the everlasting arms;
O, how bright the path grows from day to day,
Leaning on the everlasting arms.

What have I to dread, what have I to fear,
Leaning on the everlasting arms?
I have blessed peace with my Lord so near,
Leaning on the everlasting arms.

Elisha Albright Hoffman (1839-1929)

One afternoon in 1887, music teacher A. J. Showalter dismissed his class and returned to his rooming house in Hartsville, Alabama. There he found letters from two former students, each with a similar story. Both of them had lost their wives, and both wives had died on the same day. Showalter began writing letters of condolence. The Scripture that came to mind was from Deuteronomy, the assurance of God's "everlasting arms" supporting us.

Then he wrote a third letter, to Elisha Hoffman, a hymnwriter in Pennsylvania. Showalter suggested that Hoffman write a hymn on that theme. He even suggested the wording of the chorus. Hoffman responded quickly with three stanzas, and Showalter supplied the music.

With God's arms beneath us, and His love surrounding us, we can find strength in even the most sorrowful situations.

• • • •

There is no one like the God of Israel. He rides across the heavens to help you, across the skies in majestic splendor. The eternal God is your refuge, and his everlasting arms are under you.

DEUTERONOMY 33:26-27

Let Us with a Gladsome Mind

John Milton is best known for *Paradise Lost*, the magnificent epic recounting the fall of humanity. But he also wrote other poems and hymn texts for church use. As a student at Cambridge, he wrote "On the Morning of Christ's Nativity." But even earlier, at the age of fifteen, he penned this metrical version of Psalm 136. In its original form, Milton's text had almost as many verses as the psalm, but most modern hymnbooks abbreviate it. In the psalm, each verse ends with "For his mercy endureth forever" (KJV). Milton embellished that with the stirring line "Ever faithful, ever sure."

Milton became blind when he was forty-four. His first wife died that same year. He remarried four years later, and his second wife died within fifteen months. In these later, sorrowful years, Milton wrote his greatest works. No doubt he had to cling to his faith in the enduring mercies of God, "ever faithful, ever sure."

• • • •

Give thanks to the Lord, for he is good! His faithful love endures forever. Give thanks to the God of gods. His faithful love endures forever. Give thanks to the Lord of lords. His faithful love endures forever.

PSALM 136:1-3

Let us with a gladsome mind
Praise the Lord, for He is kind:
For His mercies shall endure,
Ever faithful, ever sure.

Let us sound His name abroad,
For of gods He is the God:
For His mercies shall endure,
Ever faithful, ever sure.

He, with all-commanding might,
Filled the new-made world with light:
For His mercies shall endure,
Ever faithful, ever sure.

All things living He doth feed;
His full hand supplies their need:
For His mercies shall endure,
Ever faithful, ever sure.

Let us then with gladsome mind
Praise the Lord, for He is kind:
For His mercies shall endure,
Ever faithful, ever sure.

John Milton (1608-1674)

Children of the Heavenly Father

Children of the heav'nly Father
Safely in His bosom gather;
Nestling bird nor star in heaven
Such a refuge e'er was given.

God His own doth tend and nourish,
In His holy courts they flourish;
From all evil things He spares them,
In His mighty arms He bears them.

Neither life nor death shall ever
From the Lord His children sever;
Unto them His grace He showeth,
And their sorrows all He knoweth.

Praise the Lord in joyful numbers,
Your protector never slumbers;
At the will of your Defender
Ev'ry foe-man must surrender.

Though He giveth or He taketh,
God His children ne'er forsaketh;
His the loving purpose solely
To preserve them pure and holy.

More secure is no one ever
Than the loved ones of the Savior;
Not yon star on high abiding
Nor the bird in home-nest hiding.

Carolina Sandell Berg (1832-1903)

Translated by Ernst W. Olson (1870-1958)

Text copyright © Board of Publication, Lutheran Church of America. Reprinted by permission of Augsburg Fortress.

During the last half of the nineteenth century, Carolina (Lina) Sandell Berg was Sweden's greatest hymnwriter. She was born on October 3, 1832, in Fröderyd, Sweden, the daughter of the parish pastor. As a young child, she became bedridden with a mysterious paralysis. Her doctors could do nothing for her and believed her case to be hopeless.

One Sunday morning when Lina was twelve, her parents went to church and left her at home so she could rest. She spent that time alone in prayer. When her parents came home, they were astonished to find her dressed and walking around the house! From that time on, she began to write hymns and poems, and at sixteen she published her first collection. While bedridden, Berg discovered God's comfort; in her miraculous healing, she learned of God's loving power. These experiences did much to shape her childlike trust in God, a prominent feature in many of her hymns.

• • • •

See how very much our Father loves us, for he calls us his children, and that is what we are! But the people who belong to this world don't recognize that we are God's children because they don't know him.

I JOHN 3:1

The God of Abraham Praise

Orphaned at a young age, Thomas Olivers was converted when he heard George Whitefield preach on Zechariah 3:2, "This man is like a burning stick that has been snatched from the fire." At John Wesley's urging, Olivers became an evangelist and preached extensively in England and Ireland. One day in London, he strolled into a Jewish synagogue and heard a Jewish cantor, Meyer Leoni, sing a doxology from a medieval Hebrew liturgy. Impressed by both the music and the words, Olivers adapted both for use in Christian worship. Many stanzas of the original are not included in hymnals today, including one that Olivers regarded as his own personal testimony: "The God of Abraham praise, whose all-sufficient grace shall guide me all my happy days in all His ways! He calls a worm His friend; He calls Himself my God! And He shall save me to the end, through Jesus' blood."

• • • •

The Lord is king! Let the nations tremble!
He sits on his throne between the cherubim.
Let the whole earth quake! The Lord sits
in majesty in Jerusalem, exalted above all
the nations. Let them praise your great and
awesome name. Your name is holy!

PSALM 99:1-3

The God of Abraham praise,
Who reigns enthroned above;
Ancient of everlasting days,
And God of love.
Jehovah, great I AM,
By earth and heaven confessed;
I bow and bless the sacred name,
Forever blest.

The God of Abraham praise,
At whose supreme command
From earth I rise, and seek the joys
At His right hand.
I all on earth forsake,
Its wisdom, fame, and power;
And Him my only portion make,
My shield and tower.

He by Himself hath sworn,
I on His oath depend,
I shall, on eagles' wings upborne,
To heaven ascend;
I shall behold His face,
I shall His power adore,
And sing the wonders of His grace
Forevermore.

The whole triumphant host
Give thanks to God on high;
"Hail, Father, Son and Holy Ghost!"
They ever cry.
Hail, Abraham's God and mine!
I join the heavenly lays;
All might and majesty are Thine,
And endless praise.

Thomas Olivers (1725-1799)

Take My Life and Let It Be

Take my life and let it be
Consecrated, Lord, to Thee;
Take my moments and my days—
Let them flow in ceaseless praise,
Let them flow in ceaseless praise.

Take my hands and let them move
At the impulse of Thy love;
Take my feet and let them be
Swift and beautiful for Thee,
Swift and beautiful for Thee.

Take my voice and let me sing
Always, only, for my King;
Take my lips and let them be
Filled with messages from Thee,
Filled with messages from Thee.

Take my silver and my gold—
Not a mite would I withhold;
Take my intellect and use
Ev'ry pow'r as Thou shalt choose,
Ev'ry pow'r as Thou shalt choose.

Take my will and make it Thine—
It shall be no longer mine;
Take my heart—it is Thine own,
It shall be Thy royal throne,
It shall be Thy royal throne.

Take my love—my Lord, I pour
At Thy feet its treasure store;
Take myself—and I will be
Ever, only, all for Thee,
Ever, only, all for Thee.

Frances Ridley Havergal (1836-1879)

The prolific British hymnwriter Frances Ridley Havergal wrote this hymn on February 4, 1874. "I went for a little visit of five days to Areley House," she explained. "There were ten persons in the house, some unconverted and long prayed for, some converted but not rejoicing Christians. He gave me the prayer, 'Lord, give me all in this house!' And He just did. Before I left the house, everyone had got a blessing. The last night of my visit I was too happy to sleep, and passed most of the night in praise and renewal of my own consecration, and these little couplets formed themselves and chimed in my heart one after another, till they finished with 'Ever, only, ALL for Thee.'" As Frances wrote the words, she capitalized ALL.

Two months earlier, she had made a complete surrender of herself to Christ and experienced "the blessedness of true consecration." She wrote, "I just yielded myself to Him, and utterly trusted Him to keep me."

• • • •

And so, dear brothers and sisters, I plead with you to give your bodies to God because of all he has done for you. Let them be a living and holy sacrifice—the kind he will find acceptable. This is truly the way to worship him.
ROMANS 12:1

It Is Well with My Soul

Knowing that his friend Dwight L. Moody was going to be preaching in evangelistic campaigns in England in the fall of 1871, Horatio G. Spafford decided to take his family to England. His wife and four daughters went ahead on the SS *Ville du Havre*, and he planned to follow in a few days.

But on the Atlantic Ocean the ship was struck by an iron sailing vessel and sank within twelve minutes. Two hundred and twenty-six lives were lost—including the Spaffords' four daughters. When the survivors were brought to shore at Cardiff, Wales, Mrs. Spafford cabled her husband, "Saved alone."

Spafford booked passage on the next ship. As they were crossing the Atlantic, the captain pointed out the place where he thought the *Ville du Havre* had gone down. That night, Spafford penned the words "When sorrows like sea billows roll . . . it is well, it is well with my soul."

• • • •

We can rejoice, too, when we run into problems and trials, for we know that they help us develop endurance. And endurance develops strength of character, and character strengthens our confident hope of salvation.
ROMANS 5:3-4

When peace like a river attendeth my way,
When sorrows like sea-billows roll;
Whatever my lot, Thou hast taught me to say,
"It is well, it is well with my soul."

It is well with my soul,
It is well, it is well with my soul.

Though Satan should buffet, tho' trials should come,
Let this blest assurance control,
That Christ has regarded my helpless estate,
And hath shed His own blood for my soul.

My sin—O, the bliss of this glorious thought,
My sin—not in part but the whole,
Is nailed to the cross and I bear it no more,
Praise the Lord, praise the Lord, O my soul!

And, Lord, haste the day when the faith shall be sight,
The clouds be rolled back as a scroll,
The trump shall resound and the Lord shall descend,
"Even so"—it is well with my soul.

Horatio Gates Spafford (1828-1888)

At Even, Ere the Sun Was Set

At even, ere the sun was set,
The sick, O Lord, around Thee lay;
O in what divers pains they met!
O with what joy they went away!

Once more 'tis eventide, and we,
Oppressed with various ills, draw near;
What if Thy form we cannot see?
We know and feel that Thou art here.

O Savior Christ, our woes dispel;
For some are sick, and some are sad,
And some have never loved Thee well,
And some have lost the love they had;

And none, O Lord, have perfect rest,
For none are wholly free from sin;
And they who fain would serve Thee best
Are conscious most of wrong within.

O Savior Christ, Thou too art man;
Thou hast been troubled, tempted, tried;
Thy kind but searching glance can scan
The very wounds that shame would hide.

Thy touch has still its ancient power;
No word from Thee can fruitless fall;
Hear, in this solemn evening hour,
And in Thy mercy heal us all.

Henry Twells (1823–1900)

Matthew, Mark, and Luke all emphasize one particular day in Jesus' life when He came to Capernaum. Though it was a Sabbath day, it was a busy one for the Lord. It began in the synagogue, where the people were amazed at the authority of His teaching, and continued as He cast out a demon from a demon-possessed man. Then He went to Peter's house and healed Peter's mother-in-law. By that time, people were flocking to Jesus, bringing others who were sick and asking Him to touch them.

We, too, says the hymnwriter, come to Jesus with all our troubles. Some of these are physical, some are spiritual, some are emotional, and some are a mixture of many things. He understands our troubles better than we do ourselves.

"At even, ere the sun is set," we can line up at the door and ask for the divine touch, which "has still its ancient power."

• • • •

That evening after sunset, many sick and demon-possessed people were brought to Jesus. The whole town gathered at the door to watch. So Jesus healed many people who were sick with various diseases, and he cast out many demons.
MARK 1:32-34

In the Hour of Trial

James Montgomery faced various trials, even as a young person. His missionary parents died when he was twelve. Soon after that, he was asked to leave school because he couldn't turn in his assignments on time. After working at a couple of bakeries, he left for London, where he thought he could sell his poetry. Instead, he got a job with a newspaper. And when the editor fled England to avoid prosecution, twenty-three-year-old James Montgomery assumed that role. After he commemorated the fall of the Bastille, he was fined, imprisoned, and called "a wicked, malicious and seditious person."

In time he was honored by the British government for his outspoken advocacy of humanitarian causes, especially the abolition of slavery. As he read the story of Simon Peter in the Gospels, he identified with that disciple. "I have pleaded in prayer for you, Simon, that your faith should not fail," Jesus told Peter (Luke 22:32).

• • • •

Since [Jesus] himself has gone through suffering and testing, he is able to help us when we are being tested.

HEBREWS 2:18

In the hour of trial, Jesus, plead for me;
Lest by base denial, I depart from Thee.
When Thou seest me waver, with a look recall,
Nor for fear or favor suffer me to fall.

With forbidden pleasures would this vain world charm,
Or its sordid treasures spread to work me harm;
Bring to my remembrance sad Gethsemane,
Or, in darker semblance, cross-crowned Calvary.

Should Thy mercy send me sorrow, toil, and woe,
Or should pain attend me on my path below,
Grant that I may never fail Thy hand to see:
Grant that I may ever cast my care on Thee.

When my last hour cometh, fraught with strife and pain,
When my dust returneth to the dust again,
On Thy truth relying, through that mortal strife:
Jesus, take me, dying, to eternal life.

James Montgomery (1771–1854)

Altered by Frances A. Hutton (1811–1877)

Soldiers of Christ, Arise

Soldiers of Christ, arise,
And put your armor on,
Strong in the strength which God supplies
Through His eternal Son;
Strong in the Lord of hosts,
And in His mighty power,
Who in the strength of Jesus trusts
Is more than conqueror.

Stand, then, in His great might,
With all His strength endued;
But take, to arm you for the fight,
The panoply of God:
That, having all things done,
And all your conflicts passed,
Ye may o'ercome through Christ alone,
And stand entire at last.

From strength to strength go on,
Wrestle and fight and pray;
Tread all the powers of darkness down,
And win the well-fought day.
Still let the Spirit cry,
In all His soldiers, "Come!"
Till Christ the Lord descends from high,
And takes the conquerors home.

Charles Wesley (1707-1788)

The early Methodists took their lives in their hands when they announced themselves as followers of John and Charles Wesley. One writer declared, "They were outrageously treated—stoned, mauled, ducked, hounded with bulldogs, threatened, homes looted, businesses ruined. Anyone who walked through a town could pick out by their ruinous condition the houses where Methodists lived." In one incident at Devizes in February 1747, a crowd surrounded the house where the Methodist leaders were staying, breaking the windows and ripping off the shutters.

In 1749, Charles wrote this hymn under the title "The Whole Armor of God," and it was used to confirm new converts. Spiritual warfare is no less a reality today than it was in the Wesleys' day—or in the apostle Paul's.

• • • •

Therefore, put on every piece of God's armor so you will be able to resist the enemy in the time of evil. Then after the battle you will still be standing firm.
EPHESIANS 6:13

We Give Immortal Praise

Isaac Watts had much to complain about. He was only five feet tall, and his big head made his body look even smaller. He had a long, hooked nose. And he was sickly from his teenage years, when smallpox nearly killed him.

One woman fell in love with his poetry and wanted to marry him. Watts proposed to her, but his physical appearance caused her to reject him. One source says, "Though she loved the jewel, she could not admire the casket [case] which contained it." He remained a bachelor all his life.

For his last thirty-six years he was an invalid, preaching only occasionally as his health would permit. But he wrote hymns continually, hymns of praise to God "for all our comforts here, and better hopes above." As Isaac Watts knew so well, when we give praise to God, our personal concerns are put into proper perspective.

• • • •

For at just the right time Christ will be revealed from heaven by the blessed and only almighty God, the King of all kings and Lord of all lords. He alone can never die, and he lives in light so brilliant that no human can approach him.

I TIMOTHY 6:15-16

We give immortal praise
To God the Father's love,
For all our comforts here,
And better hopes above.
He sent His own eternal Son,
To die for sins that man had done.

To God the Son belongs
Immortal glory too,
Who bought us with His Blood
From everlasting woe;
And now He lives and now He reigns,
And sees the fruit of all His plans.

To God the Spirit's name
Immortal worship give,
Whose new-creating power
Makes the dead sinner live.
His work completes the great design,
And fills the soul with joy divine.

Almighty God, to Thee
Be endless honors done,
The undivided Three,
And the mysterious One.
Where reason fails, with all her powers,
There faith prevails, and love adores.

Isaac Watts (1674-1748)

How Firm a Foundation

How firm a foundation, ye saints of the Lord,
Is laid for your faith in His excellent Word!
What more can He say than to you He hath said,
To you who for refuge to Jesus have fled?

"Fear not, I am with thee; O be not dismayed,
For I am thy God, and will still give thee aid;
I'll strengthen thee, help thee, and cause thee to
stand,
Upheld by My righteous, omnipotent hand.

"When through the deep waters I call thee to go,
The rivers of woe shall not thee overflow;
For I will be with thee thy troubles to bless,
And sanctify to thee thy deepest distress.

"When through fiery trials thy pathways shall lie,
My grace, all-sufficient, shall be thy supply;
The flame shall not hurt thee; I only design
Thy dross to consume, and thy gold to refine.

"The soul that on Jesus still leans for repose,
I will not, I will not desert to his foes;
That soul, though all hell should endeavor to shake,
I'll never, no, never, no, never forsake!"

"K" in Rippon's A Selection of Hymns, 1787

Most hymnals simply list the author of this hymn as "K" because he wanted to remain anonymous. The hymn was first published in 1787 in a hymnbook put together by John Rippon, a Baptist minister in London. While the author remained a mystery for a while, most musicologists now agree that John Rippon's assistant, Robert Keene, was probably the author.

The title of the hymn was "Scripture Promises," and in that 1787 hymnbook these words from 2 Peter 1:4 were printed above the first stanza: "Great and precious promises." Each stanza of the hymn emphasizes a different promise in God's Word, with the great climax coming on the last verse, "The soul that on Jesus still leans for repose . . . I'll never, no, never, no, never forsake!"

• • • •

Do not be afraid, for I have ransomed you. I have called you by name; you are mine. When you go through deep waters, I will be with you. When you go through rivers of difficulty, you will not drown. When you walk through the fire of oppression, you will not be burned up; the flames will not consume you.

ISAIAH 43:1-2

Near to the Heart of God

Where do you turn when unexpected tragedy strikes? Cleland McAfee, a Presbyterian minister in Chicago, had just received word that his brother and sister-in-law had lost both of their daughters to diphtheria within twenty-four hours. Grief-stricken, McAfee couldn't think of deep theological issues; he could only think of verses in the book of Psalms that brought comfort and rest to those who sought refuge in the Lord. As he meditated on God's Word, he wrote the words and music to this simple hymn.

At the double funeral, outside the darkened, quarantined house of his brother, Cleland McAfee with a choking voice sang this hymn publicly for the first time. The following Sunday, his church choir sang it from their pastor's handwritten copy.

There is a place of quiet rest
Near to the heart of God,
A place where sin cannot molest,
Near to the heart of God.

O Jesus, blest Redeemer,
Sent from the heart of God,
Hold us who wait before Thee
Near to the heart of God.

There is a place of comfort sweet
Near to the heart of God,
A place where we our Savior meet,
Near to the heart of God.

There is a place of full release
Near to the heart of God,
A place where all is joy and peace,
Near to the heart of God.

Cleland Boyd McAfee (1866–1944)

• • • •

God is our refuge and strength, always ready to help in times of trouble. . . . "Be still, and know that I am God! I will be honored by every nation. I will be honored throughout the world." The Lord of Heaven's Armies is here among us; the God of Israel is our fortress.

PSALM 46:1, 10-11

Jesus, I My Cross Have Taken

Jesus, I my cross have taken,
All to leave and follow Thee;
Destitute, despised, forsaken,
Thou, from hence, my all shalt be.
Perish every fond ambition,
All I've sought or hoped or known;
Yet how rich is my condition:
God and heaven are still my own!

Let the world despise and leave me;
They have left my Savior, too.
Human hearts and looks deceive me;
Thou art not, like man, untrue.
And, while Thou shalt smile upon me,
God of wisdom, love, and might,
Foes may hate, and friends may shun me;
Show Thy face, and all is bright.

Man may trouble and distress me,
'Twill but drive me to Thy breast;
Life with trials hard may press me;
Heaven will bring me sweeter rest.
O 'tis not in grief to harm me
While Thy love is left to me;
O 'twere not in joy to charm me,
Were that joy unmixed with Thee.

Haste thee on from grace to glory,
Armed by faith and winged by prayer;
Heaven's eternal day's before thee,
God's own hand shall guide thee there.
Soon shall close thy earthly mission;
Swift shall pass thy pilgrim days;
Hope shall change to glad fruition,
Faith to sight, and prayer to praise.

Henry Francis Lyte (1793–1847)

It may have been the story of a Methodist woman named Mary Bosenquet that inspired Henry Lyte to write this hymn. Mary was the daughter of a wealthy English merchant and enjoyed the finest of clothing and jewelry—until she attended some Methodist meetings and was converted. Then she was disinherited by her father and lived in a two-room house furnished with a borrowed table and chairs. As a member of the persecuted Methodists, she was threatened with injury, and the windows of her house were frequently broken.

Lyte is perhaps better known as the writer of "Abide with Me" (January 27), but the words to this hymn are no less powerful. While the language is archaic, the sentiment is one that is timeless: "O 'tis not in grief to harm me, while Thy love is left to me; O 'twere not in joy to charm me, were that joy unmixed with Thee."

• • • •

Then, calling the crowd to join his disciples, [Jesus] said, "If any of you wants to be my follower, you must turn from your selfish ways, take up your cross, and follow me. If you try to hang on to your life, you will lose it. But if you give up your life for my sake and for the sake of the Good News, you will save it."
MARK 8:34-35

Must Jesus Bear the Cross Alone?

This hymn was written, at least in part, by Thomas Shepherd in 1693. At the time, he was a minister of the Church of England and struggling with a major decision. He first used the hymn after preaching a sermon on Simon Peter. According to tradition, Peter was crucified in Rome upside down because he considered himself unworthy of dying in the same way as his Lord. Shepherd's hymn originally began, "Shall Simon bear the cross alone, and other saints be free?" Later the hymn was altered to refer to Jesus bearing the cross. But the message of the song is that there's a cross for every one of us. The Lord may lead us down a difficult road. Cross bearing precedes crown wearing.

And Shepherd's decision? He made it the next year. He left the Church of England, the handsome church building in which he preached and the security that it provided, to become an independent preacher in a Nottingham barn.

• • • •

My old self has been crucified with Christ. It is no longer I who live, but Christ lives in me. So I live in this earthly body by trusting in the Son of God, who loved me and gave himself for me.

GALATIANS 2:20

Must Jesus bear the cross alone
And all the world go free?
No, there's a cross for ev'ryone,
And there's a cross for me.

The consecrated cross I'll bear
Till death shall set me free,
And then go home my crown to wear,
For there's a crown for me.

Upon the crystal pavement, down
At Jesus' pierced feet,
Joyful I'll cast my golden crown
And His dear name repeat.

O precious cross! O glorious crown!
O resurrection day!
Ye angels, from the stars come down
And bear my soul away.

Thomas Shepherd (1665–1739)

Lord Jesus Christ, My Life, My Light

Lord Jesus Christ, my Life, my Light,
My Strength by day, my Trust by night,
On earth I'm but a passing guest
And sorely with my sins opprest.

Far off I see my fatherland,
Where thro' Thy blood I hope to stand.
But ere I reach that Paradise,
A weary way before me lies.

My heart sinks at the journey's length,
My wasted flesh has little strength;
My soul alone still cries in me:
"Lord, take me home, take me to Thee!"

Oh, let Thy suff'rings give me pow'r
To meet the last and darkest hour!
Thy blood refresh and comfort me;
Thy bonds and fetters make me free.

Oh, let Thy holy wounds for me
Clefts in the rock forever be
Where as a dove my soul can hide
And safe from Satan's rage abide.

And when my spirit flies away,
Thy dying words shall be my stay.
Thy cross shall be my staff in life,
Thy holy grave my rest from strife.

Martin Behm (1557–1622)

Translated by Catherine Winkworth (1827–1878)

Imagine being uprooted from your homeland and forced to flee to a new land. Imagine being forbidden to worship in your church. Imagine being threatened with imprisonment and even death just because of what you believe. And imagine that your tormentors are not atheist scoundrels but people who claim to be Christians themselves. Where can you turn for help? Only to God.

In the upheaval that followed the Protestant Reformation, many devout Christians were caught between the warring Protestants and Catholics. It quickly became a political struggle that had little to do with true faith. Believers could only hope that God would somehow give them a place to hide. They found comfort and strength in focusing on their personal relationship with God and their eternal home in heaven. This hymn reflects that sentiment.

• • • •

"My Lord and my God!" Thomas exclaimed. Then Jesus told him, "You believe because you have seen me. Blessed are those who believe without seeing me."
JOHN 20:28-29

Out of the Depths I Cry to Thee

Although Martin Luther was born into a poor mining community, his intelligence and his father's hard work earned him a university education. He began a law career at Erfurt University but suddenly left his studies to enter a nearby Augustinian monastery. Luther soon became painfully aware of his guilt before God but could find no relief from his despair. In time, he went to teach at the university in Wittenberg, where he discovered in Scripture that God had a perfect solution for his guilt—gracious forgiveness through Jesus Christ. This discovery freed Luther from the depths of his despair and became the driving force in the ensuing Reformation.

Luther's musical gifts have often been overlooked. He wrote over thirty hymns and composed music for many of them. He once said, "I wish to compose sacred hymns so that the Word of God may dwell among the people also by means of songs."

• • • •

Have mercy on me, O God, because of your unfailing love. Because of your great compassion, blot out the stain of my sins. Wash me clean from my guilt. Purify me from my sin. For I recognize my rebellion; it haunts me day and night.

PSALM 51:1-3

Out of the depths I cry to Thee:
Lord, hear me, I implore Thee;
Bend down Thy gracious ear to me,
Let my prayer come before Thee!
On my misdeeds in mercy look,
O deign to blot them from Thy book,
And let me come before Thee.

Thy sov'reign grace and boundless love
Show Thee, O Lord, forgiving;
My purest thoughts and deeds but prove
Sin in my heart is living:
None guiltless in Thy sight appear,
All who approach Thy throne must fear,
And humbly trust Thy mercy.

Thou canst be merciful while just,
This is my hope's foundation;
In Thy redeeming grace I trust,
O grant me Thy salvation.
Upheld by Thee I stand secure:
Thy word is firm, Thy promise sure,
And I rely upon Thee.

Like those who watch for midnight's hour
To hail the dawning morrow,
I wait for Thee, I trust Thy pow'r,
Unmoved by doubt or sorrow.
So let Thy people hope in Thee,
And they shall find Thy mercy free,
And Thy redemption plenteous.

Martin Luther (1483-1546)

Translated by Benjamin Latrobe (1725-1786)

Break Thou the Bread of Life

Break Thou the bread of life,
Dear Lord, to me,
As Thou didst break the loaves
Beside the sea;
Beyond the sacred page
I seek Thee, Lord;
My spirit pants for Thee,
O living Word!

Bless Thou the truth, dear Lord,
To me, to me,
As Thou didst bless the bread
By Galilee;
Then shall all bondage cease,
All fetters fall;
And I shall find my peace,
My all-in-all.

Mary Artemisia Lathbury (1841–1913)

While this hymn is often sung during Communion, it is really intended to prepare the heart for Bible study. The author, Mary Lathbury, was better known as a commercial artist than as a poet. Her illustrations regularly appeared in the popular magazines of the nineteenth century. She was a devout Christian who often vacationed at Lake Chautauqua, where she became one of the founders of a new movement. Mixing Christian inspiration, culture, and education, the Chautauqua movement spread across the country. She was asked by the leader of the movement to write a Vespers hymn, which she did ("Day Is Dying in the West," August 5), and then a Bible study hymn. As she sat with her Bible, overlooking Lake Chautauqua, she thought of the disciples at the Sea of Galilee and wrote this hymn.

• • • •

Jesus took the five loaves and two fish, looked up toward heaven, and blessed them. Then, breaking the loaves into pieces, he kept giving the bread to the disciples so they could distribute it to the people. He also divided the fish for everyone to share. They all ate as much as they wanted, and afterward, the disciples picked up twelve baskets of leftover bread and fish.

MARK 6:41-43

Lenten Hymn

We don't know a lot about the forty days Jesus spent in the desert before His temptation. We know it was a time of fasting and probably of prayer. When the devil came to Him, the conquering words of Scripture were quick on Jesus' tongue, so it may have been a time of meditation, a time of special communion with his Father.

This song draws the comparison between Jesus' forty days in the desert and the forty days of Lent. Traditionally, the Lenten season is a time of fasting. People "give up" something for Lent. The idea is not to punish ourselves, but to put aside something that may distract us from our communion with God. It is a time for special devotion to God, a time when He may "abide with us" in a special way. Lent is a time to refocus on our relationship with Christ.

• • • •

The Spirit then compelled Jesus to go into the wilderness, where he was tempted by Satan for forty days. He was out among the wild animals, and angels took care of him.

MARK 1:12-13

Lord, who throughout these forty days
For us didst fast and pray,
Teach us with Thee to mourn our sins,
And close by Thee to stay.

As Thou with Satan didst contend
And didst the victory win,
O give us strength in Thee to fight,
In Thee to conquer sin.

As Thou didst hunger bear and thirst,
So teach us, gracious Lord,
To die to self, and chiefly live
By Thy most holy Word.

And through these days of penitence,
And through Thy Passiontide,
Yea, evermore, in life and death,
Jesus! with us abide.

Abide with us, that so this life
Of suffering overpast,
An Easter of unending joy
We may attain at last!

Claudia Frances Hernaman (1838–1898)

O Love, How Deep, How Broad, How High

O love, how deep, how broad, how high,
How passing thought and fantasy,
That God, the Son of God, should take
Our mortal form for mortals' sake.

For us baptized, for us He bore
His holy fast, and hungered sore;
For us temptations sharp He knew,
For us the tempter overthrew.

For us He prayed, for us He taught,
For us His daily works He wrought,
By words and signs and actions, thus
Still seeking not Himself, but us.

For us to wicked men betrayed,
Scourged, mocked, in purple robe arrayed,
He bore the shameful cross and death,
For us gave up His dying breath.

For us He rose from death again,
For us He went on high to reign;
For us He sent His Spirit here
To guide, to strengthen, and to cheer.

All glory to our Lord and God
For love so deep, so high, so broad:
The Trinity, whom we adore
For ever and for evermore.

Latin Hymn (fifteenth century)

Translated by Benjamin Webb (1819–1885)

This ancient hymn weaves together threads of different Scriptures. Paul prays that the Ephesians might have "the power to understand . . . how wide, how long, how high, and how deep [God's] love is," and then dedicates them to God, "who is able . . . to accomplish infinitely more than we might ask or think" (Ephesians 3:18, 20). Incredible power and immeasurable love—it's a great combination.

Paul reminds the Philippians that Christ "gave up his divine privileges" and took on human form, dying a criminal's death (Philippians 2:6-7). This is the thrust of the Good News: Jesus came to seek and save those who were lost. He was not living for Himself, but for us. Every word, every healing, every gentle touch was for us. And His painful death was also for us, even when our sin made us His enemies.

• • • •

God showed his great love for us by sending Christ to die for us while we were still sinners. And since we have been made right in God's sight by the blood of Christ, he will certainly save us from God's condemnation.
ROMANS 5:8-9

Here, O My Lord, I See Thee Face to Face

The Lord's Supper has always been a special time for Christians. It is a time of soul-searching, but also joy. We remember Christ's death, but also His resurrection. Christ is the host of this meal; we have fellowship with Him as we eat and drink.

Different denominations have adopted different practices concerning the Lord's Supper. And in every tradition, it is possible for the sacrament to lose its meaning. For Horatius Bonar, a maverick Scottish Presbyterian, the important thing was that it would be a personal encounter with Christ. You can sense the rich interaction in these lines, the flux of emotions, and the warm devotion to the Lord, his "shield and sun."

• • • •

For I pass on to you what I received from the Lord himself. On the night when he was betrayed, the Lord Jesus took some bread and gave thanks to God for it. Then he broke it in pieces and said, "This is my body, which is given for you. Do this to remember me."

I CORINTHIANS 11:23-24

Here, O my Lord, I see Thee face to face;
Here would I touch and handle things unseen,
Here grasp with firmer hand eternal grace,
And all my weariness upon Thee lean.

This is the hour of banquet and of song;
This is the heavenly table spread for me;
Here let me feast, and feasting, still prolong
The hallowed hour of fellowship with Thee.

Here would I feed upon the bread of God,
Here drink with Thee the royal wine of heaven.
Here would I lay aside each earthly load,
Here taste afresh the calm of sin forgiven.

Too soon we rise: the symbols disappear;
The feast, though not the love, is past and gone.
The bread and wine remove: but Thou art here,
Nearer than ever, still my shield and sun.

Feast after feast thus comes and passes by;
Yet, passing, points to the glad feast above,
Giving sweet foretaste of the festal joy,
The Lamb's great bridal feast of bliss and love.

Horatius Bonar (1808-1889)

Hail, Thou Once Despised Jesus

Hail, Thou once despised Jesus!
Hail, Thou Galilean King!
Thou didst suffer to release us;
Thou didst free salvation bring.
Hail, Thou universal Savior,
Who hast borne our sin and shame!
By Thy merits we find favor;
Life is given through Thy name.

Paschal Lamb, by God appointed,
All our sins on Thee were laid;
By almighty love appointed,
Thou hast full atonement made.
Every sin may be forgiven,
Through the virtue of Thy blood;
Opened is the gate of heaven;
Peace is made twixt man and God.

Worship, honor, power, and blessing
Christ is worthy to receive;
Loudest praises, without ceasing,
Meet it is for us to give.
Help, ye bright angelic spirits,
Bring your sweetest, noblest lays;
Help to sing of Jesus' merits,
Help to chant Emmanuel's praise!

Probably by John Bakewell (1721–1819)

Probably altered by Martin Madan (1726–1790)

"He was despised and rejected," says Isaiah, prophesying about the Suffering Servant who would come centuries later. "He was . . . crushed for our sins." The prophecy was clearly fulfilled in Jesus, who was arrested, tried, convicted, and crucified. "He was beaten so we could be whole" (Isaiah 53:3, 5). As John put it, "He came to his own people, and even they rejected him" (John 1:11).

But there's another act to this drama. Even Isaiah foresaw that God the Father would be "satisfied" by the Servant's suffering and "give him the honors of a victorious soldier" (Isaiah 53:11-12). Paul proclaims that Jesus has been given a name that is above every name and that every knee will bow to Him. The rejection of the past becomes the glory of the future. When all is said and done, Christ will be hailed for His sacrificial suffering.

• • • •

Then I looked again, and I heard the voices of thousands and millions of angels around the throne and of the living beings and the elders. And they sang in a mighty chorus: "Worthy is the Lamb who was slaughtered— to receive power and riches and wisdom and strength and honor and glory and blessing."
REVELATION 5:11-12

Tell Me the Story of Jesus

The story of Jesus cannot be kept quiet. From the very beginning, it had to be told. The shepherds "told everyone" about the angels and the Christ child (Luke 2:17). As the adult Jesus began healing people, "news about him spread as far as Syria" (Matthew 4:24). After Jesus' death, resurrection, and ascension, the authorities ordered the disciples to stop preaching about Him. They responded, "We cannot stop telling about everything we have seen and heard" (Acts 4:20).

It's the same way today. Christians naturally tell others "the story of Jesus." As Jesus has changed their own lives, they feel compelled to tell others. They are still fulfilling Jesus' prediction that His followers would be "witnesses."

We do not need to use special techniques of persuasion to lead others to Christ; we must simply tell the story of Jesus.

• • • •

[Jesus said,] "You will receive power when the Holy Spirit comes upon you. And you will be my witnesses, telling people about me everywhere—in Jerusalem, throughout Judea, in Samaria, and to the ends of the earth."
ACTS 1:8

Tell me the story of Jesus,
Write on my heart every word;
Tell me the story most precious,
Sweetest that ever was heard.
Tell how the angels in chorus
Sang as they welcomed His birth,
"Glory to God in the highest!
Peace and good tidings to earth."

**Tell me the story of Jesus,
Write on my heart every word;
Tell me the story most precious,
Sweetest that ever was heard.**

Fasting alone in the desert,
Tell of the days that are past,
How for our sins He was tempted,
Yet was triumphant at last.
Tell of the years of His labor,
Tell of the sorrow He bore,
He was despised and afflicted,
Homeless, rejected and poor.

Tell of the cross where they nailed Him,
Writhing in anguish and pain;
Tell of the grave where they laid Him,
Tell how He liveth again.
Love in that story so tender
Clearer than ever I see:
Lord, may I always remember
Love paid the ransom for me.

Fanny Jane Crosby (1820-1915)

Forty Days and Forty Nights

Forty days and forty nights
Thou wast fasting in the wild;
Forty days and forty nights
Tempted, and yet undefiled.

Sunbeams scorching all the day;
Chilly dewdrops nightly shed;
Prowling beasts about Thy way;
Stones Thy pillow, earth Thy bed.

Shall not we Thy sorrow share,
And from earthly joys abstain,
Fasting with unceasing prayer,
Glad with Thee to suffer pain?

And if Satan, vexing sore,
Flesh or spirit should assail,
Thou, his vanquisher before,
Grant we may not faint nor fail.

Keep, O keep us, Savior dear,
Ever constant by Thy side;
That with Thee we may appear
At th'eternal Eastertide.

George Hunt Smyttan (1822–1870)

When Jesus was tempted, He was probably in the Judean desert—a cruel, hot, barren place with craggy canyons. In biblical times, wild jackals and other beasts may have roamed the area. David hid out in caves there when he ran from King Saul.

This hymn gives a feeling for Jesus' surroundings as He fasted in the desert. Day in and day out, it must have been very uncomfortable. Yet Jesus had a greater purpose; comfort was not important. He was preparing for a crucial showdown with the devil that would set the tone for his whole ministry.

The Bible says that we can count on Jesus because "he faced all of the same testings we do, yet he did not sin" (Hebrews 4:15). His strength to overcome temptation is available to us as we face temptations. He has been there before us and has won the battle. That assurance can help us not to "faint nor fail."

• • • •

For forty days and forty nights [Jesus] fasted and became very hungry. During that time the devil came and said to him, "If you are the Son of God, tell these stones to become loaves of bread." But Jesus told him, "No! The Scriptures say, 'People do not live by bread alone, but by every word that comes from the mouth of God.'"
MATTHEW 4:2-4

Wake, Awake, for Night Is Flying

In this hymn, Philipp Nicolai calls us to be prepared for the imminent return of Christ, the Bridegroom. It was natural that Nicolai was eager for Christ's return. He was the pastor in Unna, Germany, when an awful plague hit the town (1597–1598). He watched and often participated in the burial of friends and parishioners each day. It was during this difficult time that he wrote this hymn.

He looked forward to a day when disease and death would be past, when rejoicing and feasting would carry the day. Christ had given him an eternal perspective on this present life.

Whether we are now prospering or suffering, we need Philipp Nicolai's perspective. It will awaken us from lethargy when times are good; it will lift us from despair when everything looks dark. "Wake, awake, for night is flying!"

• • • •

At midnight they were roused by the shout, "Look, the bridegroom is coming! Come out and meet him!". . . Then those who were ready went in with him to the marriage feast, and the door was locked.
MATTHEW 25:6, 10

"Wake, awake, for night is flying,"
The watchmen on the heights are crying;
"Awake, Jerusalem, at last!"
Midnight hears the welcome voices,
And at the thrilling cry rejoices:
"Come forth, ye virgins, night is past!
The Bridegroom comes; awake,
Your lamps with gladness take; Alleluia!
And for His marriage feast prepare,
For you must go to meet Him there."

Zion hears the watchmen singing,
And all her heart with joy is springing;
She wakes, she rises from her gloom:
For her Lord comes down all glorious,
The Strong in grace, in truth Victorious,
Her Star is ris'n, her Light is come!
Ah, come, Thou blessed Lord,
O Jesus, Son of God, Alleluia!
We follow till the halls we see
Where Thou hast bid us sup with Thee.

Now let all the heav'ns adore Thee,
And men and angels sing before Thee,
With harp and cymbal's clearest tone;
Of one pearl each shining portal,
Where we are with the choir immortal
Of angels round Thy dazzling throne;
Nor eye hath seen, nor ear
Hath yet attained to hear
What there is ours;
But we rejoice, and sing to Thee
Our hymn of joy eternally.

Philipp Nicolai (1556–1608)

Translated by Catherine Winkworth (1827–1878)

The Lord Jehovah Reigns

The Lord Jehovah reigns,
His throne is built on high;
The garments He assumes
Are light and majesty;
His glories shine with beams so bright,
No mortal eye can bear the sight.

The thunders of His hand
Keep the wide world in awe;
His wrath and justice stand
To guard His holy law;
And where His love resolves to bless,
His truth confirms and seals the grace.

Through all His mighty works
Amazing wisdom shines,
Confounds the powers of hell,
And breaks their dark designs;
Strong is His arm, and shall fulfill
His great decrees and sovereign will.

And will this sovereign King
Of glory condescend;
And will He write His name
My Father and my Friend?
I love His name, I love His Word,
Join all my powers to praise the Lord!

Isaac Watts (1674-1748)

Our God is an awesome God. In the Psalms, we continually read of the mighty acts of the sovereign Lord. He created the heavens and the earth. He hung the stars in the sky and gives orders to the sun and moon. Some psalms even speak of thunder as God's voice. And Isaac Watts picks up that theme here. The fact is, the greatness of God is a terribly fearful thing.

But the psalms have a softer theme as well, one that is developed broadly in the New Testament. And Isaac Watts, the latter-day psalmist, presents this to us as well. Our Lord is a tender Shepherd. He is one who cares for us. In the context of God's greatness, the last stanza of today's hymn is quite stunning. The sovereign King does "condescend." He does call Himself our Father and Friend. This is the essence of the gospel: the mighty God seeks a relationship with the people He created.

· · · ·

The Lord will reign forever. He will be your God, O Jerusalem, throughout the generations. Praise the Lord!
PSALM 146:10

Come, Thou Almighty King

Presidents, kings, and other ruling officials should be honored and prayed for. So wrote the apostles Peter and Paul, who lived under the Roman emperors. But we must never forget that the King of kings and Lord of lords deserves our ultimate honor and complete allegiance.

This hymn appeared anonymously in George Whitefield's *Hymn Book*, published in 1757. It is usually attributed to Charles Wesley, but was probably published anonymously for a good reason. Scholars think Wesley wrote this hymn as an imitation of the English national anthem, "God Save Our Gracious King." The national anthem had just been written, and it had become popular throughout England. This hymn may have been Wesley's way of keeping priorities straight.

• • • •

Come, let us sing to the Lord! Let us shout joyfully to the Rock of our salvation. Let us come to him with thanksgiving. Let us sing psalms of praise to him. For the Lord is a great God, a great King above all gods.

PSALM 95:1-3

Come, Thou Almighty King,
Help us Thy name to sing,
Help us to praise:
Father! all-glorious,
O'er all victorious,
Come, and reign over us,
Ancient of Days.

Come, Thou Incarnate Word,
Gird on Thy mighty sword,
Our prayer attend!
Come, and Thy people bless,
And give Thy word success:
Spirit of holiness,
On us descend.

Come, Holy Comforter,
Thy sacred witness bear
In this glad hour!
Thou, who almighty art,
Now rule in ev'ry heart
And ne'er from us depart,
Spirit of pow'r.

To Thee, great One in Three,
Eternal praises be,
Hence evermore;
Thy sov'reign majesty
May we in glory see,
And to eternity
Love and adore.

Author unknown

O Day of Rest and Gladness

O day of rest and gladness,
O day of joy and light,
O balm of care and sadness,
Most beautiful, most bright:
On thee the high and lowly,
Through ages joined in tune,
Sing holy, holy, holy,
To the great God Triune.

On thee, at the creation,
The light first had its birth;
On thee for our salvation
Christ rose from depths of earth;
On thee our Lord victorious
The Spirit sent from heaven,
And thus on thee most glorious
A triple light was given.

Today on weary nations
The heavenly manna falls;
To holy convocations
The silver trumpet calls,
Where Gospel light is glowing
With pure and radiant beams,
And living water flowing
With soul-refreshing streams.

New graces ever gaining
From this our day of rest,
We reach the rest remaining
To spirits of the blest.
To Holy Ghost be praises,
To Father, and to Son;
The Church her voice upraises
To Thee, blest Three in One.

Christopher Wordsworth (1807–1885)

"It is the first duty of a hymn," said Christopher Wordsworth, "to teach sound doctrine and thence to save souls." He opposed the trend of nineteenth-century hymnists to write about personal experiences. As the nephew of the noted English poet William Wordsworth, he might have been expected to be a poet as well. But after distinguishing himself as a scholar and athlete at Cambridge, he went into the ministry, eventually becoming a Church of England bishop. He was a recognized Greek scholar and wrote a commentary on the entire Bible as well as a hymnal including 117 original hymns. The second stanza of this hymn is a good example of the way Wordsworth used his hymns to teach doctrine. On the first day of the week God created light; on the first day of the week, Christ arose; and on the first day of the week the Holy Spirit was given. Thus, Sunday is a day honored three times.

• • • •

This is the day the Lord has made. We will rejoice and be glad in it.
PSALM 118:24

Day by Day and with Each Passing Moment

God is always with us, even during our most painful experiences. Carolina Sandell Berg understood this truth personally. She was never strong as a child, so she spent much time in her father's study and grew especially close to him. When she was twenty-six, she accompanied her father, who was a parish pastor in Fröderyd, Sweden, on a voyage to Göteborg. As they stood on deck, the boat lurched and spilled Pastor Sandell overboard. The crew was unable to save him, and he drowned as his daughter looked on.

Berg was already well known for hymns she had published as a young girl, but this tragedy inspired many more. At the loss of her earthly father, she drew even closer to her heavenly Father. She discovered that even during the times of greatest loss, God's comforting presence was near.

• • • •

We are pressed on every side by troubles, but we are not crushed. We are perplexed, but not driven to despair. We are hunted down, but never abandoned by God. We get knocked down, but we are not destroyed.

2 CORINTHIANS 4:8-9

Day by day and with each passing moment,
    Strength I find to meet my trials here;
  Trusting in my Father's wise bestowment,
    I've no cause for worry or for fear.
  He whose heart is kind beyond all measure
  Gives unto each day what He deems best—
    Lovingly, its part of pain and pleasure,
    Mingling toil with peace and rest.

  Ev'ry day the Lord Himself is near me
    With a special mercy for each hour;
All my cares He fain would bear, and cheer me,
    He whose name is Counsellor and Pow'r.
  The protection of His child and treasure
    Is a charge that on Himself He laid;
"As thy days, thy strength shall be in measure,"
    This the pledge to me He made.

  Help me then in ev'ry tribulation
    So to trust Thy promises, O Lord,
  That I lose not faith's sweet consolation
    Offered me within Thy holy Word.
Help me, Lord, when toil and trouble meeting,
    E'er to take, as from a father's hand,
  One by one, the days, the moments fleeting,
    Till I reach the promised land.

Carolina Sandell Berg (1832-1903)

———————————

Translated by Andrew L. Skoog (1856-1934)

I'll Praise My Maker While I've Breath

I'll praise my Maker while I've breath;
  And when my voice is lost in death,
Praise shall employ my nobler pow'rs;
  My days of praise shall ne'er be past,
While life, and thought, and being last,
    Or immortality endures.

Happy the man whose hopes rely
  On Israel's God! He made the sky,
And earth, and sea, with all their train:
  His truth for ever stands secure;
He saves the oppressed, He feeds the poor,
  And none shall find His promise vain.

The Lord gives eyesight to the blind;
  The Lord supports the fainting mind;
He sends the laboring conscience peace;
  He helps the stranger in distress,
    The widow and the fatherless
And grants the prisoner sweet release.

I'll praise Him while He lends me breath;
  And when my voice is lost in death,
Praise shall employ my nobler pow'rs;
  My days of praise shall ne'er be past,
While life, and thought, and being last,
    Or immortality endures.

Isaac Watts (1674–1748)

In Westminster Abbey stands a statue of Isaac Watts with a pen in his hand. Not far from Watts, John Wesley is also honored. Today's hymn has connections to both men.

As John Wesley lay dying, he surprised the friends gathered around his bedside by singing in a clear voice this hymn of Isaac Watts: "I'll praise my Maker while I've breath, and when my voice is lost in death, praise shall employ my nobler powers."

The next day he tried to sing the hymn again, but he could not. Two or three times he began, but could only say the words "I'll praise." With those words on his lips, he was ushered into glory.

The hymn is a paraphrase of Psalm 146. Many of Watts's hymns are similarly based on psalms: "O God, Our Help in Ages Past" (January 29) is based on Psalm 90, "Jesus Shall Reign" (June 1) is from Psalm 72, and "Joy to the World" (December 25) is from Psalm 98.

• • • •

Praise the Lord! Let all that I am praise the Lord. I will praise the Lord as long as I live. I will sing praises to my God with my dying breath. . . . But joyful are those who have the God of Israel as their helper, whose hope is in the Lord their God.
PSALM 146:1-2, 5

Sing Praise to God Who Reigns Above

One hundred years after Martin Luther, the Lutheran church in Germany needed a revival. God used a Lutheran pastor in Frankfurt, Philip Jacob Spener, to begin the Pietist movement and breathe life into dead orthodoxy. Spener emphasized the importance of personal commitment to Jesus Christ as well as a continuing devotional life. Johann Schütz, a prominent Frankfurt lawyer and an authority in civil and canon law, helped Spener establish cell groups throughout the area. Schütz also wrote several hymns and was responsible for a number of religious publications.

The warmth and personal application of the Pietist movement exudes from Schütz's hymns. Notice the third stanza. "The Lord is never far away" displays the Pietist emphasis on the nearness of God in our daily affairs. "As with a mother's tender hand, He leads His own" reveals the emotional power of the movement.

• • • •

Sing to the Lord, for he has done wonderful things. Make known his praise around the world. Let all the people of Jerusalem shout his praise with joy! For great is the Holy One of Israel who lives among you.

ISAIAH 12:5-6

Sing praise to God who reigns above,
The God of all creation,
The God of pow'r, the God of love,
The God of our salvation.
With healing balm my soul He fills,
And ev'ry faithless murmur stills:
To God all praise and glory!

What God's almighty pow'r hath made
His gracious mercy keepeth,
By morning glow or evening shade
His watchful eye ne'er sleepeth.
Within the kingdom of His might,
Lo! all is just and all is right:
To God all praise and glory!

The Lord is never far away,
But, through all grief distressing,
An ever-present help and stay,
Our peace and joy and blessing.
As with a mother's tender hand
He leads His own, His chosen band:
To God all praise and glory!

Thus all my toilsome way along
I sing aloud His praises,
That men may hear the grateful song
My voice unwearied raises.
Be joyful in the Lord, my heart!
Both soul and body bear your part:
To God all praise and glory!

Johann Jakob Schütz (1640-1690)

Translated by Frances Elizabeth Cox (1812-1897)

Ah, Holy Jesus

Ah, holy Jesus, how hast Thou offended,
That man to judge Thee hath in hate pretended?
By foes derided, by Thine own rejected,
O most afflicted!

Who was the guilty? Who brought this upon Thee?
Alas, my treason, Jesus, hath undone Thee!
'Twas I, Lord Jesus, I it was denied Thee:
I crucified Thee.

Lo, the good Shepherd for the sheep is offered;
The slave hath sinned, and the Son hath suffered;
For man's atonement, while he nothing heedeth,
God intercedeth.

For me, kind Jesus, was Thy incarnation,
Thy mortal sorrow, and Thy Life's oblation;
Thy death of anguish and Thy bitter passion,
For my salvation.

Therefore, kind Jesus, since I cannot pay Thee,
I do adore Thee, and will ever pray Thee,
Think on Thy pity and Thy love unswerving,
Not my deserving.

Johann Heermann (1585-1647)

Translated by Robert Seymour Bridges (1844-1930)

In 1611 Johann Heermann became the Lutheran pastor in Köben, Germany, and during his years there, the village suffered numerous disasters. During the Thirty Years' War, plunder by both Catholic and Protestant armies and devastation by fire and plague decimated the population. More than once Heermann narrowly escaped with his life, and several times he lost everything he owned. During these years of horror, he turned to hymnwriting for consolation, especially after throat trouble forced him to stop preaching.

Heermann drew inspiration for this hymn from a Latin text attributed variously to Augustine (354–430) and Jean de Fécamp (c. 1000–1079). As we look toward the Cross this Easter season, we might well ask, "Why did Jesus have to suffer?" This hymn pronounces the simple answer: "For me . . ."

• • • •

He was despised and rejected—a man of sorrows, acquainted with deepest grief. We turned our backs on him and looked the other way. He was despised, and we did not care. Yet it was our weaknesses he carried; it was our sorrows that weighed him down.
ISAIAH 53:3-4

All Hail the Power of Jesus' Name

Edward Perronet was not an easy person to get along with. After being a minister in the Anglican church for some time, he became fed up with what he felt was the church's "nonsense" and became a Methodist, joining up with the Wesleys. As a Methodist he faced persecution. On at least one occasion, "Edward Perronet was thrown down and rolled in mud and mire," as John Wesley recorded.

Perronet soon broke with the Wesleys over the issue of who could administer the sacraments. He joined a group called the Connexion but later broke with them as well. It was as a minister of an independent church in Canterbury that he wrote this majestic hymn.

Whether Perronet intended the implication or not, the hymn points to the time all believers in Christ—regardless of petty disagreements—will join together in a celestial chorus.

• • • •

Then I saw heaven opened, and a white horse was standing there. Its rider was named Faithful and True, for he judges fairly and wages a righteous war. His eyes were like flames of fire, and on his head were many crowns.

REVELATION 19:11-12

All hail the pow'r of Jesus' name!
Let angels prostrate fall;
Bring forth the royal diadem,
And crown Him Lord of all;
Bring forth the royal diadem,
And crown Him Lord of all!

Ye chosen seed of Israel's race,
Ye ransomed from the fall,
Hail Him who saves you by His grace,
And crown Him Lord of all;
Hail Him who saves you by His grace,
And crown Him Lord of all!

Let ev'ry kindred, ev'ry tribe,
On this terrestrial ball,
To Him all majesty ascribe,
And crown Him Lord of all;
To Him all majesty ascribe,
And crown Him Lord of all!

O that with yonder sacred throng
We at His feet may fall!
We'll join the everlasting song,
And crown Him Lord of all;
We'll join the everlasting song,
And crown Him Lord of all!

Edward Perronet (1726-1792)

Altered by John Rippon (1751-1836)

According to Thy Gracious Word

According to Thy gracious word,
In meek humility,
This will I do, my dying Lord,
I will remember Thee.

Thy body, broken for my sake,
My bread from heaven shall be;
Thy testamental cup I take,
And thus remember Thee.

Remember Thee, and all Thy pains,
And all Thy love to me;
Yea, while a breath, a pulse remains,
Will I remember Thee!

And when these failing lips grow dumb,
And mind and memory flee,
When Thou shalt in Thy kingdom come,
Then, Lord, remember me!

James Montgomery (1771-1854)

As a London newspaper editor, James Montgomery remembered the poor and downtrodden. He worked hard for the abolition of slavery and was imprisoned twice for his strong editorials.

It would have been easy for this busy journalist to get caught up in the vital issues of the day and to forget the vital issues of eternity. But Montgomery resolved that he would never become too busy to remember what Jesus had done for him.

There are many earthly concerns that press into our lives, some of national or international importance, others affecting only ourselves or our families. They can become so important that they overshadow eternal issues. Let us, with James Montgomery, resolve never to forget our Lord.

• • • •

After supper he took another cup of wine and said, "This cup is the new covenant between God and his people—an agreement confirmed with my blood, which is poured out as a sacrifice for you."
LUKE 22:20

Jesus, Priceless Treasure

Jesus told a story about a man who found treasure buried in a field. The man sold all he had to buy that field. A merchant found a pearl of great price and sold his fortune to claim it. That, Jesus said, is what the Kingdom of God is all about—giving up everything to gain eternity.

A rich man came to Jesus and asked what he had to do in order to gain eternal life. Jesus told him to sell all he had and give it to the poor, then he could come and follow Jesus.

Such a complete sacrifice scares most of us. We cling to our possessions and relationships and habits. We can't imagine life without them. We assume that a life totally sold out to Jesus would be dry and joyless. But that couldn't be further from the truth. Jesus is our "purest pleasure." Possessions rust and wear out, but Jesus gives joy forever.

• • • •

O God, you are my God; I earnestly search for you. My soul thirsts for you; my whole body longs for you in this parched and weary land where there is no water. I have seen you in your sanctuary and gazed upon your power and glory.
PSALM 63:1-2

Jesus, priceless treasure,
Source of purest pleasure,
Truest friend to me,
Long my heart hath panted,
Till it well-nigh fainted,
Thirsting after Thee.
Thine I am, O spotless Lamb,
I will suffer naught to hide Thee,
Ask for naught beside Thee.

In Thine arm I rest me;
Foes who would molest me
Cannot reach me here.
Though the earth be shaking,
Every heart be quaking,
God dispels our fear;
Sin and hell in conflict fell
With their heaviest storms assail us;
Jesus will not fail us.

Hence, all thoughts of sadness!
For the Lord of gladness,
Jesus, enters in;
Those who love the Father,
Though the storms may gather,
Still have peace within;
Yea, whate'er we here must bear,
Still in Thee lies purest pleasure,
Jesus, priceless treasure!

Johann Franck (1618-1677)

Translated by Catherine Winkworth (1827-1878)

Before Jehovah's Awful Throne

Before Jehovah's awful throne,
Ye nations, bow with sacred joy; .
Know that the Lord is God alone;
He can create, and He destroy.

We are His people, we His care,
Our souls and all our mortal frame;
What lasting honors shall we rear,
Almighty Maker, to Thy name?

We'll crowd Thy gates with thankful songs,
High as the heavens our voices raise;
And earth with her ten thousand tongues
Shall fill Thy courts with sounding praise.

Wide as the world is Thy command,
Vast as eternity Thy love;
Firm as a rock Thy truth must stand,
When rolling years shall cease to move.

Isaac Watts (1674-1748)

Jehovah's *awful* throne? Isaac Watts did not think that God's throne was *bad*, as we understand the word *awful* today. It was full of awe, awe-inspiring, and (as a generation of teenagers might say) "Awesome!"

One British Christian of the 1800s told of a service in which Charles Haddon Spurgeon led a congregation of nearly ten thousand in this hymn. "It is scarcely possible," he wrote, "to give any idea of the sublime effect produced by those ten thousand voices as they swelled the massive harmonies of that grand tune with a fullness of sound rarely heard." As the crowd sang, "not a voice was mute, save where occasionally someone's nerves were overpowered by the massive rolling chorus that rose on every side. Never did we before realize what congregational singing might become." But we will all find out on that day when we surround Jehovah's throne.

. . . .

Shout with joy to the Lord, all the earth!
Worship the Lord with gladness. Come before
him, singing with joy. . . . Enter his gates with
thanksgiving; go into his courts with praise.
Give thanks to him and praise his name.
PSALM 100:1-2, 4

There Is a Balm in Gilead

After Joseph's brothers beat him up and threw him into a pit, they sold him to a caravan passing through. The merchants were traveling from Gilead to Egypt, with spices, balm, and myrrh. Gilead, the area just east of the Jordan near Galilee, was famous for its medicinal balms.

When Jeremiah cried out for the healing of his people, he looked for a cure in Gilead but found none. The people were rebellious, obstinate, willfully blind to what God was doing.

The disease was sin. We all suffer from "sin-sick souls." We are unable to live righteous lives. This is the human condition, the plague of Adam's curse—a terminal illness.

Fortunately, this song answers Jeremiah's question with a resounding *yes*. There *is* a balm in Gilead, and it rests in the simple truth that Jesus died for all, and He alone can heal the soul sick with sin.

There is a balm in Gilead
To make the wounded whole;
There is a balm in Gilead
To heal the sin-sick soul.

Sometimes I feel discouraged,
And think my work's in vain,
But then the Holy Spirit
Revives my soul again.

If you cannot preach like Peter,
If you cannot pray like Paul,
You can tell the love of Jesus,
And say, "He died for all."

Traditional spiritual

• • • •

I hurt with the hurt of my people. I mourn and am overcome with grief. Is there no medicine in Gilead? Is there no physician there? Why is there no healing for the wounds of my people?
JEREMIAH 8:21-22

Bread of Heaven, on Thee We Feed

Bread of heaven, on Thee we feed,
For Thy Flesh is meat indeed;
Ever may our souls be fed
With this true and living Bread;
Day by day with strength supplied,
Through the life of Him who died.

Vine of heaven, Thy Blood supplies
This blest cup of sacrifice;
Lord, Thy wounds our healing give,
To Thy cross we look and live:
Jesus, may we ever be
Grafted, rooted, built in Thee.

Josiah Conder (1789–1855), altered

This is a Communion hymn, and Communion has been one of the most divisive issues in Christendom. Do the bread and wine merely represent the body and blood of Christ, or is there some mystical way in which they *are* the body and blood? Is the purpose of the Lord's Supper to remind us of our Lord's sacrifice or somehow to welcome us into participation with it?

This hymn steers clear of the controversial areas and centers on Christ Himself. Whatever the Lord's Supper is or means, it is part of our whole interaction with Christ. We take the bread in the church service, but we enjoy our "daily bread" every time Christ provides the strength or wisdom we need. We drink the wine of Communion, but we also rejoice in the benefits of His death. We are healed by His wounds. And as a growing tree derives nourishment from its deep roots, so we find sustenance as we are rooted in Christ.

• • • •

Jesus said, "I tell you the truth, Moses didn't give you bread from heaven. My Father did. And now he offers you the true bread from heaven. . . . I am the bread of life. Whoever comes to me will never be hungry again. Whoever believes in me will never be thirsty.
JOHN 6:32, 35

O Love That Will Not Let Me Go

George Matheson went completely blind when he was eighteen years old. Still, he went on to become a great preacher in the Church of Scotland, assisted by his sister, who learned Greek and Hebrew to help with his research.

This hymn was written on the evening of June 6, 1882. Matheson later wrote, "It was the day of my sister's marriage. . . . Something happened to me, which was known only to myself, and which caused me the most severe mental suffering. The hymn was the fruit of that suffering."

What was it that happened to him? Some think he was remembering the time his fiancée broke their engagement when she learned that he was going blind. Or perhaps it was difficult for him to have his devoted sister getting married. In any case, he was led to ponder God's eternal love, which would turn his "flick'ring torch" into blazing daylight.

• • • •

I am convinced that nothing can ever separate us from God's love. Neither death nor life, neither angels nor demons, neither our fears for today nor our worries about tomorrow—not even the powers of hell can separate us from God's love.

ROMANS 8:38

O Love that will not let me go,
I rest my weary soul in Thee;
I give Thee back the life I owe,
That in Thine ocean depths its flow
May richer, fuller be.

O Light that foll'west all my way,
I yield my flick'ring torch to Thee;
My heart restores its borrowed ray,
That in Thy sunshine's blaze its day
May brighter, fairer be.

O Joy that seekest me through pain,
I cannot close my heart to Thee;
I trace the rainbow through the rain,
And feel the promise is not vain
That morn shall tearless be.

O Cross that liftest up my head,
I dare not ask to fly from Thee;
I lay in dust life's glory dead,
And from the ground there blossoms red
Life that shall endless be.

George Matheson (1842–1906)

Awake, My Soul, and with the Sun

Awake, my soul, and with the sun
    Thy daily stage of duty run:
Shake off dull sloth, and joyful rise
    To pay thy morning sacrifice.

Wake, and lift up thyself, my heart,
    And with the angels bear thy part,
Who all night long unwearied sing
    High praise to the eternal King.

All Praise to Thee, who safe has kept,
    And hast refreshed me while I slept:
Grant, Lord, when I from death shall wake
    I may of endless life partake.

Lord, I my vows to Thee renew;
    Disperse my sins as morning dew;
Guard my first springs of thought and will,
    And with Thyself my spirit fill.

Direct, control, suggest, this day,
    All I design, or do, or say,
That all my powers, with all their might,
    In Thy sole glory may unite.

Praise God, from whom all blessings flow;
    Praise Him, all creatures here below;
Praise Him above, ye heavenly host;
    Praise Father, Son, and Holy Ghost.

Thomas Ken (1637–1711)

Bishop Thomas Ken wrote this hymn to remind the students of Winchester College of their daily duties. While his students may not always have appreciated these admonitions, they probably echoed the conclusion—the well-known doxology. In fact, Ken ended three different hymns with this concluding stanza. In his private devotions, Ken used all the stanzas of this hymn (he wrote thirteen), accompanying himself on the lute.

The bishop had a checkered career, caused mostly by the fact that he wasn't intimidated by royalty and condemned immorality when he saw it. He died in poverty, leaving behind only an old lute and an old horse. But he did manage to pass along some memorable hymns and a doxology that is sung in churches around the world. He was buried early in the morning as the sun was beginning to rise. Those present sang all thirteen stanzas of this hymn.

• • • •

What mighty praise, O God, belongs to you in Zion. We will fulfill our vows to you, for you answer our prayers. All of us must come to you. Though we are overwhelmed by our sins, you forgive them all.
PSALM 65:1-3

O the Deep, Deep Love of Jesus

How deep is the love of Jesus? This hymn tries to express something of its magnitude. It is an ocean and more. It is a "heaven of heavens." But what does that mean? How does knowing of this deep, deep love affect the way we live each day?

Perhaps most important, it reassures us. When the apostle Paul says that nothing can separate us from the love of Christ, we know that even our own sin will not stop Jesus from loving us. He continually offers His loving forgiveness. Christ's love also motivates us. "Spread his praise from shore to shore!" The deep, deep love of Jesus is so great, we just have to tell someone! This "love of every love the best" makes Christ the highest priority in our lives. All other longings fall by the wayside as we bask and bathe in the vast ocean of Jesus' love for us.

• • • •

May you have the power to understand, as all God's people should, how wide, how long, how high, and how deep his love is. May you experience the love of Christ, though it is too great to understand fully.

EPHESIANS 3:18-19

O the deep, deep love of Jesus,
Vast, unmeasured, boundless, free!
Rolling as a mighty ocean
In its fullness over me,
Underneath me, all around me,
Is the current of Thy love;
Leading onward, leading homeward
To my glorious rest above.

O the deep, deep love of Jesus,
Spread His praise from shore to shore!
How He loveth, ever loveth,
Changeth never, nevermore;
How He watches o'er His loved ones,
Died to call them all His own;
How for them He intercedeth,
Watcheth o'er them from the throne.

O the deep, deep love of Jesus,
Love of every love the best;
'Tis an ocean vast of blessing,
'Tis a haven sweet of rest,
O the deep, deep love of Jesus,
'Tis a heav'n of heav'ns to me;
And it lifts me up to glory,
For it lifts me up to Thee.

Samuel Trevor Francis (1834-1925)

Come, Christians, Join to Sing

Come, Christians, join to sing,
  Alleluia! Amen!
Loud praise to Christ our King;
  Alleluia! Amen!
Let all, with heart and voice,
Before His throne rejoice;
Praise is His gracious choice:
  Alleluia! Amen!

Come, lift your hearts on high,
  Alleluia! Amen!
Let praises fill the sky;
  Alleluia! Amen!
He is our Guide and Friend;
To us He'll condescend;
His love shall never end:
  Alleluia! Amen!

Praise yet our Christ again,
  Alleluia! Amen!
Life shall not end the strain;
  Alleluia! Amen!
On heaven's blissful shore
His goodness we'll adore,
Singing forevermore,
  "Alleluia! Amen!"

Christian H. Bateman (1813–1889)

This hymn was originally written as a Sunday school song with the title "Come, *Children*, Join to Sing." But since adults, too, found great joy in the song, the title was changed.

After studying to become a minister in a Moravian church, Christian Bateman pastored several Congregational churches in England and Scotland and finally ended up in the Church of England. It was as if his whole career welcomed all believers, of all denominations, to "join to sing, Alleluia! Amen!"

The words *alleluia* and *amen* are both from the Bible. We find *alleluia* (or *hallelujah*) frequently in the Psalms. It means, "Praise the Lord!" We find *amen* at the end of prayers and at the beginning of some of Jesus' statements. Whenever He says, "Truly, truly I say to you," in the original language it's "Amen, amen I say to you." *Amen* means "assuredly," "indeed," or "so be it."

• • • •

Be filled with the Holy Spirit, singing psalms and hymns and spiritual songs among yourselves, and making music to the Lord in your hearts. And give thanks for everything to God the Father in the name of our Lord Jesus Christ.

EPHESIANS 5:18-20

A Wonderful Savior Is Jesus My Lord

As a blind person, Fanny Crosby faced daily insecurity. That is why she found so much comfort in the book of Psalms, and why so many of her hymns point to the security we have in the Lord. Perhaps that is why this gospel song was one of her favorites. Like David in the desert, she sometimes felt alone and vulnerable. But she found comfort in the psalmist's figures of speech. In the words of Scripture she prayed, "Hide me," and many psalms would come to mind (e.g., Psalm 17:8; 27:5; 31:20; 32:7). She seemed to focus on Psalms 62–64.

Another psalm image, "the cleft of the Rock," has special meaning for Christians because we know that Jesus is the Rock who was broken for us. When we consider how the hand of God covers us, shielding us from harm, we can only express praise to God. "O glory to God for such a Redeemer as mine!" What wonderful security we have in Him!

• • • •

The one thing I ask of the Lord—the thing I seek most—is to live in the house of the Lord all the days of my life. . . . For he will conceal me there when troubles come; he will hide me in his sanctuary. He will place me out of reach on a high rock.

PSALM 27:4-5

A wonderful Savior is Jesus my Lord,
A wonderful Savior to me;
He hideth my soul in the cleft of the rock,
Where rivers of pleasure I see.

He hideth my soul in the cleft of the rock
That shadows a dry, thirsty land;
He hideth my life in the depths of His love,
And covers me there with His hand,
And covers me there with His hand.

A wonderful Savior is Jesus my Lord,
He taketh my burden away;
He holdeth me up, and I shall not be moved,
He giveth me strength as my day.

With numberless blessings each moment He crowns,
And, filled with His fulness divine,
I sing in my rapture, "O glory to God
For such a Redeemer as mine!"

When clothed in His brightness transported I rise,
To meet Him in clouds of the sky,
His perfect salvation, His wonderful love,
I'll shout with the millions on high.

Fanny Jane Crosby (1820–1915)

The Heavens Declare Thy Glory, Lord

The heavens declare Thy glory, Lord;
In every star Thy wisdom shines;
But when our eyes behold Thy Word,
We read Thy name in fairer lines.

The rolling sun, the changing light,
And nights and days, Thy power confess;
But the blest Volume Thou hast writ
Reveals Thy justice and Thy grace.

Sun, moon, and stars convey Thy praise
Round the whole earth, and never stand;
So when Thy truth began its race,
It touched and glanced on every land.

Nor shall Thy spreading gospel rest
Till through the world Thy truth has run;
Till Christ has all the nations blest
That see the light, or feel the sun.

Isaac Watts (1674–1748)

Isaac Watts was tired of singing dull songs. In his time, churches sang only psalms, and the English translations were wooden and confusing. "Tho' the Psalms of David are a Work of admirable and divine Composure," he wrote, "tho' they contain the noblest Sentiments of Piety, and breathe a most exalted Spirit of Devotion, yet when the best of Christians attempt to sing many of them in our common Translations, that Spirit of Devotion vanishes and is lost, the Psalm dies upon their Lips, and they feel scarce any thing of the holy Pleasure."

Watts felt it was important to bring out the spiritual impact of each psalm and to bring in the New Testament fulfillment of ancient longings. Just as the heavens declared God's glory in a fixed but ever-turning way, so Watts could present God's truth clearly to a new generation.

• • • •

The heavens proclaim the glory of God. The skies display his craftsmanship. . . . Yet their message has gone throughout the earth, and their words to all the world.
PSALM 19:1, 4

I Am Thine, O Lord

Cincinnati, Ohio, was the birthplace of this favorite hymn. Fanny Crosby, the prolific blind poetess, was visiting her friend and collaborator William H. Doane in his home. The sun was setting, and though Crosby could not see the changing light, she could certainly hear and feel the hush of twilight. Their conversation turned to the nearness of God. Crosby was touched by their talk and wrote the words of this hymn before she retired that night. Doane added the music in the morning.

It may be that the "friend to friend" communion of the third stanza is an allusion to Crosby's fine friendship with Doane. If a mere human can be such a friend, how much greater would a friendship be with the Author of love, the Lord of all?

Crosby had a talent for focusing attention on Christ, and on the glories of eternal life with Him. In that way, she opened the eyes of believers everywhere.

I am Thine, O Lord, I have heard Thy voice,
And it told Thy love to me;
But I long to rise in the arms of faith,
And be closer drawn to Thee.

Draw me nearer, nearer, blessed Lord,
To the cross where Thou hast died;
Draw me nearer, nearer, nearer, blessed Lord,
To Thy precious, bleeding side.

Consecrate me now to Thy service, Lord,
By the pow'r of grace divine;
Let my soul look up with a steadfast hope,
And my will be lost in Thine.

O, the pure delight of a single hour
That before Thy throne I spend,
When I kneel in prayer, and with Thee, my God,
I commune as friend with friend!

There are depths of love that I cannot know
Till I cross the narrow sea;
There are heights of joy that I may not reach
Till I rest in peace with Thee.

Fanny Jane Crosby (1820–1915)

• • • •

So humble yourselves before God. Resist the devil, and he will flee from you. Come close to God, and God will come close to you.
JAMES 4:7-8

Turn Your Eyes upon Jesus

O soul, are you weary and troubled?
No light in the darkness you see?
There's light for a look at the Savior,
And life more abundant and free!

Turn your eyes upon Jesus,
Look full in His wonderful face,
And the things of earth will grow strangely dim
In the light of His glory and grace.

Through death into life everlasting
He passed, and we follow Him there;
Over us sin no more hath dominion—
For more than conquerors we are!

His word shall not fail you—He promised;
Believe Him, and all will be well:
Then go to a world that is dying,
His perfect salvation to tell!

Helen Howarth Lemmel (1864–1961)

Copyright © 1922. Singspiration Music/ASCAP. All rights reserved. Used by permission of Benson Music Group, Inc.

Helen Lemmel was already a noted Christian singer and voice teacher on that day in 1918 when a friend of hers, a missionary, handed her a tract called "Focused." It said, "So then, turn your eyes upon Him, look full into His face and you will find that the things of earth will acquire a strange new dimness."

The tract struck a chord in Lemmel. "Suddenly," she said later, "as if commanded to stop and listen, I stood still, and singing in my soul and spirit was the chorus, with not one conscious moment of putting word to word to make rhyme, or note to note to make melody. The verses were written the same week, after the usual manner of composition."

Later the same year, the song was published in London in pamphlet form. It quickly became a favorite of Christians in England (especially at the Keswick Convention), then in America, and around the world.

• • • •

Since you have been raised to new life with Christ, set your sights on the realities of heaven, where Christ sits in the place of honor at God's right hand. Think about the things of heaven, not the things of earth. For you died to this life, and your real life is hidden with Christ in God.

COLOSSIANS 3:1–3

I Am His, and He Is Mine

Does Christ make a difference here on earth? Does He change the earthly lives of those who love Him?

Yes! Life as a Christian is infinitely richer, more joyful, and more secure. Christians know the Creator, and that changes everything.

The sky is bluer, the grass greener, the birds cheerier, the flowers more beautiful. Why? At face value, we might compare this hymn to your standard love song—"everything seems better because you put me in a good mood." And certainly there is a "romantic" element here; the key phrase is even borrowed from the Song of Songs. But there's more to Robinson's thesis than just a good mood. We can appreciate the blue sky and green grass even more because we recognize that these are gifts from the God who loves us. They are expressions of who He is, and we love Him with all our heart.

• • • •

I am the good shepherd; I know my own sheep, and they know me, just as my Father knows me and I know the Father. . . . My sheep listen to my voice; I know them, and they follow me. . . . No one can snatch them away from me.

JOHN 10:14-15, 27-28

Loved with everlasting love,
Led by grace that love to know;
Spirit, breathing from above,
Thou hast taught me it is so!
Oh, this full and perfect peace!
Oh, this transport all divine!
In a love which cannot cease,
I am His, and He is mine.

Heav'n above is softer blue,
Earth around is sweeter green!
Something lives in ev'ry hue
Christless eyes have never seen:
Birds with gladder songs o'erflow
Flow'rs with deeper beauties shine,
Since I know, as now I know,
I am His, and He is mine.

Things that once were wild alarms
Cannot now disturb my rest;
Closed in everlasting arms,
Pillowed on the loving breast.
Oh, to lie forever here,
Doubt, and care, and self resign,
While He whispers in my ear—
I am His, and He is mine.

His forever, only His;
Who the Lord and me shall part?
Ah, with what a rest of bliss,
Christ can fill the loving heart!
Heav'n and earth may fade and flee,
First born light in gloom decline;
But while God and I shall be,
I am His, and He is mine.

George Wade Robinson (1838–1877)

Amazing Grace

Amazing grace! how sweet the sound—
That saved a wretch like me!
I once was lost but now am found,
Was blind but now I see.

'Twas grace that taught my heart to fear,
And grace my fears relieved;
How precious did that grace appear
The hour I first believed!

The Lord has promised good to me,
His word my hope secures;
He will my shield and portion be
As long as life endures.

Through many dangers, toils and snares
I have already come;
'Tis grace hath brought me safe thus far,
And grace will lead me home.

When we've been there ten thousand years,
Bright shining as the sun,
We've no less days to sing God's praise
Than when we'd first begun.

John Newton (1725-1807)

Stanza 5, John P. Rees (1828-1900)

The gift of forgiveness is often best appreciated by those who need it the most. The Reverend John Newton experienced this truth firsthand. His tombstone tells the story: "John Newton, clerk, once an infidel and Libertine, a servant of slavers in Africa, was, by the rich mercy of our Lord and Savior Jesus Christ, preserved, restored, pardoned, and appointed to preach the faith he had so long labored to destroy." These words were written by Newton himself, a testimony to God's transforming power. After years as a hardened slave trader, that "wretch" met Jesus Christ and abruptly turned to defend the gospel he had so long despised.

When it was suggested Newton retire (at age eighty-two!) due to poor health and a failing memory, he responded, "My memory is nearly gone, but I remember two things: that I am a great sinner, and that Christ is a great Savior!"

• • • •

God saved you by his grace when you believed. And you can't take credit for this; it is a gift from God. Salvation is not a reward for the good things we have done, so none of us can boast about it.
EPHESIANS 2:8-9

Jesus, Keep Me near the Cross

This is another Fanny Crosby/William H. Doane collaboration (see March 14). But with this hymn Doane's tune came first and Crosby's words came later. When hymns are composed this way, the words sometimes seem stilted and unnatural, but not here. Crosby was masterful at hearing the message in the music. She would often say, "That tune says to me . . . ," and then write a stirring text.

Once again, the focus is the cross of Christ. Crosby realized that the Cross is the central point of history. Even in Crosby's time, some scholars and preachers were beginning to focus on the moral teaching of Jesus, the virtue and goodness that He modeled for us. This was all well and good, but they were also seriously downplaying Jesus' sacrificial crucifixion. But Crosby echoed the apostle Paul, "May I never boast about anything except the cross of our Lord Jesus Christ" (Galatians 6:14).

• • • •

Through [Christ] God reconciled everything to himself. He made peace with everything in heaven and on earth by means of Christ's blood on the cross.

COLOSSIANS 1:20

Jesus, keep me near the cross—
There a precious fountain,
Free to all, a healing stream,
Flows from Calv'ry's mountain.

In the cross, in the cross
Be my glory ever,
Till my raptured soul shall find
Rest, beyond the river.

Near the cross, a trembling soul,
Love and mercy found me;
There the Bright and Morning Star
Sheds its beams around me.

Near the cross! O Lamb of God,
Bring its scenes before me;
Help me walk from day to day
With its shadow o'er me.

Near the cross I'll watch and wait,
Hoping, trusting ever,
Till I reach the golden strand
Just beyond the river.

Fanny Jane Crosby (1820–1915)

Jesus Paid It All

I hear the Savior say,
"Thy strength indeed is small!
Child of weakness, watch and pray,
Find in Me thine all in all."

Jesus paid it all,
All to Him I owe;
Sin had left a crimson stain—
He washed it white as snow.

Lord, now indeed I find
Thy pow'r, and Thine alone,
Can change the leper's spots
And melt the heart of stone.

For nothing good have I
Whereby Thy grace to claim—
I'll wash my garments white
In the blood of Calv'ry's Lamb.

And when before the throne
I stand in Him complete,
"Jesus died my soul to save,"
My lips shall still repeat.

Elvina Mabel Hall (1820-1889)

What do you do when the pastor rambles on too long? Elvina Hall wrote a hymn. Seated in the choir loft at the Monument Street Methodist Church of Baltimore, she had no paper to write on—only the fly-leaf of the hymnal. There she wrote these stanzas.

The composer of the well-known tune to this hymn, John T. Grape, was the organist and choir director at the church. Professionally, he was a successful coal merchant, but he "dabbled in music," as he liked to say. He had come up with this tune, which he called "All to Christ I Owe." His wife liked it, but no one else seemed to.

It was the pastor, George Schrick, who put the words and tune together (we don't know how he responded to the fact that Hall had been writing while he was preaching). Hall's stanzas fit part of Grape's tune, and she probably added the chorus to fit with his tune title.

• • • •

"Come now, let's settle this," says the Lord. "Though your sins are like scarlet, I will make them as white as snow. Though they are red like crimson, I will make them as white as wool."
ISAIAH 1:18

There Is a Green Hill Far Away

From her childhood, Cecil Frances Alexander wrote poetry, and as an adult she wrote primarily for children. She felt that the truths of Christianity could best be taught through hymns, and so she tackled major doctrines with simple words. One project was a series of hymns based on the Apostles' Creed. She wrote "All Things Bright and Beautiful" (May 5) to teach about God the Father as "maker of heaven and earth." Today's hymn was written to teach about Jesus as He "suffered under Pontius Pilate, was crucified, dead and buried."

Along with her husband, Reverend William Alexander, Cecil cared for the poor families in their parish in Ireland. "From one poor home to another she went," her husband wrote. "Christ was ever with her, and in her, and all felt her influence." She reportedly wrote this song while sitting at a child's sickbed.

• • • •

Carrying the cross by himself, [Jesus] went to the place called Place of the Skull (in Hebrew, Golgotha). There they nailed him to the cross. Two others were crucified with him, one on either side, with Jesus between them.

JOHN 19:17-18

There is a green hill far away,
Without a city wall,
Where the dear Lord was crucified,
Who died to save us all.

**Oh, dearly, dearly has He loved,
And we must love Him too,
And trust in His redeeming blood,
And try His works to do.**

We may not know, we cannot tell
What pains He had to bear;
But we believe it was for us
He hung and suffered there.

He died that we might be forgiv'n,
He died to make us good,
That we might go at last to heav'n,
Saved by His precious blood.

There was no other good enough
To pay the price of sin;
He only could unlock the gate
Of heav'n, and let us in.

Cecil Frances Alexander (1818–1895)

Were You There?

Were you there when they crucified my Lord?
Were you there when they crucified my Lord?
O! Sometimes it causes me to tremble,
tremble, tremble!
Were you there when they crucified my Lord?

Were you there when they nailed Him to the tree?
Were you there when they nailed Him to the tree?
O! Sometimes it causes me to tremble,
tremble, tremble!
Were you there when they nailed Him to the tree?

Were you there when they laid Him in the tomb?
Were you there when they laid Him in the tomb?
O! Sometimes it causes me to tremble,
tremble, tremble!
Were you there when they laid Him in the tomb?

Were you there when He rose up from the dead?
Were you there when He rose up from the dead?
O! Sometimes I feel like shouting glory, glory, glory!
Were you there when He rose up from the dead?

Traditional spiritual

This favorite hymn comes from the rich American spiritual tradition, probably developed in the early 1800s by African-American slaves. As in most spirituals, the words are simple, seizing on one central theme or concept.

Spirituals tend to have a lot of emotional appeal. As a result, this hymn, like few others, puts the singer *there*. We experience the "tremble" as we sing it. And in the triumphant final stanza, we experience the glory of a risen Lord. We are called out of the cold analysis of Christ's death, burial, and resurrection into the moment of living it. We are called out of the theological debate and into the stark reality. We hear the nails pounded into the cross, we see the onlookers wagging their heads, we smell the burial spices, and we feel the rumble of the stone rolling away. And we tremble . . . tremble . . . tremble.

• • • •

When the Roman officer overseeing the execution saw what had happened, he worshiped God and said, "Surely this man was innocent." And when all the crowd that came to see the crucifixion saw what had happened, they went home in deep sorrow.
LUKE 23:47-48

Behold the Savior of Mankind

On February 9, 1709, a fire ripped through a rectory in the village of Epworth, England. The Wesley family lost nearly everything. Miraculously, their six-year-old boy named John (who would later found the Methodist church) was saved from the fire, as was a piece of paper bearing this hymn, written by the rector, Samuel Wesley.

Samuel Wesley, father of John and Charles (and seventeen other children), was scholarly and stern. His major academic project was a study of the book of Job. And he faced a great deal of suffering himself.

This hymn, however, shows us a slightly different side of Samuel Wesley. The theme of suffering is strong, but there's an attitude of love, of devotion. Apparently he taught his famous sons more than just discipline, but also a deep appreciation for what Christ accomplished through His suffering.

Behold the Savior of mankind
Nailed to the shameful tree!
How vast the love that Him inclined
To bleed and die for thee!

Hark, how He groans, while nature shakes,
And earth's strong pillars bend!
The temple's veil in sunder breaks;
The solid marbles rend.

'Tis done! the precious ransom's paid!
"Receive my soul!" He cries;
See where He bows His sacred head!
He bows His head and dies!

But soon He'll break death's envious chain,
And in full glory shine;
O Lamb of God, was ever pain,
Was ever love, like Thine?

Samuel Wesley (1662-1735)

• • • •

By this time it was noon, and darkness fell across the whole land until three o'clock. The light from the sun was gone. And suddenly, the curtain in the sanctuary of the Temple was torn down the middle. Then Jesus shouted, "Father, I entrust my spirit into your hands!"

LUKE 23:44-46

Come, Ye Faithful, Raise the Strain

Come, ye faithful, raise the strain
Of triumphant gladness;
God hath brought His Israel
Into joy from sadness;
Loosed from Pharaoh's bitter yoke
Jacob's sons and daughters;
Led them with unmoistened foot
Through the Red Sea waters.

'Tis the spring of souls today;
Christ hath burst His prison,
And from three days' sleep in death
As a sun hath risen;
All the winter of our sins,
Long and dark, is flying
From His light, to whom we give
Laud and praise undying.

Now the queen of seasons, bright
With the day of splendor,
With the royal feast of feasts,
Comes its joy to render;
Comes to glad Jerusalem,
Who with true affection
Welcomes in unwearied strains
Jesus' resurrection.

"Alleluia!" now we cry
To our King immortal,
Who, trimphant, burst the bars
Of the tomb's dark portal;
"Alleluia" with the Son,
God the Father praising;
"Alleluia!" yet again
To the Spirit raising.

John of Damascus (eighth century)

Translated by John Mason Neale (1818–1866)

John of Damascus was an artist in a time of censorship. The Christian emperor Leo of the Byzantine Empire was trying to destroy all Christian art because he felt that such works promoted idolatry. John argued strongly in favor of art. According to tradition, the emperor punished John by (falsely) informing the Muslim caliph that John was a spy working for the Christian empire.

Not long afterwards, John left public life for the monastery at Mar Saba. There he continued his studies and also took up music. Some say he did for Eastern Christianity what Gregory the Great did in the West, organizing and codifying Christian hymns. And he wrote some himself as well.

This hymn artistically draws parallels between Israel's exodus, Christ's resurrection, and the season of spring. The ancient Greek is translated beautifully by the prolific scholar John Neale.

• • • •

Then the angel spoke to the women. "Don't be afraid!" he said. "I know you are looking for Jesus, who was crucified. He isn't here! He is risen from the dead, just as he said would happen."
MATTHEW 28:5-6

The Old Rugged Cross

"The inspiration came to me one day in 1913, when I was staying in Albion, Michigan," George Bennard wrote about the composition of this hymn. "I began to write 'The Old Rugged Cross.' I completed the melody first. The words that I first wrote were imperfect. The words of the finished hymn were put into my heart in answer to my own need. Shortly thereafter it was introduced at special meetings in Pokagon, Michigan, on June 7, 1913."

Bennard had served with the Salvation Army before being ordained in the Methodist Episcopal church. By this time he was carrying on revival services throughout the Midwest. After its debut at Pokagon, the song was presented at an evangelistic convention in Chicago. Participants then took it back to their homes throughout the country.

• • • •

He did not retaliate when he was insulted, nor threaten revenge when he suffered. He left his case in the hands of God, who always judges fairly. He personally carried our sins in his body on the cross so that we can be dead to sin and live for what is right.

I PETER 2:23-24

On a hill far away stood an old rugged cross,
The emblem of suffering and shame;
And I love that old cross where the dearest and best
For a world of lost sinners was slain.

**So I'll cherish the old rugged cross,
'Til my trophies at last I lay down;
I will cling to the old rugged cross,
And exchange it some day for a crown.**

O that old rugged cross, so despised by the world,
Has a wondrous attraction for me;
For the dear Lamb of God left His glory above
To bear it to dark Calvary.

In the old rugged cross, stained with blood so divine,
A wondrous beauty I see;
For 'twas on that old cross Jesus suffered and died
To pardon and sanctify me.

To the old rugged cross I will ever be true,
Its shame and reproach gladly bear;
Then He'll call me some day to my home far away,
Where His glory forever I'll share.

George Bennard (1873-1958)

At Calvary

Years I spent in vanity and pride,
Caring not my Lord was crucified,
Knowing not it was for me He died
On Calvary.

Mercy there was great and grace was free,
Pardon there was multiplied to me,
There my burdened soul found liberty—
At Calvary.

By God's Word at last my sin I learned—
Then I trembled at the law I'd spurned,
Till my guilty soul imploring turned
To Calvary.

Now I've giv'n to Jesus ev'rything,
Now I gladly own Him as my King,
Now my raptured soul can only sing
Of Calvary.

O the love that drew salvation's plan!
O the grace that bro't it down to man!
O the mighty gulf that God did span
At Calvary.

William Reed Newell (1868–1956)

William R. Newell was best known as a Bible teacher, commentator, pastor, and professor. Yet while on his way to teach a class at Moody Bible Institute one day, the words of this hymn began to form in his mind. He didn't want to forget these ideas, so he went into an unoccupied classroom and there scribbled the words on the back of an envelope. A few minutes later he gave the words to Daniel B. Towner, the director of music at the school. Within an hour Towner had composed music for them.

The first three stanzas tell the testimony of the Christian; the final stanza praises God for the greatness of divine love, the depth of grace, and the breadth of mercy. Since Newell is best known for a commentary on the book of Romans, it is no surprise that the last stanza bears a resemblance to Romans 11:33, "Oh, how great are God's riches and wisdom and knowledge!"

• • • •

We praise God for the glorious grace he has poured out on us who belong to his dear Son. He is so rich in kindness and grace that he purchased our freedom with the blood of his Son and forgave our sins.
EPHESIANS 1:6-7

In the Cross of Christ I Glory

Tradition has it that John Bowring—linguist, author, and British governor of Hong Kong—was inspired to write this hymn by the sight of a huge cross on the ruins of a cathedral at Macao on the south Chinese coast. Apparently the cathedral, built by Portuguese colonists, had been leveled by a typhoon, but the wall with this bronze cross remained standing. The story is unverified, but the image is a strong one—the cross "towering o'er the wrecks of time" above the shore at Macao.

• • • •

When I first came to you, dear brothers and sisters, I didn't use lofty words and impressive wisdom to tell you God's secret plan. For I decided that while I was with you I would forget everything except Jesus Christ, the one who was crucified. . . . And my message and my preaching were very plain. Rather than using clever and persuasive speeches, I relied only on the power of the Holy Spirit. I did this so you would trust not in human wisdom but in the power of God.

I CORINTHIANS 2:1-2, 4-5

In the cross of Christ I glory,
Towering o'er the wrecks of time;
All the light of sacred story
Gathers round its head sublime.

When the woes of life o'ertake me,
Hopes deceive, and fears annoy,
Never shall the cross forsake me:
Lo! it glows with peace and joy.

When the sun of bliss is beaming
Light and love upon my way,
From the Cross the radiance streaming
Adds more luster to the day.

Bane and blessing, pain and pleasure,
By the Cross are sanctified;
Peace is there, that knows no measure,
Joys that through all time abide.

In the cross of Christ I glory,
Towering o'er the wrecks of time;
All the light of sacred story
Gathers round its head sublime.

John Bowring (1792-1872)

All Glory, Laud, and Honor

All glory, laud, and honor
To Thee, Redeemer, King,
To whom the lips of children
Made sweet hosannas ring:
Thou art the King of Israel,
Thou David's royal Son,
Who in the Lord's name comest,
The King and blessed One!

The company of angels
Are praising Thee on high,
And mortal men and all things
Created make reply:
The people of the Hebrews
With palms before Thee went;
Our praise and prayer and anthems
Before Thee we present.

To Thee, before Thy passion,
They sang their hymns of praise;
To Thee, now high exalted,
Our melody we raise:
Thou didst accept their praises—
Accept the praise we bring,
Who in all good delightest,
Thou good and gracious King!

Theodulf of Orléans (c. 750–821)

Translated by John Mason Neale (1818–1866)

When Jesus entered Jerusalem riding on a donkey, hopeful crowds filled the streets waving palm branches and praising God. But less than a week later, when it became clear that Jesus was not the political and military revolutionary they expected, this same crowd demanded His crucifixion.

When life keeps pace with expectations, praise comes quite easily. But for Theodulf, whom King Charlemagne had made bishop of Orléans in the late 700s, praise was born of painful circumstances. After Charlemagne's death, Theodulf was exiled to Angers, France, on charges of conspiracy. In the dark prison at Angers, Theodulf apparently wrote the text of this hymn, which has become the great Palm Sunday processional of the Western church—a celebration of God's grace sung by millions throughout the centuries.

• • • •

Jesus was in the center of the procession, and the people all around him were shouting, "Praise God! Blessings on the one who comes in the name of the Lord! Blessings on the coming Kingdom of our ancestor David! Praise God in highest heaven!"

MARK 11:9-10

O Sacred Head, Now Wounded

Although Bernard was one of the most influential Christians of the Middle Ages, settling disputes between kings and influencing the selection of popes, he remained a devout monk, single-minded in his devotion to Christ. Even the great reformer Martin Luther, who as a rule disliked medieval theologians, said, "Bernard loved Jesus as much as anyone can."

"O Sacred Head, Now Wounded" comes from a poem originally having seven sections, each focusing on a wounded part of the crucified Savior's body—His feet, knees, hands, side, breast, heart, and head. The text of this hymn compels us to gaze at the cross until the depth of God's love overwhelms us. Bernard's hymn pictures God's love, not as an abstract theological statement, but as a profoundly personal and awesome vision of the suffering Christ.

• • • •

Yet it was our weaknesses he carried; it was our sorrows that weighed him down. . . . He was pierced for our rebellion, crushed for our sins. He was beaten so we could be whole. He was whipped so we could be healed.

ISAIAH 53:4-5

O sacred Head, now wounded,
With grief and shame weighed down,
Now scornfully surrounded
With thorns Thine only crown:
How pale Thou art with anguish,
With sore abuse and scorn!
How does that visage languish
Which once was bright as morn!

What Thou, my Lord, has suffered
Was all for sinners' gain;
Mine, mine was the transgression,
But Thine the deadly pain.
Lo, here I fall, my Savior!
'Tis I deserve Thy place;
Look on me with Thy favor,
Vouchsafe to me Thy grace.

What language shall I borrow
To thank Thee, dearest Friend,
For this Thy dying sorrow,
Thy pity without end?
O make me Thine forever;
And should I fainting be,
Lord, let me never, never
Outlive my love to Thee.

Attributed to Bernard of Clairvaux (1091-1153)

———————————

Translated from Latin into German by Paul Gerhardt (1607-1676)

Translated into English by John Waddell Alexander (1804-1859)

And Can It Be?

And can it be that I should gain
An interest in the Savior's blood?
Died He for me, who caused His pain?
For me, who Him to death pursued?

Amazing love! how can it be
That Thou, my Lord, shouldst die for me?

He left His Father's throne above,
So free, so infinite His grace!
Emptied Himself of all but love,
And bled for Adam's helpless race!
'Tis mercy all, immense and free,
For, O my God, it found out me.

'Tis mystery all! th' Immortal dies!
Who can explore His strange design?
In vain the firstborn seraph tries
To sound the depths of love divine.
'Tis mercy all! let earth adore;
Let angel minds inquire no more.

Long my imprisoned spirit lay
Fast bound in sin and nature's night.
Thine eye diffused a quickening ray;
I woke—the dungeon flamed with light!
My chains fell off, my heart was free,
I rose, went forth, and followed Thee.

No condemnation now I dread;
Jesus, and all in Him is mine;
Alive in Him, my living Head,
And clothed in righteousness divine,
Bold I approach th' eternal throne,
And claim the crown, through Christ my own.

Charles Wesley (1707-1788)

Charles Wesley is probably the greatest hymnwriter the church has ever known. From the time of his conversion in 1738, Wesley wrote an average of two hymns a week every week for fifty years, composing between five and six thousand hymns during his lifetime. Most of these hymns were written on horseback as he traveled with his brother John, preaching and ministering to the poor.

The Wesleys broke with the conventions of their day and did the unthinkable—preaching the gospel outdoors. Traveling the highways and byways of England, they brought the Good News of Christ to thousands of poor farmers and illiterate coal miners. These were people at the margins of society, people most churches did not bother to think about. It was for them that Charles Wesley composed his hymns, bringing theology to the heart, where people experienced the love of God in profound ways.

• • • •

So now there is no condemnation for those who belong to Christ Jesus. . . . [God] sent his own Son in a body like the bodies we sinners have. And in that body God declared an end to sin's control over us by giving his Son as a sacrifice for our sins.
ROMANS 8:1, 3

The Day of Resurrection

It is said that John of Damascus started his hymnwriting career with a funeral hymn for a fellow monk. The monk wasn't dead yet, but everyone thought death was near. So John prepared his song and was singing it loudly in his room, testing it out. Suddenly the monk for whom it was written burst into the room and scolded John for raising such a racket. Tradition says that John was expelled from the monastery briefly for causing this disturbance, but then the Lord told the abbot that John would be doing great things with music, so the abbot welcomed John back.

And John did some great things, collecting and organizing the great hymns of the Greek-speaking church. His major accomplishment was the writing of the Golden Canon, an Easter liturgy still used in the Orthodox church and from which this hymn is taken. Scholars have called his text the finest sacred poetry in the Greek language.

• • • •

And [Jesus] said, "Yes, it was written long ago that the Messiah would suffer and die and rise from the dead on the third day. It was also written that this message would be proclaimed . . . : 'There is forgiveness of sins for all who repent.'"

LUKE 24:46-47

The day of resurrection!
Earth, tell it out abroad;
The passover of gladness,
The passover of God.
From death to life eternal,
From earth unto the sky,
Our Christ hath brought us over
With hymns of victory.

Our hearts be pure from evil,
That we may see aright
The Lord in rays eternal
Of resurrection light;
And listening to His accents,
May hear, so calm and plain,
His own "All hail!" and, hearing,
May raise the victor strain.

Now let the heavens be joyful!
Let earth her song begin!
Let the round world keep triumph,
And all that is therein!
Let all things seen and unseen
Their notes in gladness blend,
For Christ the Lord hath risen,
Our joy that hath no end.

John of Damascus (eighth century)

Translated by John Mason Neale (1818–1866)

Hosanna, Loud Hosanna

Hosanna, loud hosanna
The little children sang;
Through pillared court and temple
The lovely anthem rang;
To Jesus, who had blessed them
Close folded to His breast,
The children sang their praises,
The simplest and the best.

From Olivet they followed
Mid an exultant crowd,
The victor palm branch waving,
And chanting clear and loud;
The Lord of men and angels
Rode on in lowly state,
Nor scorned that little children
Should on His bidding wait.

"Hosanna in the highest!"
That ancient song we sing,
For Christ is our Redeemer,
The Lord of heaven our King.
O may we ever praise Him
With heart and life and voice,
And in His blissful presence
Eternally rejoice!

Jeannette Threlfall (1821–1880)

The triumphal entry into Jerusalem was the scene of a curious exchange between Jesus and the religious leaders of the day. A crowd was following Jesus, waving palms and singing, "Hosanna!" This term, literally "Lord, save us!" was also a cry of praise.

This crowd included a number of children, no doubt caught up in the excitement of the day. The leaders asked Jesus to tell the children to stop. "Do you hear what these children are saying?" they asked Jesus. Yes, Jesus said, quoting Psalm 8:2, "You have taught children and infants to give you praise" (Matthew 21:16).

Jeannette Threlfall had many reasons *not* to praise God. Orphaned young, shuttled among relatives, she was injured in an accident and became an invalid. Yet she remained cheery and faithful, penning many Christian poems and hymns.

• • • •

A large crowd of Passover visitors took palm branches and went down the road to meet [Jesus]. They shouted, "Praise God! Blessings on the one who comes in the name of the Lord! Hail to the King of Israel!"
JOHN 12:12-13

Go to Dark Gethsemane

Step by step James Montgomery takes us through Christ's passion. We go with our Lord to the garden of Gethsemane. It was a difficult time, and in Montgomery's simple text we feel each drop of sweat. At Jesus' trial—a shabby excuse for justice if ever there was one—He bore the beating and badgering without speaking a word. He was carrying our sins with Him to the Cross. At the Cross we can only fall at His feet in worship.

When we finally reach the tomb we find He is not there. There is a moment of confusion—who has taken Him?—before the truth dawns on us. He is risen!

At each point of this journey we have much to learn from our Savior. We can learn to pray when tempted and to endure suffering with patience. And Christ teaches us to rise in newness of life, to live in a way that honors Him, and ultimately to join Him in glory.

• • • •

They stripped him and put a scarlet robe on him. They wove thorn branches into a crown and put it on his head, and they placed a reed stick in his right hand as a scepter. Then they knelt before him in mockery and taunted, "Hail! King of the Jews!"

MATTHEW 27:28-29

Go to dark Gethsemane,
Ye that feel the tempter's power;
Your Redeemer's conflict see;
Watch with Him one bitter hour;
Turn not from His griefs away;
Learn of Jesus Christ to pray.

See Him at the judgment hall,
Beaten, bound, reviled, arraigned;
See Him meekly bearing all!
Love to man His soul sustained.
Shun not suffering, shame, or loss;
Learn of Christ to bear the cross.

Calvary's mournful mountain climb;
There adoring at His feet,
Mark that miracle of time,
God's own sacrifice complete;
"It is finished!" hear Him cry;
Learn of Jesus Christ to die.

Early hasten to the tomb
Where they laid His breathless clay:
All is solitude and gloom;
Who hath taken Him away?
Christ is risen! He meets our eyes.
Savior, teach us so to rise.

James Montgomery (1771-1854)

Jesus Lives, and So Shall I

Jesus lives, and so shall I:
Death, thy sting is gone forever!
He for me hath deigned to die,
Lives the bands of death to sever.
He shall raise me from the dust:
Jesus is my hope and trust.

Jesus lives and reigns supreme:
And, His kingdom still remaining,
I shall also be with Him,
Ever living, ever reigning.
God has promised—be it must:
Jesus is my hope and trust.

Jesus lives—and by His grace,
Vict'ry o'er my passions giving,
I will change my heart and ways,
Ever to His glory living.
Me He raises from the dust:
Jesus is my hope and trust.

Jesus lives—I know full well
Naught from Him my heart can sever,
Life nor death nor pow'rs of hell,
Joy nor grief, henceforth forever.
None of all His saints is lost:
Jesus is my hope and trust.

Jesus lives—and death is now
But my entrance into glory;
Courage, then, my soul, for thou
Hast a crown of life before thee.
Thou shalt find thy hopes were just:
Jesus is my hope and trust.

Christian Furchtegott Gellert (1715-1769)

Translated by Philip Schaff (1819-1893)

Jesus *had to* rise, as Peter eloquently stated at Pentecost. It was impossible for death to defeat the Lord of life. The Resurrection proves that Jesus was the Son of God. Our faith is built on this solid foundation. As Paul wrote, "If Christ has not been raised, then your faith is useless and you are still guilty of your sins. . . . And if our hope in Christ is only for this life, we are more to be pitied than anyone in the world" (1 Corinthians 15:17, 19). But He *has* risen! And as Jesus promised His disciples, "Since I live, you also will live" (John 14:19).

Without Christ, human life is merely prolonged death. Everything is decaying. But Jesus gives us eternal life, which radically changes our life on earth. Not only do we have eternity to look forward to, but we have the power to live in right relationship with God and others right now in our daily lives. Jesus is our hope for the future and our trust for each day. Praise Him!

• • • •

When our dying bodies have been transformed into bodies that will never die, this Scripture will be fulfilled: "Death is swallowed up in victory. O death, where is your victory? O death, where is your sting?"

I CORINTHIANS 15:54-55

Christ the Lord Is Risen Today

The grave has been "boasting" of its power since Eden. But now it has finally met its match. It wraps Jesus up at the Cross and "forbids Him rise," but our Champion, Jesus Christ, fought and won. Where is your sting now, O Death? Christ has won the final victory.

We know that whatever boasting we do is not in ourselves, but in the power of Christ. He has won the victory, and now we're just soaring where Christ has led. We bask in the benefits of the Cross, and we look past the grave to our heavenly reunion with Him. Alleluia!

• • • •

Christ has been raised from the dead. He is the first of a great harvest of all who have died. . . . Just as everyone dies because we all belong to Adam, everyone who belongs to Christ will be given new life.

I CORINTHIANS 15:20, 22

Christ the Lord is risen today, Alleluia!
Sons of men and angels say, Alleluia!
Raise your joys and triumphs high, Alleluia!
Sing, ye heavens, and earth reply, Alleluia!

Lives again our glorious King, Alleluia!
Where, O death, is now thy sting? Alleluia!
Once He died, our souls to save, Alleluia!
Where's thy victory, boasting grave? Alleluia!

Love's redeeming work is done, Alleluia!
Fought the fight, the battle won, Alleluia!
Death in vain forbids Him rise, Alleluia!
Christ hath opened paradise, Alleluia!

Soar we now where Christ has led, Alleluia!
Following our exalted Head, Alleluia!
Made like Him, like Him we rise, Alleluia!
Ours the cross, the grave, the skies, Alleluia!

Charles Wesley (1707–1788) and others

Bread of the World, in Mercy Broken

Bread of the world, in mercy broken,
Wine of the soul, in mercy shed,
By whom the words of life were spoken,
And in whose death our sins are dead:
Look on the heart by sorrow broken,
Look on the tears by sinners shed;
And be Thy feast to us the token
That by Thy grace our souls are fed.

Reginald Heber (1783-1826)

Reginald Heber wrote this hymn specifically for use in the service before the Eucharist. Its simple lines focus first on Christ and then on the attitude of the singer. Christ has spoken words of life and has taken our sins to the cross with Him. We are sorry for our sins and take this "feast" of bread and wine as a "token" of the forgiveness that Christ offers.

For sixteen years Heber served as a parish priest in the village of Hodnet in western England. Three times he was asked to become the bishop of Calcutta, India, and twice he turned it down. Finally at the age of forty, he accepted the call and sailed for India with his wife and two daughters. Three years later, after preaching to a crowded church near Hindu shrines to Vishnu and Siva, he suffered a stroke and died.

While Heber's hymns initially met with official church resistance, many of them were eventually published shortly before his death.

• • • •

[Jesus said,] "For my flesh is true food, and my blood is true drink. Anyone who eats my flesh and drinks my blood remains in me, and I in him. I live because of the living Father who sent me; in the same way, anyone who feeds on me will live because of me."
JOHN 6:55-57

When I Survey the Wondrous Cross

Few believers ever learn to truly love the cross of Christ. For though it offers great deliverance, it also demands great sacrifice. Isaac Watts drives this truth home through the words and music of this powerful hymn. Watts was deeply disappointed with the hymns of his day, which failed to inspire his parishioners to genuine worship and holy living. His dissatisfaction led him to compose more than six hundred hymns, all designed to call his congregation to a deeper knowledge and worship of God. This hymn was written in 1707 for use in a Communion service.

The music of this hymn was borrowed from Gregorian chant. Its rich, grave tones call those who sing it to realize the seriousness of Christ's sacrificial death. What shall we offer to God in grateful return for His gracious gift? All that we are and have is but a small offering in return for such great love.

. . . .

I once thought these things were valuable, but now I consider them worthless because of what Christ has done. . . . For his sake I have discarded everything else, counting it all as garbage, so that I could gain Christ and become one with him.

PHILIPPIANS 3:7-9

When I survey the wondrous cross
On which the Prince of glory died,
My richest gain I count but loss,
And pour contempt on all my pride.

Forbid it, Lord, that I should boast,
Save in the death of Christ, my God;
All the vain things that charm me most—
I sacrifice them to His blood.

See, from His head, His hands, His feet,
Sorrow and love flow mingled down;
Did e'er such love and sorrow meet,
Or thorns compose so rich a crown?

Were the whole realm of nature mine,
That were a present far too small:
Love so amazing, so divine,
Demands my soul, my life, my all.

Isaac Watts (1674-1748)

Cross of Jesus, Cross of Sorrow

Cross of Jesus, cross of sorrow,
Where the blood of Christ was shed,
Perfect man on thee did suffer,
Perfect God on thee has bled!

Here the King of all the ages,
Throned in light ere worlds could be,
Robed in mortal flesh is dying,
Crucified by sin for me.

O mysterious condescending!
O abandonment sublime!
Very God Himself is bearing
All the sufferings of time!

Cross of Jesus, cross of sorrow,
Where the blood of Christ was shed,
Perfect man on thee did suffer,
Perfect God on thee has bled!

William John Sparrow-Simpson (1860–1952)

The Crucifixion was more than merely a martyr's death. Rather, it was a tear in the fabric of history, and part of a great overarching eternal plan.

William Sparrow-Simpson captures some of the outrageousness of the Cross in these lines. This was not just a good man on a cross, but a perfect man, and more, perfect God. The King of all the ages, very God Himself, died on a hand-hewn wooden cross. Viewed from this perspective, the story no longer refers to a gentle reformer overpowered by a vicious religious or political machine. Our loving God allowed Himself to be bound and killed by people He created. It is mysterious condescending, abandonment sublime.

This song is part of John Stainer's cantata *The Crucifixion.* Sparrow-Simpson wrote the entire libretto to that work, his main claim to hymnology fame. In this hymn, he reminds us all of Jesus' great love in submitting Himself to the "cross of sorrow."

• • • •

May I never boast about anything except the cross of our Lord Jesus Christ. Because of that cross, my interest in this world has been crucified, and the world's interest in me has also died.

GALATIANS 6:14

The Head That Once Was Crowned

Thomas Kelly wrote 765 hymn texts in the span of fifty-one years. That's more than one a month for half a century. Kelly was also known as a popular preacher, and many of his hymns were written to accompany his sermon texts.

Studying law at Trinity College, Dublin, Kelly had a strong conversion experience that redirected his life toward the ministry. He preached powerfully, staunchly defending the doctrine of justification by faith. The Anglican church, still in the wake of reaction against the Wesleys, wanted no more troublemakers, so they kicked Kelly out. He landed with the Congregationalists and gained an even greater reputation. He was not only a gifted preacher but was also very generous, openly contributing to the poor, especially during the Dublin famine of 1847.

• • • •

When [Jesus] appeared in human form, he humbled himself in obedience to God and died a criminal's death on a cross. Therefore, God elevated him to the place of highest honor and gave him the name above all other names, that at the name of Jesus every knee should bow.

PHILIPPIANS 2:7-10

The head that once was crowned with thorns,
Is crowned with glory now;
A royal diadem adorns
The mighty Victor's brow.

The joy of all who dwell above,
The joy of all below,
To whom He manifests His love,
And grants His name to know.

To them the cross, with all its shame,
With all its grace, is giv'n;
Their name an everlasting name,
Their joy the joy of heav'n.

The cross He bore is life and health,
Tho' shame and death to Him,
His people's hope, His people's wealth,
Their everlasting theme.

Thomas Kelly (1769–1855)

My Savior's Love

I stand amazed in the presence
Of Jesus the Nazarene,
And wonder how He could love me,
A sinner, condemned, unclean.

How marvelous! how wonderful!
And my song shall ever be:
How marvelous! how wonderful
Is my Savior's love for me!

For me it was in the garden
He prayed, "Not My will, but Thine";
He had no tears for His own griefs,
But sweat-drops of blood for mine.

In pity angels beheld Him,
And came from the world of light
To comfort Him in the sorrows
He bore for my soul that night.

He took my sins and my sorrows,
He made them His very own;
He bore the burden to Calv'ry,
And suffered and died alone.

When with the ransomed in glory
His face I at last shall see,
'Twill be my joy thru the ages
To sing of His love for me.   ·

Charles Hutchinson Gabriel (1856–1932)

In the early 1900s, Charles H. Gabriel was the king of gospel music. Gabriel wrote the words and music for a number of hymns used by popular evangelists of his day such as Billy Sunday and his songleader, Homer Rodeheaver.

Gabriel's hymns reflect a change in the style of gospel music. In the 1800s, hymns were deeply meaningful and often meditative. But with the revivals of Moody and Sunday, Christians learned to love songs that were fun to sing, highly energetic, and easy to remember. Perhaps Gabriel's most popular hymn is "O That Will Be Glory for Me" with its rousing chorus. He also wrote "Send the Light."

These songs, like "My Savior's Love," focus on a simple emotion and celebrate it. In this case, it is raw amazement at the magnitude of Christ's sacrifice. How can we help but "stand amazed" in His presence? How marvelous! How wonderful!

• • • •

When we were utterly helpless, Christ came at just the right time and died for us sinners. . . . God showed his great love for us by sending Christ to die for us while we were still sinners.

ROMANS 5:6, 8

Christ Arose

It's hard to match this hymn for sheer drama. The first stanza begins dismally, then strikes a note of hope, and then the chorus explodes with joy. The music itself comes rising up from the depths and celebrates on high.

Robert Lowry wrote both the words and music to this hymn in 1874. At the time, he was a professor of literature at Bucknell University in Pennsylvania and pastor of a nearby church. He had written other hymn tunes and texts as he practiced his passion for poetry and song. "Sometimes the music comes and the words follow," he explained once. "I watch my moods, and when anything strikes me, whether words or music, no matter where I am, at home, on the street, I jot it down. My brain is sort of a spinning machine, for there is music running through it all the time."

Low in the grave He lay,
Jesus my Savior!
Waiting the coming day,
Jesus my Lord!

Up from the grave He arose,
With a mighty triumph o'er His foes;
He arose a Victor from the dark domain,
And He lives forever with His saints to reign,
He arose! He arose!
Hallelujah! Christ arose!

Vainly they watch His bed,
Jesus my Savior!
Vainly they seal the dead,
Jesus my Lord!

Death cannot keep his prey,
Jesus my Savior!
He tore the bars away,
Jesus my Lord!

Robert Lowry (1826-1899)

• • • •

God knew what would happen, and his prearranged plan was carried out when Jesus was betrayed. With the help of lawless Gentiles, [the people of Israel] nailed him to a cross and killed him. But God released him from the horrors of death and raised him back to life.

ACTS 2:23-24

The Strife Is O'er

The strife is o'er—the battle done,
The victory of life is won;
The song of triumph has begun:
Alleluia!

The pow'rs of death have done their worst,
But Christ their legions hath dispersed;
Let shouts of holy joy outburst:
Alleluia!

The three sad days have quickly sped,
He rises glorious from the dead;
All glory to our risen Head!
Alleluia!

He closed the yawning gates of hell,
The bars from heav'n's high portals fell;
Let hymns of praise His triumphs tell:
Alleluia!

Lord, by the stripes which wounded Thee,
From death's dread sting Thy servants free,
That we may live and sing to Thee:
Alleluia!

Latin Hymn

Symphonia Serenum Selectarum, 1695
Translated by Francis Pott (1832-1909)

Note the pattern of this hymn: negative undone, positive done, our response. In each triad we see first the forces of evil that tried to conquer Christ but were beaten. Then we see a more positive expression of what has occurred. Christ has won, He rises, He opens heaven and frees slaves. Finally, we respond with songs and shouts of joy: Alleluia!

The richness of the text is matched by the majesty of the music, written by the sixteenth-century composer Giovanni de Palestrina. He was a devout Roman Catholic who created many wonderful sacred works still used in churches and secular settings. This tune was adapted from a "Gloria Patri" in one of his choral works. It first appeared with Francis Pott's translation of this Latin text in 1861.

• • • •

"O death, where is your victory? O death, where is your sting?" For sin is the sting that results in death, and the law gives sin its power. But thank God! He gives us victory over sin and death through our Lord Jesus Christ.

I CORINTHIANS 15:55-57

Never Further than Thy Cross

The coordinates are laid out in the first stanza: latitude, Jesus' cross; longitude, Jesus' feet. This is where we stay. Not that our lives are static. No, we "press onward as we can." But we keep coming back to those familiar coordinates: Jesus' cross, Jesus' feet. This text reveals an intricacy of symmetry and light contrast. One scholar compares it to the sewing of a sampler—there's sort of a light cross-stitch pattern, especially in the last two lines of each stanza.

Elizabeth Rundle Charles was the daughter of a member of Parliament, and her husband was a lawyer. She became a renowned writer, scholar, musician, and artist in her own right. For a time she was one of the most famous women in Britain. In this hymn, she points out that all we do is checked by what Christ does. This is where we belong, His devoted children, at Jesus' cross, at Jesus' feet.

• • • •

You were dead because of your sins and because your sinful nature was not yet cut away. Then God made you alive with Christ, for he forgave all our sins. He canceled the record of the charges against us and took it away by nailing it to the cross.

COLOSSIANS 2:13-14

Never further than Thy cross,
Never higher than Thy feet;
Here earth's precious things seem dross;
Here earth's bitter things grow sweet.

Here, O Christ, our sins we see,
Learn Thy love while gazing thus;
Sin, which laid the cross on Thee,
Love, which bore the cross for us.

Here we learn to serve and give,
And, rejoicing, self deny;
Here we gather love to live;
Here we gather faith to die.

Pressing onward as we can,
Still to this our hearts must tend;
Where our earliest hopes began,
There our last aspirings end.

Till amid the hosts of light,
We in Thee redeemed, complete,
Through Thy cross made pure and white,
Cast our crowns before Thy feet.

Elizabeth Rundle Charles (1828-1896)

Beneath the Cross of Jesus

Beneath the cross of Jesus
I fain would take my stand—
The shadow of a mighty Rock
Within a weary land;
A home within the wilderness,
A rest upon the way,
From the burning of the noontide heat,
And the burden of the day.

Upon that cross of Jesus
Mine eye at times can see
The very dying form of One
Who suffered there for me;
And from my smitten heart with tears
Two wonders I confess—
The wonders of redeeming love
And my unworthiness.

I take, O cross, thy shadow
For my abiding place;
I ask no other sunshine than
The sunshine of His face;
Content to let the world go by,
To know no gain nor loss,
My sinful self my only shame,
My glory all the cross.

Elizabeth Cecelia Clephane (1830–1869)

Elizabeth Cecelia Clephane spent her whole life in Scotland. Daughter of a county sheriff, she grew up in the village of Melrose. She suffered from poor health most of her life, but that didn't keep her from serving others. She regularly helped the poor and those with disabilities, even selling a horse and carriage to give more money. Her cheery attitude and selfless spirit earned her the nickname "The Sunbeam of Melrose." She wrote eight hymns, including "The Ninety and Nine."

The "two wonders" that the author confesses in this hymn are Christ's love and her own unworthiness. These are common themes for Christian writers. Even the apostle Paul suggested that someone might give his life for a good person, but marveled that God showed His love to us "while we were still sinners" (Romans 5:8).

• • • •

When Jesus had tasted it, he said, "It is finished!" Then he bowed his head and released his spirit.
JOHN 19:30

Let Us Break Bread Together

Some say that this spiritual was the password used to call slaves to secret, forbidden worship meetings in Virginia. Whether secret or not, the song calls Christians to gather and celebrate the Lord's Supper.

The posture is significant. Some churches have participants kneel to take the elements of Communion, others have them sit or stand. Whatever posture the body takes, the attitude of the heart is worship. We come in reverence before our Lord.

"The rising sun" could refer to an ancient custom of worshiping toward the east. Most cathedrals are built with the nave facing east. The rising sun has often been a symbol for God. It brings new life and light, a source of energy and hope. Malachi prophesied that the "the Sun of Righteousness will rise with healing in his wings" (Malachi 4:2), which many take as a reference to the coming Christ.

Let us break bread together on our knees;
Let us break bread together on our knees;
When I fall on my knees
With my face to the rising sun,
O Lord, have mercy on me.

Let us drink the cup together on our knees;
Let us drink the cup together on our knees;
When I fall on my knees
With my face to the rising sun,
O Lord, have mercy on me.

Let us praise God together on our knees;
Let us praise God together on our knees;
When I fall on my knees
With my face to the rising sun,
O Lord, have mercy on me.

Traditional spiritual

• • • •

Jesus said again, "I tell you the truth, unless you eat the flesh of the Son of Man and drink his blood, you cannot have eternal life within you. But anyone who eats my flesh and drinks my blood has eternal life, and I will raise that person at the last day."
JOHN 6:53-54

Alas! And Did My Savior Bleed?

Alas! and did my Savior bleed
And did my Sovereign die?
Would He devote that sacred head
For sinners such as I?

Was it for sins that I have done
He suffered on the tree?
Amazing pity! grace unknown!
And love beyond degree!

Well might the sun in darkness hide
And shut His glories in,
When Christ, the great Redeemer, died
For man the creature's sin.

Thus might I hide my blushing face
While His dear cross appears,
Dissolve my heart in thankfulness,
And melt mine eyes to tears.

But drops of grief can ne'er repay
The debt of love I owe;
Here, Lord, I give myself away—
'Tis all that I can do.

Isaac Watts (1674-1748)

We never know how deeply our actions affect the lives of others. This hymn by Isaac Watts has certainly touched the hearts of millions through the centuries. After drawing the stark contrasts between the sacrificial death of the mighty Maker and the unworthiness of the sinful creature, he concludes with the consecration, "Here, Lord, I give myself away—'Tis all that I can do."

A thirty-year-old blind woman heard a revival choir sing this simple hymn. Stanza after stanza stirred her heart, but when the choir came to the final line, "Here, Lord, I give myself away," she gave herself away to the Lord as well. That blind woman was Fanny Crosby, who went on to become the greatest writer of gospel songs in the nineteenth century. We never know how deeply our lives will touch the lives of others.

• • • •

He was pierced for our rebellion, crushed for our sins. He was beaten so we could be whole. He was whipped so we could be healed. All of us, like sheep, have strayed away. We have left God's paths to follow our own. Yet the Lord laid on him the sins of us all.

ISAIAH 53:5-6

Christ Jesus Lay in Death's Strong Bands

In his death on the cross, Christ bound Himself in the chains of sin and death. In His resurrection from the tomb, Christ broke those chains for Himself and for us all. Martin Luther celebrates Christ's conquest over sin and death in this rousing Easter hymn. The reformer was deeply aware of the spiritual battle won by Christ on that first Easter. Luther was also aware of the ongoing spiritual battle every believer must face. He once felt Satan's oppressive presence so keenly that he threw an inkpot at him. An ink spot still decorates the wall of his room in Wartburg Castle!

Luther believed that singing hymns was one of our best weapons against Satan and his evil forces. He said, "The devil, the originator of sorrowful anxieties and restless troubles, flees before the sound of music almost as much as before the Word of God."

• • • •

I also pray that you will understand the incredible greatness of God's power for us who believe him. This is the same mighty power that raised Christ from the dead and seated him in the place of honor at God's right hand in the heavenly realms.

EPHESIANS 1:19-20

Christ Jesus lay in death's strong bands
For our offenses given;
But now at God's right hand He stands,
And brings us life from heaven;
Wherefore let us joyful be,
And sing to God right thankfully
Loud songs of Alleluia! Alleluia!

It was a strange and dreadful strife
When life and death contended;
The victory remained with life;
The reign of death was ended;
Stripped of power, no more he reigns,
An empty form alone remains;
His sting is lost forever! Alleluia!

So let us keep the festival
Whereto the Lord invites us;
Christ is Himself the joy of all,
The Sun that warms and lights us;
By His grace He doth impart
Eternal sunshine to the heart;
The night of sin is ended! Alleluia!

Then let us feast this Easter Day
On the true bread of heaven;
The Word of grace hath purged away
The old and wicked leaven;
Christ alone our souls will feed;
He is our meat and drink indeed;
Faith lives upon no other! Alleluia!

Martin Luther (1483-1546)

Translated by Richard Massie (1800-1887)

Jesus Christ Is Risen Today

Jesus Christ is risen today, Alleluia!
Our triumphant holy day, Alleluia!
Who did once, upon the cross, Alleluia!
Suffer to redeem our loss. Alleluia!

Hymns of praise then let us sing, Alleluia!
Unto Christ, our heavenly King, Alleluia!
Who endured the cross and grave, Alleluia!
Sinners to redeem and save. Alleluia!

Sing we to our God above, Alleluia!
Praise eternal as His love, Alleluia!
Praise Him, all ye heavenly host, Alleluia!
Father, Son, and Holy Ghost. Alleluia!

Latin Hymn (fourteenth century)

Translated in Lyra Davidica, 1708
Stanza 2, John Arnold's Compleat Psalmodist, 1749
Stanza 3, Charles Wesley (1707-1788)

You might confuse this hymn with Charles Wesley's "Christ the Lord Is Risen Today" (April 3). The theme is the same, the structure is similar, and Wesley also had a hand in this hymn. But this hymn is based on a medieval Latin text.

Alleluia is the perfect word for Easter Sunday. It simply means "Praise the Lord." It is used throughout Scripture (especially in Psalms and Revelation) to glorify God for the mighty acts He has done. And what mightier act is there than this: the resurrection of Christ from the dead.

Interestingly, this hymn speaks more about Christ's death than His new life. Both are vital aspects of God's redeeming work. Christ endured the cross *and* rose from the dead. His death and resurrection are inseparable, and hymn singers exult in all of it. During this Easter season, let us praise the God who made it happen. Alleluia!

• • • •

Christ suffered for our sins once for all time. He never sinned, but he died for sinners to bring you safely home to God. He suffered physical death, but he was raised to life in the Spirit.
1 PETER 3:18

What Wondrous Love Is This?

This hymn has always been associated with the Appalachian area. Like most spirituals, it has been passed down through the generations and exists in several different versions. The melody, based on a six-tone scale, sounds minor to modern ears and has a haunting effect. The text adds to the effect. This is the question of the ages, and after all the glorious celebration of the Easter season, the question remains. What made Him do it? What made Him do it for me?

Every so often you'll read about a disaster where someone makes a heroic but fatal effort to save others. A man jumps into icy water to save someone. He puts the lifeline in the person's hand, but drowns. We marvel at the selflessness of such a person. What made him do it? Christ "bore the dreadful curse" for our soul, and we can ponder that for the rest of our lives. We can also resolve to devote our lives to Him, to please Him, and to praise Him through all eternity.

What wondrous love is this, O my soul, O my soul,
What wondrous love is this, O my soul!
What wondrous love is this that caused the Lord of bliss
To bear the dreadful curse for my soul, for my soul,
To bear the dreadful curse for my soul?

What wondrous love is this, O my soul, O my soul,
What wondrous love is this, O my soul!
What wondrous love is this that caused the Lord of life
To lay aside His crown for my soul, for my soul,
To lay aside His crown for my soul?

American folk hymn

• • • •

Christ has rescued us from the curse pronounced by the law. When he was hung on the cross, he took upon himself the curse for our wrongdoing. For it is written in the Scriptures, "Cursed is everyone who is hung on a tree."

GALATIANS 3:13

At the Lamb's High Feast

At the Lamb's high feast we sing
Praise to our victorious King,
Who hath washed us in the tide
Flowing from His pierced side;
Praise we Him, whose love divine
Gives His sacred Blood for wine,
Gives His Body for the feast,
Christ the victim, Christ the priest.
Where the Paschal Blood is poured,
Death's dark angel sheathes his sword;
Israel's hosts triumphant go
Through the wave that drowns the foe.
Praise we Christ, whose Blood was shed,
Paschal victim, Paschal bread;
With sincerity and love
Eat we manna from above.
Mighty Victim from the sky,
Hell's fierce powers beneath Thee lie;
Thou hast conquered in the fight,
Thou hast brought us life and light;
Now no more can death appall,
Now no more the grave enthrall;
Thou hast opened paradise,
And in Thee Thy saints shall rise.
Paschal triumph, Paschal joy,
Sin alone can this destroy;
From sin's power do Thou set free
Souls new-born, O Lord, in Thee.
Hymns of glory, songs of praise,
Father, unto Thee we raise:
Risen Lord, all praise to Thee
with the Spirit ever be.

Latin Hymn

Translated by Robert Campbell (1814–1868)

Scripture speaks of several Passover (or Paschal) feasts. The first was celebrated by the Israelites in Egypt. After the lamb was slain and blood was put on the doorposts, the Israelite families feasted while the angel of death passed over their houses.

In the upper room just prior to His death, Jesus, the Lamb of God, observed the Last Supper with His disciples. This Passover meal took on special meaning because of Jesus. This is the Eucharist—or Communion—that the Christian church continues to celebrate today.

Revelation 19 speaks of the wedding supper of the Lamb, the consummation of the Paschal feast. The Lamb that was slain, Jesus, has now been glorified. The Victim is now the Victor. This ancient hymn, translated from Latin, weaves the three feasts together into a triumphant climax.

• • • •

Praise the Lord! For the Lord our God, the Almighty, reigns. Let us be glad and rejoice, and let us give honor to him. For the time has come for the wedding feast of the Lamb, and his bride has prepared herself.
REVELATION 19:6-7

Hallelujah, What a Savior!

Philip Bliss was one of the most prominent hymnwriters in the heyday of gospel hymnwriting. Bliss grew up working on a farm and in lumber camps, but eventually became a music teacher. He sold his first song at age twenty-six and later worked for a hymn publisher. D. L. Moody urged Bliss to become a singing evangelist, and so he did, beginning in 1874. This hymn was published in 1875. In 1876, while traveling through Ohio, Bliss and his family were involved in a train wreck. Reportedly, Bliss went back into the fiery train to save his wife, but they both died.

It was a tragedy for hymn lovers around the world, but you might say that Bliss just changed his address. Certainly he continues, even now, creating new praises for our wonderful Savior in glory.

• • • •

There was nothing beautiful or majestic about his appearance, nothing to attract us to him. He was despised and rejected— a man of sorrows, acquainted with deepest grief. We turned our backs on him and looked the other way.

ISAIAH 53:2-3

"Man of Sorrows!" what a name
For the Son of God, who came
Ruined sinners to reclaim!
Hallelujah, what a Savior!

Bearing shame and scoffing rude,
In my place condemned He stood—
Sealed my pardon with His blood:
Hallelujah, what a Savior!

Guilty, vile and helpless we,
Spotless Lamb of God was He;
Full atonement! can it be?
Hallelujah, what a Savior!

Lifted up was He to die,
"It is finished!" was His cry;
Now in heav'n exalted high:
Hallelujah, what a Savior!

When He comes, our glorious King,
All His ransomed home to bring,
Then anew this song we'll sing:
Hallelujah, what a Savior!

Philip Paul Bliss (1838-1876)

There Is a Fountain Filled with Blood

There is a fountain filled with blood
Drawn from Emmanuel's veins,
And sinners, plunged beneath that flood,
Lose all their guilty stains,
Lose all their guilty stains;
And sinners, plunged beneath that flood,
Lose all their guilty stains.

The dying thief rejoiced to see
That fountain in his day;
And there may I, though vile as he,
Wash all my sins away,
Wash all my sins away;
And there may I, though vile as he,
Wash all my sins away.

E'er since, by faith, I saw the stream
Thy flowing wounds supply,
Redeeming love has been my theme,
And shall be till I die,
And shall be till I die;
Redeeming love has been my theme,
And shall be till I die.

Then in a nobler, sweeter song,
I'll sing Thy pow'r to save,
When this poor lisping, stammering tongue
Lies silent in the grave,
Lies silent in the grave;
When this poor lisping, stammering tongue
Lies silent in the grave.

William Cowper (1731–1800)

William Cowper suffered from deep depression for most of his life. In 1764 he found himself within the walls of an institution for the mentally ill. There in the asylum, William Cowper found Christ through reading the Bible.

Despite his emotional pain, or perhaps because of it, Cowper produced literature of amazing insight. He is still renowned in literary circles as one of England's greatest poets.

Today's hymn, written about 1770, is based on Zechariah 13:1. Cowper would certainly be surprised that the work of his "poor lisping, stammering tongue" has filled the mouths of millions who claim the blood of Christ as their atonement.

• • • •

On that day a fountain will be opened for the dynasty of David and for the people of Jerusalem, a fountain to cleanse them from all their sins and impurity.
ZECHARIAH 13:1

Am I a Soldier of the Cross?

In the early eighteenth century, when Isaac Watts was preaching in England, he frequently would write a hymn to illustrate his sermon. After preaching the sermon, he (or a clerk in the church) would teach the congregation the hymn.

One Sunday in 1727, Watts was preaching a sermon entitled "Holy Fortitude, or Remedies against Fear." The text was 1 Corinthians 16:13, "Be on guard. Stand firm in the faith." At that time many Nonconformist believers were imprisoned for their views, even as Watts's own father had been. In his sermon, Watts urged his congregation to "practice unfashionable virtues, plead the cause of the oppressed, be courageous before infidels and scoffers." Then, as he closed the sermon, he began the hymn "Am I a Soldier of the Cross?"

Am I a soldier of the cross?
A foll'wer of the Lamb?
And shall I fear to own His cause
Or blush to speak His name?

Must I be carried to the skies
On flow'ry beds of ease,
While others fought to win the prize
And sailed through bloody seas?

Are there no foes for me to face?
Must I not stem the flood?
Is this vile world a friend to grace,
To help me on to God?

Sure I must fight if I would reign—
Increase my courage, Lord!
I'll bear the toil, endure the pain,
Supported by Thy Word.

Isaac Watts (1674-1748)

• • • •

Endure suffering along with me, as a good soldier of Christ Jesus. Soldiers don't get tied up in the affairs of civilian life, for then they cannot please the officer who enlisted them.

2 TIMOTHY 2:3-4

Wonderful Grace of Jesus

Wonderful grace of Jesus,
Greater than all my sin;
How shall my tongue describe it,
Where shall its praise begin?
Taking away my burden,
Setting my spirit free,
For the wonderful grace of Jesus reaches me.

Wonderful the matchless grace of Jesus,
Deeper than the mighty rolling sea;
Higher than the mountain, sparkling like a fountain,
All sufficient grace for even me;
Broader than the scope of my transgressions,
Greater far than all my sin and shame;
O magnify the precious name of Jesus,
Praise His name!

Wonderful grace of Jesus,
Reaching to all the lost,
By it I have been pardoned,
Saved to the uttermost;
Chains have been torn asunder,
Giving me liberty,
For the wonderful grace of Jesus reaches me.

Wonderful grace of Jesus,
Reaching the most defiled,
By its transforming power
Making me God's dear child,
Purchasing peace and heaven
For all eternity—
And the wonderful grace of Jesus reaches me.

Haldor Lillenas (1885-1959)

In 1917, young pastor Haldor Lillenas and his wife were settling into a ministry at the Nazarene church of Auburn, Illinois. After buying a house in nearby Olivet, they had little money left to furnish it. Though they were both hymnwriters, they had no money for a piano. Then Lillenas found a "wheezy little organ" in the home of a neighbor and paid five dollars for it. Lillenas wrote a number of songs on that instrument, including this one.

This song, with its rolling melody and climbing chorus, became very popular at evangelistic meetings. Lillenas used it in his own evangelistic crusades, and others, such as the famous songleader Charles Alexander, used it often.

The message of Scripture comes through clearly here—you cannot outsin God's grace. No matter how great your guilt, God's forgiveness is greater. Praise His name.

• • • •

God can point to us in all future ages as examples of the incredible wealth of his grace and kindness toward us, as shown in all he has done for us who are united with Christ Jesus.

EPHESIANS 2:7

I Will Sing of My Redeemer

It's not easy to keep the Christian faith bottled up. Throughout history, various rulers have tried to keep Christians from preaching the gospel, but with little success. Ancient Rome would not have minded if Christians had just kept to themselves, privately enjoying their faith. But it doesn't work that way. As the apostles told the authorities in Jerusalem, "We cannot help speaking about what we have seen and heard" (Acts 4:20, NIV).

Bliss was the songleader for an evangelist known as Major Whittle, based in Chicago. This hymn text was found in Bliss's trunk after he and his wife died in a train accident in 1876. James McGranahan, who succeeded Bliss as Whittle's songleader, wrote the music and used it in their meetings.

• • • •

Praise God for the glorious grace he has poured out on us who belong to his dear Son. He is so rich in kindness and grace that he purchased our freedom with the blood of his Son and forgave our sins.

EPHESIANS 1:6-7

I will sing of my Redeemer
And His wondrous love to me;
On the cruel cross He suffered,
From the curse to set me free.

**Sing, O sing of my Redeemer,
With His blood He purchased me;
On the cross He sealed my pardon,
Paid the debt and made me free.**

I will tell the wondrous story,
How, my lost estate to save,
In His boundless love and mercy,
He the ransom freely gave.

I will praise my dear Redeemer,
His triumphant pow'r I'll tell,
How the victory He giveth
Over sin and death and hell.

I will sing of my Redeemer
And His heav'nly love to me;
He from death to life hath bro't me,
Son of God with Him to be.

Philip Paul Bliss (1838–1876)

I Know That My Redeemer Lives

I know that my Redeemer lives:
What joy the blest assurance gives!
He lives, He lives, who once was dead;
He lives, my everlasting Head!

He lives to bless me with His love;
He lives to plead for me above;
He lives my hungry soul to feed;
He lives to help in time of need.

He lives and grants me daily breath;
He lives and I shall conquer death;
He lives my mansion to prepare;
He lives to bring me safely there.

He lives, all glory to His name;
He lives, my Savior, still the same;
What joy the blest assurance gives:
I know that my Redeemer lives!

Samuel Medley (1738-1799)

Every once in a while, a verse jumps out of the Old Testament and takes on a new meaning. Job lost his fortune, family, and much of his health. In a stunning display of faith, he expressed his only remaining hope: "I know that my Redeemer lives, and he will stand upon the earth at last" (Job 19:25). The words find fulfillment in Jesus.

Jesus gave His life to redeem us, to buy us back from our slavery to sin. His death was the price of our freedom. But that's not the bottom line, thank God. As the sun rises on Easter morning, we can say with Job, "I know that my Redeemer lives." He lives! Death could not hold Him. He lives, to finish salvation's work in me.

Hymnwriter Samuel Medley often repeated words and phrases in his songs. Here, what's repeated is the most important concept: "He lives . . . He lives . . . He lives."

• • • •

But as for me, I know that my Redeemer lives, and he will stand upon the earth at last. And after my body has decayed, yet in my body I will see God! I will see him for myself. Yes, I will see him with my own eyes. I am overwhelmed at the thought!

JOB 19:25-27

Redeemed

Fanny Crosby didn't start writing hymns until she was forty, but she made up for lost time. Only a rare few have matched the number of Christian songs she's written. Blinded in infancy because of a doctor's error, Crosby demonstrates no bitterness in her songs. We find nothing but joy and longing for the Lord. "Redeemed and so happy in Jesus" is not just a line that sounds good in a hymn, it's the story of Crosby's life. Blinded to the light of this world, Fanny Crosby had a light shining in her soul.

Love is another major topic in Crosby's work. She regularly marvels at God's love. "His love is the theme of my song." Only as we come face-to-face with the overwhelming love of God can we begin to love others fully. As John says, "We love each other because he loved us first" (1 John 4:19). And Jesus said that the world would recognize his disciples by the love they had for each other.

. . . .

For you know that God paid a ransom to save you from the empty life you inherited from your ancestors. And the ransom he paid was not mere gold or silver. It was the precious blood of Christ, the sinless, spotless Lamb of God.

I PETER 1:18-19

Redeemed, how I love to proclaim it!
Redeemed by the blood of the Lamb;
Redeemed through His infinite mercy,
His child, and forever, I am.

Redeemed, redeemed,
Redeemed by the blood of the Lamb.
Redeemed, redeemed,
His child, and forever, I am.

Redeemed and so happy in Jesus,
No language my rapture can tell;
I know that the light of His presence
With me doth continually dwell.

I think of my blessed Redeemer,
I think of Him all the day long;
I sing, for I cannot be silent;
His love is the theme of my song.

I know I shall see in His beauty
The King in whose law I delight;
Who lovingly guardeth my footsteps,
And giveth me songs in the night.

Fanny Jane Crosby (1820–1915)

My Faith Looks Up to Thee

My faith looks up to Thee,
Thou Lamb of Calvary,
Savior divine!
Now hear me while I pray,
Take all my guilt away,
O let me from this day
Be wholly Thine!

May Thy rich grace impart
Strength to my fainting heart,
My zeal inspire;
As Thou hast died for me,
O may my love to Thee
Pure, warm, and changeless be,
A living fire!

While life's dark maze I tread
And griefs around me spread,
Be Thou my guide;
Bid darkness turn to day,
Wipe sorrow's tears away,
Nor let me ever stray
From Thee aside.

When ends life's passing dream,
When death's cold, threatening stream
Shall o'er me roll,
Blest Savior, then, in love,
Fear and distrust remove;
O lift me safe above,
A ransomed soul!

Ray Palmer (1808-1887)

At twenty-two, Ray Palmer was having a tough year. He wanted to go into the ministry but was stuck teaching in New York City. He was lonely, depressed, and sick. Then he found a German poem about a sinner kneeling before the cross. He translated it and added four stanzas.

"I wrote the verses with tender emotion," he said later. "There was not the slightest thought of writing for another eye, least of all writing a hymn for Christian worship."

Two years later, while visiting Boston, he ran across his friend Lowell Mason. Mason, a major figure in American music in the early 1800s, was preparing a new hymnal. He asked Palmer if he'd like to contribute anything. Palmer bashfully showed Mason these verses. "You may live many years and do many good things," Mason said, "but I think you will be best known to posterity as the author of 'My Faith Looks Up to Thee.'"

• • • •

Have you never heard? Have you never understood? The Lord is the everlasting God, the Creator of all the earth. He never grows weak or weary. No one can measure the depths of his understanding. He gives power to the weak and strength to the powerless.
ISAIAH 40:28-29

Depth of Mercy!

Life would be much tidier if Christians were suddenly made perfect, incapable of sin. Certainly by the power of God's Spirit we can walk in righteousness, but our sinful nature still drags us down. We are tempted. We go astray.

This was originally part of a thirteen-stanza hymn entitled, "After a Relapse into Sin." Charles Wesley knew that people would wander from the faith. He also knew that God welcomed them back. The first three stanzas of this compact version clearly depict the plight of the wanderer. The guilt is strong, often keeping the person from returning to Christ. It's the last stanza that answers the doubts—yes, Jesus is there, holding out His wounded hands. He is weeping, He mourns my sin, but He still loves me. It's a great picture. We have a great Savior to come home to.

Depth of mercy! can there be
Mercy still reserved for me?
Can my God His wrath forbear,
Me, the chief of sinners, spare?

I my Master have denied;
I afresh have crucified,
Oft profaned His hallowed name,
Put Him to an open shame.

Now incline me to repent;
Let me now my sins lament;
Now my foul revolt deplore,
Weep, believe, and sin no more.

There for me the Savior stands,
Holding forth His wounded hands;
God is love! I know, I feel,
Jesus weeps and loves me still.

Charles Wesley (1707-1788)

• • • •

If we claim we have no sin, we are only fooling ourselves and not living in the truth. But if we confess our sins to him, he is faithful and just to forgive us our sins and to cleanse us from all wickedness.

I JOHN 1:8-9

Let Us Love, and Sing, and Wonder

Let us love, and sing, and wonder,
    Let us praise the Savior's name!
He has hushed the Law's loud thunder,
He has quenched Mount Sinai's flame;
    He has washed us with His blood,
    He has brought us nigh to God.

Let us love the Lord who bought us,
    Pitied us when enemies,
Called us by His grace, and taught us,
    Gave us ears, and gave us eyes:
    He has washed us with His blood,
    He presents our souls to God.

Let us sing, though fierce temptations
    Threaten hard to bear us down!
For the Lord, our strong salvation,
Holds in view the conqu'ror's crown,
    He who washed us with His blood,
    Soon will bring us home to God.

Let us wonder; grace and justice
    Join, and point to mercy's store;
When through grace in Christ our trust is,
    Justice smiles and asks no more:
    He who washed us with His blood,
    Has secured our way to God.

Let us praise, and join the chorus
    Of the saints enthroned on high;
Here they trusted Him before us,
    Now their praises fill the sky:
"Thou hast washed us with Thy blood;
    Thou art worthy, Lamb of God!"

John Newton (1725-1807)

Much has been made of John Newton's move from the slave trade to the church. It was a turnaround that rivaled that of the apostle Paul, and Newton always recognized the depths of sin from which he had come. The "wretch like me" in "Amazing Grace" (March 17) was no exaggeration. Newton knew that he had sinned greatly; he also knew the greatness of God's redeeming grace.

This hymn, however, comes from later years, when Newton was a renowned preacher. It is rich with theology and biblical images. Christ has "hushed the Law's loud thunder," says Newton, evoking images of Mount Sinai.

Grace and justice join in Christ, says Newton. Normally these two words don't belong in the same sentence, but when our trust is in Christ's righteousness, both are satisfied—"justice smiles and asks no more."

• • • •

[Christ is] the ruler of all the kings of the world. All glory to him who loves us and has freed us from our sins by shedding his blood for us. He has made us a Kingdom of priests for God his Father. All glory and power to him forever and ever! Amen.

REVELATION 1:5-6

Blessed Be the Name

In ancient times, names were sacred. Names expressed character. Often we find Old Testament characters changing their names to reflect changes in their lives. Jacob ("the grabber") became Israel ("God's prince") after a divine encounter.

God's name is especially sacred. Ancient Israelite scribes revered the name of God, Yahweh, so much that they would not write it. One of the Ten Commandments was that people should not take the Lord's name in vain. Jesus echoed the idea in the Lord's Prayer, "Hallowed be your name." That is, your name is holy; we acknowledge that you are, by nature, holy.

When Isaiah predicts that the coming Redeemer "will be called: Wonderful Counselor, Mighty God, Everlasting Father, Prince of Peace" (Isaiah 9:6), he is saying that this will be Messiah's nature. When we bless God's name, we praise God for who He is.

• • • •

The Son is far greater than the angels, just as the name God gave him is greater than their names.

HEBREWS 1:4

All praise to Him who reigns above
In majesty supreme,
Who gave His Son for man to die,
That He might man redeem!

Blessed be the name! blessed be the name!
Blessed be the name of the Lord!
Blessed be the name! blessed be the name!
Blessed be the name of the Lord!

His name above all names shall stand,
Exalted more and more,
At God the Father's own right hand,
Where angel hosts adore.

Redeemer, Savior, Friend of man
Once ruined by the fall,
Thou hast devised salvation's plan,
For Thou hast died for all.

His name shall be the Counselor,
The mighty Prince of Peace,
Of all earth's kingdoms Conqueror,
Whose reign shall never cease.

William H. Clark (nineteenth century)

Ralph E. Hudson (1843–1901), refrain

Rejoice, Ye Pure in Heart

Rejoice, ye pure in heart;
Rejoice, give thanks and sing;
Your glorious banner wave on high,
The cross of Christ your King.

Rejoice, rejoice,
Rejoice, give thanks and sing.

Bright youth and snow-crowned age,
Strong men and maidens fair,
Raise high your free, exulting song,
God's wondrous praise declare.

With voice as full and strong
As ocean's surging praise,
Send forth the hymns our fathers loved,
The psalms of ancient days.

Yes, on through life's long path,
Still chanting as ye go;
From youth to age, by night and day,
In gladness and in woe.

Still lift your standard high,
Still march in firm array,
As warriors through the darkness toil
Till dawns the golden day.

Edward Hayes Plumptre (1821–1891)

This hymn was written in 1865 as the processional for a choir festival in Petersborough Cathedral in England. There are hints in the text of a marching quality ("glorious banner," "as ye go," "lift your standard," "march in firm array"). You can see an army of choir members stepping down the aisle, and this hymn seems to invite the congregation, and perhaps all Christians everywhere, to join in the song. There is a relentless sense of joy here. One observer comments on the "stately simplicity" of this work.

Edward Plumptre was a noted scholar and author in the Church of England. He wrote a major biography of Bishop Thomas Ken (also a famous hymnwriter), as well as historical works and poetry. He was also a Bible scholar. He wrote this hymn at age forty-four, somewhere between "bright youth and snow-crowned age."

• • • •

May we shout for joy when we hear of your victory and raise a victory banner in the name of our God. May the Lord answer all your prayers. . . . Some nations boast of their chariots and horses, but we boast in the name of the Lord our God.
PSALM 20:5, 7

Blessed Assurance

Fanny Crosby wrote more than eight thousand hymns and used more than two hundred pen names. Under contract to a music publisher, she wrote three new hymns each week during much of her adult life. The fact that she was blind didn't diminish her productivity. She would formulate an entire song in her mind and then dictate it to a friend or a secretary.

Phoebe Palmer Knapp, wife of the founder of Metropolitan Life Insurance Company, composed a tune in 1873 and brought it to Crosby in Brooklyn. "Play it for me on the organ," Crosby asked. Knapp did and then asked, "What does this tune say?" She turned to see Crosby kneeling in prayer. Knapp played it a second time and then a third. Then the blind woman responded, "That says, 'Blessed assurance, Jesus is mine! O what a foretaste of glory divine!'"

Blessed assurance, Jesus is mine!
O what a foretaste of glory divine!
Heir of salvation, purchase of God,
Born of His Spirit, washed in His blood.

This is my story, this is my song,
Praising my Savior all the day long;
This is my story, this is my song,
Praising my Savior all the day long.

Perfect submission, perfect delight!
Visions of rapture now burst on my sight;
Angels descending bring from above
Echoes of mercy, whispers of love.

Perfect submission—all is at rest,
I in my Savior am happy and blest;
Watching and waiting, looking above,
Filled with His goodness, lost in His love.

Fanny Jane Crosby (1820-1915)

• • • •

We can boldly enter heaven's Most Holy Place because of the blood of Jesus. By his death, Jesus opened a new and life-giving way through the curtain into the Most Holy Place.

HEBREWS 10:19-20

Rejoice, the Lord Is King!

Rejoice, the Lord is King!
Your Lord and King adore!
Rejoice, give thanks, and sing,
And triumph evermore:

Lift up your heart, lift up your voice!
Rejoice, again I say, rejoice!

Jesus, the Savior, reigns,
The God of truth and love;
When He had purged our stains,
He took His seat above:

His kingdom cannot fail,
He rules o'er earth and heaven;
The keys of death and hell
Are to our Jesus given:

Rejoice in glorious hope!
Our Lord the judge shall come,
And take His servants up
To their eternal home:

Charles Wesley (1707-1788)

The early days of Methodism were filled with persecution and hardship. It would have been natural for Wesley's followers to become discouraged and lose hope. One reason Charles Wesley wrote six thousand hymns was to encourage Methodists to be a singing, joyful people.

Paul's letter to the Philippians provided Wesley's text for this hymn. Paul was imprisoned in Rome under Emperor Nero. But the message to the Philippians is one of joy and encouragement. You can be a victor regardless of the situation because the Lord is King.

This hymn first appeared in Wesley's 1746 collection, *Hymns for Our Lord's Resurrection.* Each stanza adds another dimension to our praise: adoration, thanksgiving, and exultation.

• • • •

Always be full of joy in the Lord. I say it again—rejoice!
PHILIPPIANS 4:4

All Creatures of Our God and King

Saint Francis of Assisi is perhaps best known as a nature lover. You may recall the painting in which the Italian artist Giotto depicts him feeding the birds. One writer spoke of him this way: "With smiles he met the friendless, fed the poor, freed a trapped bird, led home a child. Although he spoke no word, his text, God's love, the town did not forget."

A soldier in his early years, Francis resolved to imitate the life of Christ, denounced his wealth, and founded the Franciscan Order of Friars. He and those who followed him became itinerant evangelists, preaching and helping the poor of Italy. He wrote sixty hymns of praise and worship and encouraged church music in every way he could.

• • • •

Praise the Lord from the earth, you creatures of the ocean depths, fire and hail, snow and clouds, wind and weather that obey him, mountains and all hills, fruit trees and all cedars, wild animals and all livestock, small scurrying animals and birds, kings of the earth and all people, rulers and judges of the earth, young men and young women, old men and children. Let them all praise the name of the Lord.

PSALM 148:7-13

All creatures of our God and King,
Lift up your voice and with us sing
Alleluia! Alleluia!
Thou burning sun with golden beam,
Thou silver moon with softer gleam!

**O praise Him, O praise Him!
Alleluia! Alleluia! Alleluia!**

Thou rushing wind that art so strong,
Ye clouds that sail in heaven along,
O praise Him! Alleluia!
Thou rising morn, in praise rejoice,
Ye lights of evening, find a voice!

Thou flowing water, pure and clear,
Make music for thy Lord to hear,
Alleluia! Alleluia!
Thou fire so masterful and bright,
Thou givest man both warmth and light!

And thou, most kind and gentle death,
Waiting to hush our latest breath,
O praise Him! Alleluia!
Thou leadest home the child of God,
And Christ our Lord the way hath trod.

Let all things their Creator bless,
And worship Him in humbleness,
O praise Him! Alleluia!
Praise, praise the Father, praise the Son,
And praise the Spirit, Three in One!

Francis of Assisi (1182-1226)

Translated by William H. Draper (1855-1933)

For the Beauty of the Earth

For the beauty of the earth,
For the glory of the skies,
For the love which from our birth
Over and around us lies:

Lord of all, to Thee we raise
This our hymn of grateful praise.

For the beauty of each hour
Of the day and of the night,
Hill and vale, and tree and flower,
Sun and moon, and stars of light:

For the joy of ear and eye,
For the heart and mind's delight,
For the mystic harmony
Linking sense to sound and sight:

For the joy of human love,
Brother, sister, parent, child,
Friends on earth, and friends above;
For all gentle thoughts and mild:

For Thy church, that evermore
Lifteth holy hands above,
Offering up on every shore
Her pure sacrifice of love:

For Thyself, best Gift Divine!
To our race so freely given;
For that great, great love of Thine,
Peace on earth, and joy in heaven:

Folliot Sanford Pierpoint (1835-1917)

Since Roman Times the town of Bath, on the banks of the Avon River in England, has been considered one of the most beautiful spots on the British Isles. Enclosed by an amphitheater of hills and blessed with warm springs, it has been both a pleasure resort and a health spa for the ailing.

Folliot Pierpoint was born in Bath but went away to attend Cambridge University, where he became a classical scholar and taught. But when he was twenty-nine years old he returned to his hometown of Bath. The beauty of the countryside in the late spring caused his heart to well up with emotion and inspired this hymn.

Each stanza thanks God for a different kind of beauty. In its original form it was a Communion hymn of eight stanzas. Each stanza concluded with the words "Christ our God, to thee we raise this our sacrifice of praise," alluding to Hebrews 13:15.

• • • •

Therefore, let us offer through Jesus a
continual sacrifice of praise to God,
proclaiming our allegiance to his name.
HEBREWS 13:15

All Things Bright and Beautiful

Cecil Alexander and her husband, William, a parish minister in Londonderry, Ireland, served in a rural area. She visited the poor families and gathered the children around her for instruction in the Bible, the catechism, and the Apostles' Creed. When she published a collection of her songs, almost all for children, she donated the profits to support disabled children in her area.

"All Things Bright and Beautiful" was written to help children understand the phrase "I believe in God the Father, Maker of Heaven and earth." Often when we think of God the Creator, we consider the vast galaxies of space and the mighty billowing oceans, but this hymn, written for boys and girls, talks of little flowers with glowing colors, little birds with tiny wings, purple-headed mountains, ripe fruits in the garden, and meadows where we play.

• • • •

In the beginning the Word already existed. The Word was with God, and the Word was God. He existed in the beginning with God. God created everything through him, and nothing was created except through him.

JOHN 1:1-3

All things bright and beautiful,
All creatures great and small,
And all things wise and wonderful;
The Lord God made them all.

Each little flow'r that opens up,
Each little bird that sings,
He made their glowing colors and
He made their tiny wings.

The purple-headed mountain,
The river running by,
The sunset and the morning light
That brightens up the sky.

The cold wind in the wintertime,
The pleasant summer sun,
The ripe fruits in the garden now,
He made them ev'ry one.

He gave us eyes to see them all,
And lips that we might tell
How great is the Almighty God
Who has made all things well.

Cecil Frances Alexander (1818–1895)

How Great Thou Art

O Lord my God!
When I in awesome wonder
Consider all the worlds Thy hands have made,
I see the stars, I hear the rolling thunder,
Thy power throughout the universe displayed,

Then sings my soul, My Savior, God, to Thee:
How great Thou art! How great Thou art!
Then sings my soul, My Savior, God, to Thee;
How great Thou art! How great Thou art!

When through the woods and forest glades I wander
And hear the birds sing sweetly in the trees,
When I look down from lofty mountain grandeur
And hear the brook and feel the gentle breeze,

And when I think that God, His Son not sparing,
Sent Him to die, I scarce can take it in;
That on the cross, my burden gladly bearing,
He bled and died to take away my sin,

When Christ shall come with shout of acclamation
And take me home, what joy shall fill my heart!
Then I shall bow in humble adoration
And there proclaim, my God, how great Thou art!

Carl Boberg (1859–1940)

Translated by Stuart K. Hine (1899–1989)

Copyright © 1953, renewed 1981 by Manna Music, Inc., 35255 Brooten Rd., Pacific City, OR 97135. International copyright secured. All rights reserved. Used by permission.

Outside USA: Copyright © 1953 Stuart K. Hine/ Kingsway's Thankyou Music, P.O. Box 75, Eastbourne, East Sussex BN23 6NW, UK.

Although this hymn is often associated with the crusades of Billy Graham, it originated in nineteenth-century Europe. In 1886 Swedish pastor Carl Boberg was caught in a sudden thunderstorm while visiting a beautiful country estate. As the storm passed, giving way to the sweet songs of birds and a green countryside glistening in sunlight, Boberg composed the nine original stanzas of this hymn.

In time the hymn was translated into German and Russian. It was noticed by a British missionary who was serving in Ukraine. That missionary, Reverend Stuart K. Hine, often sang the song with his wife as they ministered there. Later they translated three stanzas into English from the Russian, and Hine himself added a fourth.

• • • •

Look up into the heavens. Who created all the stars? He brings them out like an army, one after another, calling each by its name. Because of his great power and incomparable strength, not a single one is missing.
ISAIAH 40:26

Alleluia! Sing to Jesus

This hymn was originally entitled "Redemption through the Precious Blood." It was inspired by Revelation 5:9: "And they sang a new song with these words: "You are worthy. . . . For you were slaughtered, and your blood has ransomed people for God." William Dix, a Scottish maritime insurance agent, wrote this as a Communion hymn on Ascension Sunday, six weeks after Easter. While the first stanza reminds us of the Revelation scene, the second recalls Christ's ascension and even His comforting words in the upper room, "I will not abandon you as orphans" (John 14:18). The last stanza speaks of the ascended Christ in heaven as the great High Priest, interceding for His own.

• • • •

After this I saw a vast crowd, too great to count, from every nation and tribe and people and language, standing in front of the throne and before the Lamb. They were clothed in white robes and held palm branches in their hands. And they were shouting with a great roar, "Salvation comes from our God who sits on the throne and from the Lamb!"

REVELATION 7:9-10

Alleluia! sing to Jesus!
His the sceptre, His the throne;
Alleluia! His the triumph,
His the victory alone;
Hark! the songs of peaceful Zion
Thunder like a mighty flood;
"Jesus, out of ev'ry nation
Has redeemed us by His blood."

Alleluia! not as orphans
Are we left in sorrow now;
Alleluia! He is near us,
Faith believes, nor questions how:
Though the clouds from sight received Him
When the forty days were o'er,
Shall our hearts forget His promise,
"I am with you evermore"?

Alleluia! Bread of Heaven,
You on earth our food and stay!
Alleluia! here the sinful
Flee to You from day to day;
Intercessor, Friend of sinners,
Earth's Redeemer, plead for me,
Where the songs of all the sinless
Sweep across the crystal sea.

William Chatterton Dix (1837-1898)

All Nature's Works His Praise Declare

All nature's works His praise declare,
To whom they all belong;
There is a voice in every star,
In every breeze a song.
Sweet music fills the world abroad
With strains of love and power;
The stormy sea sings praise to God,
The thunder and the shower.

To God the tribes of ocean cry,
And birds upon the wing;
To God the powers that dwell on high
Their tuneful tribute bring.
Like them, let man the throne surround,
With them loud chorus raise,
While instruments of loftier sound
Assist his feeble praise.

Great God, to Thee we consecrate
Our voices and our skill;
We bid the pealing organ wait
To speak alone Thy will.
Lord, while the music round us floats,
May earthborn passions die;
O grant its rich and swelling notes
May lift our souls on high!

Henry Ware Jr. (1794-1843)

All of nature continually praises God. Only humans require reminders to do so. When Henry Ware's church in Boston was dedicating its new organ, he was asked to write a dedicatory hymn. As he wrote, he made sure that he did not speak of the greatness of the instrument. Instead, he emphasized the organ's purpose: to assist Christians in the praise of God. In a way, it's reminiscent of Psalm 150, which speaks of seven or eight different musical instruments, united in the praise of God. Thirteen times that psalm urges us to join in praise. We, too, are created for this purpose, to sing of God's glory.

We can thank God for our church organs and the other instruments that lead us in Sunday worship. But how often during the week do we lift our souls to God in the unaccompanied exaltation of our glorious Lord?

• • • •

Praise him with a blast of the ram's horn; praise him with the lyre and harp! Praise him with the tambourine and dancing; praise him with strings and flutes! Praise him with a clash of cymbals; praise him with loud clanging cymbals. Let everything that breathes sing praises to the Lord!
PSALM 150:3-6

I Sing the Mighty Power of God

Isaac Watts never married, yet he loved children. In his own childhood, he was precocious. He learned Latin when he was four, Greek when he was eight or nine, French when he was eleven, and Hebrew when he was thirteen. As an adult, he not only wrote books on theology, but on psychology, logic, and astronomy as well. He also wrote a book of children's songs, which included this hymn, even though it was considered a hymn for adults. His *Divine and Moral Songs for Children* was the first hymnal written for children and remained popular for more than a hundred years.

The first lesson that a child should learn is a lesson that adults should never forget: the great God who created this vast universe loves us and keeps us in His care. "I Sing the Mighty Power of God" teaches that lesson.

• • • •

For the Lord is a great God, a great King above all gods. He holds in his hands the depths of the earth and the mightiest mountains. The sea belongs to him, for he made it. His hands formed the dry land, too.

PSALM 95:3-5

I sing the mighty pow'r of God,
That made the mountains rise;
That spread the flowing seas abroad,
And built the lofty skies.
I sing the wisdom that ordained
The sun to rule the day;
The moon shines full at His command,
And all the stars obey.

I sing the goodness of the Lord,
That filled the earth with food;
He formed the creatures with His Word,
And then pronounced them good.
Lord, how Thy wonders are displayed,
Where e're I turn my eye:
If I survey the ground I tread,
Or gaze upon the sky!

There's not a plant or flow'r below,
But makes Thy glories known:
And clouds arise, and tempests blow,
By order from Thy throne;
While all that borrows life from Thee
Is ever in Thy care.
And ev'rywhere that man can be,
Thou, God, art present there.

Isaac Watts (1674-1748)

This Is My Father's World

This is my Father's world,
And to my listening ears
All nature sings, and round me rings
The music of the spheres.
This is my Father's world:
I rest me in the thought
Of rocks and trees, of skies and seas—
His hand the wonders wrought.

This is my Father's world,
The birds their carols raise,
The morning light, the lily white,
Declare their Maker's praise.
This is my Father's world:
He shines in all that's fair;
In the rustling grass I hear Him pass,
He speaks to me everywhere.

This is my Father's world,
O let me ne'er forget
That though the wrong seems oft so strong,
God is the Ruler yet.
This is my Father's world:
The battle is not done;
Jesus who died shall be satisfied,
And earth and heav'n be one.

Maltbie Davenport Babcock (1858-1901)

Maltbie Babcock was an athlete. An outstanding baseball pitcher and a champion swimmer, he kept himself in shape by running. When he was pastor of the First Presbyterian Church in Lockport, New York, he would run out in the early morning to the brow of the hill two miles away and look over at Lake Ontario. Before he left, he would tell his church staff, "I am going out to see my Father's world." From the brow of the hill, he would run two more miles to a deep ravine where as many as forty different species of birds found a sanctuary. Then he would run back.

Babcock loved athletics and nature, as well as playing music on the organ, piano, and violin. So it was not strange that he should write a hymn extolling God's handiwork in nature.

• • • •

The Lord merely spoke, and the heavens were created. He breathed the word, and all the stars were born. He assigned the sea its boundaries and locked the oceans in vast reservoirs. Let the whole world fear the Lord, and let everyone stand in awe of him.
PSALM 33:6-8

Praise Him! Praise Him!

Many of us remember when schoolteachers marked papers with grades of "good," "very good," and "excellent." There was nothing wrong with a "good" paper, but the "excellent" one went beyond expectations. It excelled.

In this hymn, Fanny Crosby urges us to praise God for His "excellent" greatness. Consider who or what, besides God, is the greatest thing in your life? Your family? Your home? Your friends? Your softball team? These may be good, even very good, but God is greater. He excels above all other aspects of our lives. His greatness exceeds our ability to praise Him.

It's hard to find a hymn richer in praise and joy. Jesus is hailed as Rock, Redeemer, Prophet, Priest, and King. But just when we begin to think He's so "excellent" that He's out of reach, we see Him as a Shepherd, carrying His little ones in His arms.

Praise Him! praise Him! Jesus, our blessed Redeemer!
Sing, O Earth, His wonderful love proclaim!
Hail Him! hail Him! highest archangels in glory;
Strength and honor give to His holy name!
Like a shepherd Jesus will guard His children,
In His arms He carries them all day long:

**Praise Him! praise Him! tell of His excellent greatness;
Praise Him! praise Him! ever in joyful song!**

Praise Him! praise Him! Jesus, our blessed Redeemer!
For our sins He suffered, and bled and died;
He our Rock, our hope of eternal salvation,
Hail Him! hail Him! Jesus the Crucified.
Sound His praises! Jesus who bore our sorrows;
Love unbounded, wonderful, deep and strong:

Praise Him! praise Him! Jesus, our blessed Redeemer!
Heav'nly portals loud with hosannas ring!
Jesus, Savior, reigneth forever and ever;
Crown Him! crown Him! Prophet and Priest and King!
Christ is coming! over the world victorious,
Pow'r and glory unto the Lord belong:

Fanny Jane Crosby (1820-1915)

• • • •

*[The angels] sang in a mighty chorus:
"Worthy is the Lamb who was slaughtered—
to receive power and riches and wisdom and
strength and honor and glory and blessing."*
REVELATION 5:12

Come, Let Us Rise with Christ

Come, let us rise with Christ our Head
And seek the things above,
By the almighty Spirit led
And filled with faith and love;
Our hearts detached from all below
Should after Him ascend,
And only wish the joy to know
Of our triumphant friend.

Enthroned at God's right hand He sits,
Maintainer of our cause,
Till every vanquished foe submits
To His victorious cross;
Worthy to be exalted thus,
The Lamb for sinners slain,
The Lord our King, who reigns for us,
And shall forever reign.

To Him our willing hearts we give
Who gives us power and peace,
And dead to sin, His members live
The life of righteousness;
The hidden life of Christ is ours
With Christ concealed above,
And tasting the celestial powers,
We banquet on His love.

Charles Wesley (1707–1788)

This hymn was based on Colossians 3:1: "Since you have been raised to new life with Christ, set your sights on the realities of heaven, where Christ sits in the place of honor at God's right hand." One year at a Christian college this verse was posted on bulletin boards throughout the campus. On one board in the student center, known for its graffiti, one sophomoric student had scrawled under the verse, "Too Platonic."

For all its disrespect, the comment had a shred of sense. Plato was the Greek philosopher who separated the physical from the mental, the life of our mundane world from the glorious ideals of the mind. Generations of followers tweaked this idea into an otherworldly attitude that considered the physical world (including human bodies) either insignificant or evil. We must never forget, though, that God loved this world so much He sent Jesus to die for it.

• • • •

For you died to this life, and your real life is hidden with Christ in God. And when Christ, who is your life, is revealed to the whole world, you will share in all his glory.
COLOSSIANS 3:3-4

A Hymn of Glory Let Us Sing

Bede is so revered that he is historically known as "the Venerable." He was a noted scholar, writing on history, nature, Scripture, and theology. Bede has been called "first among English scholars, first among English theologians, and first among English historians." His *Ecclesiastical History of the English Nation* is a remarkable work that recounts Christianity's movement to the British Isles.

The faith, he said, came with singing. The missionaries came with a simple lifestyle, and new converts believed, "admiring the simplicity of their innocent life, and the sweetness of their heavenly doctrine." In one city, he wrote, the Christians came together to "meet, to sing, to pray," and soon the king and ten thousand citizens were baptized.

It is said that when Bede was dying, on May 26, 735, he asked his friends to carry him to the room where he usually prayed, and there he sang the "Gloria Patri."

• • • •

God elevated him to the place of highest honor and gave him the name above all other names, that at the name of Jesus every knee should bow, in heaven and on earth and under the earth.

PHILIPPIANS 2:9-10

A hymn of glory let us sing,
New hymns throughout the world shall ring;
By a new way none ever trod
Christ takes His place—the throne of God.

You are a present joy, O Lord;
You will be ever our reward;
And great the light in You we see
To guide us to eternity.

O risen Christ, ascended Lord,
All praise to You let earth accord,
Who are, while endless ages run,
With Father and with Spirit, One.

The Venerable Bede (673-735)

Stanzas 1-2 translated by Elizabeth Rundle Charles (1828–1896), altered

Stanza 3 translated by Benjamin Webb (1819–1885), altered

Fairest Lord Jesus

Fairest Lord Jesus,
Ruler of all nature,
O Thou of God and man the son,
Thee will I cherish,
Thee will I honor,
Thou, my soul's glory, joy, and crown.

Fair are the meadows,
Fairer still the woodlands,
Robed in the blooming garb of spring:
Jesus is fairer,
Jesus is purer,
Who makes the woeful heart to sing.

Fair is the sunshine,
Fairer still the moonlight,
And all the twinkling starry host:
Jesus shines brighter,
Jesus shines purer,
Than all the angels heaven can boast.

Münster Gesangbuch, 1677

Translator Unknown

This hymn may have first been sung by followers of reformer John Hus, who lived near Prague around 1400. In an anti-Reformation purge, Hussites were expelled from Bohemia and went into Silesia, where they became weavers and cobblers, maintaining their faith in secret. But they had a strong tradition of hymn singing, and the most reliable tradition says that this hymn came from these humble Christians.

The hymn contains no comments on persecution, but only praise to a wonderful Savior. Whoever wrote the hymn was close to nature and adored God's creation, but recognized that even fairer than the creation is the Creator. This season as we bask in the beauties of all that God has given us to enjoy, we mustn't forget that Jesus is fairer and purer than all the blooming garb of spring.

• • • •

Praise the Lord from the heavens! Praise him from the skies! Praise him, all his angels! Praise him, all the armies of heaven! Praise him, sun and moon! Praise him, all you twinkling stars! Praise him, skies above! Praise him, vapors high above the clouds!
PSALM 148:1-4

Prayer Is the Soul's Sincere Desire

When the Reverend Edward Bickersteth had written his *Treatise on Prayer*, he turned to newspaper editor James Montgomery to write a hymn about prayer that he could use in his book. Today Rev. Bickersteth's volume has been forgotten, but the newspaperman's hymn is still being sung.

This hymn is a theological definition in poetic form. What is prayer? Bickersteth may have said it more completely, but Montgomery defined it simply. (Montgomery later said he received more praise for this hymn than anything else he had written.)

Many years after he retired, Montgomery continued to conduct family prayer meetings in his home. After he closed one such meeting of prayer, he walked quietly to his room. The next day he was found unconscious on the floor and later died. As he had written in this hymn, prayer is the Christian's "watchword at the gates of death; he enters heaven with prayer."

· · · ·

Jesus said, "This is how you should pray: Father, may your name be kept holy. May your Kingdom come soon. Give us each day the food we need, and forgive us our sins, as we forgive those who sin against us. And don't let us yield to temptation."

LUKE 11:2-4

Prayer is the soul's sincere desire,
Unuttered or expressed,
The motion of a hidden fire
That trembles in the breast.

Prayer is the burden of a sigh,
The falling of a tear,
The upward glancing of an eye,
When none but God is near.

Prayer is the simplest form of speech
That infant lips can try;
Prayer the sublimest strains that reach
The Majesty on high.

Prayer is the contrite sinner's voice,
Returning from his ways,
While angels in their songs rejoice
And cry, "Behold, he prays!"

Prayer is the Christian's vital breath,
The Christian's native air,
His watchword at the gates of death;
He enters heaven with prayer.

O Thou, by whom we come to God,
The Life, the Truth, the Way;
The path of prayer Thyself hast trod:
Lord, teach us how to pray!

James Montgomery (1771–1854)

Crown Him with Many Crowns

Crown Him with many crowns,
The Lamb upon His throne;
Hark! how the heavenly anthem drowns
All music but its own.
Awake, my soul, and sing
Of Him who died for thee,
And hail Him as thy matchless King
Through all eternity.

Crown Him the Lord of life,
Who triumphed o'er the grave,
And rose victorious in the strife
For those He came to save;
His glories now we sing
Who died and rose on high,
Who died, eternal life to bring,
And lives, that death may die.

Crown Him the Lord of peace,
Whose power a scepter sways
From pole to pole, that wars may cease,
And all be prayer and praise;
His reign shall know no end,
And round His pierced feet
Fair flowers of paradise extend
Their fragrance ever sweet.

Crown Him the Lord of love;
Behold His hands and side,
Those wounds, yet visible above,
In beauty glorified.
All hail, Redeemer, hail!
For Thou hast died for me;
Thy praise and glory shall not fail
Throughout eternity.

Matthew Bridges (1800-1894)

Godfrey Thring (1823-1903), additional stanzas

Matthew Bridges became a convert to Roman Catholicism at the age of forty-eight and published this hymn three years later under the title "The Song of the Seraphs." Godfrey Thring, an Anglican clergyman, added several stanzas to the hymn about thirty years later, with Bridges's approval. So a Roman Catholic layman and an Anglican cleric, who probably never met, were coauthors of a hymn about heaven, where Christians of every tribe and tongue, as well as of every denomination, will crown Him Lord of all.

One of the aspects that Godfrey Thring felt was missing in the original was a stanza on the Resurrection, and so it was added. "His glories now we sing who died and rose on high, who died, eternal life to bring, and lives, that death may die."

• • • •

Then I saw heaven opened, and a white horse was standing there. Its rider was named Faithful and True, for he judges fairly and wages a righteous war. His eyes were like flames of fire, and on his head were many crowns.
REVELATION 19:11-12

Spirit of God, Descend upon My Heart

George Croly, who wrote this hymn, came from Ireland to minister in a small parish church in London. During his twenty-five years of service there he had much time for writing and became known for poems, novels, biographies, and plays. Then when he was fifty years old, he was asked to reopen a church in one of London's worst slums that had been closed for more than a century. Croly's preaching soon attracted crowds. At the age of seventy-four, he prepared a new hymnal for the congregation, including this hymn under the title "Holiness Desired."

Croly had spent twenty-five years interacting with culture, and almost the same amount of time dealing with society's ills in London's slums. But to Croly what mattered most was not what a person was on the outside, but what he was on the inside. So in this hymn he shuts the door and asks for a fresh filling of the Spirit.

Spirit of God, descend upon my heart;
Wean it from earth; through all its pulses move;
Stoop to my weakness, mighty as Thou art,
And make me love Thee as I ought to love.

I ask no dream, no prophet ecstasies,
No sudden rending of the veil of clay,
No angel visitant, no opening skies;
But take the dimness of my soul away.

Hast Thou not bid me love Thee, God and King?
All, all Thine own, soul, heart and strength and mind.
I see Thy cross; there teach my heart to cling:
O let me seek Thee, and O let me find!

Teach me to feel that Thou art always nigh;
Teach me the struggles of the soul to bear,
To check the rising doubt, the rebel sigh;
Teach me the patience of unanswered prayer.

Teach me to love Thee as Thine angels love,
One holy passion filling all my frame;
The kindling of the heaven descended Dove,
My heart an altar, and Thy love the flame.

George Croly (1780–1860)

• • • •

But the Holy Spirit produces this kind of fruit in our lives: love, joy, peace, patience, kindness, goodness, faithfulness, gentleness, and self-control. There is no law against these things!

GALATIANS 5:22-23

Come Down, O Love Divine

Come down, O Love divine,
Seek Thou this soul of mine,
And visit it with Thine own ardor glowing;
O Comforter, draw near,
Within my heart appear,
And kindle it, Thy holy flame bestowing.

O let it freely burn,
Till earthly passions turn
To dust and ashes in its heat consuming;
And let Thy glorious light
Shine ever on my sight,
And clothe me round the while my path illuming.

And so the yearning strong,
With which the soul will long,
Shall far outpass the power of human telling;
For none can guess its grace,
Till he become the place
Wherein the Holy Spirit makes His dwelling.

Bianco da Siena (?-1434)

Translated by Richard F. Littledale (1833-1890)

Six hundred years ago, Bianco da Siena, living in Venice, Italy, wrote this hymn, which he entitled "The Holy Spirit Desired." It was one of ninety-two hymns he wrote in a hymnbook he called *Spiritual Praise*. In the nineteenth century, Richard Littledale—a man of broad interests who had a special interest in writing and translating hymns—discovered the hymn and translated it from Italian into English. He published it in *The People's Hymnal* in 1867. The amazing thing about Littledale is that he also translated hymns from Danish, Swedish, Greek, Latin, Syrian, and German.

This hymn is a lovely, sensitive invitation to the Holy Spirit to enter our hearts and consume all our earthly passions, transforming us into the people God wants us to be.

• • • •

Those who are controlled by the Holy Spirit think about things that please the Spirit. So letting your sinful nature control your mind leads to death. But letting the Spirit control your mind leads to life and peace.
ROMANS 8:5-6

Come, Gracious Spirit, Heavenly Dove

Hymnwriter Simon Browne often found it easier to write things on paper than to know them experientially. He wrote an English dictionary, he completed the memorable commentary of Matthew Henry after that great scholar passed away, and he wrote beautiful hymns.

But he struggled with the painful memory of an event that happened when he was forty years old. Browne was attacked by a highwayman, and in self-defense, he struck the man, knocking him down and killing him. Convinced that he was a murderer, Browne could never forgive himself; he felt God had taken his own soul from him. The prayer of his tortured heart is captured in the first line of this hymn, "Come, gracious Spirit, heavenly Dove, with light and comfort from above."

Come, gracious Spirit, heav'nly Dove,
With light and comfort from above;
Be Thou our Guardian, Thou our Guide;
O'er ev'ry thought and step preside.

To us the light of truth display,
And make us know and choose Thy way;
Plant holy fear in ev'ry heart,
That we from God may ne'er depart.

Lead us to holiness, the road
Which we must take to dwell with God;
Lead us to Christ, the living way;
Nor let us from His pastures stray.

Lead us to God, our final rest,
To be with Him forever blest;
Lead us to heav'n, its bliss to share,
Fullness of joy forever there.

Simon Browne (1680–1732)

• • • •

[Jesus said,] "If you love me, obey my commandments. And I will ask the Father, and he will give you another Advocate, who will never leave you. He is the Holy Spirit, who leads into all truth."

JOHN 14:15-17

Come, Holy Ghost, Our Hearts Inspire

Come, Holy Ghost, our hearts inspire,
Let us Thine influence prove:
Source of the old prophetic fire,
Fountain of life and love.

Come, Holy Ghost, for moved by Thee
The prophets wrote and spoke;
Unlock the truth, Thyself the key,
Unseal the sacred book.

Expand Thy wings, celestial Dove,
Brood o'er our nature's night;
On our disordered spirits move,
And let there now be light.

God, through Himself, we then shall know
If Thou within us shine,
And sound with all Thy saints below,
The depths of love divine.

Charles Wesley (1707-1788)

This hymn uses two Scripture passages: the very first biblical reference to the Holy Spirit and one of the last. In Genesis 1:2, we find the Spirit involved in Creation, "hovering over the surface of the waters." Toward the end of the New Testament, 2 Peter 1:19-21 urges readers to pay attention to the word of the prophets, "for their words are like a lamp shining in a dark place." The prophets, Peter says, were not just making this stuff up. No, they were "moved by the Holy Spirit, and they spoke from God."

As usual, Charles Wesley has woven solid theology into his hymn. The Spirit brings order out of our chaos. He shines light into our dark places. He often does this through the Scriptures. He unlocks the truth spoken by the ancient prophets so it makes sense in modern times.

• • • •

"No eye has seen, no ear has heard, and no mind has imagined what God has prepared for those who love him." But it was to us that God revealed these things by his Spirit. For his Spirit searches out everything and shows us God's deep secrets.

I CORINTHIANS 2:9-10

Blessed Quietness

On the stormy Sea of Galilee, Jesus commanded the winds and waves, "Silence, be still" (Mark 4:39), and immediately there was calm. And later in the upper room, as Jesus told His disciples that He would leave them, He promised them the Holy Spirit and peace.

Manie Payne, born in Carlow, Ireland, was a Christian, but she did not know peace. She struggled with her sinful nature until she began to experience the fullness of the Holy Spirit. This is the "blessed quietness" that she wrote about. Once that occurred, she was so happy she could hardly contain herself. Indeed, joy was flowing like a river in her life.

Later she married T. P. Ferguson and founded Peniel Missions, with branches in Egypt, China, and the west coast of the United States.

• • • •

[Jesus said,] "I am leaving you with a gift—peace of mind and heart. And the peace I give is a gift the world cannot give. So don't be troubled or afraid."

JOHN 14:27

Joys are flowing like a river
Since the Comforter has come.
He abides with us forever,
Makes the trusting heart His home.

Blessed quietness, holy quietness,
What assurance in my soul!
On the stormy sea He speaks peace to me,
How the billows cease to roll!

Bringing life and health and gladness
All around this heav'nly Guest
Banished unbelief and sadness,
Changed our weariness to rest.

Like the rain that falls from heaven,
Like the sunlight from the sky,
So the Holy Ghost is given,
Coming on us from on high.

See, a fruitful field is growing,
Blessed fruit of righteousness;
And the streams of life are flowing
In the lonely wilderness.

What a wonderful salvation,
Where we always see His face!
What a perfect habitation,
What a quiet resting place!

Manie Payne Ferguson (1850–?)

Come, Holy Spirit, Dove Divine

Come, Holy Spirit, Dove divine,
On these baptismal waters shine,
And teach our hearts, in highest strain,
To praise the Lamb for sinners slain.

We love Thy name, we love Thy laws,
And joyfully embrace Thy cause;
We love Thy cross, the shame, the pain,
O Lamb of God for sinners slain.

We sink beneath the water's face,
And thank Thee for Thy saving grace;
We die to sin and seek a grave
With Thee, beneath the yielding wave.

And as we rise with Thee to live,
O let the Holy Spirit give
The sealing unction from above,
The joy of life, the fire of love.

Adoniram Judson (1788-1850)

Adoniram Judson and his wife, Ann, served in Burma as missionaries for a long time before they saw their first converts. During those years, Adoniram worked to translate the Bible into the Burmese language. Finally, one Burmese man responded. You can sense the hesitation in Adoniram's journal as he wrote, "I begin to think that the grace of God has reached his heart."

The next step was to prepare the man for baptism, and Adoniram prayed, "Oh, may it prove the beginning of a series of baptisms in the Burman Empire which shall continue in uninterrupted succession to the end of time." When more Burmese became Christians and asked to be baptized, Judson wrote this baptismal hymn.

By the time of Judson's death, seven thousand Burmese had come to Christ. The waiting was worth it.

• • • •

When we were joined with Christ Jesus in baptism, we joined him in his death. For we died and were buried with Christ by baptism. And just as Christ was raised from the dead by the glorious power of the Father, now we also may live new lives.

ROMANS 6:3-4

Holy Spirit, Truth Divine

Henry Wadsworth Longfellow, one of the first great American poets, is renowned for works like "Evangeline," "The Song of Hiawatha," and "Tales of a Wayside Inn." About the same time that he was writing "Tales of a Wayside Inn," his brother, Samuel Longfellow, was compiling a hymnbook. In this hymnal, Samuel included a hymn he had recently written, "Holy Spirit, Truth Divine." Though Samuel was a minister in the Unitarian church, as he grew older he refused to be called a Unitarian.

The hymn itself is one that is acceptable to all Christians. The Holy Spirit is praised as truth, love, power, and right. The last stanza reminds us of the words in the Gospel of John where Jesus says that the Holy Spirit would convict the world of sin, righteousness, and judgment. The Spirit does carry on this ministry within us as that "still, small voice" that shows us the way.

Holy Spirit, Truth divine,
Dawn upon this soul of mine;
Word of God and inward light,
Wake my spirit, clear my sight.

Holy Spirit, Love divine,
Glow within this heart of mine;
Kindle every high desire;
Perish self in Thy pure fire.

Holy Spirit, Power divine,
Fill and nerve this will of mine;
By Thee may I strongly live,
Bravely hear and nobly strive.

Holy Spirit, Right divine,
King within my conscience reign;
Be my Lord, and I shall be
Firmly bound, forever free.

Samuel Longfellow (1819–1892)

• • • •

Let the Holy Spirit guide your lives. Then you won't be doing what your sinful nature craves. The sinful nature wants to do evil, which is just the opposite of what the Spirit wants.

GALATIANS 5:16-17

Lord Jesus Christ, Be Present Now

Lord Jesus Christ, be present now,
Our hearts in true devotion bow,
Thy Spirit send with grace divine,
And let Thy truth within us shine.

Unseal our lips to sing Thy praise,
Our souls to Thee in worship raise,
Make strong our faith, increase our light
That we may know Thy name aright.

Until we join the hosts that cry,
"Holy art Thou, O Lord, most high!"
And in the light of that blest place
Fore'er behold Thee face to face.

Glory to God the Father, Son,
And Holy Spirit, Three in One!
To Thee, O blessed Trinity,
Be praise throughout eternity!

German Hymn

Cantionale Sacrum, 1651
Translated by Catherine Winkworth (1827-1878)

Where is Jesus? There are several ways to answer that question. As God, He is omnipresent, all around us. He said that He was somehow present in the poor and needy people that we meet. Scripture also speaks of Him sitting at the right hand of the Father. This is a place of honor, where He waits for the right time to return to earth in triumph. Through His Spirit, He is present in our hearts.

If Jesus is in all these places, why should we invite Him to be present now? Well, there are several other Scriptures to take note of. Jesus said that where two or three gather in His name, He would be there with them. That happens each time we worship. Another verse says that the Lord inhabits His people's praise. And Christ is in some way present when we observe the Lord's Supper.

This hymn is a call to worship, inviting Christ to inspire, inhabit, and enjoy our praises.

• • • •

[Jesus said,] "If two of you agree here on earth concerning anything you ask, my Father in heaven will do it for you. For where two or three gather together as my followers, I am there among them."
MATTHEW 18:19-20

Hail the Day That Sees Him Rise

Within a year after his conversion in 1738, Charles Wesley wrote three great hymns to celebrate special days of the church: "Hark! the Herald Angels Sing" for Christmas (December 22), "Christ the Lord Is Risen Today" for Easter (April 3), and "Hail the Day That Sees Him Rise" for Ascension Day.

Charles Wesley is well known, but Martin Madan, who had a role in Wesley's hymns, has almost been forgotten. Madan was one of these who was converted through the preaching of the Wesleys and later became a preacher himself. He also became interested in music, and although he left no song that we now sing, he edited many of Charles Wesley's hymns for inclusion in his hymnal. Madan liked to insert *alleluias* into hymns, and it was probably he who put the *alleluias* into both this hymn and "Christ the Lord Is Risen Today."

Hail the day that sees Him rise, Alleluia!
To His throne above the skies; Alleluia!
Christ, the Lamb for sinners giv'n, Alleluia!
Enters now the highest heav'n. Alleluia!

There for Him high triumph waits; Alleluia!
Lift your heads, eternal gates, Alleluia!
He hath conquered death and sin, Alleluia!
Take the King of glory in! Alleluia!

See, He lifts His hands above! Alleluia!
See, He shows the prints of love! Alleluia!
Hark! His gracious lips bestow, Alleluia!
Blessings on His church below. Alleluia!

Lord, beyond our mortal sight, Alleluia!
Raise our hearts to reach Thy height, Alleluia!
There Thy face unclouded see, Alleluia!
Find our heav'n of heav'ns in Thee! Alleluia!

Charles Wesley (1707-1788)

• • • •

Then Jesus led them to Bethany, and lifting his hands to heaven, he blessed them. While he was blessing them, he left them and was taken up to heaven. So they worshiped him and then returned to Jerusalem filled with great joy.

LUKE 24:50-53

Come, Holy Spirit, Heavenly Dove

Come, Holy Spirit, Heav'nly Dove,
With all Thy quick'ning pow'rs;
Kindle a flame of sacred love
In these cold hearts of ours.

Look, how we grovel here below,
Fond of these earthly toys;
Our souls, how heavily they go,
To reach eternal joys.

In vain we tune our formal songs,
In vain we strive to rise;
Hosannas languish on our tongues,
And our devotion dies.

Father, and shall we ever live
At this poor dying rate,
Our love so faint, so cold to Thee,
And Thine to us so great?

Come, Holy Spirit, Heav'nly Dove,
With all Thy quick'ning pow'rs;
Come, shed abroad a Savior's love,
And that shall kindle ours.

Isaac Watts (1674-1748)

Isaac Watts was disturbed with "business-as-usual" Christianity. He knew that the only way Christians could be shaken out of their lethargy was if they had a fresh touch of the Spirit. Just as Jesus is described both as a meek lamb and as a fearsome lion, so the Holy Spirit is described as both a dove and fire. Sometimes Christians need to experience the Holy Spirit as a gentle dove, but often we need to know Him as a roaring fire.

One stanza that is often omitted from this hymn is "Father, and shall we ever live at this poor dying rate, our love so faint, so cold to Thee, and Thine to us so great?" It was this contrast between our love for God and God's love for us that disturbed Watts. He knew that only the fire of the Spirit could kindle our hearts into deeper love.

• • • •

Suddenly, there was a sound from heaven like the roaring of a mighty windstorm, and it filled the house where they were sitting. Then, what looked like flames or tongues of fire appeared and settled on each of them. And everyone present was filled with the Holy Spirit and began speaking in other languages, as the Holy Spirit gave them this ability.

ACTS 2:2-4

O for a Closer Walk with God

Martin Madan, the unsung inserter of *alleluias* in the hymn "Hail the Day That Sees Him Rise" (May 25), had an interesting part in this hymn as well. Madan's cousin, the poet William Cowper, had tried suicide three times and had been hospitalized twice for insanity. Through Madan's influence, Cowper became a Christian and recovered his sanity.

Cowper soon became friends with John Newton, the author of "Amazing Grace" (March 17). Besides their mutual love of poetry, they both had a sense of humor and both loved to take long walks. It was the best therapy possible for Cowper. Cowper walked at a fast pace with Newton but also loved to stroll slowly through the little town of Olney, where he visited the poor and chatted with the children.

One morning at the Newtons' house, Cowper was reading the passage that says Enoch walked "in close fellowship with God" (Genesis 5:24). It inspired him to write this hymn.

O for a closer walk with God,
A calm and heav'nly frame,
A light to shine upon the road
That leads me to the Lamb.

Where is the blessedness I knew
When first I saw the Lord?
Where is the soul-refreshing view
Of Jesus and His Word?

Return, O holy Dove, return,
Sweet messenger of rest;
I hate the sins that made Thee mourn
And drove Thee from my breast.

The dearest idol I have known,
What e'er that idol be,
Help me to tear it from Thy throne
And worship only Thee.

So shall my walk be close with God,
Calm and serene my frame;
So purer light shall mark the road
That leads me to the Lamb.

William Cowper (1731-1800)

• • • •

So humble yourselves before God. Resist the devil, and he will flee from you. Come close to God, and God will come close to you.
JAMES 4:7-8

Holy Ghost, with Light Divine

Holy Ghost, with light divine,
Shine upon this heart of mine;
Chase the shades of night away,
Turn my darkness into day.

Holy Ghost, with pow'r divine,
Cleanse this guilty heart of mine;
Long hath sin without control
Held dominion o'er my soul.

Holy Ghost, with joy divine,
Cheer this saddened heart of mine;
Bid my many woes depart,
Heal my wounded, bleeding heart.

Holy Spirit, all divine,
Dwell within this heart of mine;
Cast down ev'ry idol throne,
Reign supreme and reign alone.

Andrew Reed (1787-1862)

This hymn's tune is entitled "Mercy," and that is what the Holy Spirit accomplished through Andrew Reed, the hymn's author. A Congregational pastor in London, Reed founded six hospitals for the sick and helpless in London, including the London Orphan Asylum, the Asylum for Fatherless Children, the Hospital for Incurables, and the Asylum for Idiots. While the names of the institutions may seem strange to modern ears, they were all much-needed missions of mercy.

Andrew Reed's son wanted to write a biography of his father and asked for some biographical information. Andrew responded with these words: "I was born yesterday; I shall die tomorrow; I must not spend today in telling what I have done, but in doing what I may for Him who has done so much for me."

• • • •

You have no obligation to do what your sinful nature urges you to do. For if you live by its dictates, you will die. But if through the power of the Spirit you put to death the deeds of your sinful nature, you will live. For all who are led by the Spirit of God are children of God.
ROMANS 8:12-14

Holy, Holy, Holy

Reginald Heber was always trying to improve the music at the Anglican church he served in Hodnet, England. Though his superiors frowned on the use of anything but metrical psalms, Heber introduced hymns by Newton and Cowper and even wrote new hymns of his own. This one would impress Alfred Lord Tennyson as the world's greatest hymn.

After serving sixteen years as a parish priest in England, Heber accepted the call to become the bishop of Calcutta, India. Whether in England, as he surveyed the prevalence of vice, or in India, where he was surrounded by the worship of false gods, Heber was impressed with the holiness of God. "Only Thou art holy," he wrote. The tune to which this hymn is usually sung is called "Nicaea," named after the church council that met in AD 325, which formulated the Nicene Creed and affirmed the doctrine of the Trinity.

Holy, holy, holy! Lord God Almighty!
Early in the morning our song shall rise to Thee;
Holy, holy, holy! merciful and mighty!
God in three Persons, blessed Trinity!

Holy, holy, holy! all the saints adore Thee,
Casting down their golden crowns
around the glassy sea;
Cherubim and seraphim falling down before Thee,
Which wert and art and evermore shalt be.

Holy, holy, holy! though the darkness hide Thee,
Though the eye of sinful man Thy glory may not see;
Only Thou art holy—there is none beside Thee,
Perfect in pow'r, in love and purity.

Holy, holy, holy! Lord God Almighty!
All Thy works shall praise Thy name
in earth and sky and sea;
Holy, holy, holy! merciful and mighty!
God in three Persons, blessed Trinity!

Reginald Heber (1783–1826)

• • • •

Day after day and night after night they keep on saying, "Holy, holy, holy is the Lord God, the Almighty—the one who always was, who is, and who is still to come."

REVELATION 4:8

Christ for the World We Sing

Christ for the world we sing;
The world to Christ we bring
    With loving zeal—
The poor and them that mourn,
    The faint and over-borne,
    Sin-sick and sorrow-worn,
        For Christ to heal.

Christ for the world we sing;
The world to Christ we bring
    With fervent prayer—
The wayward and the lost,
    By restless passions tossed,
    Redeemed at countless cost
        From dark despair.

Christ for the world we sing;
The world to Christ we bring
    With one accord—
With us the work to share,
    With us reproach to dare,
    With us the cross to bear,
        For Christ our Lord.

Christ for the world we sing;
The world to Christ we bring
    With joyful song—
The newborn souls whose days,
    Reclaimed from error's ways,
    Inspired with hope and praise,
        To Christ belong.

Samuel Wolcott (1813–1886)

Samuel Wolcott wanted to be a missionary in Syria, but after two years there he had to return to America. In the United States, he pastored churches in Rhode Island, Illinois, Massachusetts, and Ohio.

While attending a YMCA convention in Cleveland, he was captivated by a huge banner with the words "Christ for the World and the World for Christ" outlined in evergreen letters above the pulpit. As Wolcott left the meeting, the words for this hymn gradually took shape in his mind.

Wolcott had learned that the "world" for whom Christ died included not only those in distant lands like Syria, where he had tried to serve, but also the poor, those that mourn, the faint, the burdened, the sin-sick and sorrow-worn in such needy places as the major cities of America where he ministered.

• • • •

I am not ashamed of this Good News about Christ. It is the power of God at work, saving everyone who believes—the Jew first and also the Gentile. This Good News tells us how God makes us right in his sight. This is accomplished from start to finish by faith. As the Scriptures say, "It is through faith that a righteous person has life."

ROMANS 1:16-17

Take Time to Be Holy

The son of a wealthy ship merchant, William Longstaff was treasurer of his church and gave liberally to Christian causes. When evangelists D. L. Moody and Ira Sankey came to England, he assisted them financially, and he also wrote reports of the meetings for the Christian press.

A few years later Longstaff heard a sermon on the text "Be ye holy, for I am holy" and wrote down what holiness meant to him. A businessman at heart, Longstaff wrote no flowery or pious-sounding verses, but these down-to-earth thoughts.

The hymn appeared in a Christian newspaper in 1882 and was promptly forgotten. But years later gospel composer George Stebbins, who was leading music in India in connection with evangelistic services there, remembered the poem when he was asked if there was a good hymn on living a holy life. Retrieving the newspaper clipping he had saved, he set the poem to music.

• • • •

Warn those who are lazy. Encourage those who are timid. Take tender care of those who are weak. Be patient with everyone. See that no one pays back evil for evil, but always try to do good to each other and to all people.

I THESSALONIANS 5:14-15

Take time to be holy,
Speak oft with thy Lord;
Abide in Him always,
And feed on His Word.
Make friends of God's children;
Help those who are weak;
Forgetting in nothing
His blessing to seek.

Take time to be holy,
The world rushes on;
Much time spend in secret
With Jesus alone;
By looking to Jesus,
Like Him thou shalt be;
Thy friends in thy conduct
His likeness shall see.

Take time to be holy,
Let Him be thy guide,
And run not before Him
Whatever betide;
In joy or in sorrow
Still follow the Lord,
And, looking to Jesus,
Still trust in His Word.

Take time to be holy,
Be calm in thy soul;
Each thought and each motive
Beneath His control;
Thus led by His Spirit
To fountains of love,
Thou soon shalt be fitted
For service above.

William Dunn Longstaff (1822–1894)

151

Jesus Shall Reign

Jesus shall reign where'er the sun
Does his successive journeys run;
His kingdom spread from shore to shore,
Till moons shall wax and wane no more.

To Him shall endless prayer be made,
And endless praises crown His head;
His name like sweet perfume shall rise
With ev'ry morning sacrifice.

People and realms of ev'ry tongue
Dwell on His love with sweetest song,
And infant voices shall proclaim
Their early blessings on His name.

Blessings abound where'er He reigns;
The prisoner leaps to loose his chains;
The weary find eternal rest,
And all the sons of want are blest.

Let every creature rise and bring
His grateful honors to our King;
Angels descend with songs again,
And earth repeat the loud amen!

Isaac Watts (1674–1748)

Isaac Watts once said that his aim was to see "David converted into a Christian." He meant singing the Psalms was good but it would be better if they were infused with the gospel. He felt some psalms were unsuitable for Christian worship because they were written before the Cross of Christ and the completion of God's redemption and revelation.

The great missionary hymn "Jesus Shall Reign" is based on Psalm 72. There was no great mission effort when Watts wrote these words. Not until sixty years later did William Carey—the father of the modern missionary movement—sail for India. Today, by means of radio and literature, as well as through the work of faithful missionaries, Christ's Kingdom has "spread from shore to shore," and "people and realms of every tongue dwell on His love with sweetest song."

• • • •

May the king's rule be refreshing like spring rain on freshly cut grass, like the showers that water the earth. May all the godly flourish during his reign. May there be abundant prosperity until the moon is no more. May he reign from sea to sea, and from the Euphrates River to the ends of the earth.

PSALM 72:6-8

Teach Me, O Lord, Thy Holy Way

Some people get the idea that the Lord's way is unexciting. As if we're children faced with a choice of peas or cotton candy. Peas are good for you, but the cotton candy is much more fun. Matson's hymn echoes the psalmist: There is "delight" in obeying the Lord. It's not just a case of doing what's good for you, like eating peas. It's finding delight and fulfillment in a growing relationship with God.

As the Lord "teaches" us His way, it's not the tedium of a dry algebra class. It's more like teaching a child to ride a bike. There will be some spills, but the end result is a whole new level of joy.

• • • •

Teach me how to live, O Lord. Lead me along the right path, for my enemies are waiting for me. Do not let me fall into their hands. For they accuse me of things I've never done; with every breath they threaten me with violence. . . . Wait patiently for the Lord. Be brave and courageous. Yes, wait patiently for the Lord.

PSALM 27:11-12, 14

Teach me, O Lord, Thy holy way,
And give me an obedient mind;
That in Thy service I may find
My soul's delight from day to day.

Guide me, O Savior, with Thy hand,
And so control my thoughts and deeds,
That I may tread the path which leads
Right onward to the blessed land.

Help me, O Savior, here to trace
The sacred footsteps Thou hast trod;
And, meekly walking with my God,
To grow in goodness, truth, and grace.

Guard me, O Lord, that I may ne'er
Forsake the right, or do the wrong:
Against temptation make me strong,
And round me spread Thy shelt'ring care.

Bless me in ev'ry task, O Lord,
Begun, continued, done for Thee:
Fulfill Thy perfect work in me;
And Thine abounding grace afford.

William T. Matson (1833–1899)

Revive Us Again

We praise Thee, O God,
For the Son of Thy love,
For Jesus who died
And is now gone above.

Hallelujah, Thine the glory!
Hallelujah, amen!
Hallelujah, Thine the glory!
Revive us again.

We praise Thee, O God,
For Thy Spirit of light,
Who has shown us our Savior
And scattered our night.

All glory and praise
To the Lamb that was slain.
Who has borne all our sins
And has cleansed ev'ry stain.

Revive us again—
Fill each heart with Thy love;
May each soul be rekindled
With fire from above.

William Paton Mackay (1839–1885)

At first, the words of this hymn may not seem to fit together. Is it a prayer for personal revival, or is it a hymn of praise? The first three stanzas are outbursts of praise to the triune God, so that the natural response is "Hallelujah, Thine the glory." Only the last stanza ties in with the title, "Revive Us Again."

But the author, William P. Mackay, a Scottish physician-turned-minister, knew what he was doing. The hymn was first published in 1875 under the inscription, "O Lord, revive Thy work." Psalm 85:6 asks, "Will you not revive us again, that your people may rejoice in you?" (NKJV). In commenting on this psalm, Charles Haddon Spurgeon wrote, "A genuine revival without joy in the Lord is as impossible as spring without flowers or daydawn without light." When surrounded by discouragement and fear, it is good to sing praise to the One "who has borne all our sins, and has cleansed every stain."

• • • •

Restore us again, O God of our salvation.
Put aside your anger against us once more.
Will you be angry with us always? Will
you prolong your wrath to all generations?
Won't you revive us again, so your people
can rejoice in you?
PSALM 85:4-6

Come, Holy Ghost, Our Souls Inspire

The Holy Spirit is often associated with fire. John the Baptist spoke of Jesus baptizing people with the Holy Spirit and with fire. Sure enough, when the Holy Spirit came at Pentecost, He appeared as tongues of fire resting on each believer.

There are seven gifts of the Spirit mentioned in Romans 12:6-8. This may be behind the "sevenfold gifts" of this hymn's first stanza. Of course 1 Corinthians 12 offers another dozen or so, and Ephesians adds a few more. So it's more likely that the author used seven as the number of perfection or completeness, as it is often used throughout Scripture.

Anointing had two purposes in Scripture. Ritually, it was used as a sign of God's special empowerment for kings, prophets, and priests. But in everyday life it was a way of refreshing and cleansing. The Spirit does all that for us, empowering us to serve God as well as offering spiritual refreshment.

Come, Holy Ghost, our souls inspire,
And lighten with celestial fire;
Thou the anointing Spirit art,
Who dost Thy sevenfold gifts impart.

Thy blessed unction from above
Is comfort, life, and fire of love;
Enable with perpetual light
The dullness of our blinded sight.

Anoint and cheer our soiled face
With the abundance of Thy grace;
Keep far our foes; give peace at home;
Where Thou art guide, no ill can come.

Teach us to know the Father, Son,
And Thee, of both, to be but One;
That through the ages all along
This, this may be our endless song:

Praise to Thy eternal merit
Father, Son, and Holy Spirit.

Attributed to Rhabanus Maurus (c. 776-856)

Translated by John Cosin (1594-1672)

• • • •

Wherever the Spirit of the Lord is, there is freedom. So all of us who have had that veil removed can see and reflect the glory of the Lord. And the Lord—who is the Spirit— makes us more and more like him as we are changed into his glorious image.

2 CORINTHIANS 3:17-18

O Zion, Haste

O Zion, haste, thy mission high fulfilling,
To tell to all the world that God is Light;
That He who made all nations is not willing
One soul should perish, lost in shades of night.

**Publish glad tidings, tidings of peace;
Tidings of Jesus, redemption, and release.**

Behold how many thousands still are lying,
Bound in the darksome prison-house of sin,
With none to tell them of the Savior's dying,
Or of the life He died for them to win.

Proclaim to every people, tongue and nation
That God, in whom they live and move, is love:
Tell how He stooped to save His lost creation,
And died on earth that man might live above.

Give of thy sons to bear the message glorious;
Give of thy wealth to speed them on their way;
Pour out thy soul for them in prayer victorious;
And all thy spending Jesus will repay.

Mary Ann Thomson (1834-1923)

One night in 1868, a worried mother sat up with one of her children who was critically ill. She prayed to the Lord to heal her child. She realized how quickly her comfortable lifestyle was jolted by the reality of something really important. And what is really important to God is the evangelization of the world. If God raised up her child, would she be willing to see him go out as a missionary to a continent like Africa, where David Livingstone was lost in the interior? Out of her inner wrestling with such questions, thirty-four-year-old Mary Ann Thomson wrote these words.

The hymn blends the messianic pronouncement of Isaiah 52 with the missionary call of Romans 10. For over a hundred years this hymn has stirred thousands to respond to God's call.

• • • •

*O Zion, messenger of good news, shout
from the mountaintops! Shout it louder,
O Jerusalem. Shout, and do not be afraid.
Tell the towns of Judah, "Your God
is coming!" Yes, the Sovereign Lord
is coming in power.*
ISAIAH 40:9-10

Onward, Christian Soldiers

Ever since the apostle Paul told the Ephesian Christians to put on the armor of God, Christian writers have used the symbolism of the soldier as a call for preparedness and courage. But when Sabine Baring-Gould, a thirty-one-year-old preacher and schoolteacher, wrote "Onward, Christian Soldiers," he simply wanted to write a marching song for his schoolchildren. Later, he apologized for the hymn: "It was written in great haste, and I am afraid that some of the rhymes are faulty."

Whitmonday was a festival day for schoolchildren in Yorkshire, and Baring-Gould's youngsters in the mill town of Horbury had to walk to a neighboring town to join other children for the celebration. "I wanted the children to sing when marching from one village to the other, but couldn't think of anything quite suitable," Baring-Gould commented, "so I sat up at night and resolved to write something myself."

• • • •

Endure suffering along with me, as a good soldier of Christ Jesus. Soldiers don't get tied up in the affairs of civilian life, for then they cannot please the officer who enlisted them.

2 TIMOTHY 2:3-4

Onward, Christian soldiers!
Marching as to war,
With the cross of Jesus
Going on before.
Christ, the royal Master,
Leads against the foe;
Forward into battle,
See His banners go!

**Onward, Christian soldiers,
Marching as to war,
With the cross of Jesus
Going on before.**

Like a mighty army
Moves the Church of God;
Brothers, we are treading
Where the saints have trod;
We are not divided,
All one body we,
One in hope and doctrine,
One in charity.

Onward, then, ye people,
Join our happy throng,
Blend with ours your voices
In the triumph song;
Glory, laud, and honor
Unto Christ the King;
This through countless ages
Men and angels sing.

Sabine Baring-Gould (1834–1924)

Channels Only

How I praise Thee, precious Savior,
That Thy love laid hold of me;
Thou hast saved and cleansed and filled me
That I might Thy channel be.

Channels only, blessed Master,
But with all Thy wondrous pow'r
Flowing thro' us, Thou canst use us
Ev'ry day and ev'ry hour.

Emptied that Thou shouldest fill me,
A clean vessel in Thy hand;
With no pow'r but as Thou givest
Graciously with each command.

Witnessing Thy pow'r to save me,
Setting free from self and sin;
Thou who boughtest to possess me,
In Thy fullness, Lord, come in.

Jesus, fill now with Thy Spirit
Hearts that full surrender know;
That the streams of living water
From our inner man may flow.

Mary E. Maxwell (1837–1915)

The original meaning of *channel* was a waterway, like the English Channel. It's related to the word *canal*. It gained a figurative meaning as any route of communication or authority: In armies and businesses, it's important to "go through the right channels" to get something done. Now it also refers to electronic frequencies that TV stations use to get their signals to your set.

So how are we to be "channels"? We are conduits for the living water of Christ. The Spirit flows within us and through us to others. Note that the channel is not the source of the water it carries. We do not create goodness or power; we merely receive it and channel it forward. Let the gospel flow freely through you in all you say and do.

• • • •

In a wealthy home some utensils are made of gold and silver, and some are made of wood and clay. The expensive utensils are used for special occasions, and the cheap ones are for everyday use. If you keep yourself pure, you will be a special utensil for honorable use. Your life will be clean, and you will be ready for the Master to use you for every good work.
2 TIMOTHY 2:20-21

I Love to Tell the Story

Kate Hankey, the daughter of a prosperous British banker, grew up in a stylish London suburb. She started a Bible class for girls in her neighborhood, and then, when she was only eighteen, Hankey went to London to teach a Bible class of "factory girls." In her twenties, she started other Bible classes for factory girls.

When she was in her early thirties, Kate Hankey became seriously ill. Doctors said she needed a year of bed rest. She was forbidden to teach her Bible classes for twelve months. During her long, slow recovery, she wrote two lengthy poems. The first, at the beginning of her convalescence, later became the hymn "Tell Me the Old, Old Story." The second, written ten months later, became "I Love to Tell the Story."

After ten months she felt strong enough to leave her bed. She soon returned to her Bible classes in London and continued teaching for many years.

• • • •

You will receive power when the Holy Spirit comes upon you. And you will be my witnesses, telling people about me everywhere—in Jerusalem, throughout Judea, in Samaria, and to the ends of the earth.

ACTS 1:8

I love to tell the story of unseen things above,
Of Jesus and His glory, of Jesus and His love;
I love to tell the story because I know 'tis true,
It satisfies my longings as nothing else can do.

I love to tell the story!
'Twill be my theme in glory—
To tell the old, old story
Of Jesus and His love.

I love to tell the story—'tis pleasant to repeat
What seems, each time I tell it,
more wonderfully sweet;
I love to tell the story, for some have never heard
The message of salvation from God's own holy Word.

I love to tell the story, for those who know it best
Seem hungering and thirsting to hear it like the rest;
And when in scenes of glory I sing the new, new song,
'Twill be the old, old story that I have loved so long.

Arabella Catherine Hankey (1834–1911)

Stand Up, Stand Up for Jesus

Stand up, stand up for Jesus,
Ye soldiers of the cross;
Lift high His royal banner,
It must not suffer loss:
From vict'ry unto vict'ry
His army shall He lead,
Till every foe is vanquished
And Christ is Lord indeed.

Stand up, stand up for Jesus,
The trumpet call obey;
Forth to the mighty conflict
In this His glorious day:
Ye that are men, now serve Him
Against unnumbered foes;
Let courage rise with danger,
And strength to strength oppose.

Stand up, stand up for Jesus,
Stand in His strength alone;
The arm of flesh will fail you;
Ye dare not trust your own.
Put on the gospel armor;
Each piece put on with prayer.
Where duty calls, or danger,
Be never wanting there.

Stand up, stand up for Jesus,
The strife will not be long.
This day the noise of battle;
The next, the victor's song.
To him that overcometh,
A crown of life shall be;
He with the King of Glory
Shall reign eternally.

George Duffield, Jr. (1818-1888)

In 1858, churches throughout Philadelphia united in a citywide evangelistic effort. Every morning and evening, services were held in churches, convention halls, and theaters. Dudley Tyng, a twenty-nine-year-old Episcopalian preacher, spoke to five thousand men; one thousand responded to the gospel invitation.

Four days later, however, Tyng was fatally injured in an accident. As he lay dying, his fellow ministers gathered around him. Tyng was still thinking about the men who had made decisions for Christ and in his last, whispered words said, "Tell them to stand up for Jesus."

Presbyterian minister George Duffield preached the next Sunday on the text "Stand therefore" and in conclusion read a poem that he had just written entitled "Stand Up for Jesus." A church member sent the poem to a Baptist newspaper, where it was eventually published.

• • • •

A final word: Be strong in the Lord and in his mighty power. Put on all of God's armor so that you will be able to stand firm against all strategies of the devil.
EPHESIANS 6:10-11

Be Thou My Vision

Between AD 500 and 700 the Irish church was synonymous with missionary fervor. One historian commented that missionary effort was "the one all-absorbing national thought and passion." Irish missionaries labored from Scotland to Switzerland. One of these missionaries was Columba of County Donegal. His biographer says, "Certain spiritual songs, which had never been heard before, he was heard to sing." He was known as one of the poets of the Irish church.

"Be Thou My Vision" is anonymous, but it comes from the seventh or eighth century, shortly after the time of Columba of Donegal. It is filled with various titles for God. The word *vision* is used to indicate not only what we focus on but also what we strive for. As we strive for a goal, we gain a long-range perspective that helps us see today's disappointments as trivial when compared to the heavenly vision.

• • • •

Lord, you alone are my inheritance, my cup of blessing. You guard all that is mine. The land you have given me is a pleasant land. What a wonderful inheritance!
PSALM 16:5-6

Be Thou my Vision, O Lord of my heart;
Nought be all else to me, save that Thou art—
Thou my best thought, by day or by night,
Waking or sleeping, Thy presence my light.

Be Thou my Wisdom, and Thou my true Word;
I ever with Thee and Thou with me, Lord;
Thou my great Father, and I Thy true son,
Thou in me dwelling, and I with Thee one.

Riches I heed not, nor man's empty praise,
Thou mine inheritance, now and always;
Thou and Thou only, first in my heart,
High King of heaven, my treasure Thou art.

High King of heaven, my victory won,
May I reach heaven's joys, O bright heaven's Sun!
Heart of my own heart, whatever befall,
Still be my Vision, O Ruler of all.

Irish hymn (eighth century)

Translated by Mary Elizabeth Byrne (1880–1931)
Versified by Eleanor Henrietta Hull (1860–1935)

Words used by permission of the Editor's Literary Estate, and Chatto & Windus, Ltd.

I Surrender All

All to Jesus I surrender,
All to Him I freely give;
I will ever love and trust Him,
In His presence daily live.

I surrender all,
I surrender all.
All to Thee, my blessed Savior,
I surrender all.

All to Jesus I surrender,
Humbly at His feet I bow,
Worldly pleasures all forsaken,
Take me, Jesus, take me now.

All to Jesus I surrender,
Make me, Savior, wholly Thine;
May Thy Holy Spirit fill me,
May I know Thy pow'r divine.

All to Jesus I surrender,
Lord, I give myself to Thee;
Fill me with Thy love and power,
Let Thy blessing fall on me.

Judson W. Van De Venter (1855–1939)

Many Christians have sung this song with their fingers crossed. But J. W. Van De Venter meant it. He was a schoolteacher by profession but an artist at heart. Teaching school allowed him to make a living while he continued his study of drawing and painting. After evangelistic meetings in his church, friends saw his gifts in counseling and working with people and urged him to become an evangelist. For five years he wavered between his love of art and what seemed to be God's calling to evangelistic ministry.

He later recalled, "At last the pivotal hour of my life came and I surrendered all. A new day was ushered into my life. I became an evangelist and discovered down deep in my soul a talent hitherto unknown to me." A few years later, Van De Venter, remembering that decisive moment, wrote this hymn.

• • • •

I once thought these things were valuable,
but now I consider them worthless because of
what Christ has done. Yes, everything else is
worthless when compared with the infinite
value of knowing Christ Jesus my Lord. For
his sake I have discarded everything else,
counting it all as garbage, so that I could
gain Christ.
PHILIPPIANS 3:7-8

Give of Your Best to the Master

Malachi had a problem. The people were bringing substandard sacrifices to the Temple, and the Lord didn't like it (Malachi 1:6-14). "Animals that are stolen and crippled and sick are being presented as offerings! Should I accept from you such offerings as these?" the Lord asked. It wasn't that they were too poor to afford healthy animals, they just didn't think sacrifices to the Lord were all that important. "You say, 'It's too hard to serve the Lord,' and you turn up your noses at my commands," the Lord charged. He went on to say that He deserved better treatment from them.

The New Testament echoes this principle and expands it. *Our whole lives* are offerings to God. Paul told the slaves at Colosse, "Work willingly at whatever you do, as though you were working for the Lord rather than for people" (Colossians 3:23). Whoever your earthly master may be, you are ultimately serving the Lord.

• • • •

He will be like a blazing fire that refines metal, or like a strong soap that bleaches clothes. He will sit like a refiner of silver, burning away the dross. He will purify the Levites, refining them like gold and silver, so that they may once again offer acceptable sacrifices to the Lord.

MALACHI 3:2-3

Give of your best to the Master,
Give of the strength of your youth;
Throw your soul's fresh, glowing ardor
Into the battle for truth.
Jesus has set the example—
Dauntless was He, young and brave;
Give Him your loyal devotion,
Give Him the best that you have.

Give of your best to the Master;
Give of the strength of your youth;
Clad in salvation's full armor,
Join in the battle for truth.

Give of your best to the Master,
Give Him first place in your heart;
Give Him first place in your service;
Consecrate every part.
Give, and to you shall be given—
God His beloved Son gave;
Gratefully seeking to serve Him,
Give Him the best that you have.

Give of your best to the Master,
Naught else is worthy His love;
He gave Himself for your ransom,
Gave up His glory above;
Laid down His life without murmur,
You from sin's ruin to save;
Give Him your heart's adoration,
Give Him the best that you have.

Howard Benjamin Grose (1851-1939)

Rescue the Perishing

Rescue the perishing, care for the dying,
Snatch them in pity from sin and the grave;
Weep o'er the erring one, lift up the fallen,
Tell them of Jesus, the mighty to save.

Rescue the perishing,
Care for the dying;
Jesus is merciful,
Jesus will save.

Though they are slighting Him, still He is waiting,
Waiting the penitent child to receive;
Plead with them earnestly, plead with them gently,
He will forgive if they only believe.

Down in the human heart, crushed by the tempter,
Feelings lie buried that grace can restore;
Touched by a loving heart, wakened by kindness,
Chords that are broken will vibrate once more.

Rescue the perishing, duty demands it—
Strength for thy labor the Lord will provide;
Back to the narrow way patiently win them,
Tell the poor wand'rer a Savior has died.

Fanny Jane Crosby (1820-1915)

Hymnwriter Fanny Crosby, though she was blind, loved to visit rescue missions in New York City. One hot summer night, she was talking to a group of working men at a mission. "I made a pressing plea," she said, "that if there was a boy present who had wandered from his mother's home and teaching, he should come to me at the end of the service. A young man of eighteen came forward and said, 'Did you mean me?'"

A few days before, Fanny Crosby had been given the suggestion to write a hymn on the theme "Rescue the Perishing," taken from Luke 14:23, where the master in one of Jesus' parables tells his servant to go out into the highways and byways and bring them in. That evening, Crosby could think of nothing else but the line, "Rescue the perishing, care for the dying," and after returning home from the mission, she wrote this hymn.

• • • •

And you must show mercy to those whose faith is wavering. Rescue others by snatching them from the flames of judgment. Show mercy to still others, but do so with great caution, hating the sins that contaminate their lives.

JUDE 1:22-23

All for Jesus, All for Jesus!

Perhaps it's best to start with the last stanza and meditate on the wonder of it. "Jesus, glorious King of kings, deigns to call me His beloved." Frequently we recall the names of our Lord. His titles are many and glorious. But it is equally amazing to see what God calls us in Scripture. We are called saints, joint heirs, friends, and coworkers. But what most impressed this hymnwriter was that, over and over in the Bible, we are called God's beloved.

The New Testament speaks of the mystery of marriage, husband and wife belonging to each other; it's a picture of Christ and the church. He has given himself to us in remarkable love. Because of His selfless sacrifice, all the privileges of royalty belong to us. And we belong to Him completely.

• • • •

Do not let sin control the way you live; do not give in to sinful desires. Do not let any part of your body become an instrument of evil to serve sin. Instead, give yourselves completely to God, for you were dead, but now you have new life. So use your whole body as an instrument to do what is right for the glory of God.

ROMANS 6:12-13

All for Jesus, all for Jesus!
All my being's ransomed pow'rs:
All my tho'ts and words and doings,
All my days and all my hours.
All for Jesus! all for Jesus!
All my days and all my hours;
All for Jesus! all for Jesus!
All my days and all my hours.

Let my hands perform His bidding,
Let my feet run in His ways;
Let my eyes see Jesus only,
Let my lips speak forth His praise.
All for Jesus! all for Jesus!
Let my lips speak forth His praise;
All for Jesus! all for Jesus!
Let my lips speak forth His praise.

Since my eyes were fixed on Jesus,
I've lost sight of all beside;
So enchained my spirit's vision,
Looking at the Crucified.
All for Jesus! all for Jesus!
Looking at the Crucified;
All for Jesus! all for Jesus!
Looking at the Crucified.

Oh, what wonder! how amazing!
Jesus, glorious King of kings,
Deigns to call me His beloved,
Lets me rest beneath His wings.
All for Jesus! all for Jesus!
Resting now beneath His wings;
All for Jesus! all for Jesus!
Resting now beneath His wings.

Mary D. James (1810–1883)

Blessed Jesus, at Thy Word

Blessed Jesus, at Thy Word
We are gathered all to hear Thee;
Let our hearts and souls be stirred
Now to seek and love and fear Thee,
By Thy teachings, sweet and holy,
Drawn from earth to love Thee solely.

All our knowledge, sense, and sight
Lie in deepest darkness shrouded
Till Thy Spirit breaks our night
With the beams of truth unclouded.
Thou alone to God canst win us;
Thou must work all good within us.

Glorious Lord, Thyself impart,
Light of Light, from God proceeding;
Open Thou our ears and heart,
Help us by Thy Spirit's pleading;
Hear the cry Thy people raises,
Hear and bless our prayers and praises.

Father, Son, and Holy Ghost,
Praise to Thee and adoration!
Grant that we Thy Word may trust
And obtain true consolation
While we here below must wander,
Till we sing Thy praises yonder.

Tobias Clausnitzer (1619-1684)

Translated by Catherine Winkworth (1827-1878)

The author of this hymn did not know peace until he was nearly thirty. The Thirty Years' War began the year before he was born, and it tore Europe apart. It was a time of princes wrestling for power, claiming religion as their motive, yet displacing innocent residents of disputed territories. In spite of all the turmoil, this period is rich with hymnody, as true believers launched their prayers and praises to the only Ruler who would listen.

This is a gathering hymn, bringing believers out of the murky world and into the presence of the Lord. It shows a justifiable cynicism about things earthly. All the "knowledge" that was gained as Europe crawled out of the Dark Ages had merely created chaos. There was a desperate need for the Spirit to shine His light on human affairs. God's people were "wandering," but they knew they were headed for a heavenly homeland.

• • • •

One of them, an expert in religious law, tried to trap him with this question: "Teacher, which is the most important commandment in the law of Moses?" Jesus replied, "You must love the Lord your God with all your heart, all your soul, and all your mind."

MATTHEW 22:35-37

Close to Thee

A Scottish minister once told Fanny Crosby that it was too bad that God had allowed her to become blind. Crosby quickly responded, "If I had been given a choice at birth, I would have asked to be blind . . . for when I get to heaven, the first face I will see will be the One who died for me." That desire to see Jesus, to be close to Him, was always foremost in her mind.

When Silas Jones Vail, who was a Long Island hatter by trade, said he had a tune for Crosby, she asked him to play it for her. As he was playing it, Crosby said, "That refrain said 'Close to Thee, close to Thee, close to Thee, close to Thee.'"

"Thou my everlasting portion" is a frequent allusion in the Psalms. The Old Testament Levites did not inherit any land in Canaan because the Lord was to be their portion. Similarly, Fanny Crosby was not given sight, but she felt blessed because the Lord was her portion.

• • • •

Let us go right into the presence of God with sincere hearts fully trusting him. For our guilty consciences have been sprinkled with Christ's blood to make us clean, and our bodies have been washed with pure water.

HEBREWS 10:22

Thou my everlasting portion,
More than friend or life to me;
All along my pilgrim journey,
Savior, let me walk with Thee.
Close to Thee, close to Thee,
Close to Thee, close to Thee;
All along my pilgrim journey,
Savior, let me walk with Thee.

Not for ease or worldly pleasure,
Nor for fame my prayer shall be;
Gladly will I toil and suffer,
Only let me walk with Thee.
Close to Thee, close to Thee,
Close to Thee, close to Thee;
Gladly will I toil and suffer,
Only let me walk with Thee.

Lead me through the vale of shadows,
Bear me o'er life's fitful sea;
Then the gate of life eternal
May I enter, Lord, with Thee.
Close to Thee, close to Thee,
Close to Thee, close to Thee;
Then the gate of life eternal
May I enter, Lord, with Thee.

Fanny Jane Crosby (1820-1915)

O Jesus, I Have Promised

O Jesus, I have promised
To serve Thee to the end;
Be Thou forever near me,
My Master and my Friend:
I shall not fear the battle
If Thou art by my side,
Nor wander from the pathway
If Thou wilt be my guide.

O let me feel Thee near me,
The world is ever near;
I see the sights that dazzle,
The tempting sounds I hear:
My foes are ever near me,
Around me and within;
But, Jesus, draw Thou nearer,
And shield my soul from sin.

O Jesus, Thou hast promised
To all who follow Thee,
That where Thou art in glory,
There shall Thy servant be;
And, Jesus, I have promised
To serve Thee to the end;
O give me grace to follow,
My Master and my Friend.

John Ernest Bode (1816-1874)

In Hebrews 10:23 there is an important parenthetical clause that reads, "God can be trusted to keep his promise." Can we be trusted to keep ours?

When John Bode served the parish of Castle Camps, near Cambridge, England, in the middle of the nineteenth century, he had the privilege of officiating at the confirmation of his daughter and two sons. This hymn was written specifically for this occasion, and originally the first line was "O Jesus, *we* have promised" because all three children were making this dedication of themselves to the Lord.

While Bode wrote the hymn for young people and referred to the alluring temptations of the world, its message applies to Christians of any age.

• • • •

Our great desire is that you will keep on loving others as long as life lasts, in order to make certain that what you hope for will come true. Then you will not become spiritually dull and indifferent. Instead, you will follow the example of those who are going to inherit God's promises because of their faith and endurance.
HEBREWS 6:11-12

God of Grace and God of Glory

It is wonderful to see what a diversity of people God has used to bring music to His church.

Harry Emerson Fosdick, one of the leaders of the liberal Protestant movement in the 1920s and 1930s, was denounced by many conservatives, some of whom now sing the hymn he wrote. In 1930, when the new building for the Riverside Church in New York City was dedicated, this hymn was sung as the dedicatory hymn.

It is a prayer of dedication that can be uttered any day. Some days in our lives are obvious turning points—a church dedication, the birth of a child, a wedding—but every day has its crucial moments. The prayer of our hearts should constantly be "Grant us wisdom, grant us courage, for the facing of this hour."

• • • •

Study this Book of Instruction continually. Meditate on it day and night so you will be sure to obey everything written in it. Only then will you prosper and succeed in all you do. This is my command—be strong and courageous! Do not be afraid or discouraged. For the Lord your God is with you wherever you go.

JOSHUA 1:8-9

God of grace and God of glory,
On Thy people pour Thy power;
Crown Thine ancient Church's story,
Bring her bud to glorious flower.
Grant us wisdom,
Grant us courage,
For the facing of this hour,
For the facing of this hour.

Lo! the hosts of evil round us
Scorn Thy Christ, assail His ways!
From the fears that long have bound us,
Free our hearts to faith and praise.
Grant us wisdom,
Grant us courage,
For the living of these days,
For the living of these days.

Cure Thy children's warring madness;
Bend our pride to Thy control;
Shame our wanton, selfish gladness,
Rich in things and poor in soul.
Grant us wisdom,
Grant us courage,
Lest we miss Thy kingdom's goal,
Lest we miss Thy kingdom's goal.

Set our feet on lofty places,
Gird our lives that they may be
Armored with all Christlike graces
In the fight to set men free.
Grant us wisdom,
Grant us courage,
That we fail not man nor Thee,
That we fail not man nor Thee.

Harry Emerson Fosdick (1878-1969)

Faith of Our Fathers

Faith of our fathers! living still
In spite of dungeon, fire, and sword;
O how our hearts beat high with joy
Whene'er we hear that glorious word!

Faith of our fathers, holy faith!
We will be true to thee till death.

Faith of our fathers! we will strive
To win all nations unto thee;
And through the truth that comes from God
Mankind shall then be truly free.

Faith of our fathers! we will love
Both friend and foe in all our strife;
And preach thee, too, as love knows how
By kindly words and virtuous life.

Frederick William Faber (1814-1863)

Whether you turn to the Old Testament and see how God called Abraham out of Ur of the Chaldeans or turn to the New Testament and see how God stopped Saul of Tarsus on the road to Damascus, the Bible is filled with things that actually happened. Our Christian faith is rooted in history.

Frederick Faber felt the new religious movements that seemed so popular in his day were dangerous. He felt there was too much emphasis on the experience of the moment. After three years as an Anglican minister, he left that church and joined the Roman Catholic church. He appreciated the continuity with the past that he found there, and he respected the martyrs who had given their lives for Christ. But as a Roman Catholic, he missed the singing he had enjoyed as an Anglican. So he wrote hymns to help fill the void.

• • • •

Therefore, since we are surrounded by such a huge crowd of witnesses to the life of faith, let us strip off every weight that slows us down, especially the sin that so easily trips us up. And let us run with endurance the race God has set before us.
HEBREWS 12:1

Sweet Hour of Prayer

According to one account, the author of this hymn was a blind preacher and curio shop owner in Coleshill, England. He carved ornaments out of ivory or wood and sold them in his small store. He also wrote poetry. One day, when a local minister stopped at the store, William Walford, the blind shop owner, mentioned that he had composed a poem in his head. He asked the minister to write it down for him. Three years later, that minister visited the United States and gave the poem to a newspaper editor.

Unfortunately, no one knows what happened to William Walford of Coleshill. Researchers have found a William Walford, a minister of Homerton, England, who wrote a book on prayer that expresses many of the same thoughts that are given in this poem. That may be the true author. But the identity of the hymnwriter is not as important as knowing a God who hears and answers prayer.

• • • •

Pray in the Spirit at all times and on every occasion. Stay alert and be persistent in your prayers for all believers everywhere.
EPHESIANS 6:18

Sweet hour of prayer! sweet hour of prayer!
That calls me from a world of care,
And bids me at my Father's throne
Make all my wants and wishes known;
In seasons of distress and grief,
My soul has often found relief,
And oft escaped the tempter's snare,
By thy return, sweet hour of prayer!

Sweet hour of prayer! sweet hour of prayer!
The joys I feel, the bliss I share
Of those whose anxious spirits burn
With strong desires for thy return!
With such I hasten to the place
Where God my Savior shows His face,
And gladly take my station there,
And wait for thee, sweet hour of prayer!

Sweet hour of prayer! sweet hour of prayer!
Thy wings shall my petition bear
To Him whose truth and faithfulness
Engage the waiting soul to bless;
And since He bids me seek His face,
Believe His Word and trust His grace,
I'll cast on Him my every care,
And wait for thee, sweet hour of prayer!

William W. Walford (1772-1850)

Dear Lord and Father of Mankind

Dear Lord and Father of mankind,
Forgive our fev'rish ways!
Reclothe us in our rightful mind;
In purer lives Thy service find,
In deeper rev'rence, praise.

In simple trust like theirs who heard,
Beside the Syrian Sea,
The gracious calling of the Lord,
Let us, like them, without a word,
Rise up and follow Thee.

O Sabbath rest by Galilee!
O calm of hills above,
Where Jesus knelt to share with thee
The silence of eternity,
Interpreted by love.

Drop Thy still dews of quietness
Till all our strivings cease;
Take from our souls the strain and stress,
And let our ordered lives confess
The beauty of Thy peace.

Breathe thru the heats of our desire
Thy coolness and Thy balm;
Let sense be dumb, let flesh retire;
Speak thru the earthquake, wind, and fire,
O still small voice of calm!

John Greenleaf Whittier (1807–1892)

The stanzas that make up John Greenleaf Whittier's hymn are taken from his longer poem "The Brewing of Soma," beginning with the twelfth stanza. In the earlier stanzas, Whittier writes about an intoxicating drink called *soma* that was brewed by a Hindu sect in India. Soma was drunk by worshipers in order "to bring the skies more near, or lift men up to heaven." Then after his description of pagan worship, Whittier writes, "In sensual transports wild as vain, we brew in many a Christian fane the heathen Soma still."

To Whittier, the ritualism and emotionalism that can accompany Christian worship were similar to drinking the Hindu soma—vain attempts to get closer to God. Instead, he called Christians back to simplicity and purity in worship.

• • • •

Pray like this: Our Father in heaven, may your name be kept holy. May your Kingdom come soon. May your will be done on earth, as it is in heaven. Give us today the food we need, and forgive us our sins, as we have forgiven those who sin against us. And don't let us yield to temptation, but rescue us from the evil one.

MATTHEW 6:9-13

Just As I Am

Charlotte Elliott seemed to have everything going for her as a young woman. She was gifted as a portrait artist and also as a writer of humorous verse. Then in her early thirties she suffered a serious illness that left her weak and depressed. During her illness a noted minister, Dr. Caesar Malan of Switzerland, came to visit her. Noticing her depression, he asked if she had peace with God. She resented the question and said she did not want to talk about it.

But a few days later she went to apologize to Dr. Malan. She said that she wanted to clean up some things in her life before becoming a Christian. Malan looked at her and answered, "Come just as you are." That was enough for Charlotte Elliott, and she yielded herself to the Lord that day.

Fourteen years later, remembering those words spoken to her by Caesar Malan in Brighton, England, she wrote this simple hymn.

• • • •

Jesus replied, "I am the bread of life. Whoever comes to me will never be hungry again. Whoever believes in me will never be thirsty. . . . Those the Father has given me will come to me, and I will never reject them."
JOHN 6:35, 37

Just as I am, without one plea,
But that Thy blood was shed for me,
And that Thou bidd'st me come to Thee,
O Lamb of God I come! I come!

Just as I am, and waiting not
To rid my soul of one dark blot,
To Thee, whose blood can cleanse each spot,
O Lamb of God I come! I come!

Just as I am, tho' tossed about
With many a conflict, many a doubt,
Fightings within, and fears without,
O Lamb of God I come! I come!

Just as I am, poor, wretched, blind,
Sight, riches, healing of the mind,
Yea, all I need, in Thee to find,
O Lamb of God I come! I come!

Just as I am, Thou wilt receive,
Wilt welcome, pardon, cleanse, relieve;
Because Thy promise I believe,
O Lamb of God I come! I come!

Just as I am, Thy love unknown
Hath broken ev'ry barrier down;
Now to be Thine, yea Thine alone,
O Lamb of God I come! I come!

Just as I am, of that free love
The breadth, length, depth, the height to prove,
Here for a season then above,
O Lamb of God I come! I come!

Charlotte Elliott (1789–1871)

All People That on Earth Do Dwell

All people that on earth do dwell,
Sing to the Lord with cheerful voice;
Him serve with fear, His praise forth tell,
Come ye before Him and rejoice.

The Lord, ye know, is God indeed;
Without our aid He did us make;
We are His flock, He doth us feed,
And for His sheep He doth us take.

O enter then His gates with praise,
Approach with joy His courts unto;
Praise, laud, and bless His name always,
For it is seemly so to do.

For why? The Lord our God is good,
His mercy is forever sure;
His truth at all times firmly stood,
And shall from age to age endure.

To Father, Son, and Holy Ghost,
The God whom heaven and earth adore,
From earth and from the angel host
Be praise and glory evermore.

William Kethe (d. 1593)

This is often called "The Old Hundredth" because it is based on Psalm 100. It is perhaps the oldest hymn of praise in the English language. William Kethe, a Scotsman, was a minister of the Church of England. But during the reign of Queen Mary (1553–1558), a reign of terror for many English Protestants, Kethe fled to Germany and then to Geneva, Switzerland, where he was influenced by John Calvin. He assisted in the translation of the Geneva Bible and helped to produce a complete English version of the metrical Psalms. From this psalter, more than four hundred years old, "The Old Hundredth" is taken. The hymn was first published in London in 1561, shortly after Queen Elizabeth came to the throne.

• • • •

Shout with joy to the Lord, all the earth! Worship the Lord with gladness. Come before him, singing with joy. Acknowledge that the Lord is God! He made us, and we are his. We are his people, the sheep of his pasture. Enter his gates with thanksgiving; go into his courts with praise. Give thanks to him and praise his name. For the Lord is good. His unfailing love continues forever, and his faithfulness continues to each generation.

PSALM 100

Praise the Lord! Ye Heavens Adore Him

One Sunday morning in the eighteenth century, Thomas Corin, a retired captain of the Merchant Navy, found an abandoned baby on the steps of St. Andrews Church in London. He and his wife took the baby home and cared for it. Later he discovered that there were many abandoned babies in London, and most of them were left to die.

Because of his efforts and his Christian commitment, a hospital for destitute and abandoned children was established. Children in the hospital were all taught to sing, and soon their singing caught public attention. The great composer George Frideric Handel presented the hospital with an organ and conducted a special performance of *Messiah* each year on the hospital's behalf.

Eventually the hospital published its own collection of hymns, which included this one.

• • • •

Praise the Lord from the heavens! Praise him from the skies! Praise him, all his angels! Praise him, all the armies of heaven! Praise him, sun and moon! Praise him, all you twinkling stars! Praise him, skies above! Praise him, vapors high above the clouds!

PSALM 148:1-4

Praise the Lord! ye heav'ns, adore Him;
Praise Him angels in the height;
Sun and moon, rejoice before Him;
Praise Him, all ye stars of light.
Praise the Lord! for He hath spoken;
Worlds His mighty voice obeyed;
Laws which never shall be broken
For their guidance He hath made.

Praise the Lord! for He is glorious;
Never shall His promise fail;
God hath made His saints victorious;
Sin and death shall not prevail.
Praise the God of our salvation!
Hosts on high, His pow'r proclaim;
Heav'n and earth and all creation,
Laud and magnify His name.

Worship, honor, glory, blessing,
Lord, we offer unto Thee;
Young and old, Thy praise expressing,
In glad homage bend the knee.
All the saints in heav'n adore Thee;
We would bow before Thy throne:
As Thine angels serve before Thee,
So on earth Thy will be done.

Foundling Hospital Collection, 1796

Stanza 3, Edward Osler (1798–1863)

Ancient of Days

Ancient of Days, who sittest throned in glory,
To Thee all knees are bent, all voices pray;
Thy love has blessed the wide world's wondrous story
With light and life since Eden's dawning day.

O holy Father, who hast led Thy children
In all the ages with fire and cloud,
Through seas dryshod,
through weary wastes bewildering,
To Thee in reverent love our hearts are bowed.

O holy Jesus, Prince of Peace and Savior,
To Thee we owe the peace that still prevails,
Stilling the rude wills of men's wild behavior,
And calming passion's fierce and stormy gales.

O Holy Ghost, the Lord and the Life-giver,
Thine is the quickening power that gives increase:
From Thee have flowed, as from a mighty river,
Our faith and hope, our fellowship and peace.

O Triune God, with heart and voice adoring,
Praise we the goodness that doth crown our days;
Pray we that Thou wilt hear us, still imploring
Thy love and favor, kept to us always.

William Croswell Doane (1832–1913)

In 1886, the city of Albany, New York, was celebrating its bicentennial. Episcopal bishop William Croswell Doane wrote this hymn for the occasion, and J. Albert Jeffery, who was in charge of music at St. Agnes School and the recently completed All Saints Cathedral, wrote the music. That new cathedral was the setting for the hymn's introduction, and Bishop Doane himself conducted the singing. It was a memorable day in Albany, as it celebrated its own "ancient days."

But the hymn draws our attention farther back, to the majesty of the triune God who existed before all time began. In stanza 1, we see the Ancient of Days, in stanza 2 the Father who leads us through the wilderness, in stanza 3 the Son who calms the storms, in stanza 4 the Holy Spirit who gives life and hope, and in stanza 5 the triune God who answers our prayers and sustains us day by day.

• • • •

I watched as thrones were put in place and the Ancient One sat down to judge. His clothing was as white as snow, his hair like purest wool. He sat on a fiery throne with wheels of blazing fire, and a river of fire was pouring out, flowing from his presence.
DANIEL 7:9-10

Holy God, We Praise Thy Name

Any hymn with roots that go as far back as this one usually has some legends connected to it, so it is difficult to know its accurate history. The hymn is derived from the Te Deum of the fourth century, a hymn of praise to God apparently written by Ambrose, the bishop of Milan, around AD 387. One story says that it was written when Augustine was baptized by Ambrose. Some scholars now feel that it was written by a fourth-century missionary bishop, Niceta.

But whatever its origin, Christians have been singing versions of this hymn for more than fifteen hundred years. The English hymn was produced by a Roman Catholic priest from Albany, New York, Clarence Walworth, who translated it from an Austrian hymnal that had been published nearly a hundred years earlier.

• • • •

Praise the Lord! Yes, give praise, O servants of the Lord. Praise the name of the Lord! Blessed be the name of the Lord now and forever. Everywhere—from east to west— praise the name of the Lord.

PSALM 113:1-3

Holy God, we praise Thy name;
Lord of all, we bow before Thee;
All on earth Thy scepter claim,
All in heaven above adore Thee.
Infinite Thy vast domain,
Everlasting is Thy reign.

Hark, the glad celestial hymn,
Angel choirs above are raising;
Cherubim and seraphim,
In unceasing chorus praising,
Fill the heavens with sweet accord:
Holy, holy, holy Lord.

Lo! the apostolic train
Joins Thy sacred name to hallow;
Prophets swell the glad refrain,
And the white-robed martyrs follow,
And from morn to set of sun,
Through the church the song goes on.

Holy Father, holy Son,
Holy Spirit: Three we name Thee,
Though in essence only One;
Undivided God we claim Thee,
And adoring bend the knee
While we own the mystery.

Attributed to Ignace Franz (1719-1790)

Translated by Clarence Walworth (1820-1900)

From Greenland's Icy Mountains

From Greenland's icy mountains,
From India's coral strand,
Where Afric's sunny fountains
Roll down their golden sand;
From many an ancient river,
From many a palmy plain,
They call us to deliver
Their land from error's chain.

What though the spicy breezes,
Blow soft o'er Ceylon's isle;
Though ev'ry prospect pleases,
And only man is vile?
In vain, with lavish kindness,
The gifts of God are strown;
The heathen, in his blindness,
Bows down to wood and stone.

Can we, whose souls are lighted
By wisdom from on high,
Can we to men benighted
The lamp of life deny?
Salvation! O salvation!
The joyful sound proclaim,
Till earth's remotest nation
Has learned Messiah's name.

Waft, waft, ye winds, His story,
And you, ye waters, roll,
Till, like a sea of glory,
It spreads from pole to pole:
Till o'er our ransomed nature
The Lamb, for sinners slain,
Redeemer, King, Creator,
In bliss returns to reign.

Reginald Heber (1783–1826)

In 1819 a royal letter was sent to all parishes of the Church of England authorizing a collection to be taken to aid "The Society for the Propagation of the Gospel in Foreign Lands." Reginald Heber's father-in-law had asked him to preach at his Sunday evening service. When the royal letter came, Heber was also asked to write a hymn that would be appropriate for the special collection. Heber went into a corner of the room for twenty minutes and then returned to show three stanzas to his father-in-law. Heber then insisted on writing a fourth stanza to give a more triumphant ending to the hymn.

When he wrote the hymn, Heber didn't know that India did not have coral strands, nor did he realize that he would soon be appointed bishop of Calcutta, India, where he would later die.

• • • •

[Jesus] said to his disciples, "The harvest is great, but the workers are few. So pray to the Lord who is in charge of the harvest; ask him to send more workers into his fields."
MATTHEW 9:37-38

Come, We That Love the Lord

Unless songwriters compose the music themselves, they usually have no control over what music accompanies their text. The prolific hymnwriter Isaac Watts wrote "Come, We That Love the Lord" and published it in 1707. In 1763 Aaron Williams put it together with a tune called "St. Thomas." However, in many denominations in the United States, the hymn underwent a transformation. Perhaps because of the popularity of Negro spirituals, gospel songs of the nineteenth and early twentieth centuries emphasized a chorus, just as the spirituals did. So the old Watts stanzas were attached to a chorus called "Marching to Zion" and set to a rousing gospel tune by Brooklyn clergyman Robert Lowry.

Lowry had a brilliant idea—let the adults sing the complicated hymn stanzas, and then let the kids join in on the familiar and lilting chorus, "We're marching to Zion, beautiful city of Zion."

Come, we that love the Lord,
And let our joys be known;
Join in a song with sweet accord,
And thus surround the throne.

Let those refuse to sing
Who never knew our God;
But children of the heav'nly King
May speak their joys abroad.

The men of grace have found
Glory begun below;
Celestial fruit on earthly ground
From faith and hope may grow.

The hill of Zion yields
A thousand sacred sweets
Before we reach the heav'nly fields,
Or walk the golden streets.

Then let our songs abound,
And every tear be dry;
We're marching thro' Emmanuel's ground
To fairer worlds on high.

Isaac Watts (1674–1748)

• • • •

Praise the Lord! Sing to the Lord a new song. Sing his praises in the assembly of the faithful. O Israel, rejoice in your Maker. O people of Jerusalem, exult in your King. Praise his name with dancing, accompanied by tambourine and harp.

PSALM 149:1-3

Who Is on the Lord's Side?

Who is on the Lord's side? Who will serve the King?
Who will be His helpers, other lives to bring?
Who will leave the world's side? Who will face the foe?
Who is on the Lord's side? Who for Him will go?
By Thy call of mercy, by Thy grace divine,
We are on the Lord's side, Savior, we are Thine.

Not for weight of glory, not for crown and palm,
Enter we the army, raise the warrior psalm;
But for love that claimeth lives for whom He died;
He whom Jesus nameth must be on His side.
By Thy love constraining, by Thy grace divine,
We are on the Lord's side, Savior, we are Thine.

Jesus, Thou hast bought us, not with gold or gem,
But with Thine own lifeblood, for Thy diadem.
With Thy blessing filling each who comes to Thee,
Thou hast made us willing, Thou hast made us free.
By Thy grand redemption, by Thy grace divine,
We are on the Lord's side, Savior, we are Thine.

Fierce may be the conflict, strong may be the foe,
But the King's own army none can overthrow.
Round His standard ranging; vict'ry is secure;
For His truth unchanging makes the triumph sure.
Joyfully enlisting by Thy grace divine,
We are on the Lord's side, Savior, we are Thine.

Frances Ridley Havergal (1836-1879)

For someone who struggled with illness much of her life, Frances Ridley Havergal wrote a remarkable number of vigorous, robust hymns. The last manuscript she worked on was *Starlight through the Shadows,* a book for invalids. She died before she could complete the book, but her sister added the final chapter from Havergal's unpublished papers. That chapter is entitled "Marching Orders" and concludes with the words of this hymn.

The hymn is based on 1 Chronicles 12:1-18. In the biblical text, the early followers of David are listed: archers and slingers, experts in running and swimming. David asked them whose side they were on, and they responded: "We are yours, David! We are on your side" (1 Chronicles 12:18). Frances Havergal put the refrain like this: "We are on the Lord's side, Savior, we are Thine."

• • • •

At this point many of his disciples turned away and deserted him. Then Jesus turned to the Twelve and asked, "Are you also going to leave?" Simon Peter replied, "Lord, to whom would we go? You have the words that give eternal life."
JOHN 6:66-68

Softly and Tenderly Jesus Is Calling

Will Thompson was called the bard of Ohio. From his home in East Liverpool, Ohio, he went to New York City to sell some of the secular songs he had written. Music dealers picked them up, and soon people across the country were singing "My Home on the Old Ohio" and "Gathering Shells from the Seashore." He made so much money from his compositions that newspapers called him "the millionaire songwriter."

But Thompson, a Christian, soon began concentrating on hymnwriting and set up his own firm for publishing hymnals. Two million copies of his gospel quartet books were sold. Sometime around 1880, when Thompson was thirty-three years old, he wrote this invitation hymn, "Softly and Tenderly."

• • • •

Then Jesus said, "Come to me, all of you who are weary and carry heavy burdens, and I will give you rest. Take my yoke upon you. Let me teach you, because I am humble and gentle at heart, and you will find rest for your souls. For my yoke is easy to bear, and the burden I give you is light."

MATTHEW 11:28-30

Softly and tenderly Jesus is calling,
Calling for you and for me;
See, on the portals He's waiting and watching,
Watching for you and for me.

Come home, come home,
Ye who are weary, come home;
Earnestly, tenderly, Jesus is calling,
Calling, O sinner, come home!

Why should we tarry when Jesus is pleading,
Pleading for you and for me?
Why should we linger and heed not His mercies,
Mercies for you and for me?

Time is now fleeting, the moments are passing,
Passing from you and from me;
Shadows are gathering, death's night is coming,
Coming for you and for me.

O for the wonderful love He has promised,
Promised for you and for me!
Though we have sinned, He has mercy and pardon,
Pardon for you and for me.

William Lamartine Thompson (1847-1909)

God Is Love; His Mercy Brightens

God is love; His mercy brightens
All the path in which we rove;
Bliss He wakes and woe He lightens:
God is wisdom, God is love.

Chance and change are busy ever;
Man decays and ages move;
But His mercy waneth never:
God is wisdom, God is love.

E'en the hour that darkest seemeth
Will His changeless goodness prove;
Through the gloom His brightness streameth:
God is wisdom, God is love.

He with earthly cares entwineth
Hope and comfort from above;
Everywhere His glory shineth:
God is wisdom, God is love.

John Bowring (1792–1872)

Sir John Bowring was truly a genius. He was said to be able to speak one hundred languages and to read two hundred. Twice he was elected to Parliament, and in 1854 he was appointed governor of Hong Kong. Despite his many successes, he was to become one of the most unpopular governors Hong Kong ever had. He was described as being "full of conceit and without any very clear idea of political principles on a grand scale."

Bowring wrote this hymn when he was thirty years old, nearly twenty-five years before he became the hated, ruthless governor. He ended each stanza with this timeless reminder: "God is wisdom, God is love." Perhaps Bowring would have been a better governor had he reminded himself that, as the apostle John says, "since God loved us that much, we surely ought to love each other" (1 John 4:11).

• • • •

All who confess that Jesus is the Son of God have God living in them, and they live in God. We know how much God loves us, and we have put our trust in his love. God is love, and all who live in love live in God, and God lives in them.

1 JOHN 4:15-16

Immortal, Invisible, God Only Wise

The Great British hymnologist Erik Routley calls this hymn "full of plump polysyllables." The hymn was inspired by the apostle Paul's words to young Timothy: "Now unto the King eternal, immortal, invisible, the only wise God, be honour and glory for ever and ever" (1 Timothy 1:17, KJV). The writer of this hymn, Walter Chalmers Smith, was a pastor in the Free Church of Scotland for forty-four years (1850–1894). Smith wrote many hymns, but this is the only one still in use today. In our day of casual Christianity and almost flippant prayer, we desperately need to catch glimpses of God's unspeakable character. In these wonderful stanzas, we who "wither and perish" come face-to-face with our immortal, invisible, unchanging God. And amazingly, this great God, whom even polysyllables cannot describe, loves us dearly.

Immortal, invisible, God only wise,
In light inaccessible hid from our eyes,
Most blessed, most glorious, the Ancient of Days,
Almighty, victorious, Thy great name we praise.

Unresting, unhasting, and silent as light,
Nor wanting, nor wasting, Thou rulest in might.
Thy justice like mountains high soaring above
Thy clouds which are fountains of goodness and love.

To all, life Thou givest, to both great and small;
In all life Thou livest, the true life of all.
We blossom and flourish as leaves on the tree,
And wither and perish, but naught changeth Thee.

Great Father of glory, pure Father of light,
Thine angels adore Thee, all veiling their sight.
All praise we would render: O help us to see
'Tis only the splendor of light hideth Thee.

Walter Chalmers Smith (1824-1908)

• • • •

"Christ Jesus came into the world to save sinners"—and I am the worst of them all. But God had mercy on me so that Christ Jesus could use me as a prime example of his great patience with even the worst sinners. . . . All honor and glory to God forever and ever! He is the eternal King, the unseen one who never dies; he alone is God.

I TIMOTHY I:I5-I7

O God of Earth and Altar

O God of earth and altar,
Bow down and hear our cry,
Our earthly rulers falter,
Our people drift and die;
The walls of gold entomb us,
The swords of scorn divide,
Take not Thy thunder from us,
But take away our pride.

From all that terror teaches,
From lies of tongue and pen,
From all the easy speeches
That comfort cruel men,
From sale and profanation
Of honor, and the sword,
From sleep and from damnation,
Deliver us, good Lord!

Tie in a living tether
The prince and priest and thrall,
Bind all our lives together,
Smite us and save us all;
In ire and exultation
Aflame with faith, and free,
Lift up a living nation,
A single sword to Thee.

Gilbert Keith Chesterton (1874–1936)

G. K. Chesterton, the noted British author and journalist, blended the realms of earth and altar. He was known for writing both detective stories and profound Christian apologetics; humorous essays like "On Running after One's Hat" and deep polemical works like *Orthodoxy*; hilarious nonsense poems and hymns for worship. He always kept a sense of humor about him, whether in writing his personal testimony, which he called "My Elephantine Adventures in Pursuit of the Obvious," or in this hymn, where he asked God to "Tie in a living tether the prince and priest and thrall."

Chesterton calls for unity between the political and the spiritual, reminding us that political freedom can only find its source in God. Only as the hearts of political leaders, religious leaders, and citizens are turned to Him can a nation become "aflame with faith, and free."

• • • •

Listen! The Lord's arm is not too weak to save you, nor is his ear too deaf to hear you call. It's your sins that have cut you off from God. Because of your sins, he has turned away and will not listen anymore.
ISAIAH 59:1-2

Battle Hymn of the Republic

Julia Ward Howe wrote these lyrics in the heart of the Civil War. Her purpose was to provide some wholesome lyrics for the tune of "John Brown's Body Lies A-Moldering in the Grave." She accomplished that and more. When President Abraham Lincoln first heard the hymn, he asked to have it sung again.

The text is filled with biblical allusions. The expression "grapes of wrath" refers to Revelation 14:19; the sounding trumpet is probably from Revelation 8. For the Christian, the message of this song is that God's truth is eternal. Although circumstances may appear overwhelmingly difficult, God will still accomplish His purposes, and His truth will endure.

It can be dangerous to identify political causes or even national patriotism with God's truth. Nations may rise and fall, but God's truth remains forever. "His truth is marching on."

• • • •

After that the end will come, when he will turn the Kingdom over to God the Father, having destroyed every ruler and authority and power. For Christ must reign until he humbles all his enemies beneath his feet. And the last enemy to be destroyed is death.

I CORINTHIANS 15:24-26

Mine eyes have seen the glory of
the coming of the Lord,
He is trampling out the vintage
where the grapes of wrath are stored;
He hath loosed the fateful lightning
of His terrible swift sword—
His truth is marching on.

Glory! glory, hallelujah!
Glory! glory, hallelujah!
Glory! glory, hallelujah!
His truth is marching on.

I have seen Him in the watch fires
of a hundred circling camps,
They have builded Him an altar in
the evening dews and damps;
I can read His righteous sentence
by the dim and flaring lamps—
His day is marching on.

He has sounded forth the trumpet
that shall never sound retreat,
He is sifting out the hearts of men
before His judgment seat;
O be swift, my soul, to answer Him!
be jubilant, my feet!
Our God is marching on.

In the beauty of the lilies Christ
was born across the sea,
With a glory in His bosom that
transfigures you and me;
As He died to make men holy,
let us live to make men free,
While God is marching on.

Julia Ward Howe (1819-1910)

God of Our Fathers

God of our fathers, whose almighty hand
Leads forth in beauty all the starry band
Of shining worlds in splendor through the skies,
Our grateful songs before Thy throne arise.

Thy love divine hath led us in the past;
In this free land by Thee our lot is cast;
Be Thou our ruler, guardian, guide, and stay,
Thy Word our law, Thy paths our chosen way.

From war's alarms, from deadly pestilence,
Be Thy strong arm our ever sure defense;
Thy true religion in our hearts increase,
Thy bounteous goodness nourish us in peace.

Refresh Thy people on their toilsome way;
Lead us from night to never-ending day;
Fill all our lives with love and grace divine,
And glory, laud, and praise be ever Thine.

Daniel Crane Roberts (1841–1907)

Six years before his death in 1907, Daniel Roberts wrote, "I remain a country parson, known only within my own small world." This hymn was penned while he pastored a rural church in Brandon, Vermont. He wrote it in 1876 to commemorate the one-hundredth birthday of the Declaration of Independence, and it was sung for the first time at Brandon's Fourth of July celebration.

Because the people of Brandon enjoyed the hymn, Roberts submitted it to the committee planning the Constitution's centennial celebration. The committee chose it as the official hymn for the occasion and sent it to the organist at St. Thomas Episcopal Church in New York City to compose an original tune. The new tune, with a dramatic trumpet fanfare, helped to make this hymn unique.

• • • •

They did not conquer the land with their swords; it was not their own strong arm that gave them victory. It was your right hand and strong arm and the blinding light from your face that helped them, for you loved them.

PSALM 44:3

God the Omnipotent!

There was no war in 1842 when Henry F. Chorley, music critic of the *London Athenaeum,* wrote this hymn under the title "In Time of War." Twenty-eight years later, John Ellerton added additional stanzas as the Franco-Prussian War was being waged in Europe.

But the prayer "Give to us peace in our time, O Lord" has been uttered since the beginning of time. Wars and rumors of wars, civic unrest, riots, looting, and rampant crime have increased as humanity has supposedly become more educated and civilized.

External peace may not come, despite our efforts and our prayers. But internal peace can be a reality because our rest and our trust are in a God who is omnipotent, all-merciful, all-righteous, and all-wise. Our God is greater than the armies and ornaments of nations.

• • • •

You will keep in perfect peace all who trust in you, all whose thoughts are fixed on you!
ISAIAH 26:3

God the omnipotent! King, who ordainest
Thunder Thy clarion, the lightning Thy sword;
Show forth Thy pity on high where Thou reignest;
Give to us peace in our time, O Lord.

God the all-merciful! Earth hath forsaken
Meekness and mercy, and slighted Thy Word;
Let not Thy wrath in its terrors awaken;
Give to us peace in our time, O Lord.

God the all-righteous One! Man hath defied Thee;
Yet to eternity standeth Thy Word;
Falsehood and wrong shall not tarry beside Thee;
Give to us peace in our time, O Lord.

So shall Thy people, with thankful devotion,
Praise Him who saved them from peril and sword,
Singing in chorus from ocean to ocean,
Peace to the nations, and praise to the Lord.

Henry Fothergill Chorley (1808-1872)

Stanzas 3-4, John Ellerton (1826-1893)

O My Soul, Bless God the Father

O my soul, bless God the Father;
All within me bless His name;
Bless the Father, and forget not
All His mercies to proclaim.

Who forgiveth thy transgressions,
Thy diseases all who heals;
Who redeems thee from destruction,
Who with thee so kindly deals.

Far as east from west is distant,
He hath put away our sin;
Like the pity of a father
Hath the Lord's compassion been.

As it was without beginning,
So it lasts without an end;
To their children's children ever
Shall His righteousness extend:

Unto such as keep His covenant
And are steadfast in His way;
Unto those who still remember
His commandments, and obey.

Bless the Father, all His creatures,
Ever under His control;
All throughout His vast dominion
Bless the Father, O my soul.

United Presbyterian Book of Psalms, 1871

This hymn, a recasting of Psalm 103, contains three rich biblical images for us to ponder. The first verses of both the psalm and the hymn call upon all within us to bless and praise the Lord. There is a totality of worship demanded here.

Later, the psalmist notes that God has removed our sins "as far as the east is from the west." East and west are as far apart as you can get. What a vivid reminder that when God forgives us, our sins are truly gone!

The third image is that of a father who cares deeply for his children. Jesus used this same illustration: If a human father gives bread to his hungry child, won't our heavenly Father do this and more? A wise parent knows the limitations of his children. We don't ask five-year-old children to compute our taxes and then punish them for missing a few deductions. That would be foolish. In the same way, our heavenly Father understands our limits and has compassion when we fail.

• • • •

Let all that I am praise the Lord; with my whole heart, I will praise his holy name. Let all that I am praise the Lord; may I never forget the good things he does for me.
PSALM 103:1-2

O for a Thousand Tongues to Sing

The original title of this hymn was "For the Anniversary Day of One's Conversion"; Charles Wesley wrote it on May 21, 1749, the eleventh anniversary of his own conversion. Before they were converted, John and Charles Wesley were dubbed "methodists" because of the methods of spirituality they had introduced in their club at Oxford, the Holy Club. But later John and Charles met the German Moravians, who loved to sing, were very missions-minded, and emphasized a personal conversion experience.

One of the Moravian leaders, Peter Bohler, once said, "Had I a thousand tongues, I would praise Christ Jesus with all of them." So it was fitting for Charles Wesley to build a hymn around that quotation to celebrate the date of his conversion.

• • • •

And when he comes, he will open the eyes of the blind and unplug the ears of the deaf. The lame will leap like a deer, and those who cannot speak will sing for joy! Springs will gush forth in the wilderness, and streams will water the wasteland.

ISAIAH 35:5-6

O for a thousand tongues to sing
my great Redeemer's praise,
The glories of my God and King,
the triumphs of His grace!

My gracious Master and my God,
assist me to proclaim,
To spread thro' all the earth abroad
the honors of Thy name.

Jesus! the name that charms our fears,
that bids our sorrows cease,
'Tis music in the sinners' ears;
'tis life, and health, and peace.

He breaks the power of canceled sin,
He sets the prisoner free;
His blood can make the foulest clean;
His blood availed for me.

He speaks, and listening to His voice,
new life the dead receive;
The mournful, broken hearts rejoice;
the humble poor believe.

Hear Him, ye deaf; His praise, ye dumb,
your loosened tongues employ;
Ye blind, behold your Savior come;
and leap, ye lame, for joy.

Charles Wesley (1707-1788)

O Worship the King

O worship the King, all glorious above,
O gratefully sing His power and His love;
Our Shield and Defender, the Ancient of Days,
Pavilioned in splendor, and girded with praise.

O tell of His might, O sing of His grace,
Whose robe is the light, whose canopy space;
His chariots of wrath the deep thunderclouds form,
And dark is His path on the wings of the storm.

The earth with its store of wonders untold,
Almighty, Thy power hath founded of old,
Hath stablished it fast by a changeless decree,
And round it hath cast, like a mantle, the sea.

Thy bountiful care, what tongue can recite?
It breathes in the air, it shines in the light;
It streams from the hills, it descends to the plain,
And sweetly distills in the dew and the rain.

Frail children of dust, and feeble as frail,
In Thee do we trust, nor find Thee to fail;
Thy mercies how tender, how firm to the end,
Our Maker, Defender, Redeemer, and Friend.

Robert Grant (1779-1838)

Sir Robert Grant was acquainted with kings. His father was a member of the British Parliament and later became chairman of the East India Company. Following in his father's footsteps, young Grant was elected to Parliament and then also became a director of the East India Company. In 1834 he was appointed governor of Bombay, and in that position he became greatly loved. A medical college in India was named in his honor.

This hymn by Grant is based on Psalm 104, a psalm of praise.

• • • •

Let all that I am praise the Lord. O Lord my God, how great you are! You are robed with honor and majesty. You are dressed in a robe of light. You stretch out the starry curtain of the heavens; you lay out the rafters of your home in the rain clouds. You make the clouds your chariot; you ride upon the wings of the wind. The winds are your messengers; flames of fire are your servants.

PSALM 104:1-4

I Will Sing the Wondrous Story

Twenty-one-year-old Peter Bilhorn came to Pastor Francis Rowley one Sunday night after the evening service. The year was 1886; the place was North Adams, Massachusetts. Young Bilhorn had been converted the previous year, and already he was using his musical talents for the Lord. "Why don't you write a hymn for me to set to music?" he asked Pastor Rowley.

Rowley's response was this gospel song, which originally began "Can't you sing the wondrous story?" For Bilhorn, who was a singer as well as a pianist and organist, it was an ideal personal testimony. As an unconverted teenager, he had started his music career singing in Chicago taverns. He understood the line "I was lost but Jesus found me—found the sheep that went astray."

Bilhorn went on singing the wondrous story the rest of his life, writing two thousand songs.

• • • •

And they were singing the song of Moses, the servant of God, and the song of the Lamb: "Great and marvelous are your works, O Lord God, the Almighty. Just and true are your ways, O King of the nations."

REVELATION 15:3

I will sing the wondrous story
Of the Christ who died for me—
How He left His home in glory
For the cross of Calvary.

Yes, I'll sing the wondrous story
Of the Christ who died for me,
Sing it with the saints in glory,
Gathered by the crystal sea.

I was lost but Jesus found me—
Found the sheep that went astray,
Threw His loving arms around me,
Drew me back into His way.

Days of darkness still come o'er me,
Sorrow's paths I often tread;
But the Savior still is with me—
By His hand I'm safely led.

He will keep me till the river
Rolls its waters at my feet;
Then He'll bear me safely over,
Where the loved ones I shall meet.

Francis Harold Rowley (1854–1942)

Jesus, My Lord, My God, My All

Jesus, my Lord, my God, my All,
Hear me, blest Savior, when I call;
Hear me, and from Thy dwelling-place
Pour down the riches of Thy grace:

Jesus, my Lord, I Thee adore;
Oh, make me love Thee more and more.

Jesus, too late I Thee have sought;
How can I love Thee as I ought?
And how extol Thy matchless fame,
The glorious beauty of Thy name?

Jesus, what did Thou find in me
That Thou has dealt so lovingly?
How great the joy that Thou has brought,
So far exceeding hope or thought!

Jesus, of Thee shall be my song;
To Thee my heart and soul belong;
All that I have or am is Thine,
And Thou, blest Savior, Thou art mine.

Henry Collins (1827-1919)

Henry Collins wrote this moving prayer-hymn the year he graduated from Oxford and began his ministry as an Anglican clergyman. One writer said that it was "almost too intimate to sing in a great congregation." But the depth of the hymn is worth exploring. The second and third stanzas ask unanswerable questions: "How can I love Thee as I ought?" and "What did Thou find in me that Thou has dealt so lovingly?"

In the apostle John's first epistle, we are reminded that God's love precedes ours. "We love each other because he loved us first" (1 John 4:19). But when we start asking *why* God loves us, there are no answers except in the character of God Himself. In Ephesians 3:19, Paul reminds us that God's love "is too great to understand."

• • • •

Whom have I in heaven but you? I desire you more than anything on earth. My health may fail, and my spirit may grow weak, but God remains the strength of my heart; he is mine forever.

PSALM 73:25-26

He Giveth More Grace

Little is known of Annie Flint, but it is clear that she understood both suffering and grace. The apostle Paul understood these things, too. During his life of ministry in service of Christ, Paul was persecuted, imprisoned, beaten, and even stoned. And as if that weren't enough, he also suffered from an unidentified "thorn in the flesh"—a weakness that he could not overcome.

But amidst all his trials, Paul wrote, "Three different times I begged the Lord to take [the thorn] away. Each time he said, 'My grace is all you need. My power works best in weakness.' So now I am glad to boast about my weaknesses, so that the power of Christ can work through me" (2 Corinthians 12:8-9).

Paul discovered that God's grace and power were sufficient to overcome any trial or weakness he might encounter.

• • • •

Dear brothers and sisters, when troubles come your way, consider it an opportunity for great joy. For you know that when your faith is tested, your endurance has a chance to grow.

JAMES 1:2-3

He giveth more grace when the burden grows greater;
He sendeth more strength when the labors increase.
To added affliction He addeth His mercy;
To multiplied trials, His multiplied peace.

His love has no limit;
His grace has no measure;
His pow'r has no boundary known unto men.
For out of His infinite riches in Jesus,
He giveth, and giveth, and giveth again!

When we have exhausted our store of endurance,
When our strength has failed ere the day is half done,
When we reach the end of our hoarded resources,
Our Father's full giving is only begun.

Annie Johnson Flint (1866–1932)

Grace Greater than Our Sin

Marvelous grace of our loving Lord,
Grace that exceeds our sin and our guilt!
Yonder on Calvary's mount outpoured—
There where the blood of the Lamb was spilt.

Grace, grace, God's grace,
Grace that will pardon and cleanse within,
Grace, grace, God's grace,
Grace that is greater than all our sin!

Sin and despair, like the sea waves cold,
Threaten the soul with infinite loss;
Grace that is greater—yes, grace untold—
Points to the refuge, the mighty cross.

Dark is the stain that we cannot hide—
What can avail to wash it away?
Look! there is flowing a crimson tide—
Whiter than snow you may be today.

Marvelous, infinite, matchless grace,
Freely bestowed on all who believe!
You that are longing to see His face,
Will you this moment His grace receive?

Julia Harriette Johnston (1849–1919)

Grace is one of the hardest lessons for us to learn about God. Some show their ignorance of God's grace by working hard to be good enough. They pay lip service to the idea of God's grace but cannot stop trying to earn their own way. Others display their misunderstanding of God's grace by concluding it's inaccessible to them. They know they cannot be good enough for God, so they despair of ever having a relationship with Him.

It is this second group that Julia Johnston was writing for. She knew how important it was to understand and experience the simple, yet difficult, truth of God's gracious forgiveness. Johnston was a Sunday school teacher herself and became a noted expert in Sunday school curriculum. Though she penned texts for more than five hundred hymns, this is the only one widely known. It powerfully teaches this essential Christian truth: You cannot out-sin God's grace.

• • • •

God's law was given so that all people could see how sinful they were. But as people sinned more and more, God's wonderful grace became more abundant. So just as sin ruled over all people and brought them to death, now God's wonderful grace rules instead, giving us right standing with God and resulting in eternal life through Jesus Christ our Lord.

ROMANS 5:20-21

Arise, My Soul, Arise

One Methodist minister said he knew of more than two hundred people who had come to Christ through singing this hymn. The story of one young boy is typical of many. He had gone to a revival meeting, and when the sermon was over, he dropped to his knees. "I knew I was sorry for my sins," he said later, "and I wanted Jesus to forgive me." The congregation sang this hymn of Charles Wesley, and the boy listened carefully. Some of the stanzas he did not understand very well, but when they came to the last stanza, joy exploded inside him.

The words "with confidence" changed his life. "It was just like being introduced to someone," he said. "From a penitent, weeping boy, I arose happy and smiling." And that's what Jesus does. He brings us to the point of denouncing our sinful lives, but then gives us the confidence to enter a relationship with Him.

• • • •

But God showed his great love for us by sending Christ to die for us while we were still sinners. And since we have been made right in God's sight by the blood of Christ, he will certainly save us from God's condemnation. For since our friendship with God was restored by the death of his Son while we were still his enemies, we will certainly be saved through the life of his Son.

ROMANS 5:8-10

Arise, my soul, arise; shake off thy guilty fears;
The bleeding sacrifice in my behalf appears:
Before the throne my surety stands,
Before the throne my surety stands,
My name is written on His hands.

He ever lives above, for me to intercede;
His all-redeeming love, His precious blood,
to plead:
His blood atoned for all our race,
His blood atoned for all our race,
And sprinkles now the throne of grace.

Five bleeding wounds He bears, received on Calvary;
They pour effectual prayers;
they strongly plead for me:
"Forgive him, O forgive," they cry,
"Forgive him, O forgive," they cry,
"Nor let the ransomed sinner die!"

The Father hears Him pray, His dear anointed One;
He cannot turn away the presence of His Son:
His spirit answers to the blood,
His spirit answers to the blood,
And tells me I am born of God.

My God is reconciled; His pardoning voice I hear;
He owns me for His child; I can no longer fear:
With confidence I now draw nigh,
With confidence I now draw nigh,
And, "Father, Abba, Father," cry.

Charles Wesley (1707-1788)

I Know Whom I Have Believed

I know not why God's wondrous grace
To me He hath made known,
Nor why, unworthy, Christ in love
Redeemed me for His own.

But "I know whom I have believed,
And am persuaded that He is able
To keep that which I've committed
Unto Him against that day."

I know not how this saving faith
To me He did impart,
Nor how believing in His Word
Wrought peace within my heart.

I know not how the Spirit moves,
Convincing men of sin,
Revealing Jesus through the Word,
Creating faith in Him.

I know not when my Lord may come,
At night or noonday fair,
Nor if I'll walk the vale with Him,
Or "meet Him in the air."

Daniel Webster Whittle (1840-1901)

As a POW during the Civil War, Daniel Whittle began reading the New Testament his mother had given him as he marched off to war, and he committed his life to Jesus Christ.

After the war, Whittle was promoted to the rank of major and then became a successful businessman. In 1873 he began preaching in evangelistic services, and for a quarter-century he led revivals throughout the United States. He also encouraged some of the leading songwriters of his time and wrote many hymns himself, including "Showers of Blessing" and "Moment by Moment." Whittle penned this hymn in 1883, perhaps thinking back to questions he had asked during his imprisonment. There were still many things he didn't know, but he certainly did know Jesus.

• • • •

That is why I am suffering here in prison. But I am not ashamed of it, for I know the one in whom I trust, and I am sure that he is able to guard what I have entrusted to him until the day of his return.

2 TIMOTHY 1:12

All My Hope on God Is Founded

Joachim Neander, the writer of this hymn, became a Christian when he was twenty and died at the age of thirty. But during his short decade of faith, this German high school teacher displayed great evangelistic zeal. All Neander's hymns are notably rich in content and deep in meaning. Perhaps his best-known hymn is "Praise to the Lord, the Almighty" (August 3).

Robert Bridges, who adapted this hymn from the German, was Britain's poet laureate for a time. Wanting to raise the standard of British hymns, he translated many from German and adapted numerous German melodies for British worshipers.

This Neander hymn, as translated by Bridges, is a noble blending of the talents and dedication of these two godly men.

• • • •

But the Lord watches over those who fear him, those who rely on his unfailing love. He rescues them from death and keeps them alive in times of famine. We put our hope in the Lord. He is our help and our shield.

PSALM 33:18-20

All my hope on God is founded;
He doth still my trust renew,
Me through change and chance He guideth,
Only good and only true,
God unknown, He alone
Calls my heart to be His own.

Mortal pride and earthly glory,
Sword and crown betray our trust;
Though with care and toil we build them,
Tower and temple fall to dust.
But God's power, hour by hour,
Is my temple and my tower.

God's great goodness e'er endureth,
Deep His wisdom passing thought:
Splendor, light, and life attend Him,
Beauty springeth out of naught.
Evermore from His store
Newborn worlds rise and adore.

Daily doth the almighty Giver
Bounteous gifts on us bestow;
His desire our soul delighteth,
Pleasure leads us where we go.
Love doth stand at His hand;
Joy doth wait on His command.

Still from earth to God eternal
Sacrifice of praise be done,
High above all praises praising
For the gift of Christ, His Son.
Christ doth call one and all:
Ye who follow shall not fall.

Joachim Neander (1650-1680)

Translated by Robert Seymour Bridges (1844-1930)

Jesus, Lover of My Soul

Jesus, Lover of my soul,
let me to Thy bosom fly,
While the nearer waters roll,
while the tempest still is high;
Hide me, O my Savior, hide,
till the storm of life is past;
Safe into the haven guide;
O receive my soul at last!

Other refuge have I none;
hangs my helpless soul on Thee;
Leave, ah! leave me not alone,
still support and comfort me.
All my trust on Thee is stayed;
all my help from Thee I bring;
Cover my defenseless head with
the shadow of Thy wing.

Thou, O Christ, art all I want;
more than all in Thee I find:
Raise the fallen, cheer the faint,
heal the sick, and lead the blind.
Just and holy is Thy name;
I am all unrighteousness;
False and full of sin I am;
Thou art full of truth and grace.

Plenteous grace with Thee is found,
grace to cover all my sin;
Let the healing streams abound;
make and keep me pure within.
Thou of life the fountain art;
freely let me take of Thee:
Spring Thou up within my heart;
rise to all eternity.

Charles Wesley (1707–1788)

Written only a year after his conversion, this is one of the most famous of Charles Wesley's six thousand hymns. As he wrote it, he may have been remembering his turbulent transatlantic crossing three years earlier. He wrote in his journal, "The sea streamed in at the sides . . . it was as much as four men could do by continual pumping to keep her above water. I rose and lay down by turns, but could remain in no posture long; strove vehemently to pray, but in vain." Later in the afternoon as the storm reached its peak, he said, "In this dreadful moment, I bless God, I found the comfort of hope."

Wesley talked to another passenger about trusting God, and the passenger replied that he had no refuge in times of danger. Even though Wesley was ill and frightened, he had the awareness, as he later wrote, that he "abode under the shadow of the Almighty."

• • • •

I am praying to you because I know you will answer, O God. Bend down and listen as I pray. Show me your unfailing love in wonderful ways. By your mighty power you rescue those who seek refuge from their enemies. Guard me as you would guard your own eyes. Hide me in the shadow of your wings.
PSALM 17:6-8

There's a Wideness in God's Mercy

Brought up as a Calvinistic Anglican, Frederick Faber was ordained in the Church of England. But at the age of thirty-one, he converted to Roman Catholicism, following his friend John Henry Newman. Rebaptized as Father Wilfred, he founded a community known as "Brothers of the Will of God." In 1849 Newman asked Faber to open an oratory—a place of prayer. When Faber opened his oratory, it soon became a place of both prayer and music, much like the famous Oratory in Rome.

Faber was concerned that British Roman Catholics did not have a heritage of hymnwriters like Watts, Wesley, and Newton. He began writing hymns so that Catholics, too, could be a hymn-singing people. Just as there is "a wideness in God's mercy," so was there a breadth to Faber's hymns, which soon became more familiar to Protestants than to Catholics.

There's a wideness in God's mercy,
Like the wideness of the sea;
There's a kindness in His justice,
Which is more than liberty.
There is welcome for the sinner,
And more graces for the good;
There is mercy with the Savior;
There is healing in His blood.

For the love of God is broader
Than the measure of man's mind;
And the heart of the Eternal
Is most wonderfully kind.
If our love were but more simple,
We should take Him at His word;
And our lives would be all sunshine
In the sweetness of our Lord.

Frederick William Faber (1814-1863)

• • • •

Acknowledge that the Lord is God! He made us, and we are his. We are his people, the sheep of his pasture. Enter his gates with thanksgiving; go into his courts with praise. Give thanks to him and praise his name. For the Lord is good. His unfailing love continues forever, and his faithfulness continues to each generation.

PSALM 100:3-5

Rock of Ages

Rock of Ages, cleft for me,
Let me hide myself in Thee;
Let the water and the blood,
From Thy wounded side which flowed,
Be of sin the double cure,
Save from wrath and make me pure.

Could my tears forever flow,
Could my zeal no languor know,
These for sin could not atone;
Thou must save, and Thou alone.
In my hand no price I bring;
Simply to Thy cross I cling.

While I draw this fleeting breath,
When my eyes shall close in death,
When I rise to worlds unknown,
And behold Thee on Thy throne,
Rock of Ages, cleft for me,
Let me hide myself in Thee.

Augustus Toplady (1740-1778)

Converted under a Methodist evangelist while attending the University of Dublin, Augustus Toplady decided to prepare for the ministry. Though impressed with the spirit of Methodism, he strongly disagreed with the Wesleys' Arminian theology and waged a running battle with them through tracts, sermons, and even hymns. "Wesley," said Toplady, "is guilty of Satan's shamelessness." Wesley retorted, "I do not fight with chimney sweeps!"

Toplady wrote "Rock of Ages" to conclude a magazine article in which he emphasized that, just as England could never repay its national debt, so humans through their own efforts could never satisfy the eternal justice of God. He died of tuberculosis and overwork at the age of thirty-eight, two years after he published his own hymnal, in which "Rock of Ages" and Charles Wesley's "Jesus, Lover of My Soul" (July 17) were placed side by side.

• • • •

Let all that I am wait quietly before God, for my hope is in him. He alone is my rock and my salvation, my fortress where I will not be shaken. My victory and honor come from God alone. He is my refuge, a rock where no enemy can reach me.
PSALM 62:5-7

My Hope Is Built on Nothing Less

Many of the British hymnwriters were children of the clergy or came from middle- or upper-class backgrounds. But not Edward Mote. His parents kept a pub in London, and Mote says, "My Sundays were spent in the streets; so ignorant was I that I did not know that there was a God." He was apprenticed to a cabinetmaker who took him to church, where he heard the gospel message. Mote himself became a successful cabinetmaker in a London suburb and was active in his local church.

Mote wrote this hymn while he was working as a cabinetmaker. The chorus came to his mind as he was walking to work, and during the day the stanzas came to him. Two years later he published it in a collection of his own hymns and titled it "The Immutable Basis of a Sinner's Hope." It is a hymn that combines deep biblical theology with sincere personal experience.

My hope is built on nothing less
Than Jesus' blood and righteousness;
I dare not trust the sweetest frame,
But wholly lean on Jesus' name.

On Christ, the solid rock, I stand;
All other ground is sinking sand,
All other ground is sinking sand.

When darkness veils His lovely face,
I rest on His unchanging grace;
In every high and stormy gale,
My anchor holds within the vale.

His oath, His covenant, His blood
Support me in the whelming flood;
When all around my soul gives way,
He then is all my hope and stay.

When He shall come with trumpet sound,
O may I then in Him be found!
Dressed in His righteousness alone,
Faultless to stand before the throne!

Edward Mote (1797–1874)

• • • •

If we are living in the light, as God is in the light, then we have fellowship with each other, and the blood of Jesus, his Son, cleanses us from all sin. If we claim we have no sin, we are only fooling ourselves and not living in the truth. But if we confess our sins to him, he is faithful and just to forgive us our sins and to cleanse us from all wickedness.

I JOHN 1:7-9

Jesus, Thy Blood and Righteousness

Jesus, Thy blood and righteousness
My beauty are, my glorious dress;
Midst flaming worlds, in these arrayed,
With joy shall I lift up my head.

Bold shall I stand in Thy great day,
For who aught to my charge shall lay?
Fully absolved through these I am,
From sin and fear, from guilt and shame.

Lord, I believe Thy precious blood,
Which, at the mercy seat of God,
Forever doth for sinners plead,
For me, e'en for my soul, was shed.

Lord, I believe were sinners more
Than sands upon the ocean shore,
Thou hast for all a ransom paid,
For all a full atonement made.

Nicolaus von Zinzendorf (1700–1760)

Translated by John Wesley (1703–1791)

Count Nicolaus von Zinzendorf was one of the most remarkable persons in church history. He was born into a wealthy family in Saxony, Germany, educated at the best universities, and named counselor of the State of Saxony, but he chose to be associated with the Moravians, devout believers who had been exiled from Austria.

Of the two thousand hymns he wrote, this is perhaps the best known. His hymns were personal because he was a passionate promoter of what he called "Christianity of the heart." They were also Christ centered because his life motto was "I have but one passion, and that is He and only He."

• • • •

For you know that God paid a ransom to save you from the empty life you inherited from your ancestors. And the ransom he paid was not mere gold or silver. It was the precious blood of Christ, the sinless, spotless Lamb of God.

I PETER 1:18-19

Jesus! What a Friend for Sinners!

Jesus' detractors accused Him of being a friend of tax collectors and sinners. They couldn't have been more right.

In defense of His actions, Jesus said cryptically, "Wisdom is shown to be right by its results" (Matthew 11:19). Certainly He backed this up with His own actions. As He said later, "There is no greater love than to lay down one's life for one's friends" (John 15:13). That is precisely what He did for His friends, the sinners. Jesus gave His life so everyone can experience freedom from sin's powerful grip.

As a pastor and evangelist, J. Wilbur Chapman knew the joy of seeing scores of sinners open their hearts to the Lord. As a believer himself, he knew firsthand the joy of a sinner finding a friend in Christ.

• • • •

All praise to God, the Father of our Lord Jesus Christ, who has blessed us with every spiritual blessing in the heavenly realms because we are united with Christ. Even before he made the world, God loved us and chose us in Christ to be holy and without fault in his eyes. God decided in advance to adopt us into his own family by bringing us to himself through Jesus Christ.

EPHESIANS 1:3-5

Jesus! what a Friend for sinners!
Jesus! Lover of my soul;
Friends may fail me, foes assail me,
He, my Savior, makes me whole.

Jesus! what a Strength in weakness!
Let me hide myself in Him;
Tempted, tried, and sometimes failing,
He, my Strength, my vict'ry wins.

Jesus! what a Help in sorrow!
While the billows o'er me roll,
Even when my heart is breaking,
He, my Comfort, helps my soul.

Jesus! what a Guide and Keeper!
While the tempest still is high,
Storms about me, night o'ertakes me,
He, my Pilot, hears my cry.

Jesus! I do now receive Him,
More than all in Him I find,
He hath granted me forgiveness,
I am His, and He is mine.

J. Wilbur Chapman (1859–1918)

Ye Servants of God

Ye servants of God, your Master proclaim,
And publish abroad His wonderful name;
The name all-victorious of Jesus extol;
His kingdom is glorious and rules over all.

God ruleth on high, almighty to save;
And still He is nigh, His presence we have;
The great congregation His triumph shall sing,
Ascribing salvation to Jesus, our King.

"Salvation to God, who sits on the throne!"
Let all cry aloud and honor the Son:
The praises of Jesus the angels proclaim,
Fall down on their faces and worship the Lamb.

Then let us adore and give Him His right,
All glory and power, all wisdom and might,
All honor and blessing, with angels above,
And thanks never ceasing, and infinite love.

Charles Wesley (1707–1788)

In 1744 England was at war with France, and the British were expecting an invasion to dethrone George II and restore the House of Stuart to the throne. People suspected the Methodists of friendship with France and perhaps plotting to overthrow the king. Wesleyan meetings were broken up by mobs, and at times John and Charles Wesley themselves were arrested.

In the middle of the turmoil, the Wesleys published a collection of hymns to encourage their followers. The title was *Hymns for Times of Trouble and Persecution.* This hymn, "Ye Servants of God," was published under the heading "To Be Sung in a Tumult." The stanzas we have in our hymnals today do not suggest any turmoil, but one that was omitted reads "Men, devils engage, the billows arise and horribly rage, and threaten the skies; their fury shall never our steadfastness shock, the weakest believer is built on a rock."

• • • •

I saw a vast crowd, too great to count, . . . standing in front of the throne and before the Lamb. . . . And they were shouting with a great roar, "Salvation comes from our God who sits on the throne and from the Lamb!"
REVELATION 7:9-10

O Thou in All Thy Might So Far

Frederick Hosmer was a Unitarian minister, a graduate of Harvard Divinity School, and a student of hymns. In a time when many were intellectualizing Christianity, he maintained a personal and emotional faith, expressing his personal feelings for the almighty God. This song even demonstrates an intellectual modesty ("I know Thee but in part"), uncommon in an age when scholars were picking and probing at the traditional faith, rationally dismantling many deeply cherished doctrines, and claiming to have all the answers.

Still, as a Unitarian, Hosmer did not write much about Jesus. We can applaud Hosmer's call to "childlike faith." Yet we can also recognize that his faith was blinder than it needed to be. God *can* be known fully in the person of Jesus Christ. He is the One who leads us on the "open path" to the Father.

• • • •

Jesus replied, "Have I been with you all this time, Philip, and yet you still don't know who I am? Anyone who has seen me has seen the Father!"

JOHN 14:9

O Thou in all Thy might so far,
In all Thy love so near,
Beyond the range of sun and star,
And yet beside us here.

What heart can comprehend Thy name,
Or searching find Thee out,
Who art within, a quickening flame,
A presence round about?

Yet though I know Thee but in part,
I ask not, Lord, for more;
Enough for me to know Thou art,
To love Thee, and adore.

And dearer than all things I know
Is childlike faith to me,
That makes the darkest way I go
An open path to Thee.

Frederick Lucian Hosmer (1840-1929)

Jesus, the Very Thought of Thee

Jesus, the very thought of Thee
With sweetness fills my breast;
But sweeter far Thy face to see,
And in Thy presence rest.

Nor voice can sing, nor heart can frame,
Nor can the mem'ry find
A sweeter sound than Thy blest name,
O Savior of mankind!

O Hope of every contrite heart,
O Joy of all the meek,
To those who fall, how kind Thou art!
How good to those who seek!

But what to those who find? Ah, this
Nor tongue nor pen can show:
The love of Jesus, what it is
None but His loved ones know.

Jesus, our only joy be Thou,
As Thou our prize wilt be:
Jesus, be Thou our glory now,
And through eternity.

Attributed to Bernard of Clairvaux (1091–1153)

Translated by Edward Caswall (1814–1878)

Knowing God is a matter of the heart. This truth dominated the life of Bernard of Clairvaux. At a very early age Bernard was drawn to spiritual things, largely influenced by the piety of his mother. At twenty-two he entered a monastery at Citeaux, and three years later he founded a monastery at Clairvaux, serving as its spiritual leader until he died in 1153.

In spite of his many pressing responsibilities and frequent travel, Bernard never lost sight of what he prized most—the love of Jesus. God's love was Bernard's lifeblood, pulsing through everything he said and did. His knowledge of God was deeply personal, a mystical love affair that not only gave meaning to his life on earth but formed his vision of heaven. As Bernard said, "[God] is Himself the reward of those who love Him, the eternal reward of those who love Him for eternity."

• • • •

I decided that while I was with you I would forget everything except Jesus Christ, the one who was crucified. I came to you in weakness—timid and trembling. And my message and my preaching were very plain. Rather than using clever and persuasive speeches, I relied only on the power of the Holy Spirit. I did this so you would trust not in human wisdom but in the power of God.
I CORINTHIANS 2:2-5

God, Be Merciful to Me

King David had failed miserably. He had committed a terrible sin, and his cover-up had then led to murder.

Psalm 51, David's confession, stands as a timeless example of public humility and private repentance. This hymn faithfully paraphrases that psalm. We see the king's heartfelt sorrow. We see him struggle with the evil in his heart. We see his longing to be clean in God's eyes. And we can understand—because all of us have been there in one way or another.

• • • •

Have mercy on me, O God, because of your unfailing love. Because of your great compassion, blot out the stain of my sins. Wash me clean from my guilt. Purify me from my sin. For I recognize my rebellion; it haunts me day and night. Against you, and you alone, have I sinned; I have done what is evil in your sight. You will be proved right in what you say, and your judgment against me is just.

PSALM 51:1-4

God, be merciful to me,
On Thy grace I rest my plea;
Plenteous in compassion Thou,
Blot out my transgressions now;
Wash me, make me pure within,
Cleanse, O cleanse me from my sin.

My transgressions I confess,
Grief and guilt my soul oppress;
I have sinned against Thy grace
And provoked Thee to Thy face;
I confess Thy judgment just,
Speechless, I Thy mercy trust.

I am evil, born in sin;
Thou desirest truth within.
Thou alone my Savior art,
Teach Thy wisdom to my heart;
Make me pure, Thy grace bestow,
Wash me whiter than the snow.

Gracious God, my heart renew,
Make my spirit right and true;
Cast me not away from Thee,
Let Thy Spirit dwell in me;
Thy salvation's joy impart,
Steadfast make my willing heart.

Sinners then shall learn from me
And return, O God, to Thee;
Savior, all my guilt remove,
And my tongue shall sing Thy love;
Touch my silent lips, O Lord,
And my mouth shall praise accord.

The Psalter, 1912

We Praise Thee, O God

We praise Thee, O God, our Redeemer, Creator
In grateful devotion our tribute we bring;
We lay it before Thee, we kneel and adore Thee,
We bless Thy holy Name, glad praises we sing.

We worship Thee, God of our fathers,
we bless Thee
Thru life's storm and tempest
our Guide hast Thou been;
When perils o'ertake us, escape Thou wilt make us,
And with Thy help, O Lord, our battles we win.

With voices united our praises we offer
To Thee, great Jehovah, glad anthems we raise;
Thy strong arm will guide us, our God is beside us,
To Thee, our great Redeemer, forever be praise!

Julia Cady Cory (1882-1963)

From her student years, Julia Cady wrote Christian poems and songs. Her father, a prominent architect, was also a longtime Sunday school superintendent at New York City's Church of the Covenant.

When Julia was in her twenties, the organist at Brick Presbyterian Church asked her to write new words for a traditional Dutch Thanksgiving hymn. She produced "We Praise Thee, O God," and the new words were sung for Thanksgiving at both Brick Presbyterian and her home church.

The original Dutch hymn goes back to the 1600s. The familiar words "We Gather Together to Ask the Lord's Blessing" are an English rendering of a German version of the Dutch original. Julia Cady Cory's words express the same theme of thanks for God's blessings, but in a fresh way.

• • • •

O nations of the world, recognize the Lord, recognize that the Lord is glorious and strong. Give to the Lord the glory he deserves! Bring your offering and come into his presence. Worship the Lord in all his holy splendor.
I CHRONICLES 16:28-29

Stand Up and Bless the Lord

As a newspaper editor in Sheffield, England, James Montgomery was known as an outspoken advocate of many humanitarian causes. In fact, he was imprisoned twice for his editorials. He wrote against slavery and promoted democracy in government. Though a gentle man by nature, he was not afraid to champion unpopular causes. He didn't see why anyone who was a Christian should be ashamed to stand up and say so.

In 1824 Montgomery wrote this hymn for a Sunday school anniversary. It is based on Nehemiah 9:5, where the Levites say to the people, "Stand up and praise the Lord your God, for he lives from everlasting to everlasting!"

• • • •

Stand up and praise the Lord your God, for he lives from everlasting to everlasting! . . . May your glorious name be praised! May it be exalted above all blessing and praise! You alone are the Lord. You made the skies and the heavens and all the stars. You made the earth and the seas and everything in them. You preserve them all, and the angels of heaven worship you.

NEHEMIAH 9:5-6

Stand up and bless the Lord,
Ye people of His choice;
Stand up and bless the Lord your God
With heart and soul and voice.

Though high above all praise,
Above all blessing high,
Who would not fear His holy name,
And laud and magnify?

O for the living flame
From His own altar brought,
To touch our lips, our minds inspire,
And wing to heaven our thought!

God is our strength and song,
And His salvation ours;
Then be His love in Christ proclaimed
With all our ransomed powers.

Stand up and bless the Lord;
The Lord your God adore;
Stand up and bless His glorious name,
Henceforth forevermore.

James Montgomery (1771-1854)

Jesus! The Name High over All

Jesus! the name high over all,
In hell or earth or sky;
Angels and men before it fall,
And devils fear and fly.

Jesus! the name to sinners dear,
The name to sinners given;
It scatters all their guilty fear;
It turns their hell to heaven.

O that the world might taste and see
The riches of His grace!
The arms of love that compass me
Would all mankind embrace.

Thee I shall constantly proclaim,
Though earth and hell oppose,
Bold to confess Thy glorious name
Before a world of foes.

His only righteousness I show,
His saving grace proclaim;
'Tis all my business here below
To cry, "Behold the Lamb!"

Happy, if with my latest breath
I may but gasp His name;
Preach Him to all and cry in death,
"Behold, behold the Lamb!"

Charles Wesley (1707-1788)

Mrs. Turner was a quiet woman who had only recently come to faith in Christ. Charles Wesley was physically ill and spiritually hungry when he found refuge in her brother's home in the spring of 1738. Shyly, Mrs. Turner told him how she had come to personal faith in Christ. Then she said, "In the name of Jesus of Nazareth, arise and believe, and thou shalt be healed of thine infirmities!" That was the turning point for Charles.

Several years later, when Charles Wesley was preaching in Cornwall, England, a drunken man started opposing him. Wesley responded, "Who is this that pleads for the devil?" and he rebuked the man in the name of Jesus. That night Wesley went to bed thinking about the name of Jesus. The hymn he wrote during the night referred to that experience in the first stanza. But as he wrote the second stanza he was probably thinking of what shy Mrs. Turner had told him years earlier.

• • • •

Peter said, "I don't have any silver or gold for you. But I'll give you what I have. In the name of Jesus Christ the Nazarene, get up and walk!" Then Peter took the lame man by the right hand and helped him up. And as he did, the man's feet and ankles were instantly healed and strengthened.
ACTS 3:6-7

Joyful, Joyful, We Adore Thee

Henry Van Dyke was serving as a guest preacher at Williams College in the Berkshire Mountains of Massachusetts. He was so moved by the beauty of God's creation that he wrote this hymn of joy. The next morning he handed the poem to the college president. "Here is a hymn for you," he said. "Your mountains were my inspiration. It must be sung to the music of Beethoven's 'Hymn to Joy.'" And so it has been ever since.

Van Dyke was a Presbyterian minister; the author of many books, including the best-selling *The Other Wise Man*; professor of literature at Princeton University; Navy chaplain during World War I; and ambassador to Holland and Luxembourg under President Woodrow Wilson.

• • • •

Always be full of joy in the Lord. I say it again—rejoice! . . . Don't worry about anything; instead, pray about everything. Tell God what you need, and thank him for all he has done. Then you will experience God's peace, which exceeds anything we can understand. His peace will guard your hearts and minds as you live in Christ Jesus.

PHILIPPIANS 4:4-7

Joyful, joyful, we adore Thee,
God of glory, Lord of love;
Hearts unfold like flowers before Thee,
Opening to the sun above.
Melt the clouds of sin and sadness;
Drive the dark of doubt away;
Giver of immortal gladness,
Fill us with the light of day!

All Thy works with joy surround Thee,
Earth and heav'n reflect Thy rays,
Stars and angels sing around Thee,
Center of unbroken praise;
Field and forest, vale and mountain,
Flowery meadow, flashing sea,
Chanting bird and flowing fountain,
Call us to rejoice in Thee.

Thou art giving and forgiving,
Ever blessing, ever blest,
Wellspring of the joy of living,
Ocean depth of happy rest!
Thou our Father, Christ our brother,
All who live in love are Thine;
Teach us how to love each other,
Lift us to the joy divine.

Mortals join the mighty chorus,
Which the morning stars began;
Father love is reigning o'er us,
Brother love binds man to man.
Ever singing, march we onward,
Victors in the midst of strife;
Joyful music leads us sunward
In the triumph song of life.

Henry van Dyke (1852-1933)

When Morning Gilds the Skies

When morning gilds the skies,
My heart awaking cries,
May Jesus Christ be praised!
Alike at work and prayer,
To Jesus I repair;
May Jesus Christ be praised!

The night becomes as day,
When from the heart we say,
May Jesus Christ be praised!
The powers of darkness fear,
When this sweet chant they hear,
May Jesus Christ be praised!

Ye nations of mankind,
In this your concord find,
May Jesus Christ be praised!
Let all the earth around
Ring joyous with the sound,
May Jesus Christ be praised!

Be this, while life is mine,
My canticle divine,
May Jesus Christ be praised!
Be this th' eternal song
Through all the ages long,
May Jesus Christ be praised!

German Hymn (nineteenth century)

Stanzas 1, 2, 4 translated by Edward Caswall (1814-1878)
Stanza 3 translated by Robert Seymour Bridges (1844-1930)

An anonymous German author wrote the fourteen stanzas of this hymn, which was first printed in *Katholisches Gesangbuch* of Würtzburg in 1828. Only six stanzas were originally translated into English. Three of the others begin like this:

"My tongue shall never tire of chanting with the choir, may Jesus Christ be praised!"

"Be this at meals your grace, in every time and place, may Jesus Christ be praised!"

"And at your work rejoice, to sing with heart and voice, may Jesus Christ be praised!"

The author was pointing out that our praise to God should not be limited to church services, but should overflow to our homes and places of work.

The hymn was probably written in the lovely Franconia section of Germany, the home of fairy-tale castles, deep green forests, and lovely mountain ranges.

• • • •

So whether you eat or drink, or whatever you do, do it all for the glory of God. Don't give offense to Jews or Gentiles or the church of God. I, too, try to please everyone in everything I do. I don't just do what is best for me; I do what is best for others so that many may be saved. And you should imitate me, just as I imitate Christ.

I CORINTHIANS 10:31—11:1

Lord of All Being, Throned Afar

Oliver Wendell Holmes went to Harvard University to study law but ended up studying medicine. His fame, however, came from his literary efforts. After writing "Old Ironsides" at the age of twenty-one and launching *The Autocrat of the Breakfast-Table* series at twenty-two, he quickly gained fame as a writer.

In December 1859, the last of his papers making up *The Professor at the Breakfast-Table* appeared. He concluded with these words: "And so my year's record is finished. . . . Peace to all such as may have been vexed in spirit by any utterance the pages have repeated. They will doubtless forget for the moment the difference in the lines . . . and join in singing this hymn to the source of the light we all need to lead us."

Then he printed this hymn, which has been called "the finest statement of God's omnipresence in the English language."

• • • •

Since we are receiving a Kingdom that is unshakable, let us be thankful and please God by worshiping him with holy fear and awe. For our God is a devouring fire.

HEBREWS 12:28-29

Lord of all being, throned afar,
Thy glory flames from sun and star;
Center and soul of every sphere,
Yet to each loving heart how near!

Sun of our life, Thy quickening ray
Sheds on our path the glow of day;
Star of our hope, Thy softened light
Cheers the long watches of the night.

Our midnight is Thy smile withdrawn;
Our noontide is Thy gracious dawn;
Our rainbow arch Thy mercy's sign;
All, save the clouds of sin, are Thine!

Lord of all life, below, above,
Whose light is truth, whose warmth is love,
Before Thy ever-blazing throne
We ask no luster of our own.

Grant us Thy truth to make us free,
And kindling hearts that burn for Thee;
Till all Thy living altars claim
One holy light, one heavenly flame.

Oliver Wendell Holmes (1809-1894)

Of the Father's Love Begotten

Of the Father's love begotten,
Ere the worlds began to be,
He is Alpha and Omega,
He the source, the ending He;
Of the things that are, that have been,
And that future years shall see,
Evermore and evermore.

O ye heights of heaven, adore Him;
Angel hosts, His praises sing;
Powers, dominions, bow before Him,
And extol our God and King;
Let no tongue on earth be silent,
Every voice in concert ring,
Evermore and evermore.

Christ, to Thee with God the Father,
And, O Holy Ghost, to Thee,
Hymn and chant and high thanksgiving,
And unwearied praises be:
Honor, glory, and dominion,
And eternal victory,
Evermore and evermore.

Aurelius Clemens Prudentius (348-c. 413)

*Translated by John Mason Neale (1818-1866)
and Henry W. Baker (1821-1877)*

Since its inception, the church has been troubled by heresy. One of the most enduring heresies has been Arianism, which teaches that Jesus is not God by nature but gained His divinity because God the Father foresaw His righteous life. This heresy was condemned at the Council of Nicaea in 325, but to this day it persists in many different forms.

Aurelius Prudentius, a Spaniard by birth, lived at a time when Arianism was still in its infancy. In this hymn he presents a poetic defense for an orthodox confession of Jesus' divinity and coeternal relationship with God the Father. We can be thankful for God's many faithful saints throughout history who, like Prudentius, have passed on to us the true Christian faith.

• • • •

Through [Christ] God created everything in the heavenly realms and on earth. He made the things we can see and the things we can't see—such as thrones, kingdoms, rulers, and authorities in the unseen world. Everything was created through him and for him. He existed before anything else, and he holds all creation together. Christ is also the head of the church, which is his body. He is the beginning, supreme over all who rise from the dead. So he is first in everything.
COLOSSIANS 1:16-18

Praise to the Lord, the Almighty

As a student in Bremen, Germany, Joachim Neander lived a godless life. Then, when Neander was twenty, a preacher named Under-Eyke came to Bremen, and Neander was converted.

Four years later he became headmaster of a school in Düsseldorf, and during his time there he wrote more than sixty hymns. Because of his strong Christian views and his evangelistic activities, he displeased the authorities and was eventually removed from his position.

Despite the tensions, he wrote many hymns of praise. He often wandered through the valleys and hills near Düsseldorf, communing with his Lord. After losing his position at the school, he lived for a time in a cave and continued to write hymns. He died very young, at the age of thirty, but he left behind him a legacy of praise to God.

• • • •

Let all that I am praise the Lord; with my whole heart, I will praise his holy name. Let all that I am praise the Lord; may I never forget the good things he does for me.

PSALM 103:1-2

Praise to the Lord, the Almighty,
the King of creation!
O my soul, praise Him,
for He is thy health and salvation!
All ye who hear, now to His temple draw near;
Join me in glad adoration!

Praise to the Lord, who o'er all things
so wondrously reigneth,
Shieldeth thee under His wings,
yea, so gently sustaineth!
Hast thou not seen how thy
desires e'er have been
Granted in what He ordaineth?

Praise to the Lord, who doth prosper
thy work and defend thee;
Surely His goodness and mercy
here daily attend thee.
Ponder anew what the Almighty can do,
If with His love He befriend thee.

Praise to the Lord!
O let all that is in me adore Him!
All that hath life and breath,
come now with praises before Him!
Let the amen sound from His people again;
Gladly forever adore Him.

Joachim Neander (1650-1680)

Translated by Catherine Winkworth (1827-1878)

215

Before Thy Throne, O God, We Kneel

Before Thy throne, O God, we kneel;
Give us a conscience quick to feel,
A ready mind to understand
The meaning of Thy chastening hand;
Whate'er the pain and shame may be,
Bring us, O Father, nearer Thee.

Search out our hearts and make us true;
Wishful to give to all their due.
From love of pleasure, lust of gold,
From sins which make the heart grow cold,
Wean us and train us with Thy rod;
Teach us to know our faults, O God.

For sins of heedless word and deed,
For pride, ambitious to succeed,
For crafty trade and subtle snare
To catch the simple unaware,
For lives bereft of purpose high,
Forgive, forgive, O Lord, we cry.

Let the fierce fires which burn and try
Our inmost spirits purify:
Consume the ill; purge out the shame;
O God, be with us in the flame;
A newborn people may we rise,
More pure, more true, more nobly wise.

William Boyd Carpenter (1841–1918)

William Boyd Carpenter, bishop of Rixon, England, wrote this hymn for Christians whose consciences needed tenderizing. It is much like the words of the psalmist in Psalm 139:23: "Search me, O God, and know my heart." There is so much packed into this hymn of confession that it is difficult to sing. It is better to meditate upon it phrase by phrase.

Our lives become so busy that we lose track of sins that are accepted as normal by our society. Bishop Carpenter speaks of our need to be delivered "from love of pleasure, lust of gold, from sins which make the heart grow cold." We need to take time to kneel humbly before our holy God, to search our hearts before Him, and to ask Him to "give us a conscience quick to feel."

• • • •

Create in me a clean heart, O God. Renew a loyal spirit within me. Do not banish me from your presence, and don't take your Holy Spirit from me. Restore to me the joy of your salvation, and make me willing to obey you. Then I will teach your ways to rebels, and they will return to you.

PSALM 51:10-13

Day Is Dying in the West

"Remember, my child, that you have a gift of weaving fancies into verse and a gift with the pencil of producing visions that come to your heart; consecrate these to Me as thoroughly as you do your inmost spirit." That was what God seemed to be saying to Mary Lathbury, an artist by training, a teacher of art by profession.

She is regarded as one of the founders of the Chautauqua movement, which began as a Christian summer conference on Lake Chautauqua in western New York. The movement spread across the country, providing both Christian education and cultural development to thousands of believers.

At Chautauqua in 1877, Lathbury was asked to write an appropriate evening hymn for the conference. As she sat watching the sun disappear behind the trees, she was inspired to write the first two stanzas of this hymn. The third and fourth stanzas were written two years later.

● ● ● ●

You made the moon to mark the seasons, and the sun knows when to set. You send the darkness, and it becomes night.

PSALM 104:19-20

Day is dying in the west;
Heaven is touching earth with rest;
Wait and worship while the night
Sets her evening lamps alight
Through all the sky.

Holy, holy, holy, Lord God of Hosts!
Heaven and earth are full of Thee!
Heaven and earth are praising Thee,
O Lord most high!

Lord of life, beneath the dome
Of the universe, Thy home,
Gather us who seek Thy face
To the fold of Thy embrace,
For Thou art nigh.

While the deepening shadows fall,
Heart of love enfolding all,
Through the glory and the grace
Of the stars that veil Thy face,
Our hearts ascend.

When forever from our sight
Pass the stars, the day, the night,
Lord of angels, on our eyes
Let eternal morning rise
And shadows end.

Mary Artemisia Lathbury (1841–1913)

Grace! 'Tis a Charming Sound

Grace! 'tis a charming sound,
Harmonious to the ear;
Heaven with the echo shall resound,
And all the earth shall hear.

Grace first contrived the way
To save rebellious man;
And all the steps that grace display
Which drew the wondrous plan.

Grace led my roving feet
To tread the heavenly road;
And new supplies each hour I meet,
While pressing on to God.

Grace all the work shall crown,
Through everlasting days;
It lays in heaven the topmost stone,
And well deserves the praise.

Philip Doddridge (1702–1751)

Grace led Philip Doddridge to take some surprising steps in his life. He was a gifted student, but he turned down a scholarship to train for ministry in the Church of England. He chose instead to side with the Dissenters, the Nonconformists who emphasized personal commitment to Christ over institutional loyalty. He went to a Dissenter college, and later he pastored a Congregational church. He wrote about 370 hymns, never seeing any of them published in his lifetime.

Grace sometimes works like that, too. In His goodness, God may grant us anonymity. He may delay the rewards of public acclaim until after we die. This hymn conveys the author's strong awareness of heaven—the place where God's grace is most at home. On earth, grace is the faint underscoring of our lives. In heaven it echoes through the halls!

• • • •

God saved you by his grace when you believed. And you can't take credit for this; it is a gift from God. Salvation is not a reward for the good things we have done, so none of us can boast about it.

EPHESIANS 2:8-9

O Love Divine, That Stooped to Share

A professor of anatomy at Harvard Medical School, Oliver Wendell Holmes was highly regarded both as a pioneer researcher and as a teacher. One day in class, he held up a portion of a skeleton and said, "These, gentlemen, are the bones on which Providence destined man to sit and view the works of creation."

As a member of the elite Saturday Club, he met regularly with brilliant men like Emerson, Longfellow, Lowell, and Agassiz, and together they sharpened their wits. With a few words, Holmes could cut to the heart of any matter.

So this poet-scientist, this humorist-philosopher, wrote a perceptive hymn about God's great love that "stooped to share." As a scientist, he recognized the God of creation, but he also knew of a God who shares our burdens and in our pain tells us that He is near and that He loves us.

O Love divine, that stooped to share
Our sharpest pang, our bitterest tear,
On Thee we cast each earthborn care;
We smile at pain while Thou art near.

Though long the weary way we tread,
And sorrow crown each lingering year,
No path we shun, no darkness dread,
Our hearts still whispering, "Thou art near!"

When drooping pleasure turns to grief,
And trembling faith is changed to fear,
The murmuring wind, the quivering leaf
Shall softly tell us Thou art near!

On Thee we fling our burdening woe,
O Love divine, forever dear,
Content to suffer while we know,
Living and dying, Thou art near!

Oliver Wendell Holmes (1809-1894)

• • • •

Now you have been united with Christ Jesus. Once you were far away from God, but now you have been brought near to him through the blood of Christ.
EPHESIANS 2:13

Lo! He Comes, with Clouds Descending

Lo! He comes, with clouds descending,
Once for favored sinners slain;
Thousand, thousand saints attending
Swell the triumph of His train;
Hallelujah! Hallelujah! Hallelujah!
God appears on earth to reign,
God appears on earth to reign.

Every eye shall now behold Him,
Robed in dreadful majesty;
Those who set at naught and sold Him,
Pierced and nailed Him to the tree,
Deeply wailing, deeply wailing, deeply wailing,
Shall the true Messiah see,
Shall the true Messiah see.

The dear tokens of His passion
Still His dazzling body bears;
Cause of endless exultation
To His ransomed worshipers;
With what rapture, with what rapture,
with what rapture,
Gaze we on those glorious scars!
Gaze we on those glorious scars!

Yea, Amen! Let all adore Thee,
High on Thy eternal throne;
Savior, take the power and glory,
Claim the kingdom for Thine own;
Hallelujah! Hallelujah! Hallelujah!
Everlasting God, come down!
Everlasting God, come down!

Charles Wesley (1707–1788)

This hymn was truly a team effort. The original version was penned by John Cennick, a land surveyor from Reading, England, who became a Moravian preacher. Hymnwriter Charles Wesley adapted the Cennick version, and then it was finished by two of Wesley's followers. One of them was Thomas Olivers, who had been a London cobbler; the other was Martin Madan, who loved to embellish Wesley's hymns and probably added the *hallelujahs*.

As we await the coming of our Lord, about which this hymn is written, God's Kingdom continues to grow just as this hymn once grew. Preachers, cobblers, land surveyors, and those who embellish with *hallelujahs* build on one another's efforts for the glory of God. They are just a few of the "thousand, thousand saints attending."

• • • •

Look! He comes with the clouds of heaven. And everyone will see him—even those who pierced him. And all the nations of the world will mourn for him. Yes! Amen!
REVELATION 1:7

Almighty God, Thy Word Is Cast

In our day God's Word goes forth in many different ways, in ways that John Cawood would never have imagined. It is broadcast on radio and TV, produced in movies and recordings, and it is available in just about any translation on your computer or phone. God's Word is cast in many new ways, but hearts still need to be ready to receive it.

Our own hearts need to be tilled like good soil for the truth that God is casting there. That is why many Christians observe a "quiet time" in their personal Bible reading. It's not just a verse or two grabbed on the run, but a seed received, planted, surrounded with the soil of prayer. Why not memorize the first stanza of this hymn and pray it each time you ponder the Scriptures?

• • • •

A farmer went out to plant some seeds. As he scattered them across his field, some seeds fell on a footpath. . . . Other seeds fell on shallow soil. . . . Other seeds fell among thorns that grew up and choked out the tender plants. Still other seeds fell on fertile soil, and they produced a crop that was thirty, sixty, and even a hundred times as much as had been planted!

MATTHEW 13:3-5, 7-8

Almighty God, Thy word is cast
Like seed into the ground;
Now let the dew of heav'n descend
And righteous fruits abound.

Let not the foe of Christ and man
This holy seed remove,
But give it root in ev'ry heart,
To bring forth fruits of love.

Let not the world's deceitful cares
The rising plant destroy,
But let it yield a hundredfold
The fruits of peace and joy.

Oft as the precious seed is sown,
Thy quick'ning grace bestow,
That all whose souls the truth receive
Its saving pow'r may know.

John Cawood (1775–1852)

O Word of God Incarnate

O Word of God incarnate, O Wisdom from on high,
O Truth unchanged, unchanging,
O Light of our dark sky:
We praise Thee for the radiance
that from the hallowed page,
A lantern to our footsteps, shines on from age to age.

The Church from Thee, her Master,
received the gift divine,
And still that light she lifteth o'er all the earth to shine,
It is the sacred casket where gems of truth are stored;
It is the heaven-drawn picture of Thee, the living Word.

It floateth like a banner before God's host unfurled;
It shineth like a beacon above the darkling world.
It is the chart and compass that o'er life's surging sea,
Mid mists and rocks and quicksands,
still guides, O Christ, to Thee.

O make Thy Church, dear Savior, a lamp of purest gold,
To bear before the nations Thy true light as of old.
O teach Thy wandering pilgrims
by this their path to trace,
Till, clouds and darkness ended,
they see Thee face to face.

William Walsham How (1823–1897)

There was a down-to-earth simplicity about William Walsham How. He served a rural congregation on the Welsh border for twenty-eight years and then ministered in London's East End. He loved children and wrote hymns for them. One of them began like this: "It is a thing most wonderful, almost too wonderful to be, that God's own Son should come from heaven, and die to save a child like me."

William How also loved the Bible. On his symbolic pastoral staff, he engraved the words of St. Bernard: "*Pasce verbo, Pasce vita,*" which means "Feed with the Word, feed with the Life." So it is not surprising that he should write a hymn of praise to God's Word.

• • • •

Teach me your decrees, O Lord; I will keep them to the end. Give me understanding and I will obey your instructions; I will put them into practice with all my heart. Make me walk along the path of your commands, for that is where my happiness is found. Give me an eagerness for your laws rather than a love for money! Turn my eyes from worthless things, and give me life through your word.

PSALM 119:33-37

All Praise to Our Redeeming Lord

William Barclay once wrote that a person needs to have three conversions: first, to God; second, to other Christians; and third, to the world. Certainly there are these three crucial aspects to our faith—worship, fellowship, and ministry. Charles Wesley, the prolific Methodist hymnwriter, wrote widely on all three sides of this sacred triangle.

We have probably all noticed that many churches emphasize one of these aspects to the exclusion of the others. Some focus on personal growth or outreach, but never develop a "body life" in which Christians get to know and love each other. Others are so absorbed in Christian fellowship that they never do anything to reach out to others.

As usual, Wesley's words are rooted in Scripture. The New Testament continually weaves these three threads of Christian life together.

• • • •

He has given each one of us a special gift through the generosity of Christ. . . . Now these are the gifts Christ gave to the church: the apostles, the prophets, the evangelists, and the pastors and teachers. Their responsibility is to equip God's people to do his work and build up the church, the body of Christ.

EPHESIANS 4:7, 11-12

All praise to our redeeming Lord,
Who joins us by His grace,
And bids us, each to each restored,
Together seek His face.

The gift which He on one bestows,
We all delight to prove,
The grace through every vessel flows
In purest streams of love.

He bids us build each other up;
And, gathered into one,
To our high calling's glorious hope,
We hand in hand go on.

We all partake the joy of one;
The common peace we feel:
A peace to sensual minds unknown,
A joy unspeakable.

And if our fellowship below
In Jesus be so sweet,
What height of rapture shall we know
When round His throne we meet!

Charles Wesley (1707-1788)

Where Cross the Crowded Ways of Life

Where cross the crowded ways of life,
Where sound the cries of race and clan,
Above the noise of selfish strife,
We hear Thy voice, O Son of man!

In haunts of wretchedness and need,
On shadowed thresholds dark with fears,
From paths where hide the lures of greed,
We catch the vision of Thy tears.

From tender childhood's helplessness,
From woman's grief, man's burdened toil,
From famished souls, from sorrow's stress
Thy heart has never known recoil.

The cup of water given for Thee
Still holds the freshness of Thy grace;
Yet long these multitudes to see
The sweet compassion of Thy face.

O Master, from the mountainside,
Make haste to heal these hearts of pain;
Among these restless throngs abide,
O tread the city's streets again.

Till sons of men shall learn Thy love
And follow where Thy feet have trod;
Till, glorious from Thy heaven above,
Shall come the city of our God!

Frank Mason North (1850–1935)

"I'm not a hymnwriter!" Frank Mason North protested when he was asked to write a hymn on a missionary theme for the Methodist hymnal. He was a New York City man. He had been born there and had served as a pastor there. In 1903 he was an officer of both the New York City Mission and the National City Evangelical Mission.

North realized that the city was a great mission field. He decided to write about the city as he saw it, about "haunts of wretchedness" and "shadowed thresholds dark with fears." He wrote of Wall Street–like paths that "hide the lures of greed."

North's stirring words were published first by the Methodist City Missionary Society and later appeared in the Methodist hymnal. Let us listen to this challenge to bring Christ's loving presence to the streets of our cities.

• • • •

Come, you who are blessed by my Father, inherit the Kingdom prepared for you from the creation of the world. For I was hungry, and you fed me. I was thirsty, and you gave me a drink. I was a stranger, and you invited me into your home. I was naked, and you gave me clothing. I was sick, and you cared for me. I was in prison, and you visited me.

MATTHEW 25:34-36

Happy the Home When God Is There

On a television show, two ministers disagreed over the influence of the media on children. But then the host skeptically asked, "Can a three-year-old really know anything about Jesus?" Suddenly the ministers were in complete agreement. "Yes!" said both; and one added, "My children learned early on that Jesus loved them."

Christians may have serious debates over how we should relate to the world around us. But let us all agree on this: Let us teach our children early that Jesus loves them. Let them "lisp His fame" from an early age.

As this hymn indicates, this is done not through indoctrination, but by example. When parents exhibit a genuine love for the Lord, children will see and learn. They will still have to make their own choices, but at least they will have lived in a home where God was an important part of the family.

Happy the home when God is there,
And love fills every breast;
When one their wish, and one their prayer,
And one their heavenly rest.

Happy the home where Jesus' name
Is sweet to every ear;
Where children early lisp His fame,
And parents hold Him dear.

Happy the home where prayer is heard,
And praise is wont to rise;
Where parents love the sacred Word
And all its wisdom prize.

Lord, let us in our homes agree
This blessed peace to gain;
Unite our hearts in love to Thee,
And love to all will reign.

Henry Ware, Jr. (1794–1843)

• • • •

Commit yourselves wholeheartedly to these commands that I am giving you today. Repeat them again and again to your children. Talk about them when you are at home and when you are on the road, when you are going to bed and when you are getting up.

DEUTERONOMY 6:6-7

Blest Be the Tie That Binds

Blest be the tie that binds
Our hearts in Christian love:
The fellowship of kindred minds
Is like to that above.

Before our Father's throne
We pour our ardent prayers;
Our fears, our hopes, our aims are one,
Our comforts and our cares.

We share each other's woes,
Our mutual burdens bear,
And often for each other flows
The sympathizing tear.

When we asunder part,
It gives us inward pain;
But we shall still be joined in heart,
And hope to meet again.

John Fawcett (1740-1817)

Orphaned when he was twelve, then forced to work fourteen hours a day in a sweatshop, John Fawcett learned to read by candlelight. He was converted at sixteen under the preaching of George Whitefield, and he was ordained a Baptist minister at the age of twenty-five. He began his ministry at a poor church in Wainsgate in northern England. The small congregation could only afford to pay him a minimal salary, partly in potatoes and wool.

After seven years of ministry, Fawcett received a call to the prestigious Carter's Lane Church in London. But as he was saying his farewells and saw the tears on the faces of his people, he changed his mind and decided to stay.

Not long afterward, he wrote this hymn for the congregation at Wainsgate. He recognized that the bond of love he knew there was worth more than any material wealth.

• • • •

Make every effort to keep yourselves united in the Spirit, binding yourselves together with peace. For there is one body and one Spirit, just as you have been called to one glorious hope for the future. There is one Lord, one faith, one baptism, one God and Father.

EPHESIANS 4:3-6

The Church's One Foundation

Windsor on the Thames, with its royal castle, is one of England's most popular tourist attractions. Samuel Stone's ministry was located here, among the poorer people at the outskirts of town.

Samuel Stone was a fighter. He stood up for what he believed, and if local "toughs" threatened the neighborhood, he was not afraid to take them on. In the Church of England, Stone was regarded as a fundamentalist, opposing the liberal theological tendencies of his day. When he was twenty-seven, he wrote a collection of hymns based on the Apostles' Creed. This hymn, taken from that collection, is based on the article in the Creed regarding the church as the body of Christ.

Two years later, Anglicans from around the world met to discuss the crucial theological issues that were raging in the church. Significantly, they chose Stone's hymn as the processional for their historic conference.

• • • •

Together, we are his house, built on the foundation of the apostles and the prophets. And the cornerstone is Christ Jesus himself.

EPHESIANS 2:20

The Church's one foundation is Jesus Christ her Lord;
She is His new creation by water and the word.
From heaven He came and
sought her to be His holy bride;
With His own blood He bought her,
and for her life He died.

Elect from every nation, yet one o'er all the earth,
Her charter of salvation, one Lord,
one faith, one birth;
One holy name she blesses, partakes one holy food,
And to one hope she presses,
with every grace endued.

Mid toil and tribulation, and tumult of her war,
She waits the consummation of peace forevermore;
Till, with the vision glorious, her longing eyes are blest,
And the great Church victorious
shall be the Church at rest.

Yet she on earth hath union
with God the Three in One,
And mystic sweet communion
with those whose rest is won.
O happy ones and holy! Lord, give us grace that we,
Like them, the meek and lowly,
on high may dwell with Thee.

Samuel John Stone (1839-1900)

I Love Thy Kingdom, Lord

I love Thy kingdom, Lord,
The house of Thine abode,
The Church our blest Redeemer saved
With His own precious blood.

I love Thy Church, O God!
Her walls before Thee stand
Dear as the apple of Thine eye,
And graven on Thy hand.

For her my tears shall fall,
For her my prayers ascend,
To her my cares and toils be given,
Till toils and cares shall end.

Beyond my highest joy
I prize her heavenly ways,
Her sweet communion, solemn vows,
Her hymns of love and praise.

Sure as Thy truth shall last,
To Zion shall be given
The brightest glories earth can yield,
And brighter bliss of heaven.

Timothy Dwight (1752–1817)

Like his grandfather, theologian Jonathan Edwards, Timothy Dwight was a brilliant scholar. He could read Latin when he was six, graduated from Yale at seventeen, began teaching there at nineteen, and wrote his first book at twenty.

He enlisted in the Continental Army in 1777 as a chaplain, where he became known for writing songs to encourage the troops. After the Revolutionary War, he served as a pastor in Connecticut. Finally, in 1795, he accepted the trustees' invitation to become president of Yale.

When Dwight returned to Yale, there were probably as few as five professing Christians on campus. But with Dwight came a new spiritual emphasis, and revival soon swept over the university. This hymn, written during the revivals at Yale, is the earliest American hymn in use today.

• • • •

God has given me the responsibility of serving his church by proclaiming his entire message to you. This message was kept secret for centuries and generations past, but now it has been revealed to God's people.
COLOSSIANS 1:25-26

Blest Be the Dear Uniting Love

J. B. Gough, a famous nineteenth-century American orator, tells the story of how he left England when he was only twelve to come to America. His parents were poor and unable to apprentice him to learn a trade. So they sent him to America with neighbors who were emigrating there.

While in America, he strayed from his parents' faith. Though he was able to make money, he was a spiritual pauper. But he could not forget his mother who was "poor in purse, but rich in piety." He could not forget the Christian friends who had sung "Blest Be the Dear Uniting Love" as he left them. And he could not forget a Bible verse his mother had taught him—"He is able, once and forever, to save those who come to God through him" (Hebrews 7:25).

"Is there salvation even for me?" Gough asked. Then he said to himself the first three words of the Bible verse: "He is able. . . ."

Blest be the dear uniting love
That will not let us part;
Our bodies may far off remove,
We still are one in heart.

Joined in one spirit to our Head,
Where He appoints we go;
And still in Jesus' footsteps tread,
And show His praise below.

O may we ever walk in Him,
And nothing know beside,
Nothing desire, nothing esteem,
But Jesus crucified!

Partakers of the Savior's grace,
The same in mind and heart,
Nor joy, nor grief, nor time, nor place,
Nor life, nor death can part.

Charles Wesley (1707-1788)

• • • •

Is there any encouragement from belonging to Christ? Any comfort from his love? Any fellowship together in the Spirit? Are your hearts tender and compassionate? Then make me truly happy by agreeing wholeheartedly with each other, loving one another, and working together with one mind and purpose.

PHILIPPIANS 2:1-2

Jesus, Thy Boundless Love to Me

Jesus, Thy boundless love to me
No thought can reach, no tongue declare;
O knit my thankful heart to Thee,
And reign without a rival there!
Thine wholly, Thine alone, I'd live,
Myself to Thee entirely give.

O Love, how cheering is thy ray!
All fear before thy presence flies;
Care, anguish, sorrow melt away,
Where'er thy healing beams arise:
O Jesus, nothing may I see,
Nothing desire, or seek, but Thee!

In suffering be Thy love my peace;
In weakness be Thy love my power;
And when the storms of life shall cease,
O Jesus, in that solemn hour,
In death as life be Thou my guide,
And save me, who for me hast died.

Paul Gerhardt (1607-1676)

Translated by John Wesley (1703-1791)

Many have noted a similarity between secular love songs and Christian songs about love for God. It is interesting that Paul Gerhardt wrote this hymn near the time of his marriage to a woman he had long loved. He was a theologian with strong convictions, a student and teacher whose plans had long been frustrated by the Thirty Years' War. As a young man he had passionately argued the finer points of Lutheran theology, but with age he had mellowed. His passion turned to the overwhelming love of God. At forty-five, he found a steady job in a small village, married his sweetheart, and began publishing his hymns.

Nearly a century later, John Wesley heard Moravians singing this song in German as he sailed with them to America. Impressed by the rich hymns of the Moravians and by their deep personal devotion, Wesley translated many of their hymns into English.

• • • •

Everything else is worthless when compared with the infinite value of knowing Christ Jesus my Lord. For his sake I have discarded everything else, counting it all as garbage, so that I could gain Christ.
PHILIPPIANS 3:8

Christ Is Made the Sure Foundation

This hymn is drawn from a Latin meditation on the New Jerusalem. Some scholars think the original work may have been used as a dedication for a new church building. But in this translation, John Neale clearly identified the "temple" as the *people* of the church. This is where Christ lives, not in walls of stone, but in the hearts of people whose lives belong to Him.

Neale was a scholar in the Church of England. Though he had poor health, he ran churches, colleges, and charities. But his greatest contribution to the church was in hymnology. He unearthed a treasure trove of ancient Latin and Greek hymns, which he translated for church use. Many are widely sung today. In this way, Neale helped to "bind together" the church, new and old. Though his own body was a frail temple, he used it tirelessly to strengthen that other temple of God, the church.

• • • •

You are living stones that God is building into his spiritual temple. . . . As the Scriptures say, "I am placing a cornerstone in Jerusalem, chosen for great honor, and anyone who trusts in him will never be disgraced."

I PETER 2:5-6

Christ is made the sure foundation,
Christ the head and cornerstone,
Chosen of the Lord and precious,
Binding all the Church in one;
Holy Zion's help forever,
And her confidence alone.

To this temple, where we call Thee,
Come, O Lord of hosts, today!
With Thy wonted loving-kindness
Hear Thy people as they pray;
And Thy fullest benediction
Shed within its walls alway.

Here vouchsafe to all Thy servants
What they ask of Thee to gain:
What they gain from Thee forever
With the blessed to retain,
And hereafter in Thy glory
Evermore with Thee to reign.

Laud and honor to the Father,
Laud and honor to the Son,
Laud and honor to the Spirit,
Ever Three and ever One;
One in might, and One in glory,
While unending ages run.

Latin Hymn (seventh century)

Translated by John Mason Neale (1818–1866)

Come, Ye Sinners, Poor and Needy

Come, ye sinners, poor and needy,
Weak and wounded, sick and sore;
Jesus ready stands to save you,
Full of pity, love, and power;
He is able, He is able,
He is willing; doubt no more.

Now, ye needy, come and welcome;
God's free bounty glorify;
True belief and true repentance,
Every grace that brings you nigh;
Without money, without money,
Come to Jesus Christ and buy.

Let not conscience make you linger,
Nor of fitness fondly dream;
All the fitness He requireth
Is to feel your need of Him:
This He gives you, this He gives you;
'Tis the Spirit's glimmering beam.

Come, ye weary, heavy laden,
Bruised and mangled by the Fall;
If you tarry till you're better,
You will never come at all;
Not the righteous, not the righteous;
Sinners Jesus came to call.

Joseph Hart (1712–1768)

London-born Joseph Hart struggled against God for years. When he attended church, he went to find fault. He responded to a sermon by John Wesley by writing a tract, "The Unreasonableness of Religion." He was (in his own words) a "loose backslider, an audacious apostle, and a bold-faced rebel." Then he came under conviction. At times he was afraid to sleep, fearing he would "awake in hell." He went from church to church, but as he said, "everything served only to condemn me."

Finally at the age of forty-five he wandered into a Moravian chapel in London and heard words of hope. On returning home he knelt in prayer.

Three years later he became a minister and began writing hymns to touch the hearts of others who had experienced similar spiritual struggles.

• • • •

But when the teachers of religious law who were Pharisees saw him eating with tax collectors and other sinners, they asked his disciples, "Why does he eat with such scum?" When Jesus heard this, he told them, "Healthy people don't need a doctor—sick people do. I have come to call not those who think they are righteous, but those who know they are sinners."
MARK 2:16-17

We Give Thee but Thine Own

London's East End housed the slums of the city. That is exactly where William Walsham How wanted to serve. He had worked faithfully as pastor of the Anglican church in his farming village of Whittington for a quarter-century. He repeatedly turned down advancements and opportunities to serve as bishop in such places as South Africa, New Zealand, and Jamaica. He was not a scholar, and some people thought he lacked ambition, but when the opportunity came to serve in London's East End, he took it.

He was known as the poor man's bishop. He rode public buses rather than private coaches. He always did whatever he could to raise funds to alleviate the poverty around him. His ambition was "not to be remembered but to be helpful." He was called "a most unselfish man, with a tender fondness for children."

We give Thee but Thine own,
Whate'er the gift may be:
All that we have is Thine alone,
A trust, O Lord, from Thee.

May we Thy bounties thus
As stewards true receive,
And gladly, as Thou blessest us,
To Thee our first fruits give.

To comfort and to bless,
To find a balm for woe,
To tend the lone and fatherless,
Is angels' work below.

And we believe Thy word,
Though dim our faith may be:
Whate'er for Thine we do, O Lord,
We do it unto Thee.

William Walsham How (1823–1897)

• • • •

God saved you by his grace when you believed. And you can't take credit for this; it is a gift from God. Salvation is not a reward for the good things we have done, so none of us can boast about it. For we are God's masterpiece. He has created us anew in Christ Jesus, so we can do the good things he planned for us long ago.

EPHESIANS 2:8-10

O to Be like Thee!

O to be like Thee! blessed Redeemer,
This is my constant longing and prayer;
Gladly I'll forfeit all of earth's treasures,
Jesus, Thy perfect likeness to wear.

O to be like Thee! O to be like Thee,
Blessed Redeemer, pure as Thou art!
Come in Thy sweetness, come in Thy fullness—
Stamp Thine own image deep on my heart.

O to be like Thee! full of compassion,
Loving, forgiving, tender and kind;
Helping the helpless, cheering the fainting,
Seeking the wand'ring sinner to find.

O to be like Thee! while I am pleading,
Pour out Thy Spirit, fill with Thy love;
Make me a temple meet for Thy dwelling,
Fit me for life and heaven above.

Thomas Obadiah Chisholm (1866-1960)

When people were introduced to Thomas O. Chisholm, the author of this hymn and of "Great Is Thy Faithfulness" (October 15), he would often say, "Aw, I'm just an old shoe!"

Born in a Kentucky log cabin in 1866, Chisholm was self-educated and began teaching in a rural school when he was sixteen. At the age of twenty-seven, the Kentucky farm boy wrote this hymn, "O to Be like Thee!" He served on the staff of the *Pentecostal Herald* in Louisville until his health broke. He was accepted as a traveling preacher in the Methodist church, but once again health problems caused him to resign. Regretfully he had to leave the ministry. Eventually he became a life insurance agent.

Throughout his life he displayed many of the characteristics that he praised in Jesus in the hymns he wrote. Chisholm, who described himself as an old shoe, was perhaps more like Christ than he realized.

• • • •

Dear friends, we are already God's children, but he has not yet shown us what we will be like when Christ appears. But we do know that we will be like him, for we will see him as he really is.

I JOHN 3:2

Love Divine, All Loves Excelling

For most of his life Charles Wesley was a traveling preacher—traveling on horseback. In his pocket he carried little cards on which he scribbled hymns in shorthand as he rode.

When a horse threw him, he wrote in his journal, "My companion thought I had broken my neck; but my leg only was bruised, my hand sprained, and my head stunned, which spoiled my making hymns till the next day."

Although Charles Wesley had been a classical scholar at Oxford, few of his hymns reveal allusions to the classics. However, this one follows the meter of John Dryden's "King Arthur," referring to Camelot: "Fairest Isle, all Isles excelling, Seats of pleasure and of love." King Arthur may have dreamed of Camelot, but as Charles Wesley rode horseback from village to village, his thoughts were on Jesus, the divine love, the joy of heaven.

• • • •

We are eagerly waiting for [the Lord Jesus Christ] to return as our Savior. He will take our weak mortal bodies and change them into glorious bodies like his own, using the same power with which he will bring everything under his control.

PHILIPPIANS 3:20-21

Love divine, all loves excelling,
Joy of heaven, to earth come down;
Fix in us Thy humble dwelling;
All Thy faithful mercies crown!
Jesus, Thou art all compassion,
Pure, unbounded love Thou art;
Visit us with Thy salvation;
Enter every trembling heart.

Breathe, O breathe Thy loving spirit
Into every troubled breast!
Let us all in Thee inherit;
Let us find that second rest.
Take away our bent to sinning;
Alpha and Omega be;
End of faith, as its beginning,
Set our hearts at liberty.

Come, Almighty to deliver,
Let us all Thy life receive;
Suddenly return and never,
Nevermore Thy temples leave.
Thee we would be always blessing,
Serve Thee as Thy hosts above,
Pray and praise Thee without ceasing,
Glory in Thy perfect love.

Finish, then, Thy new creation;
Pure and spotless let us be.
Let us see Thy great salvation
Perfectly restored in Thee:
Changed from glory into glory,
Till in heaven we take our place,
Till we cast our crowns before Thee,
Lost in wonder, love, and praise.

Charles Wesley (1707-1788)

More about Jesus

More about Jesus would I know,
More of His grace to others show,
More of His saving fullness see,
More of His love who died for me.

More, more about Jesus,
More, more about Jesus;
More of His saving fullness see,
More of His love who died for me!

More about Jesus let me learn,
More of His holy will discern;
Spirit of God, my teacher be,
Showing the things of Christ to me.

More about Jesus; in His Word,
Holding communion with my Lord,
Hearing His voice in ev'ry line,
Making each faithful saying mine.

More about Jesus on His throne,
Riches in glory all His own,
More of His kingdom's sure increase,
More of His coming—Prince of Peace.

Eliza Edmunds Hewitt (1851–1920)

Eliza Hewitt wrote this hymn as she was studying the promises of God that had been fulfilled in Jesus Christ. The more she studied, the more excited she became as she saw Scripture fulfilled in every aspect of Christ's life. All of Scripture, she discovered, focused on Jesus Christ.

It is especially significant that Hewitt was so faithfully seeking God at this point in her life. At the time, she was recovering from a severe spinal injury. A schoolteacher, Hewitt had been struck with a heavy slate by one of her students.

Hewitt was never again able to teach in the public schools, but she continued to be involved with Sunday school. There she was able to combine the two great loves of her life: children and Jesus.

• • • •

May God give you more and more grace and peace as you grow in your knowledge of God and Jesus our Lord.

2 PETER 1:2

Art Thou Weary, Art Thou Languid?

John Neale specialized in discovering old Greek and Latin hymns and translating or paraphrasing them. This hymn was inspired by the life and writings of a Greek monk who lived in the Mar Sabas monastery near the Dead Sea.

In the seventh century, Islam had overrun the Middle East and North Africa. Many Christians fled to desolate areas, where monasteries were set up. Stephen the Sebaite was one of these. At Mar Sabas, he became choirmaster for a community of monks and composed a hymn, on which this one is based.

The beauty of the hymn lies in the contrast between the first couplet of each stanza (our human question or concern) and the second (Christ's divine answer). The questions posed by this ancient hymn are still relevant today—and the answers, still true.

• • • •

Come to me, all of you who are weary and carry heavy burdens, and I will give you rest. Take my yoke upon you. Let me teach you, because I am humble and gentle at heart, and you will find rest for your souls. For my yoke is easy to bear, and the burden I give you is light.

MATTHEW 11:28-30

Art thou weary, art thou languid,
Art thou sore distressed?
"Come to me," saith One, "and, coming,
Be at rest."

Hath He marks to lead me to Him,
If He be my guide?
In His feet and hands are wound prints,
And His side.

Hath He diadem, as monarch,
That His brow adorns?
Yea, a crown, in very surety,
But of thorns.

If I find Him, if I follow,
What His guerdon here?
Many a sorrow, many a labor,
Many a tear.

If I still hold closely to Him,
What hath He at last?
Sorrow vanquished, labor ended,
Jordan passed.

If I ask Him to receive me,
Will He say me nay?
Not till earth and not till heaven
Pass away.

Finding, following, keeping, struggling,
Is He sure to bless?
Saints, apostles, prophets, martyrs,
Answer yes.

Stephen the Sebaite (734-794)

Translated by John Mason Neale (1818-1866)

O for a Heart to Praise My God

O for a heart to praise my God,
A heart from sin set free,
A heart that always feels Thy blood
So freely shed for me;

A heart resigned, submissive, meek,
My great Redeemer's throne,
Where only Christ is heard to speak,
Where Jesus reigns alone;

A humble, lowly, contrite heart,
Believing, true, and clean,
Which neither life nor death can part
From Him that dwells within;

A heart in every thought renewed
And full of love divine,
Perfect and right and pure and good,
A copy, Lord, of Thine:

Thy nature, gracious Lord, impart;
Come quickly from above;
Write Thy new name upon my heart,
Thy new, best name of Love.

Charles Wesley (1707–1788)

It is not surprising that John and Charles Wesley should be concerned about the human heart. After all, they had gone through the motions of a heartless Christianity for years. It was not enough, they discovered, for a person to be religious, moral, and orthodox. They had been all that—as ordained clergymen, they knew the gospel well. But their hearts still had to be changed by an encounter with God's Word. Suddenly they saw the necessity of a personal faith that would change the heart.

This hymn, written by Charles Wesley less than four years after his conversion, is based on Psalm 51:10, "Create in me a clean heart, O God." He knew as well as anybody that that was the only way he could truly be what God wanted him to be.

• • • •

And I will give them singleness of heart and put a new spirit within them. I will take away their stony, stubborn heart and give them a tender, responsive heart, so they will obey my decrees and regulations. Then they will truly be my people, and I will be their God.

EZEKIEL 11:19-20

Lord, It Belongs Not to My Care

From this hymn and the books he wrote, like *The Saints' Everlasting Rest*, it would be easy to assume that Richard Baxter was a docile gentleman who lived quietly in a British country manor. But that was far from the case for this seventeenth-century English clergyman.

At the age of seventy, Baxter was brought before a judge and accused of writing a paraphrase of the New Testament. The judge called him "an old rogue, a hypocritical villain, a fanatical dog, and a sniveling Presbyterian." He proceeded to have Baxter whipped and jailed in the Tower of London.

This hymn was written as an expansion of Philippians 1:21—"For to me, living means living for Christ, and dying is even better." It was dedicated to Baxter's wife, who had died a few years earlier after a long and painful illness. Baxter's life was full of constant struggle, but he was content to leave matters in the hands of the Lord.

Lord, it belongs not to my care
 Whether I die or live;
To love and serve Thee is my share,
 And this Thy grace must give.

If life be long, I will be glad
 That I may long obey;
If short, yet why should I be sad
 To soar to endless day?

Christ leads me through no darker rooms
 Than He went through before;
He that into God's kingdom comes
 Must enter by this door.

Come, Lord, when grace hath made me meet
 Thy blessed face to see;
For if Thy work on earth be sweet,
 What will Thy glory be?

My knowledge of that life is small;
 The eye of faith is dim;
But 'tis enough that Christ knows all,
 And I shall be with Him.

Richard Baxter (1615-1691)

• • • •

I have learned how to be content with whatever I have. I know how to live on almost nothing or with everything. I have learned the secret of living in every situation. . . . For I can do everything through Christ, who gives me strength.

PHILIPPIANS 4:11-13

Breathe on Me, Breath of God

Breathe on me, Breath of God,
Fill me with life anew,
That I may love what Thou dost love,
And do what Thou wouldst do.

Breathe on me, Breath of God,
Until my heart is pure,
Until with Thee I will one will,
To do and to endure.

Breathe on me, Breath of God,
Till I am wholly Thine,
Till all this earthly part of me
Glows with Thy fire divine.

Breathe on me, Breath of God,
So shall I never die,
But live with Thee the perfect life
Of Thine eternity.

Edwin Hatch (1835–1889)

Edwin Hatch was a learned man who could string together sentences filled with many-syllable words. After all, he was a distinguished lecturer in ecclesiastical history at Oxford and a professor of classics at Trinity College in Quebec. His lectures "On the Organization of Early Christian Churches" were translated into German by the noted theologian Harnack. Few other English theologians had won European recognition for original research.

But when it came to expressing his faith, Hatch was "as simple and unaffected as a child." This hymn is filled with one-syllable words and is a simple, heartfelt prayer.

Hatch knew that, while the words of his hymn were simple, the meaning was profound. At man's creation, God breathed and man "became a living being" (Genesis 2:7, NIV). At our re-creation through Jesus, the breath of God brings spiritual life and power.

• • • •

The Spirit of God, who raised Jesus from the dead, lives in you. And just as God raised Christ Jesus from the dead, he will give life to your mortal bodies by this same Spirit living within you.
ROMANS 8:11

Children of the Heavenly King

John Cennick was a most unlikely candidate to become a child of the heavenly King. As he described himself, "My natural temper was obstinate and my lips full of lies." When he was sixteen, God began working in his life, and for two years he struggled with the fear of going to hell. Then at eighteen, he began to see that Christ had accomplished his salvation on the cross. "I believed there was mercy for me. . . . I heard the voice of Jesus saying, 'I am thy salvation.'" Cennick was overwhelmed by joy.

After working as a land surveyor, Cennick became involved with the ministry of the Wesleys and then became a Moravian minister. Perhaps he is best known today for his table grace, "Be present at our table, Lord."

• • • •

Since you have been raised to new life with Christ, set your sights on the realities of heaven, where Christ sits in the place of honor at God's right hand. Think about the things of heaven, not the things of earth.

COLOSSIANS 3:1-2

Children of the heavenly King,
As we journey let us sing;
Sing our Savior's worthy praise,
Glorious in His works and ways.

We are traveling home to God,
In the way our fathers trod;
They are happy now, and we
Soon their happiness shall see.

Fear not, brethren; joyful stand
On the borders of our land;
Jesus Christ, our Father's Son,
Bids us undismayed go on.

Lord, obediently we'll go,
Gladly leaving all below;
Only Thou our leader be,
And we still will follow Thee.

Lift your eyes, ye sons of light,
Zion's city is in sight;
There our endless home shall be,
There our Lord we soon shall see.

John Cennick (1718-1755)

Come, Ye Disconsolate

Come, ye disconsolate, where'er ye languish,
Come to the mercy seat, fervently kneel.
Here bring your wounded hearts,
here tell your anguish:
Earth has no sorrow that heaven cannot heal.

Joy of the desolate, light of the straying,
Hope of the penitent, fadeless and pure!
Here speaks the Comforter, tenderly saying,
"Earth has no sorrow that heaven cannot cure."

Here see the Bread of Life; see waters flowing
Forth from the throne of God, pure from above.
Come to the feast of love; come, ever knowing
Earth has no sorrow but heaven can remove.

Thomas Moore (1779-1852)

Altered by Thomas Hastings (1784-1872)

Irish poet Thomas Moore is best known for his ballads like "The Last Rose of Summer" and "Believe Me if All Those Endearing Young Charms." One writer called Moore "one of the strangest of all men to write hymns." The son of a Dublin grocer, Moore was educated at Trinity College in Dublin, but he could not graduate because he was Roman Catholic. After a short career in government, he devoted himself to writing and became known as the "Voice of Ireland." Many were surprised when Moore published his *Sacred Song-Duets* in 1824.

"Come, Ye Disconsolate," which was originally titled "Relief in Prayer," has undergone some revision since Moore wrote it, but the original version contained the same message.

• • • •

I heard a loud shout from the throne, saying, "Look, God's home is now among his people! He will live with them, and they will be his people. God himself will be with them. He will wipe every tear from their eyes, and there will be no more death or sorrow or crying or pain. All these things are gone forever."

REVELATION 21:3-4

My Jesus, I Love Thee

Sixteen-year-old William Featherston of Montreal wrote this simple hymn shortly after his conversion in 1862. He died before his twenty-seventh birthday, and this is apparently the only hymn he wrote.

Young Featherston sent the poem to his aunt in Los Angeles, who then sent it to England, where it appeared in *The London Hymnbook* of 1864. Back in Boston, Massachusetts, Baptist minister A. J. Gordon was preparing a hymnal for Baptist congregations when he saw "My Jesus, I Love Thee" in the British hymnal. He didn't like the music the words were set to, and he later wrote that "in a moment of inspiration, a beautiful new air sang itself to me." The simple tune he wrote perfectly complemented the simple words, and soon the hymn was being sung across America.

My Jesus, I love Thee, I know Thou art mine—
For Thee all the follies of sin I resign;
My gracious Redeemer, my Savior art Thou:
If ever I loved Thee, my Jesus, 'tis now.

I love Thee because Thou hast first loved me
And purchased my pardon on Calvary's tree;
I love Thee for wearing the thorns on Thy brow:
If ever I loved Thee, my Jesus, 'tis now.

I'll love Thee in life, I will love Thee in death,
And praise Thee as long as Thou lendest me breath;
And say when the death-dew lies cold on my brow,
"If ever I loved Thee, my Jesus, 'tis now."

In mansions of glory and endless delight,
I'll ever adore Thee in heaven so bright;
I'll sing with the glittering crown on my brow,
"If ever I loved Thee, my Jesus, 'tis now."

William Ralph Featherston (1846–1873)

• • • •

This is real love—not that we loved God, but that he loved us and sent his Son as a sacrifice to take away our sins. Dear friends, since God loved us that much, we surely ought to love each other.

I JOHN 4:10-11

We Gather Together

We gather together to ask the Lord's blessing;
He chastens and hastens His will to make known;
The wicked oppressing now cease from distressing,
Sing praises to His name: He forgets not His own.

Beside us to guide us, our God with us joining,
Ordaining, maintaining His kingdom divine;
So from the beginning the fight we were winning:
Thou, Lord, wast at our side, all glory be Thine!

We all do extol Thee, Thou Leader triumphant,
And pray that Thou still our Defender wilt be.
Let Thy congregation escape tribulation:
Thy name be ever praised! O Lord, make us free!

Dutch Folk Hymn

Translated by Theodore Baker (1851-1934)

No one knows who the author of this hymn was, but we can trace it to the Netherlands in the first quarter of the seventeenth century. The Dutch were praying for freedom from Spanish oppression.

This hymn was written to give thanks for the victory that was almost in sight. For these Dutch believers, "the wicked oppressing" were the Spaniards, who would "now cease from distressing." And there was no doubt that God should receive the glory for the victory.

Life is often like that. The victory may still be around the corner, but that should not keep us from giving thanks. For Holland, a golden age of prosperity—of world exploration, of artists like Rembrandt and scientists like Leeuwenhoek—was only a few decades away. And blessings like these are merely a foretaste of what God has for us in the future.

• • • •

May God be merciful and bless us. May his face smile with favor on us. May your ways be known throughout the earth, your saving power among people everywhere.
PSALM 67:1-2

Holy Bible, Book Divine

Sunday schools were introduced to England in 1780 by Robert Raikes, and they quickly spread across the country. There was no public school system, and most children could not read. Many had never even seen a Bible.

One of the first questions that the founders of Sunday schools had to answer was, "What shall we teach?" Some thought it best to have the children memorize catechisms, but Raikes and a young Sunday school teacher named John Burton taught the Bible. And if they needed to teach children to read, then they did that, too.

In 1803, when he was thirty, Burton published this hymn for children in his little book, *Youth's Monitor in Verse, a Series of Tales, Emblems, Poems and Songs.* Three years later he included it in a second book, *Hymns for Sunday Schools.*

Holy Bible, book divine,
Precious treasure, thou art mine;
Mine to tell me whence I came;
Mine to teach me what I am.

Mine to chide me when I rove;
Mine to show a Savior's love;
Mine thou art to guide and guard;
Mine to punish or reward.

Mine to comfort in distress,
Suff'ring in this wilderness;
Mine to show, by living faith,
Man can triumph over death.

Mine to tell of joys to come,
And the rebel sinner's doom;
O thou Holy Book divine,
Precious treasure, thou art mine.

John Burton (1773-1822)

• • • •

All Scripture is inspired by God and is useful to teach us what is true and to make us realize what is wrong in our lives. It corrects us when we are wrong and teaches us to do what is right. God uses it to prepare and equip his people to do every good work.
2 TIMOTHY 3:16-17

Approach, My Soul, the Mercy Seat

Approach, my soul, the mercy seat
Where Jesus answers prayer;
There humbly fall before His feet,
For none can perish there.

Thy promise is my only plea;
With this I venture nigh:
Thou callest burdened souls to Thee,
And such, O Lord, am I.

Bowed down beneath a load of sin,
By Satan sorely pressed
By war without, and fears within,
I come to Thee for rest.

Be Thou my shield and hiding place
That, sheltered near Thy side,
I may my fierce accuser face
And tell him Thou hast died.

O wondrous love! to bleed and die,
To bear the cross and shame,
That guilty sinners, such as I,
Might plead Thy gracious Name!

John Newton (1725-1807)

"Keep your relationship with God honest and personal," John Newton would say. He always remembered the days when he was a slave trader, living a debauched life. After his conversion, he lived in constant amazement that God could love him. The well-known hymn "Amazing Grace" (March 17) is his personal testimony.

When Newton became a minister, he started writing hymns. He never considered himself a poet, but he often wrote hymns for his midweek Bible study and prayer service. This was probably one of those hymns.

Newton frequently used the pronoun *I* in his hymns, reflecting his deep and personal relationship with God. He often expressed his personal questions and fears, as he does in this hymn. In his prayer life, Newton regularly struggled with the doubts thrown at him by Satan, but he knew that he belonged to Christ and that ultimately Christ was the Victor.

• • • •

Since we have a great High Priest who has entered heaven, Jesus the Son of God, let us hold firmly to what we believe. . . . Let us come boldly to the throne of our gracious God. There we will receive his mercy, and we will find grace to help us when we need it most.

HEBREWS 4:14, 16

I've Found a Friend, O Such a Friend

Sometimes the buddy-buddy approach to Christianity causes our concept of God's holiness to be diminished. But when Christ's friendship is depicted as James Small depicts it here, Christ is exalted.

Small was a minister in the Scottish Free church who loved to write hymns. His first book was *Hymns for Youthful Voices*, published in 1859. This hymn, originally called "Jesus the Friend," was published four years later in *The Revival Hymnbook*.

The hymn is full of great theological truths. From our standpoint, we sing, "I've found a Friend," but the truth is "He loved me ere I knew him," and "He drew me with the cords of love." Obviously it is Jesus who initiates this friendship. The final stanza concludes with lines that recall Romans 8:35: "Who shall separate us from the love of Christ?" (NKJV). Small concludes, "I am His forever." Such a Friend is truly worth singing about!

• • • •

There is no greater love than to lay down one's life for one's friends. You are my friends if you do what I command. I no longer call you slaves, because a master doesn't confide in his slaves. Now you are my friends, since I have told you everything the Father told me.

JOHN 15:13-15

I've found a Friend, O such a Friend!
　He loved me ere I knew Him;
　He drew me with the cords of love,
　And thus He bound me to Him.
And round my heart still closely twine
　Those ties which naught can sever;
　For I am His, and He is mine,
　Forever and forever.

I've found a Friend; O such a Friend!
　He bled, He died to save me;
　And not alone the gift of life,
　But His own self He gave me.
Naught that I have my own I call,
　I hold it for the Giver;
My heart, my strength, my life, my all,
　Are His, and His forever.

I've found a Friend; O such a Friend!
　So kind and true and tender;
　So wise a Counselor and Guide,
　So mighty a Defender!
From Him who loves me now so well,
　What pow'r my soul shall sever?
Shall life or death, shall earth or hell?
　No; I am His forever.

James Grindlay Small (1817–1888)

247

Speak, Lord, in the Stillness

Speak, Lord, in the stillness,
While I wait on Thee;
Hushed my heart to listen
In expectancy.

Speak, O blessed Master,
In this quiet hour,
Let me see Thy face, Lord,
Feel Thy touch of power.

For the words Thou speakest,
"They are life" indeed;
Living Bread from heaven,
Now my spirit feed!

All to Thee is yielded,
I am not my own;
Blissful, glad surrender,
I am Thine alone.

Fill me with the knowledge
Of Thy glorious will;
All Thine own good pleasure
In my life fulfill.

Emily May Grimes (1868-1927)

God revealed himself mightily to the prophet Elijah, sending fire to burn the sacrifice on Mount Carmel. But later, as Elijah moped on the mountain, the Lord taught him an important lesson. There was a wind, an earthquake, and a fire—but the Lord was not in any of these. Then came a still, small voice. That was how God chose to speak to His prophet.

The same is true today. We long for fire from heaven to silence skeptics once and for all, but God doesn't usually work that way. Long ago He revealed Himself as a helpless baby sleeping in a dirty feed trough, and today He speaks quietly to ordinary people like you and me—if only we are still enough to listen.

• • • •

So [Eli] said to Samuel, "Go and lie down again, and if someone calls again, say, 'Speak, Lord, your servant is listening.'" So Samuel went back to bed. And the Lord came and called as before, "Samuel! Samuel!" And Samuel replied, "Speak, your servant is listening."

I SAMUEL 3:9-10

Fight the Good Fight

Too many of us are spiritually flabby, often avoiding spiritual conflict instead of facing it. That was certainly not the apostle Paul's style, nor was it John Monsell's. Monsell was a gifted Anglican clergyman who could hold his congregation spellbound as he spoke and who advocated "more fervent and joyous" singing in his church. He once said, "We sing, but not as we should, to Him who is the chief among ten thousand, the altogether lovely."

This hymn was written to accompany the reading of Ephesians 4:17-32, where Paul outlines the nature of new life in Christ. But Monsell's hymn has allusions to many other passages of Scripture as well. Stanza 1 refers to 1 Timothy 6:12 and Philippians 4:1; stanza 2 to Hebrews 12:1, John 14:6, and Philippians 3:14; stanza 3 to 1 Peter 5:7; and stanza 4 to Galatians 6:9, Mark 5:36, John 6:29, and Colossians 3:11.

Fight the good fight with all thy might!
Christ is thy strength, and Christ thy right.
Lay hold on life, and it shall be
Thy joy and crown eternally.

Run the straight race through God's good grace;
Lift up thine eyes, and seek His face.
Life with its way before us lies;
Christ is the path, and Christ the prize.

Cast care aside, lean on thy Guide;
His boundless mercy will provide.
Trust, and thy trusting soul shall prove
Christ is its life, and Christ its love.

Faint not nor fear, His arms are near;
He changeth not, and thou art dear.
Only believe, and thou shalt see
That Christ is all in all to thee.

John Samuel Bewley Monsell (1811–1875)

• • • •

Pursue righteousness and a godly life, along with faith, love, perseverance, and gentleness. Fight the good fight for the true faith. Hold tightly to the eternal life to which God has called you, which you have confessed so well before many witnesses.

I TIMOTHY 6:11-12

The Wise May Bring Their Learning

The wise may bring their learning,
The rich may bring their wealth,
And some may bring their greatness,
And some bring strength and health;
We, too, would bring our treasures
To offer to the King;
We have no wealth or learning:
What shall we children bring?

We'll bring Him hearts that love Him;
We'll bring Him thankful praise,
And young souls meekly striving
To walk in holy ways:
And these shall be the treasures
We offer to the King,
And these are gifts that even
The poorest child may bring.

We'll bring the little duties
We have to do each day;
We'll try our best to please Him,
At home, at school, at play:
And better are these treasures
To offer to our King,
Than richest gifts without them;
Yet these a child may bring.

The Book of Praise for Children, 1881

This anonymous, probably American, hymn was written for children. But the message is for everyone—all who have "little duties" to perform each day. Jesus treasured children. He welcomed them when the disciples turned them away. He loved their praises and sought to protect them. He once used a boy's lunch to feed a multitude.

This was consistent with Jesus' topsy-turvy message. It is not the wealthy, the strong, or even the wise who are great, but the humble, the servants, the poor, the children. You cannot enter the Kingdom unless you become like a child. Wisdom, wealth, power—these are worthless currency in Christ's Kingdom. He deals in hearts of love, praise, and devotion. These are the gifts He longs to receive.

• • • •

One day some parents brought their little children to Jesus so he could touch and bless them. But when the disciples saw this, they scolded the parents for bothering him. Then Jesus called for the children and said to the disciples, "Let the children come to me. Don't stop them! For the Kingdom of God belongs to those who are like these children. I tell you the truth, anyone who doesn't receive the Kingdom of God like a child will never enter it."
LUKE 18:15-17

Now the Day Is Over

Sabine Baring-Gould wrote eighty-five books in areas as diverse as religion, travel, folklore, mythology, history, fiction, biography, sermons, and popular theology. He wrote a fifteen-volume *Lives of the Saints*. He edited a quarterly review of ecclesiastical art and literature. But he loved children, and we remember him best for his children's hymns: "Onward, Christian Soldiers" (June 6) and "Now the Day Is Over."

After graduating from Cambridge, Baring-Gould started a church in his tiny two-floor apartment. Soon, he said, "the congregation filled the room and the stairs and the kitchen. . . . The singing had to bump down the stairs, fill the kitchen, and one strain of the tune after another came up irregularly through the chinks of the floor."

• • • •

You can go to bed without fear; you will lie down and sleep soundly.

PROVERBS 3:24

Now the day is over,
Night is drawing nigh,
Shadows of the evening
Steal across the sky.

Jesus, give the weary
Calm and sweet repose;
With Thy tend'rest blessing
May our eyelids close.

Grant to little children
Visions bright of Thee;
Guard the sailors tossing
On the deep blue sea.

Thro' the long night-watches,
May Thine angels spread
Their white wings above me,
Watching round my bed.

When the morning wakens,
Then may I arise,
Pure and fresh and sinless
In Thy holy eyes.

Sabine Baring-Gould (1834-1924)

All Praise to Thee, My God, This Night

All praise to Thee, my God, this night,
For all the blessings of the light!
Keep me, O keep me, King of kings,
Beneath Thine own almighty wings.

Forgive me, Lord, for Thy dear Son,
The ill that I this day have done,
That with the world, myself, and Thee,
I, when I sleep, at peace may be.

O may my soul on Thee repose,
And with sweet sleep mine eyelids close,
Sleep that may me more vigorous make
To serve my God when I awake.

Praise God, from whom all blessings flow;
Praise Him, all creatures here below;
Praise Him above, ye heavenly host;
Praise Father, Son, and Holy Ghost.

Thomas Ken (1637–1711)

In 1673 Anglican bishop Thomas Ken wrote a *Manual of Prayers* for the students at Winchester College. The book contained a hymn for the morning, one for evening, and one for midnight. All three hymns conclude with the same stanza, "Praise God, from whom all blessings flow"—the most-sung hymn lyrics in the English language.

Thomas Ken knew well that some days are difficult to end with a doxology of praise. Orphaned as a boy, he was adopted by a noted scholar and author. He was ordained in the Church of England and became chaplain to Princess Mary of Orange. But when he spoke against the immorality of the royal court, he soon found himself without a job. Later he was imprisoned in the Tower of London by James II for refusing to read the king's Declaration of Indulgence. Still, it is said that Bishop Ken continued to use his morning and evening hymns in his personal devotions.

• • • •

The whole earth will acknowledge the Lord and return to him. All the families of the nations will bow down before him. For royal power belongs to the Lord. He rules all the nations.

PSALM 22:27-28

Peace, Perfect Peace

In 1875, while Edward Bickersteth was vacationing in Harrowgate, England, he heard a sermon on Isaiah 26:3, "You will keep in perfect peace all who trust in you, all whose thoughts are fixed on you!" The minister explained that the original Hebrew read, "You will keep in peace, peace. . . ." In Hebrew the repetition of a word indicates intensity or perfection. That afternoon Bickersteth visited a dying relative. When he found the man deeply distressed, he withdrew for a while and wrote this hymn. Then he returned to read Scripture and to share the comforting lines he had written.

As we read the first line of each stanza, we are pummeled by the problems of our modern society. But while problems are found in the first line of each stanza, there is one word that appears consistently in the second line—*Jesus.* And His presence in our problems and heartaches makes all the difference.

Peace, perfect peace, in this dark world of sin?
The blood of Jesus whispers peace within.

Peace, perfect peace, by thronging duties pressed?
To do the will of Jesus, this is rest.

Peace, perfect peace, with sorrows surging round?
On Jesus' bosom naught but calm is found.

Peace, perfect peace, our future all unknown?
Jesus we know, and He is on the throne.

Peace, perfect peace, death shadowing us and ours?
Jesus has vanquished death and all its powers.

It is enough: earth's struggles soon shall cease,
And Jesus, call us to heav'n's perfect peace.

Edward Henry Bickersteth (1825-1906)

• • • •

[Jesus said,] "I have told you all this so that you may have peace in me. Here on earth you will have many trials and sorrows. But take heart, because I have overcome the world."

JOHN 16:33

'Tis So Sweet to Trust in Jesus

'Tis so sweet to trust in Jesus,
Just to take Him at His Word,
Just to rest upon His promise,
Just to know "Thus saith the Lord."

Jesus, Jesus, how I trust Him!
How I've proved Him o'er and o'er!
Jesus, Jesus, precious Jesus!
O for grace to trust Him more!

O how sweet to trust in Jesus,
Just to trust His cleansing blood,
Just in simple faith to plunge me
'Neath the healing, cleansing flood!

Yes, 'tis sweet to trust in Jesus,
Just from sin and self to cease,
Just from Jesus simply taking
Life and rest and joy and peace.

I'm so glad I learned to trust Him,
Precious Jesus, Savior, Friend;
And I know that He is with me,
Will be with me to the end.

Louisa M. R. Stead (1850–1917)

Louisa Stead and her husband were relaxing with their four-year-old daughter on a Long Island beach when they heard a desperate child's cry. A boy was drowning, and Louisa's husband tried to rescue him. In the process, however, the boy pulled Mr. Stead under the water, and both drowned as Louisa and her daughter watched.

Louisa Stead was left with no means of support except the Lord. She and her daughter experienced dire poverty. One morning, when she had neither funds nor food for the day, she opened the front door and found that someone had left food and money on her doorstep. That day she wrote this hymn. It remains a timeless reminder and comfort to all believers who have experienced this same truth: "Jesus, Jesus, how I trust Him; how I've proved Him o'er and o'er! Jesus, Jesus, precious Jesus! O for grace to trust Him more."

• • • •

[Jesus said,] "Don't let your hearts be troubled. Trust in God, and trust also in me. There is more than enough room in my Father's home. . . . When everything is ready, I will come and get you, so that you will always be with me where I am."

JOHN 14:1-3

Lord, Speak to Me

When Frances Ridley Havergal was a child, her father nicknamed her "Little Quicksilver." She had a quick and hungry mind and as a child memorized long passages of Scripture. Her mother died when Frances was only eleven, but one of the last things her mother said to her was, "Pray God to prepare you for all He is preparing for you."

Shortly before she wrote this hymn at the age of thirty-six, she wrote in a letter, "I am always getting surprised at my own stupidity. . . . If I am to write to any good, a great deal of living must go to a very little writing." About the same time, she also wrote, "I feel like a child writing. You know a child will look up at every sentence and ask, 'What shall I say next?' This is what I do. Every line and word and rhyme comes from God." She called this hymn "A Worker's Prayer."

Lord, speak to me, that I may speak
In living echoes of Thy tone;
As Thou hast sought, so let me seek
Thy erring children lost and lone.

O teach me, Lord, that I may teach
The precious things Thou dost impart;
And wing my words, that they may reach
The hidden depths of many a heart.

O fill me with Thy fullness, Lord,
Until my very heart o'erflow
In kindling thought and glowing word
Thy love to tell, Thy praise to show.

O use me, Lord, use even me,
Just as Thou wilt and when and where;
Until Thy blessed face I see,
Thy rest, Thy joy, Thy glory share.

Frances Ridley Havergal (1836-1879)

• • • •

Work hard so you can present yourself to God
and receive his approval. Be a good worker,
one who does not need to be ashamed and
who correctly explains the word of truth.
2 TIMOTHY 2:15

Lord Jesus, Think on Me

Lord Jesus, think on me,
And purge away my sin;
From earthborn passions set me free,
And make me pure within.

Lord Jesus, think on me,
With care and woe oppressed;
Let me Thy loving servant be,
And taste Thy promised rest.

Lord Jesus, think on me,
Amid the battle's strife;
In all my pain and misery
Be Thou my health and life.

Lord Jesus, think on me,
Nor let me go astray;
Through darkness and perplexity
Point Thou the heavenly way.

Lord Jesus, think on me,
That when this life is past,
I may th'eternal brightness see,
And share Thy joy at last.

Lord Jesus, think on me,
That I may sing above
To Father, Spirit, and to Thee,
The strains of praise and love.

Synesius of Cyrene (c. 375–430)

Translated by Allen W. Chatfield (1808–1896)

Synesius was a native of Cyrene in northern Africa, the hometown of the Simon who had carried the cross for Jesus. He was more famous as a philosopher than as a Christian leader. Most of the writings of Synesius come from his pre-Christian days, including a humanist eulogy on baldness, a speech depicting the ideal Roman emperor, and a paper, *De Insomniis,* on the causes and meaning of dreams.

When he was thirty-three, Synesius married a Christian woman and later became a Christian himself. Yet he struggled with how to reconcile his philosophy with Christian doctrine. Eventually he was consecrated a bishop in the church, but his philosophical struggle continued.

This hymn was derived from an ode written by Synesius, and in it can be seen his sincere desire for God to shed light on his path.

• • • •

We keep on praying for you, asking our God to enable you to live a life worthy of his call. May he give you the power to accomplish all the good things your faith prompts you to do.
2 THESSALONIANS 1:11

O Master, Let Me Walk with Thee

Washington Gladden believed that Christians should be involved in the world's problems—and he wasn't afraid to say so. A newspaperman-turned-clergyman, he crusaded against injustice. He fought against the infamous Tweed Ring that controlled New York City politics. He objected to John D. Rockefeller's gift to his denomination's foreign mission board because of the millionaire's policies at Standard Oil. In his various churches, he often preached a social gospel, trying to rouse his congregation to the social and labor problems that were engulfing the country.

When Gladden wrote this hymn in 1879, he said the poem had no theological significance, but that it was an honest cry of human need and of the need for divine companionship. If our friendship with Jesus does not lead us to concern for our fellowman, then we'd better check to see how closely we are walking with the Master.

• • • •

Imitate God, therefore, in everything you do, because you are his dear children. Live a life filled with love, following the example of Christ. He loved us and offered himself as a sacrifice for us, a pleasing aroma to God.
EPHESIANS 5:1-2

O Master, let me walk with Thee
In lowly paths of service free;
Tell me Thy secret; help me bear
The strain of toil, the fret of care.

Help me the slow of heart to move
By some clear, winning word of love;
Teach me the wayward feet to stay,
And guide them in the homeward way.

Teach me Thy patience; still with Thee
In closer, dearer company,
In work that keeps faith sweet and strong,
In trust that triumphs over wrong,

In hope that sends a shining ray
Far down the future's broadening way,
In peace that only Thou canst give,
With Thee, O Master, let me live.

Washington Gladden (1836-1918)

Praise the Savior, Ye Who Know Him

Praise the Savior, ye who know Him!
Who can tell how much we owe Him?
Gladly let us render to Him
All we are and have.

Jesus is the name that charms us,
He for conflict fits and arms us;
Nothing moves and nothing harms us
While we trust in Him.

Trust in Him, ye saints forever—
He is faithful, changing never;
Neither force nor guile can sever
Those He loves from Him.

Keep us, Lord, O keep us cleaving
To Thyself, and still believing,
Till the hour of our receiving
Promised joys with Thee.

Then we shall be where we would be,
Then we shall be what we should be;
Things that are not now, nor could be,
Soon shall be our own.

Thomas Kelly (1769–1855)

There was nothing wishy-washy about Thomas Kelly. He was an Irishman through and through, from Kellywatle, Ireland. He studied to be a lawyer like his father, but in the process began to read Christian doctrine. Under conviction of sin, he struggled to find peace with God through fasting and asceticism, but it didn't work. Eventually, he trusted Jesus Christ for the free gift of salvation through faith. He was ordained a minister in the established church, but because of his strong views on salvation by grace, he moved on to serve in independent chapels.

It is said that most of his hymns were focused on Jesus Christ, praising Him for His work on the cross and the glories of heaven. In a way, Kelly writes simply, and yet because his rhyme schemes are unusual, the words become more memorable. This hymn is typical of Kelly, beginning with grateful praise to his Savior and ending with a meditation on heaven.

• • • •

Because we are united with Christ, we have received an inheritance from God, for he chose us in advance, and he makes everything work out according to his plan.
EPHESIANS 1:11

Cleanse Me

In 1936, at the age of twenty-four, evangelist J. Edwin Orr wrote this hymn during an Easter evangelistic campaign in New Zealand. During that campaign, revival fell on the people of New Zealand. Midnight services had to be added to accommodate the crowds; many were converted, and revival fires spread across the island-nation.

As Orr was about to leave New Zealand, four Maori girls came and sang him their native song of farewell. Impressed by the tune and still stirred by the revival he had witnessed, Orr quickly scribbled the stanzas of this hymn on the back of an envelope as he waited in the post office of Ngaruawahia, New Zealand.

Orr, a brilliant man who would go on to earn doctorates from universities in Europe, Asia, Africa, and America, studied revival movements for the next fifty years and chronicled them in numerous books.

Search me, O God, and know my heart today;
Try me, O Savior, know my thoughts, I pray.
See if there be some wicked way in me;
Cleanse me from every sin, and set me free.

I praise Thee, Lord, for cleansing me from sin;
Fulfill Thy Word, and make me pure within.
Fill me with fire, where once I burned with shame;
Grant my desire to magnify Thy name.

Lord, take my life, and make it wholly Thine;
Fill my poor heart with Thy great love divine.
Take all my will, my passion, self and pride;
I now surrender, Lord—in me abide.

O Holy Ghost, revival comes from Thee;
Send a revival, start the work in me.
Thy Word declares Thou wilt supply our need;
For blessings now, O Lord, I humbly plead.

James Edwin Orr (1912–1987)

• • • •

Search me, O God, and know my heart; test me and know my anxious thoughts. Point out anything in me that offends you, and lead me along the path of everlasting life.

PSALM 139:23-24

My Faith Has Found a Resting Place

My faith has found a resting place—
Not in device or creed:
I trust the Ever-Living One—
His wounds for me shall plead.

**I need no other argument,
I need no other plea;
It is enough that Jesus died,
And that He died for me.**

Enough for me that Jesus saves—
This ends my fear and doubt;
A sinful soul I come to Him—
He'll never cast me out.

My heart is leaning on the Word—
The written Word of God:
Salvation by my Savior's name—
Salvation through His blood.

My great Physician heals the sick—
The lost He came to save;
For me His precious blood He shed—
For me His life He gave.

Lidie H. Edmunds (nineteenth century)

The pioneering radio preacher Donald Grey Barnhouse used to ask, "When you get to the pearly gates and God asks, 'Why should I let you into my Heaven?' what will you say?" This song is an answer to that question.

God does not run heaven like a country club or a successful corporation. We cannot get in on *our own* qualifications. The door is barred to all who try to earn their entry. But it swings wide open for the simple saint who affirms in faith, "I need no other argument, I need no other plea; it is enough that Jesus died, and that He died for me."

• • • •

Make sure that your own hearts are not evil and unbelieving, turning you away from the living God. You must warn each other every day, while it is still "today," so that none of you will be deceived by sin and hardened against God. For if we are faithful to the end, trusting God just as firmly as when we first believed, we will share in all that belongs to Christ.

HEBREWS 3:12-14

Rise Up, O Men of God

The hymn has been criticized because it speaks only of men of God and not women of God. Many contemporary hymnals have changed the words to "saints of God." Yet William Merrill's notion was not to discriminate against women, but to challenge men. Women in his day already had numerous church organizations and groups like the Women's Christian Temperance Union, but there were no Christian movements for men that could rival the various fraternal organizations proclaiming a brotherhood that was only pseudo-Christian.

Merrill's hymn is full of exclamation points and military-sounding commands. The Christian message still comes to us—both men and women—with exclamation points and definite commands. Followers of Christ are called to be soldiers, not just passive recipients of God's blessings.

Rise up, O men of God!
Have done with lesser things;
Give heart and soul and mind and strength
To serve the King of kings.

Rise up, O men of God!
His kingdom tarries long;
Bring in the day of brotherhood
And end the night of wrong.

Rise up, O men of God!
The Church for you doth wait,
Her strength unequal to her task:
Rise up and make her great.

Lift high the cross of Christ,
Tread where His feet have trod;
As brothers of the Son of man,
Rise up, O men of God!

William Pierson Merrill (1867–1954)

• • • •

These are the gifts Christ gave to the church: the apostles, the prophets, the evangelists, and the pastors and teachers. Their responsibility is to equip God's people to do his work and build up the church, the body of Christ. This will continue until we all come to such unity in our faith and knowledge of God's Son that we will be mature in the Lord, measuring up to the full and complete standard of Christ.

EPHESIANS 4:11-13

Come, Thou Fount of Every Blessing

Come, Thou Fount of ev'ry blessing,
Tune my heart to sing Thy grace;
Streams of mercy never ceasing,
Call for songs of loudest praise:
Teach me some melodious sonnet,
Sung by flaming tongues above;
Praise the mount—O fix me on it,
Mount of God's unchanging love.

Here I raise mine Ebenezer;
Hither by Thy help I'm come;
And I hope, by Thy good pleasure,
Safely to arrive at home:
Jesus sought me when a stranger,
Wand'ring from the fold of God;
He, to save my soul from danger,
Interposed His precious blood.

O, to grace how great a debtor
Daily I'm constrained to be!
Let that grace, Lord, like a fetter,
Bind my wand'ring heart to Thee.
Prone to wander, Lord, I feel it;
Prone to leave the God I love;
Here's my heart; Lord, take and seal it;
Seal it for Thy courts above.

Robert Robinson (1735–1790)

Robert Robinson had always been prone to wander. Apprenticed to a barber at fourteen, he spent more time reading and playing with friends than cutting hair. Then, still a teen, he went to a George Whitefield meeting, intending to ridicule it—and instead was converted. After his apprenticeship was over, Robinson went into the ministry. He wrote this hymn at the age of twenty-three as he served at the Calvinistic Methodist church in Norfolk, England.

Late in life, Robinson did stray from the faith. Once, in a stagecoach, he sat by a lady who was reading a hymnbook. She showed him "Come, Thou Fount," saying how wonderful it was. He tried to change the subject, but couldn't. Finally he said, "Madam, I am the unhappy man who wrote that hymn many years ago, and I would give a thousand worlds to enjoy the feelings I had then."

• • • •

Samuel then took a large stone and placed it between the towns of Mizpah and Jeshanah. He named it Ebenezer (which means "the stone of help"), for he said, "Up to this point the Lord has helped us!"

I SAMUEL 7:12

Nearer, My God, to Thee

Sarah Adams had to say farewell often, but she never liked it. Her mother had died when Sarah was only five—that was her first farewell. At thirty-two, as an actress playing Lady Macbeth in London's Richmond Theater, she said farewell to the stage. She wanted to continue, but her health was failing. The health of her sister was also poor, and Adams feared the day when she would have to bid her farewell. She began to question her faith. Why did God seem so far away?

When Adams's pastor asked her and her sister to help him prepare a hymnal, the two responded eagerly, writing thirteen texts and sixty-two new tunes. As the sisters were finishing their work, their pastor mentioned that he was planning a sermon about Jacob's dream of a ladder ascending to heaven and he needed an appropriate hymn. Adams soon completed the five stanzas of "Nearer, My God, to Thee."

• • • •

Jacob found a stone to rest his head against and lay down to sleep. As he slept, he dreamed of a stairway that reached from the earth up to heaven. And he saw the angels of God going up and down the stairway. . . . He named that place Bethel (which means "house of God").

GENESIS 28:11-12, 19

Nearer, my God, to Thee, nearer to Thee!
E'en though it be a cross that raiseth me;
Still all my song shall be, nearer, my God, to Thee,
Nearer, my God, to Thee, nearer to Thee.

Though like the wanderer, the sun gone down,
Darkness be over me, my rest a stone;
Yet in my dreams I'd be nearer, my God, to Thee,
Nearer, my God, to Thee, nearer to Thee.

There let the way appear steps unto heav'n;
All that Thou sendest me in mercy giv'n;
Angels to beckon me nearer, my God, to Thee,
Nearer, my God, to Thee, nearer to Thee.

Then, with my waking thoughts bright
with Thy praise,
Out of my stony griefs, Bethel I'll raise;
So by my woes to be nearer, my God, to Thee,
Nearer, my God, to Thee, nearer to Thee.

Or if on joyful wing, cleaving the sky,
Sun, moon, and stars forgot, upward I fly,
Still all my song shall be nearer, my God, to Thee,
Nearer, my God, to Thee, nearer to Thee.

Sarah Flower Adams (1805-1848)

More Love to Thee, O Christ

More love to Thee, O Christ,
More love to Thee!
Hear Thou the prayer I make
On bended knee;
This is my earnest plea:
More love, O Christ, to Thee,
More love to Thee,
More love to Thee!

Once earthly joy I craved,
Sought peace and rest;
Now Thee alone I seek,
Give what is best;
This all my prayer shall be:
More love, O Christ, to Thee,
More love to Thee,
More love to Thee!

Then shall my every breath
Sing out Your praise;
This be the only song
My heart shall raise;
This still my prayer shall be:
More love, O Christ, to Thee,
More love to Thee,
More love to Thee!

Elizabeth Payson Prentiss (1818–1878)

Elizabeth Payson Prentiss came from a godly home. Her father, Edward Payson, was a brilliant Bible teacher and a loving father. Her husband, a gifted Presbyterian minister, later became a seminary professor. But despite her many blessings, Prentiss's life was not easy. She suffered from severe headaches and chronic insomnia. One of her children suddenly died, and a short time later a second child died. At this, Prentiss cried out in anguish, "Our home is broken up, our lives wrecked, our hopes shattered, our dreams dissolved. I don't think I can stand living for another moment."

In her room with a Bible and hymnal in hand, she sought comfort. She stopped at Sarah Adams's hymn "Nearer, My God, to Thee" and read it several times. As she prayed, words came to her: "More Love to Thee, O Christ."

• • • •

This is my commandment: Love each other in the same way I have loved you. There is no greater love than to lay down one's life for one's friends. You are my friends if you do what I command. I no longer call you slaves, because a master doesn't confide in his slaves. Now you are my friends, since I have told you everything the Father told me.
JOHN 15:12-15

May the Grace of Christ, Our Savior

The apostle Paul concluded one of his letters to the troubled Corinthian church with this benediction: "May the grace of the Lord Jesus Christ, the love of God, and the fellowship of the Holy Spirit be with you all" (2 Corinthians 13:14). It is a remarkable verse because it mentions the work of God on our behalf through each person of the Trinity—Father, Son, and Holy Spirit.

John Newton, the former slave trader whose life was touched by God's amazing grace, became a loving pastor. He loved his congregation, and they loved him. He was not a great preacher, but that did not matter. He had special services for children and special services for senior citizens, teaching the Bible faithfully and singing songs that he had just written.

One writer said, "Newton was more remarkable for his goodness than for his greatness." Newton would have loved that assessment.

May the grace of Christ, our Savior,
And the Father's boundless love,
With the Holy Spirit's favor,
Rest upon us from above.

Thus may we abide in union
With each other and the Lord,
And possess, in sweet communion,
Joys which earth cannot afford.

John Newton (1725–1807)

• • • •

My old self has been crucified with Christ. It is no longer I who live, but Christ lives in me. So I live in this earthly body by trusting in the Son of God, who loved me and gave himself for me. I do not treat the grace of God as meaningless. For if keeping the law could make us right with God, then there was no need for Christ to die.

GALATIANS 2:20-21

How Sweet the Name of Jesus Sounds

How sweet the name of Jesus sounds
In a believer's ear!
It soothes his sorrows, heals his wounds,
And drives away his fear.

It makes the wounded spirit whole
And calms the troubled breast;
'Tis manna to the hungry soul
And to the weary, rest.

Dear name! the rock on which I build,
My shield and hiding place;
My never-failing treasure, filled
With boundless stores of grace!

Jesus, my Shepherd, Brother, Friend,
My Prophet, Priest, and King,
My Lord, my Life, my Way, my End,
Accept the praise I bring.

Till then I would Thy love proclaim
With ev'ry fleeting breath;
And may the music of Thy name
Refresh my soul in death.

John Newton (1725–1807)

At the age of eighty, John Newton was quite deaf and almost blind, but he still continued to preach. For his final messages, Newton brought an aide to the pulpit. The aide would read the next point of Newton's sermon outline, and Newton would then expound on that point.

On one particular Sunday, not long before Newton's death, the assistant read the first point and Newton said to the congregation, "Jesus Christ is precious." He paused and waited until the aide read the second point. Newton said again, "Jesus Christ is precious."

The aide reminded Newton that he had already said that. "Yes, I said it twice," the aged pastor replied, "and I'll say it again! Jesus Christ is precious." Then he asked the congregation to sing the hymn he had written many years before, "How Sweet the Name of Jesus Sounds."

• • • •

Jesus is the one referred to in the Scriptures, where it says, "The stone that you builders rejected has now become the cornerstone." There is salvation in no one else! God has given no other name under heaven by which we must be saved.

ACTS 4:11-12

Savior, like a Shepherd Lead Us

Of all the names and titles given to Jesus, perhaps the most beloved is *Shepherd,* a title Jesus gave himself in John 10. The Good Shepherd knows His sheep, guards His sheep, and even gives His life for His sheep. Scripture also says that He knows His sheep by name.

Unfortunately we don't know the author of this hymn by name. The hymn was first published in a book of songs and poems by Dorothy Thrupp of Paddington Green, England. The poems that she contributed are followed by her initials, D.A.T., but this one has no initials. Either she forgot to initial it, or it came from another source. Dorothy Thrupp's book was *Hymns for the Young,* and so the hymn is often identified as a children's hymn, though its message applies to people of all ages.

• • • •

I am the good shepherd; I know my own sheep, and they know me, just as my Father knows me and I know the Father. So I sacrifice my life for the sheep.

JOHN 10:14-15

Savior, like a shepherd lead us,
Much we need Thy tender care;
In Thy pleasant pastures feed us,
For our use Thy folds prepare:
Blessed Jesus, blessed Jesus!
Thou hast bought us, Thine we are.

We are Thine, do Thou befriend us,
Be the guardian of our way;
Keep Thy flock, from sin defend us,
Seek us when we go astray:
Blessed Jesus, blessed Jesus!
Hear, O hear us, when we pray.

Thou hast promised to receive us,
Poor and sinful though we be;
Thou hast mercy to relieve us,
Grace to cleanse and power to free:
Blessed Jesus, blessed Jesus!
Early let us turn to Thee.

Early let us seek Thy favor,
Early let us do Thy will;
Blessed Lord and only Savior,
With Thy love our bosoms fill:
Blessed Jesus, blessed Jesus!
Thou hast loved us, love us still.

Hymns for the Young, 1836

Attributed to Dorothy A. Thrupp (1779–1847)

Sun of My Soul, Thou Savior Dear

Sun of my soul, Thou Savior dear,
It is not night if Thou be near;
O may no earthborn cloud arise
To hide Thee from Thy servant's eyes.

When the soft dews of kindly sleep
My wearied eyelids gently steep,
Be my last thought, how sweet to rest
Forever on my Savior's breast.

Abide with me from morn till eve,
For without Thee I cannot live;
Abide with me when night is nigh,
For without Thee I dare not die.

If some poor wandering child of Thine
Has spurned, today, the voice divine,
Now, Lord, the gracious work begin;
Let him no more lie down in sin.

Watch by the sick; enrich the poor
With blessings from Thy boundless store;
Be every mourner's sleep tonight,
Like infants' slumbers, pure and light.

Come near and bless us when we wake,
Ere through the world our way we take,
Till in the ocean of Thy love
We lose ourselves in heaven above.

John Keble (1792–1866)

The prophet Malachi called the Messiah the Sun of Righteousness, who would rise with healing in His wings. So John Keble was using a familiar title for Jesus when he wrote this poem. Keble first published "Sun of my Soul" in a book called *The Christian Year*, which included poems to be used by believers for worship throughout the church year. An extremely modest man, Keble published this book anonymously. He used the proceeds from the sale of his book to maintain the small village church near Oxford in which he served for more than three decades.

Throughout his ministry, Keble was known as an outstanding preacher and a careful Bible scholar. He wrote over seven hundred hymns. In 1869 Keble College was founded at Oxford University as a tribute to him.

• • • •

For you who fear my name, the Sun of Righteousness will rise with healing in his wings. And you will go free, leaping with joy like calves let out to pasture.

MALACHI 4:2

The King of Love My Shepherd Is

The twenty-third psalm has been sung in hundreds of different forms since King David wrote the words some three thousand years ago. The version from the 1650 *Scottish Psalter*, "The Lord's My Shepherd, I'll Not Want" (January 5), has certainly stood the test of time. But when Henry Baker, an Anglican clergyman, was asked to compile a new hymnal for his church, he added this hymn, a paraphrase of Psalm 23, to the appendix of the hymnal. The fact that his hymnal sold more than sixty million copies indicates that he did his job well.

As Baker was dying, his last words came from the third stanza of this hymn: "Perverse and foolish, oft I strayed, but yet in love He sought me."

• • • •

Even when I walk through the darkest valley, I will not be afraid, for you are close beside me. Your rod and your staff protect and comfort me. You prepare a feast for me in the presence of my enemies. You honor me by anointing my head with oil. My cup overflows with blessings. Surely your goodness and unfailing love will pursue me all the days of my life, and I will live in the house of the Lord forever.

PSALM 23:4-6

The King of love my Shepherd is,
Whose goodness faileth never;
I nothing lack if I am His,
And He is mine forever.

Where streams of living water flow,
My ransomed soul He leadeth,
And where the verdant pastures grow,
With food celestial feedeth.

Perverse and foolish, oft I strayed,
But yet in love He sought me,
And on His shoulder gently laid,
And home, rejoicing, brought me.

In death's dark vale I fear no ill
With Thee, dear Lord, beside me;
Thy rod and staff my comfort still,
Thy cross before to guide me.

Thou spread'st a table in my sight;
Thy unction grace bestoweth;
And O what transport of delight
From Thy pure chalice floweth!

And so through all the length of days
Thy goodness faileth never:
Good Shepherd, may I sing Thy praise
Within Thy house forever.

Henry Williams Baker (1821–1877)

What a Friend We Have in Jesus

What a Friend we have in Jesus,
All our sins and griefs to bear!
What a privilege to carry
Everything to God in prayer!
O what peace we often forfeit,
O what needless pain we bear,
All because we do not carry
Everything to God in prayer!

Have we trials and temptations?
Is there trouble anywhere?
We should never be discouraged,
Take it to the Lord in prayer.
Can we find a friend so faithful
Who will all our sorrows share?
Jesus knows our every weakness,
Take it to the Lord in prayer.

Are we weak and heavy-laden,
Cumbered with a load of care?
Precious Savior, still our refuge—
Take it to the Lord in prayer.
Do thy friends despise, forsake thee?
Take it to the Lord in prayer;
In His arms He'll take and shield thee,
Thou wilt find a solace there.

Joseph Medlicott Scriven (1819-1886)

Not far from Port Hope, Ontario, stands a monument with this inscription: "Four miles north, in Pengally's Cemetery, lies the philanthropist and author of this great masterpiece, written at Port Hope, 1857." Above the inscription are the words of this beloved hymn. Joseph Scriven, its author, was a man who had experienced the friendship of Jesus through a life filled with personal tragedy.

When Scriven was a young man in Ireland, his fiancée accidentally drowned the evening before their wedding. Soon after this, he set sail for Canada. He seemed destined to live his life alone, with Jesus as his only close friend.

Scriven never intended to publish this hymn. He wrote the words to accompany a letter to his mother, who was ill in far-off Ireland. He had no material resources to send her; only a reminder that the most perfect of friends, Jesus Himself, was nearby.

• • • •

Don't worry about anything; instead, pray about everything. Tell God what you need, and thank him for all he has done. Then you will experience God's peace, which exceeds anything we can understand. His peace will guard your hearts and minds as you live in Christ Jesus.
PHILIPPIANS 4:6-7

Almighty God, Thy Lofty Throne

This hymn is based on Psalm 89:14-18, a passage that lifts praise to God for His justice and righteousness. But this psalm was not written in victorious days—Jerusalem may have been under siege at the time. King David's dynasty was in danger of being lost forever. That is why the psalmist ends with a plea for the Lord to act. "O Lord, how long will this go on? Will you hide yourself forever?. . . Lord, where is your unfailing love? You promised it to David with a faithful pledge" (Psalm 89:46, 49).

Even in times when God seems far from us, when our prayers don't seem to be getting through, it is good for us to sing hymns of praise.

• • • •

Righteousness and justice are the foundation of your throne. Unfailing love and truth walk before you as attendants. Happy are those who hear the joyful call to worship, for they will walk in the light of your presence, Lord. They rejoice all day long in your wonderful reputation. They exult in your righteousness. You are their glorious strength. It pleases you to make us strong. Yes, our protection comes from the Lord, and he, the Holy One of Israel, has given us our king.

PSALM 89:14-18

Almighty God, Thy lofty throne
Has justice for its cornerstone,
And shining bright before Thy face
Are truth and love and boundless grace.

With blessing is the nation crowned
Whose people know the joyful sound;
They in the light, O Lord, shall live,
The light Thy face and favor give.

Thy Name with gladness they confess,
Exalted in Thy righteousness;
Their fame and might to Thee belong,
For in Thy favor they are strong.

All glory unto God we yield,
Jehovah is our help and shield;
All praise and honor we will bring
To Israel's Holy One, our King.

The Psalter, 1912

Join All the Glorious Names

Join all the glorious names
Of wisdom, love, and pow'r,
That ever mortals knew,
That angels ever bore:
All are too poor to speak His worth,
Too poor to set my Savior forth.

Great Prophet of my God,
My tongue would bless Thy name:
By Thee the joyful news
Of our salvation came,
The joyful news of sins forgiv'n,
Of hell subdued and peace with heav'n.

Jesus, my great High Priest,
Offered His blood, and died;
My guilty conscience seeks
No sacrifice beside:
His pow'rful blood did once atone
And now it pleads before the throne.

Thou art my Counselor,
My Pattern, and my Guide,
And Thou my Shepherd art;
O keep me near Thy side;
Nor let my feet e'er turn astray
To wander in the crooked way.

My Savior and my Lord,
My Conqu'ror and my King,
Thy sceptre and Thy sword,
Thy reigning grace, I sing:
Thine is the pow'r; behold I sit
In willing bonds beneath Thy feet.

Isaac Watts (1674-1748)

Isaac Watts originally wrote twelve stanzas for this hymn and included seventeen different names for Christ. Watts wrote several hymns on the same theme, but his final analysis was "Earth is too narrow to express His worth, His glory, or His grace."

One such hymn starts each stanza with a question: "Is He a Rose?" "Is He a Vine?" After eighteen stanzas Watts concludes, "His beauties we can never trace till we behold Him face to face." And still another of his hymns begins, "'Tis from the treasure of His Word I borrow titles for my Lord. Nor art, nor nature, can supply sufficient forms of majesty." Watts understood that no matter how many titles he might ascribe to Jesus Christ, all of them together would still be inadequate to express His greatness.

• • • •

I also pray that you will understand the incredible greatness of God's power for us who believe him. This is the same mighty power that raised Christ from the dead and seated him in the place of honor at God's right hand in the heavenly realms. Now he is far above any ruler or authority or power or leader or anything else—not only in this world but also in the world to come.

EPHESIANS 1:19-21

Glorious Things of Thee Are Spoken

This hymn by John Newton is aptly sung to the tune called "Austria," written by Franz Joseph Haydn, whose eighteenth-century life span coincided with that of Newton. Haydn once wrote, "When I think of the divine Being, my heart is so full of joy that the notes fly off as from a spindle, and as I have a cheerful heart, He will pardon me if I serve Him joyfully."

Newton would have liked that. One of the stanzas of this hymn that is often omitted ends with the lines, "Fading is the worldling's pleasure, all his boasted pomp and show; solid joys and lasting treasure, none but Zion's children know." Newton had tasted the pleasures of the world and was left with a bitter taste in his mouth. He much preferred the joys of Zion.

• • • •

You will see Zion as a place of holy festivals. You will see Jerusalem, a city quiet and secure. . . . The Lord will be our Mighty One. He will be like a wide river of protection that no enemy can cross, that no enemy ship can sail upon. For the Lord is our judge, our lawgiver, and our king. He will care for us and save us.

ISAIAH 33:20-22

Glorious things of thee are spoken,
　　Zion, city of our God;
He whose word cannot be broken
　　Formed thee for His own abode:
On the Rock of Ages founded,
　　What can shake thy sure repose?
With salvation's walls surrounded,
　　Thou may'st smile at all thy foes.

See, the streams of living waters,
　　Springing from eternal love,
Well supply thy sons and daughters,
　　And all fear of want remove.
Who can faint while such a river
　　Ever flows their thirst to assuage?
Grace which, like the Lord, the Giver,
　　Never fails from age to age!

Round each habitation hovering,
　　See the cloud and fire appear
For a glory and a covering,
　　Showing that the Lord is near!
Thus deriving from their banner
　　Light by night and shade by day,
Safe they feed upon the manna
　　Which He gives them when they pray.

John Newton (1725-1807)

At the Name of Jesus

At the name of Jesus
Every knee shall bow,
Every tongue confess Him
King of glory now;
'Tis the Father's pleasure
We should call Him Lord,
Who from the beginning
Was the mighty Word.

At His voice creation
Sprang at once to sight,
All the angel faces,
All the hosts of light,
Thrones and dominations,
Stars upon their way,
All the heavenly orders,
In their great array.

Humbled for a season,
To receive a name
From the lips of sinners
Unto whom He came,
Faithfully He bore it
Spotless to the last,
Brought it back victorious
When from death He passed.

In your hearts enthrone Him;
There let Him subdue
All that is not holy,
All that is not true:
Crown Him as your captain
In temptation's hour;
Let His will enfold you
In its light and power.

Caroline Maria Noel (1817–1877)

As a young woman, Caroline Noel tried to write poems, but she gave it up by the age of twenty. Then when she was bedridden with a serious illness at forty, she took up her pen once again. Eventually, her poetry was published in a little book called *At the Name of Jesus, and Other Verses for the Sick and Lonely.*

You might think the tone of her work would be comforting and devotional, but this hymn is more theological in nature. It focuses attention on Jesus and His power, rather than on sickness and loneliness. Actually, the poem is a beautiful paraphrase of Philippians 2:4-11, an early-church hymn that shows Jesus humbling Himself on earth and being glorified in heaven.

• • • •

When he appeared in human form, he humbled himself in obedience to God and died a criminal's death on a cross. Therefore, God elevated him to the place of highest honor and gave him the name above all other names, that at the name of Jesus every knee should bow, in heaven and on earth and under the earth, and every tongue confess that Jesus Christ is Lord, to the glory of God the Father.

PHILIPPIANS 2:7-11

How Lovely Is Thy Dwelling Place

This hymn is a very close rendering of Psalm 84, which focuses on the Temple in Jerusalem. Some scholars believe the psalm was written by an exiled Levite who may have been prevented from reaching the Temple when Jerusalem was under siege by the Assyrian army. In any case, the writer longs to be in the Temple again.

The birds add a beautiful touch to the psalm and hymn. Ancient sources indicate that sparrows and swallows did build nests in temples. Perhaps the psalmist envied the freedom of being able to fly to the Temple. Certainly he wished that he, too, could find a home there. Yet the verse also calls to mind some New Testament allusions—especially "Not a single sparrow can fall to the ground without your Father knowing it" (Matthew 10:29). God cares enough for sparrows to give them a home in His presence; He does the same for us.

• • • •

How lovely is Thy dwelling place,
O Lord of hosts, to me!
The tabernacles of Thy grace
How pleasant, Lord, they be!

My thirsty soul longs ardently,
Yea, faints Thy courts to see;
My very heart and flesh cry out,
O living God, for Thee.

Behold, the sparrows findeth out
A house wherein to rest;
The swallow also for herself
Provided hath a nest;

Even Thine own altars, where she safe
Her young ones forth may bring,
O Thou almighty Lord of hosts,
Who art my God and King.

Blest are they in Thy house that dwell,
They ever give Thee praise.
Blest is the man whose strength Thou art,
In whose heart are Thy ways.

Scottish Psalter, 1850

How lovely is your dwelling place, O Lord of Heaven's Armies. . . . Even the sparrow finds a home, and the swallow builds her nest and raises her young at a place near your altar, O Lord of Heaven's Armies, my King and my God!

PSALM 84:1, 3

Great God, Attend, While Zion Sings

Great God, attend, while Zion sings
The joy that from Thy presence springs;
To spend one day with Thee on earth
Exceeds a thousand days of mirth,
Exceeds a thousand days of mirth.

Might I enjoy the meanest place
Within Thy house, O God of grace,
Nor tents of ease, nor thrones of power,
Should tempt my feet to leave Thy door,
Should tempt my feet to leave Thy door.

God is our sun, He makes our day;
God is our shield, He guards our way
From all th'assaults of hell and sin,
From foes without and foes within,
From foes without and foes within.

O God, our King, whose sovereign sway
The glorious hosts of heaven obey,
And devils at Thy presence flee;
Blest is the man that trusts in Thee,
Blest is the man that trusts in Thee.

Isaac Watts (1674-1748)

Isaac Watts found inspiration for this hymn in the final verses of Psalm 84. But unlike most English hymnwriters of his day, he was not a slave to the Hebrew poetic lines. He would rather the message be fresh and powerful than a word-for-word English reproduction of the original that ended up sounding wooden and obscure. He was the first hymnwriter to successfully challenge the long tradition of strict psalm-singing in the English church.

Watts was motivated to write hymns by the lifeless singing he heard in his services. He once said, "The singing of God's praise is the part of worship most closely related to heaven; but its performance among us is the worst on earth." With this somber assessment, he set to work writing hymns that would help his parishioners to worship better.

• • • •

A single day in your courts is better than a thousand anywhere else! I would rather be a gatekeeper in the house of my God than live the good life in the homes of the wicked. For the Lord God is our sun and our shield. He gives us grace and glory. The Lord will withhold no good thing from those who do what is right.

PSALM 84:10-11

A Charge to Keep I Have

If we wanted to write a hymn, most of us would not turn to the book of Leviticus for inspiration. But Charles Wesley wrote sixteen hymns derived from that Old Testament book. This hymn was composed after he had been reading Matthew Henry's commentary on Leviticus 8:35.

In that verse the Hebrew priests were commanded to be faithful in their duties in the tabernacle. "Keep the charge of the Lord, that ye die not," Moses had said (KJV). Matthew Henry commented, "We have every one of us a charge to keep, an eternal God to glorify, an immortal soul to provide for, a needful duty to be done, our generation to serve, and it must be our daily care to keep this charge, for it is the charge of the Lord our Master, who will shortly call us to an account about it, and it is our utmost peril if we neglect it."

• • • •

Now stay at the entrance of the Tabernacle day and night for seven days, and do everything the Lord requires. If you fail to do this, you will die, for this is what the Lord has commanded.

LEVITICUS 8:35

A charge to keep I have,
A God to glorify,
A never-dying soul to save,
And fit it for the sky.

To serve the present age,
My calling to fulfill;
O may it all my powers engage
To do my Master's will!

Arm me with jealous care,
As in Thy sight to live,
And O, Thy servant, Lord, prepare
A strict account to give!

Help me to watch and pray,
And on Thyself rely,
Assured, if I my trust betray,
I shall forever die.

Charles Wesley (1707–1788)

I Heard the Voice of Jesus Say

I heard the voice of Jesus say,
"Come unto Me and rest;
Lay down, thou weary one, lay down
Thy head upon My breast."
I came to Jesus as I was,
Weary and worn and sad;
I found in Him a resting place,
And He has made me glad.

I heard the voice of Jesus say,
"Behold, I freely give
The living water; thirsty one,
Stoop down and drink and live."
I came to Jesus, and I drank
Of that life-giving stream;
My thirst was quenched, my soul revived,
And now I live in Him.

I heard the voice of Jesus say,
"I am this dark world's light;
Look unto Me, thy morn shall rise,
And all thy day be bright."
I looked to Jesus, and I found
In Him my star, my sun;
And in that light of life I'll walk
Till traveling days are done.

Horatius Bonar (1808-1889)

Horatius Bonar loved to doodle as he wrote his hymns. On the sheet where this hymn first took shape, the lines are abbreviated, edited, and added to, and several doodles are scratched in the margins. Many of Bonar's ideas came to him during long country walks in his native Scotland, and he often fleshed out his ideas while riding a train. All told, Bonar wrote more than six hundred hymns and became known as "the prince of Scottish hymnwriters."

Bonar was a brilliant Bible scholar, an outstanding devotional writer, and an active church leader. He knew how to communicate profound truths to children through hymns. In so doing he helped adults to understand as well. The invitation of Christ to "come" is simple enough for a child to respond to. But after accepting that invitation, it takes a lifetime to probe the depths of what it means to come to Him, to drink the living water, and to walk in the Light.

• • • •

Jesus spoke to the people once more and said, "I am the light of the world. If you follow me, you won't have to walk in darkness, because you will have the light that leads to life."
JOHN 8:12

Blessing and Honor and Glory and Power

Do we seek to bless God in our worship? That is the focus of this hymn by Horatius Bonar, based on the worship songs in the book of Revelation.

How do we bless God? The original word for *bless* means to say good things to or about someone. Let us proclaim good things about God. How do we honor God? We honor our parents by obeying them and making them proud of us. Let us honor God by a life of obedience. How do we give God glory? It involves turning the spotlight on God and turning the light away from ourselves. Let us shine the spotlight on God and His wonderful deeds. How do we praise Him? By telling Him everything we love about Him.

As we come to worship our beautiful Lord, we must learn to focus on what we can give to God.

Blessing and honor and glory and power,
Wisdom and riches and strength evermore
Give ye to Him who our battle hath won,
Whose are the kingdom, the crown, and the throne.

Soundeth the heaven of the heavens with His name;
Ringeth the earth with His glory and fame;
Ocean and mountain, stream, forest, and flower
Echo His praises and tell of His power.

Ever ascendeth the song and the joy;
Ever descendeth the love from on high;
Blessing and honor and glory and praise—
This is the theme of the hymns that we raise.

Give we the glory and praise to the Lamb;
Take we the robe and the harp and the palm;
Sing we the song of the Lamb that was slain,
Dying in weakness, but rising to reign.

Horatius Bonar (1808-1889)

• • • •

Then I looked again, and I heard the voices of thousands and millions of angels around the throne and of the living beings and the elders. And they sang in a mighty chorus: "Worthy is the Lamb who was slaughtered— to receive power and riches and wisdom and strength and honor and glory and blessing."
REVELATION 5:11-12

Come, Let Us Tune Our Loftiest Song

Come, let us tune our loftiest song
And raise to Christ our joyful strain;
Worship and thanks to Him belong,
Who reigns, and shall forever reign.

His sovereign power our bodies made;
Our souls are His immortal breath;
And when His creatures sinned, He bled,
To save us from eternal death.

Burn every breast with Jesus' love;
Bound every heart with rapturous joy;
And saints on earth, with saints above,
Your voices in His praise employ.

Extol the Lamb with loftiest song;
Ascend for Him our cheerful strain;
Worship and thanks to Him belong,
Who reigns and shall forever reign.

Robert A. West (1809-1865)

Thomas Tuller, a seventeenth-century English theologian, wished he could sing better. Once he prayed, "Hadst Thou given me a better voice, I would have praised Thee with a better voice. . . . Yea, Lord, create in me a new heart, therein to make melody, and I will be contented with my old voice until in Thy due time, being admitted unto the choir of heaven, I have another, more harmonious, bestowed upon me."

God's tuning fork doesn't tune human vocal chords; it is more concerned that human hearts be tuned to heaven. That is what Robert West had in mind when he wrote this hymn. West loved music, and within five years of arriving in America from England in 1843, he was appointed to a committee to compile a new Methodist hymnal. One of the hymns included in that hymnal was this one—from beginning to end, a hymn of praise to Jesus Christ.

• • • •

Now all glory to God, who is able to keep you from falling away and will bring you with great joy into his glorious presence without a single fault. All glory to him who alone is God, our Savior through Jesus Christ our Lord. All glory, majesty, power, and authority are his before all time, and in the present, and beyond all time! Amen.
JUDE 1:24-25

Brethren, We Have Met to Worship

What does it mean to meet for worship? One part of worship involves adoring the Lord our God, which includes the idea of gazing lovingly. We come to meet our God and to consider how wonderful He is. Our worship also usually involves preaching and prayer. This hymn presents these two aspects of worship together.

And what is the result of prayerful worship? We are blessed by "holy manna"—bread from heaven. In the Old Testament God provided the Israelites with manna as they wandered in the wilderness. In the New Testament, Jesus gave His body as the Bread of Life through which we can receive spiritual nourishment. As we worship we participate in the eternal banquet of Christ's presence. We celebrate God's provision and thank Him for it.

• • • •

O nations of the world, recognize the Lord, recognize that the Lord is glorious and strong. Give to the Lord the glory he deserves! Bring your offering and come into his presence. Worship the Lord in all his holy splendor.

I CHRONICLES 16:28-29

Brethren, we have met to worship
And adore the Lord our God;
Will you pray with all your power,
While we try to preach the Word?
All is vain unless the Spirit
Of the Holy One comes down;
Brethren, pray, and holy manna
Will be showered all around.

Brethren, see poor sinners round you
Slumbering on the brink of woe;
Death is coming, hell is moving—
Can you bear to let them go?
See our fathers and our mothers
And our children sinking down;
Brethren, pray, and holy manna
Will be showered all around.

Sisters, will you join and help us?
Moses' sister aided him;
Will you help the trembling mourners
Who are struggling hard with sin?
Tell them all about the Savior—
Tell them that He will be found;
Sisters, pray, and holy manna
Will be showered all around.

Let us love our God supremely,
Let us love each other too;
Let us love and pray for sinners
Till our God makes all things new.
Then He'll call us home to heaven,
At His table we'll sit down;
Christ will gird Himself and serve us
With sweet manna all around.

George Atkins (eighteenth century)

I Am Not Skilled to Understand

I am not skilled to understand
What God hath willed, what God hath planned;
I only know at His right hand
Stands One who is my Savior.

I take Him at His word and deed:
"Christ died to save me," this I read;
And in my heart I find a need
Of Him to be my Savior.

That He should leave His place on high
And come for sinful man to die,
You count it strange? so once did I
Before I knew my Savior.

And O that He fulfilled may see
The travail of His soul in me,
And with His work contented be,
As I with my dear Savior!

Yes, living, dying, let me bring
My strength, my solace, from this spring,
That He who lives to be my King
Once died to be my Savior!

Dora Greenwell (1821–1882)

No doubt there were many things that Dora Greenwell could not understand. Though she was born into a well-to-do English family, her father died when she was young, and the family estate had to be sold. She struggled with fragile health as she lived alone in London. Why hadn't God given her an easier life? She worked with children who had physical and intellectual disabilities. Why did they have to suffer so?

When she was thirty-nine, Greenwell wrote her first book, *The Patience of Hope*. She was beginning to see how important patience is for dealing with life's hard questions. But she didn't want to dwell on the unanswered questions; she preferred to think about God's glorious exclamations. So when she compiled her book *Songs of Salvation*, she included this poem, "I Am Not Skilled to Understand."

• • • •

Therefore, it was necessary for [Jesus] to be made in every respect like us, his brothers and sisters, so that he could be our merciful and faithful High Priest before God. Then he could offer a sacrifice that would take away the sins of the people. Since he himself has gone through suffering and testing, he is able to help us when we are being tested.
HEBREWS 2:17-18

Jesus Loves Me

Anna Warner and her sister, Susan, grew up near West Point Military Academy, where they became known for leading Sunday school services for the young men there. After the death of their father, a New York lawyer, the sisters supported themselves with their various literary endeavors. Susan became known as a best-selling novelist. Anna also wrote novels and published two collections of poems. She wrote this simple hymn in 1860 to be included in one of her sister's novels. In the story, it was a poem of comfort spoken to a dying child.

Today millions of voices around the world sing these words: "Yes, Jesus loves me!" Once, when asked to summarize the essential truths of the Christian faith, the great Swiss theologian Karl Barth gave this simple answer: "Jesus loves me, this I know, for the Bible tells me so." This profound yet simple truth is certainly worth singing about!

• • • •

God loved the world so much that he gave his one and only Son, so that everyone who believes in him will not perish but have eternal life. God sent his Son into the world not to judge the world, but to save the world through him.

JOHN 3:16-17

Jesus loves me! this I know,
For the Bible tells me so;
Little ones to Him belong,
They are weak but He is strong.

Yes, Jesus loves me!
Yes, Jesus loves me!
Yes, Jesus loves me!
The Bible tells me so.

Jesus loves me! He who died
Heaven's gate to open wide;
He will wash away my sin,
Let His little child come in.

Jesus loves me! He will stay
Close beside me all the way;
Thou hast bled and died for me,
I will henceforth live for Thee.

Anna Bartlett Warner (1820-1915)

Trust and Obey

When we walk with the Lord in the light of His Word,
What a glory He sheds on our way!
While we do His good will He abides with us still,
And with all who will trust and obey.

**Trust and obey, for there's no other way
To be happy in Jesus, but to trust and obey.**

Not a shadow can rise, not a cloud in the skies,
But His smile quickly drives it away;
Not a doubt nor a fear, not a sigh nor a tear,
Can abide while we trust and obey.

Not a burden we bear, not a sorrow we share,
But our toil He doth richly repay;
Not a grief nor a loss, not a frown nor a cross,
But is blest if we trust and obey.

But we never can prove the delights of His love
Until all on the altar we lay;
For the favor He shows and the joy He bestows
Are for them who will trust and obey.

Then in fellowship sweet we will sit at His feet,
Or we'll walk by His side in the way;
What He says we will do, where He sends we will go—
Never fear, only trust and obey.

John H. Sammis (1846-1919)

This song was written after a D. L. Moody evangelistic meeting in Brockton, Massachusetts. Daniel Towner was the song leader that night in 1886, and he asked the people to share how they had been saved. Several stood and spoke of how certain they felt of their salvation. But then a young man rose and said, "I am not quite sure, but I am going to trust, and I am going to obey."

Towner couldn't forget that testimony. He jotted it down and sent it to John Sammis, who had recently left a career in business to enter the ministry, with the hope that Sammis would find in it the inspiration for a hymn text. Towner was not disappointed.

• • • •

Everyone who believes that Jesus is the Christ has become a child of God. And everyone who loves the Father loves his children, too. We know we love God's children if we love God and obey his commandments. Loving God means keeping his commandments, and his commandments are not burdensome.

I JOHN 5:1-3

Jesus Calls Us

Cecil Alexander was the wife of a parish minister in an impoverished rural area of northern Ireland. She loved the people. "From one house to another, from one bed of sickness to another, from one sorrow to another she went," wrote one historian.

She especially loved children, and most of her hymns were written for them. Two that are well known are "All Things Bright and Beautiful" (May 5) and "Once in Royal David's City" (December 12). "Jesus Calls Us" was one of the few hymns she wrote for adults, and it illustrates her ability to apply Scripture forcefully and devotionally. She wrote the hymn at her husband's request, to accompany a sermon he was preaching about the calling of Andrew by Jesus on the shores of Galilee.

Jesus calls us; o'er the tumult
Of our life's wild, restless sea,
Day by day His sweet voice soundeth,
Saying, "Christian, follow Me."

Jesus calls us from the worship
Of the vain world's golden store,
From each idol that would keep us,
Saying, "Christian, love Me more."

In our joys and in our sorrows,
Days of toil and hours of ease,
Still He calls in cares and pleasures,
"Christian, love Me more than these."

Jesus calls us: by Thy mercies,
Savior, may we hear Thy call,
Give our hearts to Thine obedience,
Serve and love Thee best of all.

Cecil Frances Alexander (1818–1895)

• • • •

One day as Jesus was walking along the shore of the Sea of Galilee, he saw two brothers— Simon, also called Peter, and Andrew— throwing a net into the water, for they fished for a living. Jesus called out to them, "Come, follow me, and I will show you how to fish for people!"

MATTHEW 4:18-19

God of Our Fathers, Known of Old

God of our fathers, known of old,
Lord of our far-flung battle-line,
Beneath whose awful hand we hold
Dominion over palm and pine;
Lord God of hosts, be with us yet,
Lest we forget—lest we forget!

The tumult and the shouting dies;
The captains and the kings depart;
Still stands Thine ancient sacrifice,
An humble and a contrite heart.
Lord God of hosts, be with us yet,
Lest we forget—lest we forget!

Far-called, our navies melt away;
On dune and headland sinks the fire:
Lo, all our pomp of yesterday
Is one with Nineveh and Tyre!
Judge of the nations, spare us yet,
Lest we forget—lest we forget!

If, drunk with sight of power, we loose
Wild tongues that have not Thee in awe,
Such boastings as the Gentiles use,
Or lesser breeds without the law—
Lord God of hosts, be with us yet,
Lest we forget—lest we forget!

For heathen heart that puts her trust
In reeking tube and iron shard,
All valiant dust that builds on dust,
And, guarding, calls not Thee to guard,
For frantic boast and foolish word—
Thy mercy on Thy people, Lord!

Rudyard Kipling (1865-1936)

Rudyard Kipling is not known as a hymn-writer. In the 1890s he became famous for his poetry and for books like *Barrack-Room Ballads* and *The Jungle Book*. In 1897, when England was celebrating the Diamond Jubilee of Queen Victoria's reign, the *Times* of London asked Rudyard Kipling to write a special poem for the occasion.

The poem created quite a stir. Instead of praising his country's military strength, Kipling sounded almost like an Old Testament prophet calling for mercy from a just and righteous God.

It seemed uncharacteristic for Kipling, who was associated with British colonialism, to write, "All our pomp of yesterday is one with Nineveh and Tyre!" Kipling's hymn serves as a powerful sermon to all who are tempted to elevate the glory and power of their nation above that of the sovereign Creator.

• • • •

[Nebuchadnezzar] said, "Look at this great city of Babylon! By my own mighty power, I have built this beautiful city. . . ." While these words were still in his mouth, a voice called down from heaven, "O King Nebuchadnezzar, this message is for you! You are no longer ruler of this kingdom. You will be driven from human society . . . until you learn that the Most High rules over the kingdoms of the world and gives them to anyone he chooses."

DANIEL 4:30-32

Fill Thou My Life, O Lord My God

"Is Bonar the hymnwriter still alive?" asked a visitor who walked into Bonar's Edinburgh church. "I always understood he was a medieval saint." This confusion may be understandable. Horatius Bonar was descended from a long line of Scottish preachers, and his hymns are reminiscent of the monastic hymns of Bernard of Cluny.

But Bonar was not a monk, shut away from the hard realities of life. He began his ministry in the slums, writing hymns for children. He was deeply involved in a movement of evangelicals that pulled out of the national Church of Scotland to form the Free Church. And through it all, he worked incessantly. One biographer says, "He was unbelievably immersed in work." He loved to travel; he loved his family.

Though his life was busy and filled with the cares of family and congregation, he prayed that, most of all, his life might be filled with "praise in every part."

• • • •

Do you have the gift of speaking? Then speak as though God himself were speaking through you. Do you have the gift of helping others? Do it with all the strength and energy that God supplies. Then everything you do will bring glory to God through Jesus Christ.

I PETER 4:11

Fill Thou my life, O Lord my God,
In ev'ry part with praise,
That my whole being may proclaim
Thy being and Thy ways.

Not for the lip of praise alone,
Nor e'en the praising heart
I ask, but for a life made up
Of praise in ev'ry part;

Praise in the common things of life,
Its goings out and in,
Praise in each duty and each deed,
However small and mean.

Fill ev'ry part of me with praise;
Let all my being speak
Of Thee and of Thy love, O Lord,
Poor though I be, and weak.

So shalt Thou, Lord, from me, e'en me,
Receive the glory due,
And so shall I begin on earth
The song forever new.

So shall no part of day or night
From sacredness be free:
But all my life, in ev'ry step,
Be fellowship with Thee.

Horatius Bonar (1808–1889)

Great Is Thy Faithfulness

Great is Thy faithfulness, O God my Father,
There is no shadow of turning with Thee;
Thou changest not, Thy compassions they fail not;
As Thou hast been Thou forever wilt be.

Great is Thy faithfulness!
Great is Thy faithfulness!
Morning by morning new mercies I see;
All I have needed Thy hand hath provided—
Great is Thy faithfulness, Lord, unto me!

Summer and winter, and springtime and harvest,
Sun, moon and stars in their courses above
Join with all nature in manifold witness
To Thy great faithfulness, mercy and love.

Pardon for sin and a peace that endureth,
Thy own dear presence to cheer and to guide;
Strength for today and bright hope for tomorrow,
Blessings all mine, with ten thousand beside!

Thomas Obadiah Chisholm (1866–1960)

Copyright © 1923. Renewal 1951 by Hope Publishing Company, Carol Stream, IL 60188. All rights reserved. Used by permission.

Insurance agent Thomas O. Chisholm certainly had his share of disappointments in life. His health had been fragile, forcing him to resign as a Methodist minister after only one year of service. But he enjoyed writing and submitted his poetry to various Christian magazines. Sometimes he got rejection slips, sometimes acceptances, but he seldom received any money. He earned his meager living selling life insurance.

When he was seventy-five, he wrote, "My income has not been large at any time due to impaired health in the earlier years which has followed me on until now. Although I must not fail to record here the unfailing faithfulness of a covenant-keeping God and that He has given me many wonderful displays of His providing care, for which I am filled with astonishing gratefulness."

• • • •

The faithful love of the Lord never ends! His mercies never cease. Great is his faithfulness; his mercies begin afresh each morning. I say to myself, "The Lord is my inheritance; therefore, I will hope in him!" The Lord is good to those who depend on him, to those who search for him.

LAMENTATIONS 3:22-25

Have Thine Own Way, Lord!

At forty, Adelaide Pollard was trying unsuccessfully to raise support to go to Africa as a missionary. She wondered why the Lord could so burden her with the needs of Africa but not make it possible for her to go. During this time of discouragement, she attended a small prayer meeting where an elderly woman prayed, "Lord, it doesn't matter what You bring into our lives, just have Your way with us."

That night Pollard went home and read the story of Jeremiah's visit to the potter's house, and later that evening she wrote this hymn. She said that she had always felt the Lord was molding her and preparing her for His service. Then all of a sudden, He seemed to have deserted her.

"Perhaps," she reasoned, "my questioning of God's will shows a flaw in my life. So God decided to break me, as the potter broke the defective vessel, and then to mold my life again in His own pattern."

• • • •

I . . . found the potter working at his wheel. But the jar he was making did not turn out as he had hoped, so he crushed it into a lump of clay again and started over. Then the Lord gave me this message: "O Israel, can I not do to you as this potter has done to his clay? As the clay is in the potter's hand, so are you in my hand."

JEREMIAH 18:3-6

Have Thine own way, Lord! Have Thine own way!
Thou art the potter; I am the clay.
Mold me and make me after Thy will,
While I am waiting, yielded and still.

Have Thine own way, Lord! Have Thine own way!
Search me and try me, Master, today!
Whiter than snow, Lord, wash me just now,
As in Thy presence humbly I bow.

Have Thine own way, Lord! Have Thine own way!
Wounded and weary, help me, I pray!
Power, all power, surely is Thine!
Touch me and heal me, Savior divine!

Have Thine own way, Lord! Have Thine own way!
Hold o'er my being absolute sway!
Fill with Thy Spirit till all shall see
Christ only, always, living in me!

Adelaide Addison Pollard (1862–1934)

To God Be the Glory

To God be the glory—great things He hath done!
So loved He the world that He gave us His Son,
Who yielded His life an atonement for sin,
And opened the life-gate that all may go in.

**Praise the Lord, praise the Lord,
Let the earth hear His voice!
Praise the Lord, praise the Lord,
Let the people rejoice!
O come to the Father through Jesus the Son,
And give Him the glory—great things He hath done!**

O perfect redemption, the purchase of blood!
To ev'ry believer the promise of God;
The vilest offender who truly believes,
That moment from Jesus a pardon receives.

Great things He hath taught us,
great things He hath done,
And great our rejoicing through Jesus the Son;
But purer, and higher, and greater will be
Our wonder, our transport, when Jesus we see.

Fanny Jane Crosby (1820–1915)

It was hard to discourage Fanny Crosby. Joy was a characteristic of her life. When English hymnwriter Frances Ridley Havergal asked someone about Crosby, she received the reply, "She is a blind lady whose heart can see splendidly in the sunshine of God's love." Crosby herself acknowledged, "Darkness may throw a shadow over my outer vision, but there is no cloud that can keep the sunlight of hope from a trustful soul."

Probably written in 1872, this song was taken to England by Ira Sankey, who led the singing for D. L. Moody's evangelistic campaigns. The hymn became immediately popular in England but was published in only a few American hymnals until Billy Graham rediscovered the song during his 1952 British crusade. It then became as popular in America as it had been in England.

• • • •

I will exalt you, my God and King, and praise your name forever and ever. . . . Great is the Lord! He is most worthy of praise! No one can measure his greatness. Let each generation tell its children of your mighty acts; let them proclaim your power.
PSALM 145:1, 3-4

Shepherd of Eager Youth

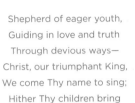

Clement of Alexandria was a scholar of the first order. He was probably born to pagan parents but came to believe in Christ through his studies. He was very familiar with the secular philosophies of his day. In Alexandria he ran a philosophical school that employed both Christian and non-Christian teachers. There he taught a young man named Origen, who later became one of the greatest thinkers in Christian history.

We may see a hint of Clement's love of philosophy in the line "the all-subduing Word." While John's Gospel presents Jesus as the Word, it was a concept borrowed from Greek philosophers, most notably Philo of Alexandria, one of Clement's favorites. In the marketplace of ideas, Jesus the *Logos* had truly conquered all other attempts to explain the nature of God.

• • • •

Christ lives in you. This gives you assurance of sharing his glory. So we tell others about Christ, warning everyone and teaching everyone with all the wisdom God has given us. We want to present them to God, perfect in their relationship to Christ.

COLOSSIANS 1:27-28

Shepherd of eager youth,
Guiding in love and truth
Through devious ways—
Christ, our triumphant King,
We come Thy name to sing;
Hither Thy children bring
Tributes of praise.

Thou art our Holy Lord,
The all-subduing Word;
Healer of strife;
Thou didst Thyself abase
That from sin's deep disgrace
Thou mightest save our race
And give us life.

Ever be near our side,
Our shepherd and our guide,
Our staff and song;
Jesus, Thou Christ of God,
By Thy enduring Word
Lead us where Thou hast trod,
Make our faith strong.

Clement of Alexandria (c. 170–c. 220)

Translated by Henry Martyn Dexter (1821–1890)

Under His Wings I Am Safely Abiding

Under His wings I am safely abiding;
Though the night deepens and tempests are wild,
Still I can trust Him—I know He will keep me;
He has redeemed me and I am His child.

Under His wings, under His wings,
Who from His love can sever?
Under His wings my soul shall abide,
Safely abide forever.

Under His wings, what a refuge in sorrow!
How the heart yearningly turns to His rest!
Often when earth has no balm for my healing,
There I find comfort and there I am blest.

Under His wings, O what precious enjoyment!
There will I hide till life's trials are o'er;
Sheltered, protected, no evil can harm me;
Resting in Jesus I'm safe evermore.

William Orcutt Cushing (1823–1902)

"O Lord, give me something to do for Thee." That was the cry of William O. Cushing when he suddenly lost his voice. He had been a pastor of several churches in New York and had enjoyed fruitful ministry. Then a paralysis affected his voice so he could no longer preach.

Not yet fifty years old, Cushing wondered how God could possibly use him. But God did. Cushing wrote texts for more than three hundred hymns and gospel songs and teamed up with some of the best-known gospel composers of the day.

When he was seventy-three, this prolific hymnwriter was moved by the words of Psalm 17:8, "Hide me in the shadow of your wings," and thought about God's care for him even when everything seemed dark. This song was the result. Though he could not speak with an audible voice, God multiplied his words for generations to come.

• • • •

Those who live in the shelter of the Most High will find rest in the shadow of the Almighty. This I declare about the Lord: He alone is my refuge, my place of safety; he is my God, and I trust him. For he will rescue you from every trap and protect you from deadly disease. He will cover you with his feathers. He will shelter you with his wings.
PSALM 91:1-4

Not What These Hands Have Done

When Horatius Bonar was called to lead the great Chambers Memorial Church in Edinburgh, people wondered if he would change his style. But he didn't. A visitor to his church once wrote, "His voice was low, quiet, and impressive. Once he paused and addressed the Sunday school children who sat by themselves on one side of the pulpit. He is just like his hymns—not great, but tender, sweet, and tranquil."

A hard worker like Bonar might have been tempted to think his deeds were worth something to God, but he knew better. God "saved us, not because of the righteous things we had done, but because of his mercy," Paul wrote to young Titus (3:5). And "salvation is not a reward for the good things we have done, so none of us can boast about it," he wrote to the Ephesians (2:9). Bonar, like Paul, knew that God wants us to come to Him humbly, as little children, trusting completely in what He has accomplished through Jesus Christ.

Not what these hands have done
Can save this guilty soul;
Not what this toiling flesh has borne
Can make my spirit whole.

Not what I feel or do
Can give me peace with God;
Not all my prayers and sighs and tears
Can bear my awful load.

Thy work alone, O Christ,
Can ease this weight of sin;
Thy blood alone, O Lamb of God,
Can give me peace within.

Thy grace alone, O God,
To me can pardon speak;
Thy power alone, O Son of God,
Can this sore bondage break.

I bless the Christ of God,
I rest on love divine,
And with unfaltering lip and heart,
I call this Savior mine.

Horatius Bonar (1808–1889)

• • • •

But God is so rich in mercy, and he loved us so much, that even though we were dead because of our sins, he gave us life when he raised Christ from the dead. (It is only by God's grace that you have been saved!)

EPHESIANS 2:4-5

Let Thy Blood in Mercy Poured

Let Thy blood in mercy poured,
Let Thy gracious body broken,
Be to me, O gracious Lord,
Of boundless love the token.

Thou didst give Thyself for me,
Now I give myself to Thee.

Thou didst die that I might live;
Blessed Lord, Thou cam'st to save me;
All that love of God could give,
Jesus by His sorrows gave me.

By the thorns that crowned Thy brow,
By the spear wound and the nailing,
By the pain and death, I now
Claim, O Christ, Thy love unfailing.

Wilt Thou own the gift I bring?
All my penitence I give Thee;
Thou art my exalted King,
Of Thy matchless love forgive me.

Greek Hymn (sixth–ninth century?)

Translated by John Brownlie (1859–1925)

A transaction occurs when we come to Christ, and this hymn beautifully captures it. We receive Jesus, and Jesus receives us.

In a way, each time we come to worship we review this transaction. In the worship service we hear again of the amazing sacrifice of Christ. We hear how He gave up His heavenly glory to become a man. We hear how He loved us enough to die for us. We hear of the power of His resurrection and the Spirit who now lives in us, empowering us each day. We hear of the promise of eternal life.

But we should also be renewing our vows to the Lord. We should take every opportunity—our songs, our offerings, our words to others, our attentive listening, our standing, sitting, kneeling, or proceeding—to remind the Lord that we belong to Him and will live for Him. We are not our own; we were bought with a price—the precious blood of Jesus.

• • • •

When we were utterly helpless, Christ came at just the right time and died for us sinners. Now, most people would not be willing to die for an upright person, though someone might perhaps be willing to die for a person who is especially good. But God showed his great love for us by sending Christ to die for us while we were still sinners.

ROMANS 5:6-8

O Jesus, King Most Wonderful

Bernard of Clairvaux was a remarkable man of God. Luther called him "the best monk that ever lived."

In 1115, at the age of twenty-five, he was sent to start a new monastery in a place called the Valley of Wormwood. Bernard and his followers changed the name to Clairvaux and transformed the desolate land, which had been a haunt for robbers, into a haven of blessing. Peasants were taught about agriculture and vine culture, and the valley began to blossom. Other monasteries were established, other poverty-stricken areas revived—within Bernard's lifetime there were 162 such monasteries established, bringing spiritual and economic health with them.

Above all else, Bernard was a student of Scripture and a lover of Jesus Christ.

• • • •

For the Lord is the Spirit, and wherever the Spirit of the Lord is, there is freedom. So all of us who have had that veil removed can see and reflect the glory of the Lord. And the Lord—who is the Spirit—makes us more and more like him as we are changed into his glorious image.

2 CORINTHIANS 3:17-18

O Jesus, King most wonderful!
Thou Conqueror renowned!
Thou Sweetness most ineffable,
In whom all joys are found!

When once Thou visitest the heart,
Then truth begins to shine,
Then earthly vanities depart,
Then kindles love divine.

O Jesus! Light of all below,
Thou Fount of life and fire!
Surpassing all the joys we know,
All that we can desire.

Thy wondrous mercies are untold,
Through each returning day;
Thy love exceeds a thousandfold,
Whatever we can say.

Thee may our tongues forever bless;
Thee may we love alone;
And ever in our lives express
The image of Thine own.

Bernard of Clairvaux (1091-1153)

Translated by Edward Caswall (1814-1878)

O Splendor of God's Glory Bright

O splendor of God's glory bright,
O Thou that bringest light from light,
O Light of light, light's living spring,
O Day all days illumining.

O Thou true Sun, on us Thy glance
Let fall in royal radiance;
The Spirit's sanctifying beam
Upon our earthly senses stream.

The Father, too, our prayers implore,
Father of glory evermore;
The Father of all grace and might,
To banish sin from our delight.

To guide whate'er we nobly do,
With love all envy to subdue,
To make ill fortune turn to fair,
And give us grace our wrongs to bear.

Ambrose of Milan (340-397)

Translated by Robert Seymour Bridges (1844-1930)

In many ways, Ambrose of Milan was an unlikely hero of the church. As a lawyer and government leader, he was so well respected that he was asked to be a bishop even before he had been baptized.

Ambrose stood against the Roman emperor when the political ruler tried to pressure the church. An edict of banishment was issued against Ambrose, but he refused to accept it. When Ambrose threatened to excommunicate the soldiers who surrounded the church, they left. Ambrose had won.

But Ambrose's biggest battle was theological. His foe was the heresy of Arianism, which held that Jesus Christ was a created being. Condemned by church councils, this false teaching enjoyed continued popularity among the people. Ambrose wrote hymns upholding the deity of Christ so that believers might have the truth embedded in their hearts.

• • • •

We preach that Jesus Christ is Lord, and we ourselves are your servants for Jesus' sake. For God, who said, "Let there be light in the darkness," has made this light shine in our hearts so we could know the glory of God that is seen in the face of Jesus Christ.
2 CORINTHIANS 4:5-6

The Lord Is King!

When Josiah Conder left school in 1802 at the age of thirteen, he didn't leave the world of books. His father was a bookseller in London, and young Conder joined his father's business. At twenty-five he became publisher of a magazine and later the editor of a newspaper. An evangelical, he frequently opposed the action of the established church and faced determined opposition. He said his best hymns were written in times of trial or change.

When Conder lay dying at the age of sixty-six, he asked to have his poems read. The last stanza of one of them, which he asked to have read three times, is "Beset with fears and cares, in Him my heart is strong. All things in life and death are theirs, who to the Lord belong." One of his children said after the third reading, "Now you can sleep on that." "Oh yes," responded Josiah, "and die upon it."

The Lord is King! Lift up Thy voice,
O earth; and all ye heav'ns, rejoice:
From world to world the joy shall ring,
"The Lord omnipotent is King!"

The Lord is King! Who then shall dare
Resist His will, distrust His care,
Or murmur at His wise decrees,
Or doubt His royal promises?

The Lord is King! Child of the dust,
The Judge of all the earth is just;
Holy and true are all His ways:
Let ev'ry creature speak His praise.

Alike pervaded by His eye,
All parts of His dominion lie;
This world of ours, and worlds unseen,
And thin the boundary between.

One Lord, one empire, all secures;
He reigns, and life and death are yours:
Through earth and heav'n one song shall ring,
"The Lord omnipotent is King!"

Josiah Conder (1789–1855)

• • • •

Then I heard again what sounded like the shout of a vast crowd or the roar of mighty ocean waves or the crash of loud thunder: "Praise the Lord! For the Lord our God, the Almighty, reigns."
REVELATION 19:6

Open My Eyes, That I May See

Open my eyes, that I may see
Glimpses of truth Thou hast for me;
Place in my hands the wonderful key,
That shall unclasp and set me free.
Silently now I wait for Thee,
Ready, my God, Thy will to see;
Open my eyes, illumine me,
Spirit divine!

Open my ears, that I may hear
Voices of truth Thou sendest clear;
And while the wave-notes fall on my ear,
Ev'rything false will disappear.
Silently now I wait for Thee,
Ready, my God, Thy will to see;
Open my ears, illumine me,
Spirit divine!

Open my mouth, and let it bear
Gladly the warm truth ev'rywhere;
Open my heart, and let me prepare
Love with Thy children thus to share.
Silently now I wait for Thee,
Ready, my God, Thy will to see;
Open my heart, illumine me,
Spirit divine!

Clara H. Scott (1841-1897)

In our busy lives we often miss the quiet promptings of God's Spirit. And when we do hear God speak, we often ignore the message. "I'm too busy now," we say. "I have more important things to do." This hymn calls us to watch and listen, and then to act on what we have seen and heard, sharing it with others.

Clara Scott was a music teacher who composed a great deal of instrumental and vocal music. She became known for her book of anthems, *The Royal Anthem Book*, which was published in 1882. Her productive life of composing and teaching at the Women's Seminary in Lyons, Iowa, is evidence that her eyes and ears were open to God's leading and that she was ready to share what God gave her. We should be ready to do the same.

• • • •

Be good to your servant, that I may live and obey your word. Open my eyes to see the wonderful truths in your instructions. I am only a foreigner in the land. Don't hide your commands from me! I am always overwhelmed with a desire for your regulations.
PSALM 119:17-20

Just a Closer Walk with Thee

A father left his son a note that read, "Will be in Far East on your birthday, but back Saturday with gift. What would you like—video game, bike, phone?" The boy circled the item he wanted—"Saturday."

The boy could have chosen any plaything he wanted, but most of all he wanted to know his father. That's the heart of this familiar spiritual. "Just a closer walk with Thee," that's all we ask. As Paul said, "Everything else is worthless when compared with the infinite value of knowing Christ Jesus my Lord" (Philippians 3:8).

Fortunately, we don't have an "absentee" heavenly Father. He is there for us and will grant this request. He is happy to walk with us, to share our burdens, to guide us safely to the shore of His Kingdom.

• • • •

Those who live in the shelter of the Most High will find rest in the shadow of the Almighty. This I declare about the Lord: He alone is my refuge, my place of safety; he is my God, and I trust him.

PSALM 91:1-2

I am weak but Thou art strong;
Jesus, keep me from all wrong;
I'll be satisfied as long
As I walk, let me walk close to Thee.

Just a closer walk with Thee,
Grant it, Jesus, is my plea,
Daily, walking close to Thee,
Let it be, dear Lord, let it be.

Through this world of toil and snares,
If I falter, Lord, who cares?
Who with me my burden shares?
None but Thee, dear Lord, none but Thee.

When my feeble life is o'er,
Time for me will be no more;
Guide me gently, safely o'er
To Thy kingdom shore, to Thy shore.

Author unknown

Lamb of God!

♫♪

Lamb of God! Our souls adore Thee,
  While upon Thy face we gaze;
There the Father's love and glory
  Shine in all their brightest rays;
Thine Almighty pow'r and wisdom
  All creation's works proclaim;
Heav'n and earth alike confess Thee
  As the ever great "I AM."

Lamb of God! Thy Father's bosom
  Ever was Thy dwelling place;
His delight, in Him rejoicing,
  One with Him in pow'r and grace;
Oh, what wondrous love and mercy!
  Thou didst lay Thy glory by;
And for us didst come from heaven
  As the Lamb of God to die.

Lamb of God! When we behold Thee
  Lowly in the manger laid,
Wand'ring as a homeless stranger
  In the world Thy hands had made;
When we see Thee in the garden
  In Thine agony of blood
At Thy grace we are confounded,
  Holy, spotless, Lamb of God!

Lamb of God! Thou soon in glory
  Wilt to this sad earth return;
All Thy foes shall quake before Thee,
  All that now despise Thee mourn;
Then Thy saints all gather'd to Thee,
  With Thee in Thy kingdom reign;
Thine the praise and Thine the glory,
  Lamb of God, for sinners slain!

James G. Deck (1802–1884)

In Isaiah 53, the prophet compares the Messiah to a quiet lamb. He also reminds us that we have all gone astray "like sheep," but that this lamblike Servant will bear the weight of our sins. That fits, of course, with the Jewish tradition of sacrifice. An animal was offered in place of the person; the animal died so the person could live. At the first Passover, it was the blood of a slain lamb, swabbed on the doorposts, that saved the Israelites from the angel of death.

When John the Baptist saw Jesus, he called Him the Lamb of God. Already Jesus' atoning death was on the horizon. It came soon enough, three Passovers later, fulfilling Isaiah's prophecy. The Lamb figures prominently in the book of Revelation. This Lamb is not a victim but a victor. The foes "will go to war against the Lamb, but the Lamb will defeat them" (Revelation 17:14). The Lamb receives songs of praise and ends this book with an invitation to His wedding feast.

• • • •

The next day John saw Jesus coming toward him and said, "Look! The Lamb of God who takes away the sin of the world! . . . I saw this happen to Jesus, so I testify that he is the Chosen One of God."
JOHN 1:29, 34

My God, How Wonderful Thou Art

Frederick Faber moved from the Anglican church to the Roman Catholic fold at thirty-one. He missed the hymns of Wesley, Newton, and Cowper that had meant so much in his youth. So he wrote 150 hymns over the following eighteen years, including "Faith of Our Fathers" (June 19) and "There's a Wideness in God's Mercy" (July 18).

We often use the word *wonderful* quite carelessly, but Faber was speaking of God as "full of wonder." It is only when we take time to consider God's greatness, as Faber does in this hymn, that we truly begin to worship. The hymn takes us step by step through the sense of adoration, of fear, of love, and of devotion, as we see all the great attributes of God displayed. The stanza of consecration, often omitted from our hymnals, reads, "Oh, then, this worse than worthless heart in pity deign to take, and make it love Thee for Thyself and for Thy glory's sake."

• • • •

The high and lofty one who lives in eternity, the Holy One, says this: "I live in the high and holy place with those whose spirits are contrite and humble. I restore the crushed spirit of the humble and revive the courage of those with repentant hearts."

ISAIAH 57:15

My God, how wonderful Thou art,
Thy majesty how bright,
How beautiful Thy mercy seat,
In depths of burning light!

How dread are Thine eternal years,
O everlasting Lord,
By prostrate spirits day and night
Incessantly adored!

O how I fear Thee, living God,
With deepest, tenderest fears,
And worship Thee with trembling hope
And penitential tears!

Yet I may love Thee too, O Lord,
Almighty as Thou art,
For Thou hast stooped to ask of me
The love of my poor heart.

No earthly father loves like Thee;
No mother e'er so mild,
Bears and forbears as Thou hast done
With me, Thy sinful child.

How wonderful, how beautiful,
The sight of Thee must be,
Thine endless wisdom, boundless power,
And awful purity!

Frederick William Faber (1814-1863)

Thee Will I Love, My Strength

Thee will I love, my strength, my tow'r,
Thee will I love, my joy, my crown,
Thee will I love with all my pow'r
In all my works and Thee alone,
Thee will I love 'til sacred fire
Fills my whole soul with pure desire.

I thank Thee uncreated Sun
That Thy bright beams on me have shined;
I thank Thee, who hast overthrown
My foes, and healed my wounded mind:
I thank Thee whose enlivening voice
Bids my freed heart in Thee rejoice.

Uphold me in the doubtful race,
Nor suffer me again to stray;
Strengthen my feet with steady pace
Still to press forward in Thy way:
That all my pow'rs, with all their might,
In Thy sole glory may unite.

Thee will I love, my joy, my crown;
Thee will I love, my Lord, my God;
Thee will I love, beneath Thy frown
Or smile, Thy sceptre or Thy rod;
What though my flesh and heart decay,
Thee shall I love in endless day.

Johann Scheffler (1624–1677)

Translated by John Wesley (1703–1791)

John Wesley's life is confusing because he ministered in the church *before* his well-known conversion. But he would say that he was just working for God and not loving God.

Years later, John and Charles Wesley went to Georgia as ministers of the Church of England. They were devoutly following the letter of the law in regard to Christian teaching, but the spirit was still missing. On the boat trip to America, Wesley met a group of Moravian Christians who impressed him greatly. There was great joy in their faith, and they were always singing. This Scheffler hymn may have been introduced to Wesley by those Moravians.

But it wasn't until 1738, back in England, that Wesley himself felt the "sacred fire" within him. His faith was no longer just an agenda of spiritual activities. Now he could sing, "Thee will I love, my joy, my crown."

• • • •

Jesus replied, "What does the law of Moses say? How do you read it?" The man answered, "'You must love the Lord your God with all your heart, all your soul, all your strength, and all your mind.' And, 'Love your neighbor as yourself.'" "Right!" Jesus told him. "Do this and you will live!"

LUKE 10:26-28

Thy Works, Not Mine, O Christ

There is religion, and then there is faith. Religion is humanity reaching for God. Different religions in their different ways try to reach their God or gods. Rituals, lifestyles, philosophies are all aimed at attaining the favor of deity.

Faith, by contrast, is merely taking the hand of God, who is reaching out to us. We enter into a relationship that is His doing, not ours. This is the Good News of Christianity. Some people take the elements of Christianity and try to make a religion out of them, but it is, pure and simple, a matter of faith—receiving what God has done.

That's why we need strong and simple songs like this one. Bonar echoes a recurring strain in Scripture. "No righteousness avails save that which is of Thee."

• • • •

When God our Savior revealed his kindness and love, he saved us, not because of the righteous things we had done, but because of his mercy. He washed away our sins, giving us a new birth and new life through the Holy Spirit. He generously poured out the Spirit upon us through Jesus Christ our Savior. Because of his grace he declared us righteous and gave us confidence that we will inherit eternal life.

TITUS 3:4-7

Thy works, not mine, O Christ,
Speak gladness to this heart;
They tell me all is done;
They bid my fear depart.

To whom, save Thee, who canst alone
For sin atone, Lord, shall I flee?

Thy pains, not mine, O Christ,
Upon the shameful tree,
Have paid the law's full price
And purchased peace for me.

Thy cross, not mine, O Christ,
Has borne the awful load
Of sins that none in heav'n
Or earth could bear but God.

Thy righteousness, O Christ,
Alone can cover me:
No righteousness avails
Save that which is of Thee.

Horatius Bonar (1808-1889)

A Mighty Fortress Is Our God

A mighty fortress is our God, a bulwark never failing;
Our helper He amid the flood of mortal ills prevailing.
For still our ancient foe doth seek to work us woe—
His craft and pow'r are great,
and, armed with cruel hate,
On earth is not his equal.

Did we in our own strength confide,
our striving would be losing,
Were not the right man on our side,
the man of God's own choosing.
Dost ask who that may be? Christ Jesus, it is He—
Lord Sabaoth His name, from age to age the same,
And He must win the battle.

And though this world, with devils filled,
should threaten to undo us,
We will not fear, for God hath willed His
truth to triumph through us.
The prince of darkness grim, we tremble not for him—
His rage we can endure, for lo! his doom is sure:
One little word shall fell him.

That word above all earthly pow'rs,
no thanks to them, abideth;
The Spirit and the gifts are ours
through Him who with us sideth.
Let goods and kindred go, this mortal life also—
The body they may kill; God's truth abideth still:
His kingdom is forever.

Martin Luther (1483-1546)

Translated by Frederick H. Hedge (1805-1890)

After posting his ninety-five theses on the door of Wittenberg's Castle Church in October 1517, Martin Luther faced many years of trials and persecution. And during the years of the ensuing Protestant Reformation, Luther came to know better than most the gracious power of God's sheltering hand. He confidently stepped forward to defend the truth he found in God's Word, despite excommunication from the Roman church, continual threats to his life and freedom, and times of intense spiritual battle.

In the comforting words of Psalm 46, Luther found the inspiration for this hymn that would become the battle cry of the Protestant Reformation. Many who suffered for their faith during that time found solid comfort in Luther's words of faith and praise. "A mighty fortress is our God!"

• • • •

God is our refuge and strength, always ready to help in times of trouble. So we will not fear when earthquakes come and the mountains crumble into the sea. Let the oceans roar and foam. Let the mountains tremble as the waters surge!

PSALM 46:1-3

For All the Saints

In 1864 Bishop William How wrote this hymn for All Saints Day. He cited Hebrews 12:1 in his original title, but he drew on all of Hebrews 11 for inspiration. That's the famous "faith chapter," which praises the faithful deeds of a score of Old Testament heroes.

The author might be considered a hero of the faith himself. He was a man of the people, regularly reaching out to minister to the poor and needy in his area. Once he listed the characteristics that a minister should have; among them was being "wholly without thought of self." Those who knew him said that Bishop How was like that, selflessly caring for others.

• • • •

Together, we are his house, built on the foundation of the apostles and the prophets. And the cornerstone is Christ Jesus himself. We are carefully joined together in him, becoming a holy temple for the Lord.

EPHESIANS 2:20-21

For all the saints, who from their labors rest,
Who Thee by faith before the world confessed,
Thy name, O Jesus, be forever blest.
Alleluia, Alleluia!

Thou wast their rock, their fortress, and their might;
Thou, Lord, their captain in the well-fought fight;
Thou, in the darkness drear, their one true light.
Alleluia, Alleluia!

O may Thy soldiers, faithful, true, and bold,
Fight as the saints who nobly fought of old,
And win with them the victor's crown of gold.
Alleluia, Alleluia!

O blest communion, fellowship divine!
We feebly struggle, they in glory shine;
Yet all are one in Thee, for all are Thine.
Alleluia, Alleluia!

And when the strife is fierce, the warfare long,
Steals on the ear the distant triumph song,
And hearts are brave again, and arms are strong.
Alleluia, Alleluia!

From earth's wide bounds, from ocean's farthest coast,
Through gates of pearl streams in the countless host,
Singing to Father, Son, and Holy Ghost.
Alleluia, Alleluia!

William Walsham How (1823–1897)

Zion, to Thy Savior Singing

Zion, to thy Savior singing,
To thy Prince and Shepherd bringing
Sweetest hymns of love and praise,
Thou wilt never reach the measure
Of His worth, by all the treasures
Of thy most ecstatic lays.

Of all wonders that can thrill thee,
And with adoration fill thee,
What than this can greater be,
That Himself to thee He giveth?
He that eateth ever liveth,
For the Bread of Life is He.

Fill thy lips to overflowing
With sweet praise, His mercy showing
Who this heav'nly table spread:
On this day so glad and holy,
To each longing spirit lowly
Giveth He the living Bread.

Here the King hath spread His table,
Whereon eyes of faith are able
Christ our Passover to trace:
Shadows of the law are going,
Light and life and truth inflowing,
Night to day is giving place.

O Good Shepherd, Bread life-giving,
Us, Thy grace and life receiving,
Feed and shelter evermore;
Thou on earth our weakness guiding,
We in heav'n with Thee abiding
With all saints will Thee adore.

Thomas Aquinas (c. 1225–1274)

Translated by Alexander R. Thompson (1822–1895)

Thomas Aquinas is among the greatest Christian thinkers in the history of the church. During the Middle Ages, he anchored Christian theology to Aristotle's philosophy and recovered the role of reason in church life. In this way he paved the way for the Reformation and Renaissance. Not that everyone agrees with all aspects of his theology. His teachings were suspect within the church at first, and later the Reformers took issue with some of his assertions. But he remains one of the most influential Christian thinkers of all time, an intellectual light during the Dark Ages.

Despite Aquinas's intellectual brilliance, his hymn is not bathed in intellectualism. It is a simple Communion hymn, a meditation on the Lord's Table. After speaking of the surpassing wonder of Christ, he marvels that Christ offers His own body and blood for us.

• • • •

Anyone who eats my flesh and drinks my blood remains in me, and I in him. I live because of the living Father who sent me; in the same way, anyone who feeds on me will live because of me.
JOHN 6:56-57

God of the Earth, the Sky, the Sea

Samuel Longfellow, brother of the famous poet Henry Wadsworth Longfellow, loved the seashore. He once compiled a book called *Thalatta*, including "all the charming bits of poetry in the language about the sea and the seashore."

Like many of the psalms, this hymn praises God for His involvement in nature. Paul wrote that the invisible qualities of God are clearly seen in what God has created. Longfellow echoes Paul's message here. God's love, life, power, and even His law are seen in the events of nature.

• • • •

He is the God who made the world and everything in it. Since he is Lord of heaven and earth, he doesn't live in man-made temples, and human hands can't serve his needs—for he has no needs. He himself gives life and breath to everything, and he satisfies every need. From one man he created all the nations throughout the whole earth. He decided beforehand when they should rise and fall, and he determined their boundaries. His purpose was for the nations to seek after God and perhaps feel their way toward him and find him—though he is not far from any one of us. For in him we live and move and exist.

ACTS 17:24-28

God of the earth, the sky, the sea,
Maker of all above below,
Creation lives and moves in Thee,
Thy present life through all doth flow.

Thy love is in the sunshine's glow,
Thy life is in the quickening air;
When lightnings flash and storm winds blow,
There is Thy power; Thy law is there.

We feel Thy calm at evening's hour,
Thy grandeur in the march of night;
And when the morning breaks in power,
We hear Thy word, "Let there be light!"

But higher far, and far more clear,
Thee in man's spirit we behold;
Thine image and Thyself are there,
Th'indwelling God, proclaimed of old.

Samuel Longfellow (1819-1892)

Teach Me, My God and King

Teach me, my God and King,
In all things Thee to see,
And what I do in anything,
To do it as for Thee.

A man that looks on glass,
On it may stay his eye,
Or, if he pleaseth, through it pass,
And then the heav'n espy.

All may of Thee partake:
Nothing can be so mean
Which with this motive, "For Thy sake,"
Will not grow bright and clean.

This is the famous stone
That turneth all to gold;
For that which God doth touch and own
Cannot for less be told.

George Herbert (1593–1633)

George Herbert was a brilliant and privileged young man who gave his all for God's glory. From a noted Welsh family, he went to Cambridge University at age fifteen and specialized in rhetoric and oratory. Herbert became a country priest and wrote about his experiences. He also wrote poetry, focusing on the Christian's heart as a temple of God.

Shortly before his death he sent a manuscript of his poems to a fellow churchman. He asked him to publish the poems if he thought anybody could benefit. But if not, he told him to burn them. He concluded, "I and [the poems] are the least of God's mercies."

The last stanza here alludes to the medieval belief in a "philosopher's stone" that would touch a baser metal and turn it to gold. Herbert says that doing things for God's sake *is* that stone, because God takes what is offered to Him and makes it precious. That was the story of George Herbert's life.

• • • •

So whether you eat or drink, or whatever you do, do it all for the glory of God. Don't give offense to Jews or Gentiles or the church of God. I, too, try to please everyone in everything I do. I don't just do what is best for me; I do what is best for others so that many may be saved.

I CORINTHIANS 10:31-33

O Christ, Our King, Creator, Lord

"Keep on seeking, and you will find," said Jesus (Matthew 7:7). "Seek the Lord while you can find him," said Isaiah (Isaiah 55:6). And God said through Amos, "Come back to me and live!" (Amos 5:4). The Bible encourages people to look for the Lord, and as this hymn puts it, God is "to them who seek [Him] ever near."

Gregory the Great was the influential pope who reminded the church of how to sing. Ray Palmer was a schoolteacher, pastor, and hymnal editor who also wrote "My Faith Looks Up to Thee" (April 26) and translated "Jesus, Thou Joy of Loving Hearts" (November 18). It is helpful to remember that even these great Christians struggled with "inbred sin" and searched for freedom in Christ.

• • • •

Seek the Lord while you can find him. Call on him now while he is near. Let the wicked change their ways and banish the very thought of doing wrong. Let them turn to the Lord that he may have mercy on them. Yes, turn to our God, for he will forgive generously.

ISAIAH 55:6-7

O Christ, our King, Creator, Lord,
Savior of all who trust Thy Word,
To them who seek Thee ever near,
Now to our praises bend Thine ear.

In Thy dear cross a grace is found—
It flows from every streaming wound—
Whose pow'r our inbred sin controls,
Breaks the firm bond, and frees our souls.

Thou didst create the stars of night;
Yet Thou hast veiled in flesh Thy light,
Hast deigned a mortal form to wear,
A mortal's painful lot to bear.

When Thou didst hang upon the tree,
The quaking earth acknowledged Thee;
When Thou didst there yield up Thy breath,
The world grew dark as shades of death.

Now in the Father's glory high,
Great Conqueror, nevermore to die,
Us by Thy mighty pow'r defend,
And reign through ages without end.

Gregory the Great (540-604)

Translated by Ray Palmer (1808-1887)

O Christ, Our True and Only Light

O Christ, our true and only Light,
Illumine those who sit in night;
Let those afar now hear Thy voice,
And in Thy fold with us rejoice.

And all who else have strayed from Thee,
O gently seek; Thy healing be
To ev'ry wounded conscience giv'n;
And let them also share Thy heav'n.

O make the deaf to hear Thy Word;
And teach the dumb to speak, dear Lord,
Who dare not yet the faith avow,
Though secretly they hold it now.

Shine on the darkened and the cold;
Recall the wand'rers from Thy fold;
Unite those now who walk apart;
Confirm the weak and doubting heart.

So they with us may evermore
Such grace with wond'ring thanks adore,
And endless praise to Thee be giv'n
By all the church in earth and heav'n.

Johann Heermann (1585-1647)

Translated by Catherine Winkworth (1827-1878)

This hymn reminds us that God seeks those who are lost. Jesus told the story of the Prodigal's father, who watched for the return of his runaway son. God is like that, "gently seeking" those who have strayed, offering his healing to those who will receive it.

This may be the earliest missionary hymn we have. Johann Heermann was a Lutheran pastor in the German village of Köben. This town was at the center of conflict during the Thirty Years' War, which pitted Protestants against Catholics throughout central Europe. Historians estimate that half the population of Germany died in the fighting. And there, as the smoke cleared, Heermann was calling for lost souls to come to the Savior.

• • • •

I am the good shepherd; I know my own sheep, and they know me, just as my Father knows me and I know the Father. So I sacrifice my life for the sheep. I have other sheep, too, that are not in this sheepfold. I must bring them also. They will listen to my voice, and there will be one flock with one shepherd.

JOHN 10:14-16

Gentle Jesus, Meek and Mild

The story is told of a little girl named Becca, who lived in an institution for troubled children. She had never spoken, and her behavior was quite violent. This was in the 1800s, when treatment for emotional problems was still quite primitive. But there was a nurse who showed love to this little girl. And slowly Becca calmed down. Still, she wouldn't speak.

One summer evening, the nurse put Becca to bed early. The sun had just gone down, and some birds were singing outside. Then the nurse heard another voice along with the birds. It was Becca. Alone in her room she was singing a song she had heard the other children sing: "Gentle Jesus, meek and mild, look upon a little child; pity my simplicity; suffer me to come to Thee."

• • • •

Gentle Jesus, meek and mild,
Look upon a little child;
Pity my simplicity,
Suffer me to come to Thee.

Lamb of God, I look to Thee;
Thou shalt my example be:
Thou art gentle, meek and mild;
Thou wast once a little child.

Fain I would be as Thou art;
Give me Thine obedient heart:
Thou art pitiful and kind;
Let me have Thy loving mind.

Loving Jesus, gentle Lamb,
In Thy gracious hands I am;
Make me, Savior, what Thou art,
Live Thyself within my heart.

Charles Wesley (1707–1788)

One day some parents brought their little children to Jesus so he could touch and bless them. But when the disciples saw this, they scolded the parents for bothering him. Then Jesus called for the children and said to the disciples, "Let the children come to me. Don't stop them! For the Kingdom of God belongs to those who are like these children. I tell you the truth, anyone who doesn't receive the Kingdom of God like a child will never enter it."

LUKE 18:15-17

Praise, My Soul, the King of Heaven

Praise, my soul, the King of heaven,
To His feet thy tribute bring;
Ransomed, healed, restored, forgiven,
Evermore His praises sing.
Alleluia! Alleluia! Praise the everlasting King.

Praise Him for His grace and favor
To our fathers in distress;
Praise Him, still the same as ever,
Slow to chide, and swift to bless,
Alleluia! Alleluia! Glorious in His faithfulness.

Fatherlike, He tends and spares us;
Well our feeble frame He knows;
In His hands He gently bears us,
Rescues us from all our foes.
Alleluia! Alleluia! Widely yet His mercy flows.

Angels in the height, adore Him;
Ye behold Him face to face;
Saints triumphant, bow before Him,
Gathered in from every race.
Alleluia! Alleluia! Praise with us the God of grace.

Henry Francis Lyte (1793–1847)

In 1834 the British clergyman Henry Francis Lyte published a collection of 280 hymns based on the book of Psalms. He called it *The Spirit of the Psalms* because these hymns were not strictly translations (like the old psalters still in use at that time) or even paraphrases (like much of Isaac Watts's work), but texts loosely inspired by the psalms. This hymn was included as a development of Psalm 103. There are many points of comparison.

The psalmist urges us not to forget the Lord's benefits; Lyte lists those benefits—"ransomed, healed, restored, forgiven." And as the psalmist indicates that God is "slow to chide," Lyte adds that he is also "swift to bless."

Queen Elizabeth II chose this hymn to be sung at her wedding in 1947. It is an apt song for any occasion, as we join our voices in this great "Alleluia!"

• • • •

Let all that I am praise the Lord; with my whole heart, I will praise his holy name. Let all that I am praise the Lord; may I never forget the good things he does for me. He forgives all my sins and heals all my diseases.
PSALM 103:1-3

In Christ There Is No East or West

John Oxenham's real name was William Arthur Dunkerley. He ran a successful wholesale grocery company and served as a deacon in a Congregational church. He was also a writer, working for newspapers and magazines. Like many journalists, he longed to do more creative work. Perhaps a bit embarrassed about these efforts, he used the name Julian Ross when he wrote some short stories. He borrowed the name John Oxenham from an adventure novel and used it for his poems and hymns. Many of his friends never knew about his triple identity.

Oxenham's writing was very popular. When he couldn't find a publisher for his book *Bees in Amber*, which included this hymn, he published it himself—and sold 286,000 copies!

In Christ there is no east or west,
In Him no south or north;
But one great fellowship of love
Throughout the whole wide earth.

In Him shall true hearts everywhere
Their high communion find;
His service is the golden cord
Close binding all mankind.

Join hands, then, brothers of the faith,
Whate'er your race may be.
Who serves my Father as a son
Is surely kin to me.

In Christ now meet both east and west,
In Him meet south and north;
All Christly souls are one in Him
Throughout the whole wide earth.

John Oxenham (1852–1941)

• • • •

There is no longer Jew or Gentile, slave or free, male and female. For you are all one in Christ Jesus. And now that you belong to Christ, you are the true children of Abraham. You are his heirs, and God's promise to Abraham belongs to you.

GALATIANS 3:28-29

God, in the Gospel of His Son

God, in the gospel of His Son,
Makes His eternal counsels known;
Where love in all its glory shines,
And truth is drawn in fairest lines.

Here sinners of a humble frame
May taste His grace, and learn His Name;
May read, in characters of blood,
The wisdom, pow'r, and grace of God.

The pris'ner here may break his chains;
The weary rest from all his pains;
The captive feel his bondage cease;
The mourner find the way of peace.

Here faith reveals to mortal eyes
A brighter world beyond the skies;
Here shines the light which guides our way
From earth to realms of endless day.

O grant us grace, Almighty Lord,
To read and mark Thy holy Word;
Its truths with meekness to receive,
And by its holy precepts live.

Benjamin Beddome (1717-1795)

Thomas Cotterill (1779-1823)

Sometimes those who have been Christians for a long time take the Bible for granted. But what joy the newcomer finds there! Each page of Scripture reveals fresh and eternal truths. It brings strength and hope into dismal lives. It announces a message of freedom—freedom from sin, freedom from aimlessness, and freedom to love God with all our heart, soul, and mind. God's Word shines light into the darkness of people's lives.

This hymn reminds us that Scripture helps us to recognize the name of our loving Lord. For some this search for the heavenly Father is as desperate as that of an adopted child for his or her birth parents. There's a voice in a dream, faintly calling, but who is it? Then the Good Book opens, and the lost child sees the name that has lived in his hopes—almighty Lord, loving Savior, Friend, and Guide.

• • • •

All Scripture is inspired by God and is useful to teach us what is true and to make us realize what is wrong in our lives. It corrects us when we are wrong and teaches us to do what is right. God uses it to prepare and equip his people to do every good work.
2 TIMOTHY 3:16-17

How Lovely Shines the Morning Star

When Philipp Nicolai was pastor at Unna, Germany, an awful plague hit the town. His window overlooked the cemetery. There were sometimes as many as thirty burials in a single day. It seemed that every home in the town was mourning for a stricken family member. It was a difficult time to be a pastor. How did he get through it?

"There seemed to me nothing more sweet, delightful, and agreeable," Nicolai wrote, "than the contemplation of the noble, sublime doctrine of Eternal Life obtained through the Blood of Christ. This I allowed to dwell in my heart day and night." Christ enlarges our scope of vision. We serve Him as much as possible here on earth, but we realize there's another chapter to come, an eternal existence in heaven with Him.

• • • •

[Jesus] went first to Nazareth, then left there and moved to Capernaum, beside the Sea of Galilee, in the region of Zebulun and Naphtali. This fulfilled what God said through the prophet Isaiah: "In the land of Zebulun and of Naphtali, beside the sea, beyond the Jordan River, in Galilee where so many Gentiles live, the people who sat in darkness have seen a great light. And for those who lived in the land where death casts its shadow, a light has shined."

MATTHEW 4:13-16

How lovely shines the Morning Star!
The nations see and hail afar
The light in Judah shining.
Thou David's Son of Jacob's race,
My Bridegroom and my King of Grace,
For Thee my heart is pining.
Lowly, Holy, Great and glorious,
Thou victorious Prince of graces,
Filling all the heav'nly places.

Now richly to my waiting heart,
O Thou, my God, deign to impart
The grace of love undying.
In Thy blest body let me be,
E'en as the branch is in the tree,
Thy life my life supplying.
Sighing, crying, for the savor
Of Thy favor; resting never
Till I rest in Thee forever.

Thou, mighty Father, in Thy Son
Didst love me ere Thou hadst begun
This ancient world's foundation.
Thy Son hath made a friend of me,
And when in spirit Him I see,
I joy in tribulation.
What bliss is this! He that liveth
To me giveth Life forever;
Nothing me from Him can sever.

Philipp Nicolai (1556-1608)

_____

Composite Translation

O Lord, How Shall I Meet Thee

O Lord, how shall I meet Thee,
How welcome Thee aright?
Thy people long to greet Thee,
My Hope, my heart's Delight!
O kindle, Lord most holy,
Thy lamp within my breast
To do in spirit lowly
All that may please Thee best.

Love caused Thine incarnation,
Love brought Thee down to me;
Thy thirst for my salvation
Procured my liberty.
O love beyond all telling,
That led Thee to embrace,
In love all love excelling,
Our lost and fallen race!

Rejoice, then, ye sad-hearted,
Who sit in deepest gloom,
Who mourn o'er joys departed
And tremble at your doom.
Despair not, He is near you,
Yea, standing at the door,
Who best can help and cheer you
And bids you weep no more.

Sin's debt, that fearful burden,
Let not your souls distress;
Your guilt the Lord will pardon
And cover by His grace.
He comes, for men procuring
The peace of sin forgiv'n,
For all God's sons securing
Their heritage in heav'n.

Paul Gerhardt (1607–1676)

Composite Translation

If Martin Luther was the mind of German hymnwriting, Paul Gerhardt was its heart. Gerhardt wrote devotional songs of love and commitment—133 hymns in all, including "Jesus, Thy Boundless Love to Me" (August 18).

Not that Gerhardt's life was all peaceful contemplation. Far from it! Like many other hymnwriters of his era, he faced the Thirty Years' War, which devastated Germany. Four of his children died in infancy, and he lost his wife after only thirteen years of marriage. Gerhardt also walked a rocky road professionally. He was a popular Lutheran pastor, but after defying an order of the secular ruler, Elector Frederick William I, he was banished from his thriving ministry in Berlin.

In spite of his troubles, his hymns still ring with love for the Lord. He seemed truly to strive "to do in spirit lowly all that may please" the Lord.

• • • •

The Kingdom of Heaven will be like ten bridesmaids who took their lamps and went to meet the bridegroom. Five of them were foolish, and five were wise. The five who were foolish didn't take enough olive oil for their lamps, but the other five were wise enough to take along extra oil. When the bridegroom was delayed, they all became drowsy and fell asleep. At midnight they were roused by the shout, "Look, the bridegroom is coming! Come out and meet him!"

MATTHEW 25:1-6

O Dearest Jesus

Jean de Fécamp was a Benedictine monk who lived and wrote over a thousand years ago. Fécamp was head of a monastic colony in Normandy for half a century. Later in his career, he decided to visit the Holy Land. While there, he was arrested and imprisoned by the ruling Turks. You might imagine him in that dank Turkish jail, as he remembered another innocent man imprisoned in Palestine by an occupying army—Jesus Christ.

It is no surprise that Lutheran pastor Johann Heermann should translate this hymn and develop the theme as his German town of Köben was ravaged by the Thirty Years' War.

• • • •

He had done no wrong and had never deceived anyone. But he was buried like a criminal; he was put in a rich man's grave. But it was the Lord's good plan to crush him and cause him grief. Yet when his life is made an offering for sin, he will have many descendants. He will enjoy a long life, and the Lord's good plan will prosper in his hands. When he sees all that is accomplished by his anguish, he will be satisfied. And because of his experience, my righteous servant will make it possible for many to be counted righteous, for he will bear all their sins.

ISAIAH 53:9-11

O dearest Jesus, what law hast Thou broken
That such sharp sentence should on Thee be spoken?
Of what great crime hast Thou to make confession,
What dark transgression?

They crown Thy head with thorns, they smite,
they scourge Thee;
With cruel mockings to the cross they urge Thee;
They give Thee gall to drink, they still decry Thee;
They crucify Thee.

Whence come these sorrows,
whence this mortal anguish?
It is my sins for which Thou, Lord, must languish;
Yea, all the wrath, the woe, Thou dost inherit,
This I do merit.

What punishment so strange is suffered yonder!
The Shepherd dies for sheep that loved to wander;
The Master pays the debt His servants owe Him,
Who would not know Him.

Jean de Fécamp (c. 1000-1079)

_____

Johann Heermann (1585–1647)
Translated by Catherine Winkworth (1827–1878)

Savior of the Nations, Come

Savior of the nations, come,
Virgin's Son, make here Thy home!
Marvel now, O heav'n and earth,
That the Lord chose such a birth.

Not of flesh and blood the Son,
Offspring of the Holy One;
Born of Mary ever blest
God in flesh is manifest.

Wondrous birth! O wondrous Child
Of the virgin undefiled!
Though by all the world disowned,
Still to be in heav'n throned.

From the Father forth He came
And returneth to the same,
Captive leading death and hell,
High the song of triumph swell!

Thou, the Father's only Son,
Hast o'er sin the vict'ry won.
Boundless shall Thy kingdom be;
When shall we its glories see?

Praise to God the Father sing,
Praise to God the Son, our King,
Praise to God the Spirit be
Ever and eternally.

Ambrose of Milan (340–397)

Translated into German by Martin Luther (1483–1546)
Translated into English by William M. Reynolds (1812–1876)

In the late 300s there was a fierce cultural struggle going on. Though the government of the Roman Empire was officially Christian, pagan ways were still strong. Far too many citizens were nominally Christian—for social or political advancement. Ambrose, as bishop of Milan, strengthened the church in many ways, taking strong theological stands, standing up to emperors, and introducing many hymns for his congregation to sing.

It is interesting that an early translation of this Ambrose hymn was made by Martin Luther, another leader who strengthened the church through singing. When we consider the "Savior of the nations," who reigns eternally, we certainly have a lot to sing about.

• • • •

In the beginning the Word already existed. The Word was with God, and the Word was God. He existed in the beginning with God. God created everything through him, and nothing was created except through him.

JOHN 1:1-3

Who Is This So Weak and Helpless?

Christianity is a faith of great irony. We honor our great Creator, Lord of heaven and earth, great Judge of all. But when He appears on earth, He is a baby in a borrowed bed, born among cattle. He grows up as a working man and wanders as a homeless preacher. He dies a criminal's death, abandoned by His closest followers. William Walsham How's hymn brilliantly displays this irony. The first four lines of each stanza ask for the identity of this poor, mistreated person. The final four lines always answer in the most glorious terms.

Even Christians get caught up in the world's idea of greatness. We often seek the glamour of a glory-filled life. But that was not our Lord's pattern, as How reminds us. Bishop How himself practiced what he preached: he was known for his ministry to the poor in some of England's worst communities.

• • • •

He came into the very world he created, but the world didn't recognize him. He came to his own people, and even they rejected him. But to all who believed him and accepted him, he gave the right to become children of God. They are reborn—not with a physical birth resulting from human passion or plan, but a birth that comes from God. So the Word became human and made his home among us. He was full of unfailing love and faithfulness. And we have seen his glory, the glory of the Father's one and only Son.

JOHN 1:10-14

Who is this so weak and helpless,
Child of lowly Hebrew maid,
Rudely in a stable sheltered,
Coldly in a manger laid?
'Tis the Lord of all creation,
Who this wondrous path hath trod;
He is God from everlasting,
And to everlasting God.

Who is this, a Man of Sorrows,
Walking sadly life's hard way,
Homeless, weary, sighing, weeping
Over sin and Satan's sway?
'Tis our God, our glorious Savior,
Who above the starry sky
Now for us a place prepareth,
Where no tear can dim the eye.

Who is this? Behold Him shedding
Drops of blood upon the ground!
Who is this, despised, rejected,
Mocked, insulted, beaten, bound?
'Tis our God, who gifts and graces
On His Church now poureth down;
Who shall smite in holy vengeance
All His foes beneath His throne.

Who is this that hangeth dying
While the rude world scoffs and scorns,
Numbered with the malefactors,
Torn with nails, and crowned with thorns?
'Tis the God who ever liveth
'Mid the shining ones on high,
In the glorious golden city,
Reigning everlastingly.

William Walsham How (1823–1897)

Songs of Thankfulness and Praise

Songs of thankfulness and praise,
Jesus, Lord, to Thee we raise,
Manifested by the star
To the sages from afar;
Branch of royal David's stem
In Thy birth at Bethlehem;
Anthems be to Thee addressed,
God in man made manifest.

Manifest at Jordan's stream,
Prophet, Priest, and King supreme;
And at Cana, wedding guest,
In Thy Godhead manifest;
Manifest in power divine,
Changing water into wine;
Anthems be to Thee addressed,
God in man made manifest.

Manifest in making whole
Palsied limbs and fainting soul;
Manifest in valiant fight,
Quelling all the devil's might;
Manifest in gracious will,
Ever bringing good from ill;
Anthems be to Thee addressed,
God in man made manifest.

Christopher Wordsworth (1807–1885)

Christopher Wordsworth took after his father, a scholar, and his uncle, the famous poet William Wordsworth. Christopher became a school headmaster, church vicar, and eventually a bishop in the Church of England. As a Greek scholar, he wrote a commentary on the Bible. But his uncle's poetic spark was in him, too, and he wrote more than a hundred hymns for church use.

Wordsworth tried to combine teaching and poetry in his hymns. He wanted his hymns to teach about Jesus and to call those who sang them to praise Him. This hymn, for instance, succinctly surveys Christ's early ministry, from birth to baptism, from first miracle to temptation. But as it teaches about the person of Christ, it also calls us to praise Him.

The key word in this hymn is *manifest*. God made Himself manifest—He revealed Himself—in Jesus. For this He deserves our constant praise.

• • • •

Without question, this is the great mystery of our faith: Christ was revealed in a human body and vindicated by the Spirit. He was seen by angels and announced to the nations. He was believed in throughout the world and taken to heaven in glory.

I TIMOTHY 3:16

O Perfect Love

Dorothy Blomfield's sister was getting married. One evening the whole family was gathered around singing hymns. After one hymn, the sister said that she'd love to have that tune sung at her wedding, if only it had appropriate words. Then she turned to Dorothy and said, "What's the use of having a sister who composes poetry if she cannot write me new words to this tune?"

Dorothy took up the challenge. The writing "was no effort whatever," she said later, "after the initial idea had come to me of the two-fold aspect of perfect union—love and life—and I have always felt that God helped me write it."

Ironically, the tune that prompted the writing of this hymn is not the music used for it today. The modern tune was composed fifteen years later in 1898 by Joseph Barnby for the marriage of Queen Victoria's granddaughter.

O perfect Love, all human thought transcending,
Lowly we kneel in prayer before Thy throne,
That theirs may be the love which knows no ending,
Whom Thou forevermore dost join in one.

O perfect Life, be Thou their full assurance
Of tender charity and steadfast faith,
Of patient hope and quiet, brave endurance,
With childlike trust that fears no pain nor death.

Grant them the joy which brightens earthly sorrow;
Grant them the peace which calms all earthly strife,
And to life's day the glorious unknown morrow
That dawns upon eternal love and life.

Dorothy Frances Blomfield Gurney (1858–1932)

• • • •

May you have the power to understand, as all God's people should, how wide, how long, how high, and how deep his love is. May you experience the love of Christ, though it is too great to understand fully.

EPHESIANS 3:18-19

Jesus, Thou Joy of Loving Hearts

Jesus, Thou joy of loving hearts!
Thou fount of life! Thou light of men!
From the best bliss that earth imparts,
We turn unfilled to Thee again.

Thy truth unchanged hath ever stood;
Thou savest those that on Thee call;
To them that seek Thee, Thou art good;
To them that find Thee, all-in-all.

We taste Thee, O Thou living bread,
And long to feast upon Thee still;
We drink of Thee, the fountainhead,
And thirst our souls from Thee to fill!

Our restless spirits yearn for Thee
Where'er our changeful lot is cast,
Glad, when Thy gracious smile we see,
Blest, when our faith can hold Thee fast.

O Jesus, ever with us stay;
Make all our moments calm and bright;
Chase the dark night of sin away;
Shed o'er the world Thy holy light!

Attributed to Bernard of Clairvaux (1091–1153)

Translated by Ray Palmer (1808–1887)

Bernard of Clairvaux knew what he was talking about. A nobleman by birth, he gave up his life of luxury to follow Christ. So when he writes about being "unfilled" by "the best bliss that earth imparts," he knows.

The monastic life was often one of withdrawal. Monks had their own communities, which were largely self-sufficient. Thus they could work and pray in relative solitude. But Bernard broke out of that system and became an unusually public figure for a monk. He challenged popes and political leaders to live righteously. He urged professors to teach truth. He launched evangelistic campaigns.

We can learn much from Bernard's example. We do need time for "calm and bright" moments alone with Christ. But we also need to let Him send us forth in service.

• • • •

Everything else is worthless when compared with the infinite value of knowing Christ Jesus my Lord. For his sake I have discarded everything else, counting it all as garbage, so that I could gain Christ.
PHILIPPIANS 3:8

O Lord of Heaven and Earth and Sea

This was originally an offertory hymn. Two extra stanzas, which are now usually omitted, made it very clear that since God has given us so much, putting some money in the offering plate is the least we can do. Without that specific emphasis, however, this becomes an excellent Thanksgiving hymn.

It begins by acknowledging God's gifts in creation. He has given us a beautiful world to enjoy and beautiful vegetation for nourishment and pleasure. God also gives us peace and health, which we enjoy and praise Him for. But in the fourth stanza, Wordsworth remembers God's greatest gift of all, Jesus Christ, who brought us redemption and forgiveness. And when it comes down to it, we derive "all" from Him—even our ability to give back to Him.

• • • •

Give thanks to the Lord, for he is good! His faithful love endures forever. Has the Lord redeemed you? Then speak out! Tell others he has redeemed you from your enemies. For he has gathered the exiles from many lands, from east and west, from north and south.

PSALM 107:1-3

O Lord of heaven and earth and sea,
To Thee all praise and glory be!
How shall we show our love to Thee,
Who givest all?

The golden sunshine, vernal air,
Sweet flowers, and fruit Thy love declare;
When harvests ripen, Thou art there,
Who givest all.

For peaceful homes and healthful days,
For all the blessings earth displays,
We owe Thee thankfulness and praise,
Who givest all.

For souls redeemed, for sins forgiven,
For means of grace and hopes of heaven:
What can to Thee, O Lord, be given,
Who givest all?

To Thee, from whom we all derive
Our life, our gifts, our power to give:
O may we ever with Thee live,
Who givest all!

Christopher Wordsworth (1807-1885)

Hark! A Thrilling Voice Is Sounding

Hark! a thrilling voice is sounding.
"Christ is nigh," it seems to say;
"Cast away the works of darkness,
O ye children of the day."

Wakened by the solemn warning,
From earth's bondage let us rise;
Christ, our sun, all sloth dispelling,
Shines upon the morning skies.

Lo! the Lamb, so long expected,
Comes with pardon down from heaven;
Let us haste, with tears of sorrow,
One and all to be forgiven;

So when next He comes with glory,
And the world is wrapped in fear,
May He with His mercy shield us,
And with words of love draw near.

Honor, glory, might, and blessing
To the Father and the Son,
With the everlasting Spirit
While unending ages run.

Latin Hymn (sixth century)

From Hymns Ancient and Modern, 1861, altered

Like many good works of poetry, this ancient hymn is not easy to understand. It takes a little thinking to sort it out.

What is the "thrilling voice" that's sounding? If we read this in chronological order, it must be the voice of the Old Testament prophets. In many ways they announced to their people, "Christ is nigh!" and they urged them to reform their ways. The mention of Christ as "our sun" in the second stanza may allude to Malachi 4:2, the last of the messianic prophecies in the Old Testament.

The third stanza, of course, refers to Christ in His first coming as the Lamb who came to be our sacrifice. We find forgiveness as we come to Him. At His next coming, as the world shudders with fear, we will receive mercy and love. And we'll join in the eternal praise invoked by the final stanza.

• • • •

The day of the Lord's return will come unexpectedly, like a thief in the night. When people are saying, "Everything is peaceful and secure," then disaster will fall on them as suddenly as a pregnant woman's labor pains begin.

I THESSALONIANS 5:2-3

Thanks to God for My Redeemer

It is easy to thank God for roses. It is much harder to thank Him for the thorns. This hymn offers a mature approach to thanksgiving, showing appreciation for pain and pleasure, joy and sorrow.

August Storm wrote this hymn in 1891 while still a young man of twenty-nine. He worked for the Salvation Army in Sweden and published this hymn in the organization's periodical, *The War Cry.*

Just eight years after writing this hymn, Storm was stricken with a back problem that left him crippled for the rest of his life. He managed to continue his Salvation Army work, and he maintained a thankful spirit even during this most difficult time. If anything, his troubles gave more power and credibility to his sermons and writings.

• • • •

Give thanks to the Lord and proclaim his greatness. Let the whole world know what he has done. Sing to him; yes, sing his praises. Tell everyone about his wonderful deeds. Exult in his holy name; rejoice, you who worship the Lord. Search for the Lord and for his strength; continually seek him.

PSALM 105:1-4

Thanks to God for my Redeemer,
Thanks for all Thou dost provide!
Thanks for times now but a memory,
Thanks for Jesus by my side!
Thanks for pleasant, balmy springtime,
Thanks for dark and dreary fall!
Thanks for tears by now forgotten,
Thanks for peace within my soul!

Thanks for prayers that Thou hast answered,
Thanks for what Thou dost deny!
Thanks for storms that I have weathered,
Thanks for all Thou dost supply!
Thanks for pain and thanks for pleasure,
Thanks for comfort in despair!
Thanks for grace that none can measure,
Thanks for love beyond compare!

Thanks for roses by the wayside,
Thanks for thorns their stems contain!
Thanks for home and thanks for fireside,
Thanks for hope, that sweet refrain!
Thanks for joy and thanks for sorrow,
Thanks for heav'nly peace with Thee!
Thanks for hope in the tomorrow,
Thanks through all eternity!

August Ludwig Storm (1862-1914)

Translated by Carl E. Backstrom (1901-?)

We Plow the Fields

We plow the fields and scatter
The good seed on the land,
But it is fed and watered
By God's almighty hand.
He sends the snow in winter,
The warmth to swell the grain,
The breezes and the sunshine,
And soft, refreshing rain.

All good gifts around us
Are sent from heaven above;
Then thank the Lord,
O thank the Lord for all His love.

He only is the Maker
Of all things near and far;
He paints the wayside flower,
He lights the evening star.
The winds and waves obey Him,
By Him the birds are fed;
Much more, to us His children,
He gives our daily bread.

We thank Thee then, O Father,
For all things bright and good:
The seedtime and the harvest,
Our life, our health, our food.
Accept the gifts we offer
For all Thy love imparts,
And, what Thou most desirest,
Our humble thankful hearts.

Matthias Claudius (1740-1815)

Translated by Jane M. Campbell (1817-1878)

Matthias Claudius had no intention of writing a hymn. A German journalist, he was merely writing a poem about a group of peasants gathering for a banquet. The poem, originally entitled "Paul Erdmann's Fest," in seventeen stanzas depicts friends coming over to Paul Erdmann's house and enjoying themselves. It praises both Paul Erdmann for his hospitality and God as the ultimate source of the feast.

It was Jane Campbell, a British music teacher, who made the free translation of this poem into its present English form. She contributed it to a new hymnal in 1861, along with some other translations from German. It has become a favorite harvest hymn in modern churches.

• • • •

Whatever is good and perfect comes down to us from God our Father, who created all the lights in the heavens. He never changes or casts a shifting shadow. He chose to give birth to us by giving us his true word. And we, out of all creation, became his prized possession.

JAMES 1:17-18

Sing to the Lord of the Harvest

For an Anglican minister, John Monsell had a stirring speaking style. Most Anglican preachers of his day read from carefully prepared texts—and put their churches to sleep. But Monsell preached without notes and kept his people on the edge of their seats.

Like Monsell's preaching, this hymn might have been considered too informal, almost irreverent. What is this about seasons "rolling" and "happy love"? And do we really want to think about the hills "leaping up in gladness" while "the valleys laugh and sing"? But Monsell didn't care what the critics thought. He knew that the church's singing needed to be "more fervent and joyous." If God is as great as we claim He is, Monsell said, we should show it by the way we sing.

• • • •

When he saw the crowds, he had compassion on them because they were confused and helpless, like sheep without a shepherd. He said to his disciples, "The harvest is great, but the workers are few. So pray to the Lord who is in charge of the harvest; ask him to send more workers into his fields."

MATTHEW 9:36-38

Sing to the Lord of the harvest,
Sing songs of love and praise;
With joyful heart and voices
Your hallelujahs raise;
By Him the rolling seasons
In fruitful order move;
Sing to the Lord of the harvest
A song of happy love.

By Him the clouds drop fatness,
The deserts bloom and spring,
The hills leap up in gladness,
The valleys laugh and sing;
He filleth with His fullness
All things with large increase;
He crowns the year with goodness,
With plenty and with peace.

Heap on His sacred altar
The gifts His goodness gave,
The golden sheaves of harvest,
The souls He died to save;
Your hearts lay down before Him
When at His feet ye fall,
And with your lives adore Him
Who gave His life for all.

John Samuel Bewley Monsell (1811–1875)

Come, Ye Thankful People, Come

Come, ye thankful people, come,
Raise the song of harvest home;
All is safely gathered in,
Ere the winter storms begin;
God, our Maker, doth provide
For our wants to be supplied;
Come to God's own temple, come,
Raise the song of harvest home.

All the world is God's own field,
Fruit unto His praise to yield;
Wheat and tares together sown,
Unto joy or sorrow grown;
First the blade, and then the ear,
Then the full corn shall appear;
Lord of harvest, grant that we
Wholesome grain and pure may be.

For the Lord our God shall come,
And shall take His harvest home;
From His field shall in that day
All offenses purge away,
Give His angels charge at last
In the fire the tares to cast,
But the fruitful ears to store
In His garner evermore.

Even so, Lord, quickly come,
Bring Thy final harvest home;
Gather Thou Thy people in,
Free from sorrow, free from sin,
There, forever purified,
In Thy presence to abide;
Come, with all Thine angels, come,
Raise the glorious harvest home.

Henry Alford (1810–1871)

Many Christians are in the habit of giving thanks before meals. It is said that Henry Alford also gave thanks *after* meals, standing and offering his gratitude to God for the blessings just received. He also did this at the end of the day. Indeed, Alford was one of the "thankful people."

But this song isn't just about thanksgiving. It is also about work completed, a job well done. It is about aching muscles and full barns, sun-reddened faces and meals of plenty. It was written to be used at harvest festivals in villages throughout England. Each village observed a celebration whenever it brought in its harvest, and Alford, one of the leading churchmen in England in the nineteenth century, provided this hymn of thanks. It was originally called "After Harvest."

• • • •

Sing out your thanks to the Lord; sing praises to our God with a harp. He covers the heavens with clouds, provides rain for the earth, and makes the grass grow in mountain pastures. He gives food to the wild animals and feeds the young ravens when they cry.

PSALM 147:7-9

Now Thank We All Our God

With the exception of "A Mighty Fortress Is Our God" (October 31), this is the most widely sung hymn in Germany. Like so many other great hymns, it was forged in the crucible of the Thirty Years' War. Martin Rinkart was the only pastor in the walled city of Eilenberg. Many refugees fled there, hoping the walls would protect them, only to see the city overrun by Swedes, Austrians, and Swedes again. In the crowded conditions, hunger and plague were chronic problems. In 1637 Rinkart conducted funerals for five thousand residents—including his wife. So when he prays, "Guide us when perplexed," he is not talking about minor inconveniences.

Yet thanksgiving erupts from this stately song. The tune, by Johann Cruger, was introduced with the text in 1644 while the war still raged. It has a majesty and a resolve that few other works can match.

• • • •

Thank the Lord! Praise his name! Tell the nations what he has done. Let them know how mighty he is! Sing to the Lord, for he has done wonderful things. Make known his praise around the world. Let all the people of Jerusalem shout his praise with joy!

ISAIAH 12:4-6

Now thank we all our God
With heart and hands and voices,
Who wondrous things hath done,
In whom His world rejoices;
Who, from our mothers' arms,
Hath blessed us on our way
With countless gifts of love,
And still is ours today.

O may this bounteous God
Through all our life be near us,
With ever joyful hearts
And blessed peace to cheer us;
And keep us in His grace,
And guide us when perplexed,
And free us from all ills
In this world and the next.

All praise and thanks to God
The Father now be given,
The Son, and Him who reigns
With them in highest heaven,
The one eternal God,
Whom earth and heaven adore;
For thus it was, is now,
And shall be evermore. Amen.

Martin Rinkart (1586-1649)

Translated by Catherine Winkworth (1827-1878)

Immanuel, to Thee We Sing

Immanuel, to Thee we sing,
Thou Prince of life, almighty King;
That Thou, expected ages past,
Didst come to visit us at last.

For Thee, since first the world was made,
Men's hearts have waited, watched and prayed;
Prophets and patriarchs, year by year,
Have longed to see Thy light appear.

All glory, worship, thanks and praise,
That Thou art come in these our days!
Thou heavenly Guest, expected long,
We hail Thee with a joyful song.

Paul Gerhardt (1607–1676)

Translated by Ludolph Ernst Schlicht (1714–1769)

Isaiah prophesied that a virgin would bear a child and name him Immanuel. Skeptics look at the Christmas story and say, "Mary named her baby Jesus! What's all this about Immanuel? Aren't prophecies supposed to be fulfilled exactly?"

It helps to understand how names were used in Bible times and what the name *Immanuel* means. A name was not just what you were called, it was *who you were*. A name was an indication of your nature. Thus, in Acts, we find a man named Joseph taking on the name *Barnabas*, "Encourager." In this case *Immanuel* means "God with us," and that is probably the best description of Jesus that can be given. Jesus was indeed God, but "with us" in human flesh, facing our struggles.

• • • •

All of this occurred to fulfill the Lord's message through his prophet: "Look! The virgin will conceive a child! She will give birth to a son, and they will call him Immanuel, which means 'God is with us.'"
MATTHEW 1:22-23

Comfort, Comfort Ye My People

Johannes Olearius was an influential church leader, well connected in the noble courts of Germany. He compiled and wrote for the major hymnal used in Germany in his time. He also wrote devotional books and a commentary on the Bible. In many ways he was similar to the prophet Isaiah. Isaiah seems to have been associated with Judah's royal court in some way. He also wrote both poetry and prose, both words of devotion and theology. And Isaiah's world, like that of Olearius, was shattered by war.

From our perspective, we see that Isaiah's words shoot past Babylon to John the Baptist, announcing the arrival of Jesus the Messiah. It is a word of hope and comfort that again rang out in seventeenth-century Germany and still rings out today. People in darkness can see the light as they focus their faith on Jesus Christ.

• • • •

"Comfort, comfort my people," says your God. "Speak tenderly to Jerusalem. Tell her that her sad days are gone and her sins are pardoned."
ISAIAH 40:1-2

Comfort, comfort ye My people
Speak ye peace, thus saith our God;
Comfort those who sit in darkness,
Mourning 'neath their sorrow's load.
Speak ye to Jerusalem
Of the peace that waits for them;
Tell her that her sins I cover,
And her warfare now is over.

Yea, her sins our God will pardon,
Blotting out each dark misdeed;
All that well deserved His anger
He no more will see or heed.
She hath suffered many a day
Now her griefs have passed away;
God will change her pining sadness
Into ever-springing gladness.

For the herald's voice is crying
In the desert far and near,
Bidding all men to repentance,
Since the kingdom now is here.
O that warning cry obey!
Now prepare for God a way;
Let the valleys rise to meet Him,
And the hills bow down to greet Him.

Make ye straight what long was crooked,
Make the rougher places plain;
Let your hearts be true and humble,
As befits His holy reign.
For the glory of the Lord
Now o'er earth is shed abroad;
And all flesh shall see the token,
That His Word is never broken.

Johannes Olearius (1611–1684)

Translated by Catherine Winkworth (1827–1878)

Lo! How a Rose E'er Blooming

Lo, how a Rose e'er blooming
From tender stem hath sprung!
Of Jesse's lineage coming
As men of old have sung.
It came, a Flower bright,
Amid the cold of winter,
When half-spent was the night.

Isaiah 'twas foretold it,
The Rose I have in mind;
With Mary we behold it,
The virgin mother kind.
To show God's love aright
She bore to men a Savior,
When half-spent was the night.

This Flower, whose fragrance tender
With sweetness fills the air,
Dispels with glorious splendor
The darkness everywhere.
True man, yet very God,
From sin and death He saves us
And lightens every load.

German Carol (sixteenth century)

---

*Stanzas 1 and 2 translated by Theodore Baker
(1851–1934)*

Stanza 3 translated by Harriet Krauth Spaeth (1845–1925)

"I am a rose of Sharon," says Song of Songs 2:1 (NIV). Medieval interpreters assigned these words to Christ, and the rose became another epithet for our Lord. In Isaiah 11, one of the best-known messianic prophecies speaks of a shoot coming up from "the stump of Jesse" (NIV).

This beautiful hymn, which may go back even as far as the fourteenth century, takes the rose image and the branch prophecy and weaves a lovely meditation. The repeated "half-spent was the night" gives us the sense of a beautiful event going almost unnoticed. It also suggests a more theological point, that the night is still with us. This Rose sprouted and blossomed in the middle of the night, and its fragrance is already wafting through the world. But the world will not see it in all its beauty until morning, when Christ is fully revealed as Ruler of all.

• • • •

Out of the stump of David's family will grow a shoot—yes, a new Branch bearing fruit from the old root. And the Spirit of the Lord will rest on him—the Spirit of wisdom and understanding, the Spirit of counsel and might, the Spirit of knowledge and the fear of the Lord.

ISAIAH 11:1-2

The People That in Darkness Sat

The prophecy of Isaiah expounded in this hymn is quite astonishing. Isaiah was writing in the southern kingdom of Judah when it was being threatened by the northern kingdom of Israel. God was promising Judah that He would remove the threat and that He would punish the northern kingdom by bringing the mighty Assyrians to defeat them.

But even in this harsh judgment there was hope. Isaiah 9 opens with a promise to honor the region of Galilee—which was in the northern kingdom! Isaiah's readers in the south might have expected great promises to Jerusalem and Judah, but Galilee? Yet these are "the people walking in darkness"—northerners who would see the light of Christ.

Jesus fulfilled this prophecy, conducting most of His public ministry around the Sea of Galilee. He was the Child born to recover David's kingdom, not physically but spiritually.

• • • •

For a child is born to us, a son is given to us. The government will rest on his shoulders. And he will be called: Wonderful Counselor, Mighty God, Everlasting Father, Prince of Peace. His government and its peace will never end.

ISAIAH 9:6-7

The people that in darkness sat
A glorious light have seen;
The light has shined on them who long
In shades of death have been.

For unto us a child is born,
To us a son is given,
And on His shoulder ever rests
All power on earth and heaven.

His name shall be the Prince of Peace
Forevermore adored,
The Wonderful, the Counselor,
The great and mighty Lord.

His righteous government and power
Shall over all extend;
On judgment and on justice based,
His reign shall have no end.

John Morison (1750-1798)

Scottish Paraphrases, 1781

Lift Up Your Heads, Ye Mighty Gates

Lift up your heads, ye mighty gates:
Behold, the King of glory waits!
The King of kings is drawing near,
The Savior of the world is here.

O blest the land, the city blest,
Where Christ the ruler is confessed!
O happy hearts and happy homes
To whom this King of triumph comes!

Fling wide the portals of your heart:
Make it a temple, set apart
From earthly use for heav'n's employ,
Adorned with prayer and love and joy.

Redeemer, come! I open wide
My heart to Thee: here, Lord, abide!
Let me Thy inner presence feel:
Thy grace and love in us reveal.

So come, my Sov'reign, enter in!
Let new and nobler life begin!
Thy Holy Spirit guide us on,
Until the glorious crown be won.

Georg Weissel (1590-1635)

———————————————

Translated by Catherine Winkworth (1827-1878)

The words King David used in Psalm 24 to celebrate the arrival of God's presence in Jerusalem inspired this beautiful Christmas hymn. Georg Weissel recognized that Jesus' birth in Bethlehem was the ultimate fulfillment of the ancient psalmist's praise. On that first Christmas, God came to be with us in a new way. He was Immanuel—"God with us."

Weissel was a German scholar, teacher, and pastor who died at the height of the Thirty Years' War—a period of unspeakable horror in Germany. Due to the war, repeated plagues, and other disasters, the population of sixteen million dwindled to only six million in thirty short years. Despite the horrors that surrounded him, Weissel found a reason for rejoicing because of God's arrival in our world in the person of Jesus Christ. •

• • • •

Open up, ancient gates! Open up, ancient doors, and let the King of glory enter. Who is the King of glory? The Lord, strong and mighty; the Lord, invincible in battle.
PSALM 24:7-8

Watchman, Tell Us of the Night

This is an unusual hymn from an unusual man. John Bowring was a brilliant linguist, scholar, and politician. In later life he became an extremely unpopular British governor of Hong Kong. Here he displays his flair for poetry.

The hymn is unusual in that it shows more than it tells. Most hymns tell things about the nature of God or about personal experience or about how to live. Bowring himself did that sort of thing in his hymn "In the Cross of Christ I Glory" (March 26). This hymn, in contrast, offers a single image and builds it for dramatic effect.

Bowring borrows the watchman from an obscure reference in Isaiah. The watchman, perhaps representing the longing soul, perhaps the watchful wise men, or perhaps the prophet himself, watches for the coming of the day as heralded by the morning star.

• • • •

"Watchman, how much longer until morning? When will the night be over?" The watchman replies, "Morning is coming, but night will soon return. If you wish to ask again, then come back and ask."

ISAIAH 21:11-12

Watchman, tell us of the night,
What its signs of promise are.
Traveler, o'er yon mountain's height
See that glory-beaming star!
Watchman, doth its beauteous ray
Aught of joy or hope foretell?
Traveler, yes; it brings the day,
Promised day of Israel.

Watchman, tell us of the night;
Higher yet that star ascends.
Traveler, blessedness and light,
Peace and truth, its course portends.
Watchman, will its beams alone
Gild the spot that gave them birth?
Traveler, ages are its own;
See, it bursts o'er all the earth!

Watchman, tell us of the night,
For the morning seems to dawn.
Traveler, darkness takes its flight;
Doubt and terror are withdrawn.
Watchman, let thy wandering cease;
Hide thee to thy quiet home!
Traveler, lo, the Prince of Peace,
Lo, the Son of God is come!

John Bowring (1792-1872)

Come, Thou Long-Expected Jesus

Come, Thou long-expected Jesus,
Born to set Thy people free;
From our fears and sins release us;
Let us find our rest in Thee.
Israel's strength and consolation,
Hope of all the earth Thou art;
Dear desire of every nation,
Joy of every longing heart.

Born Thy people to deliver,
Born a child and yet a King,
Born to reign in us forever,
Now Thy gracious kingdom bring.
By Thine own eternal spirit
Rule in all our hearts alone;
By Thine all sufficient merit,
Raise us to Thy glorious throne.

Charles Wesley (1707–1788)

Prolific hymnwriter Charles Wesley penned eighteen Christmas songs, but he was never happy with simply painting the picture of the manger scene. In this hymn he begins by alluding to scriptural prophecies of Christ. Moving on to personal application, he continues: Christ is not only the "desire of every nation"; He is the "joy of every longing heart."

Such personal application was a hallmark of the Wesleys' ministry. Charles and his brother John challenged the staid Anglican traditions of their time. The church of their day had great scholarship; its theology was orthodox. Christians sang hymns straight from Scripture. But the Wesleys seemed to ask, "Does this mean anything *to you*? Is the biblical story about long-ago events or about what is going on *in your life*?" They urged people to meet Christ personally and to include Him in every part of their lives.

• • • •

"Joseph, son of David," the angel said, "do not be afraid to take Mary as your wife. For the child within her was conceived by the Holy Spirit. And she will have a son, and you are to name him Jesus, for he will save his people from their sins."

MATTHEW 1:20-21

Hail to the Lord's Anointed

In April 1822 James Montgomery was speaking in Liverpool at a Methodist missionary meeting. It was a time when the English were waking up to foreign missions, and numerous meetings like this one were presenting worldwide needs and commissioning new workers. Montgomery himself was a Moravian and already a noted hymnwriter. He loved to promote missionary zeal wherever he could.

As the hymnwriter spoke, the lights suddenly went out in the building. Then there was a loud crash as the back of a seat was broken in the darkness. For a moment it seemed that mass panic might ensue. But then the chairman of the meeting called out, "There is still light within," and Montgomery resumed speaking. The crowd calmed down, listening in the darkness. Montgomery concluded his words by reciting this newly written hymn, "Hail to the Lord's Anointed."

• • • •

Give your love of justice to the king, O God, and righteousness to the king's son. Help him judge your people in the right way; let the poor always be treated fairly. May the mountains yield prosperity for all, and may the hills be fruitful.

PSALM 72:1-3

Hail to the Lord's Anointed,
Great David's greater Son!
Hail in the time appointed,
His reign on earth begun!
He comes to break oppression,
To set the captive free;
To take away transgression,
And rule in equity.

He comes with succor speedy
To those who suffer wrong;
To help the poor and needy,
And bid the weak be strong;
To give them songs for sighing,
Their darkness turn to light,
Whose souls, condemned and dying,
Are precious in His sight.

He shall come down like showers
Upon the fruitful earth;
Love, joy, and hope, like flowers,
Spring in His path to birth.
Before Him, on the mountains,
Shall peace, the herald, go,
And righteousness, in fountains,
From hill to valley flow.

To Him shall prayer unceasing
And daily vows ascend;
His kingdom still increasing,
A kingdom without end.
The tide of time shall never
His covenant remove;
His name shall stand forever;
That name to us is love.

James Montgomery (1771–1854)

O Come, O Come, Emmanuel

O come, O come, Emmanuel,
And ransom captive Israel,
That mourns in lonely exile here
Until the Son of God appear.

Rejoice! Rejoice! Emmanuel
Shall come to thee, O Israel!

O come, Thou Wisdom from on high,
And order all things, far and nigh;
To us the path of knowledge show,
And cause us in her ways to go.

O come, Desire of nations, bind
All peoples in one heart and mind;
Bid envy, strife, and quarrels cease;
Fill the whole world with heaven's peace.

O come, Thou Dayspring, come and cheer
Our spirits by Thine advent here;
Disperse the gloomy clouds of night,
And death's dark shadows put to flight.

Latin Hymn (twelfth century)

---

*Stanzas 1 and 4 translated by John Mason Neale
(1818–1866)*

*Stanzas 2 and 3 translated by Henry S. Coffin
(1877–1954)*

This hymn is ancient, not only in its text, but also in its music. While the tune used today was not really finalized until the 1800s, it is based on plainsong, which was used in the church during medieval times. The lack of strict rhythmic measures gives the tune a free-flowing style. You can almost imagine the simple intervals echoing through a stone cathedral.

The text developed without the chorus as a series of liturgical phrases used during Advent. Each stanza concentrates on a different biblical name for Christ, making this hymn a rich source for Christian meditation. Jesus is Emmanuel—"God with us"; Wisdom from on high; Desire of nations; Lord of might; Rod of Jesse; Dayspring; and Key of David. As we approach Christmas, let us take some time to think about the nature of the Christ whose coming we celebrate.

• • • •

[Zechariah prophesied,] "And you, my little son, will be called the prophet of the Most High, because you will prepare the way for the Lord. You will tell his people how to find salvation through forgiveness of their sins. Because of God's tender mercy, the morning light from heaven is about to break upon us."
LUKE 1:76–78

Good Christian Men, Rejoice

As with "O Come, O Come, Emmanuel," both text and music for this hymn go back many centuries. In 1601, Bartholomaeus Gesius adapted the previously existing music and called it *In Dulci Jubilo*, which means "With Sweet Shouting." Later Bach arranged it for the organ, and later still John Stainer did a choral version. The words come from Latin, but very early on the Germans were already translating it and adding thoughts. Many other language groups have freely adapted this song for their own use. Though the great translator John Neale standardized the hymn in English, it is truly a folk song with many different forms and traditions.

It is reported that in Bethlehem, Pennsylvania, in 1745 a gathering of Moravian missionaries sang this song in thirteen different European and native American languages.

• • • •

When God our Savior revealed his kindness and love, he saved us, not because of the righteous things we had done, but because of his mercy. He washed away our sins, giving us a new birth and new life through the Holy Spirit.

TITUS 3:4-5

Good Christian men, rejoice,
With heart and soul and voice;
Give ye heed to what we say:
Jesus Christ is born today.
Ox and ass before Him bow,
He is in the manger now.
Christ is born today,
Christ is born today!

Good Christian men, rejoice,
With heart and soul and voice;
Now ye hear of endless bliss;
Jesus Christ was born for this!
He hath oped the heavenly door,
And man is blessed evermore.
Christ was born for this,
Christ was born for this!

Good Christian men, rejoice,
With heart and soul and voice;
Now ye need not fear the grave;
Jesus Christ was born to save!
Calls you one and calls you all,
To gain His everlasting hall,
Christ was born to save,
Christ was born to save!

Latin Hymn (fourteenth century)

Paraphrase by John Mason Neale (1818-1866)

All Praise to Thee, Eternal Lord

All praise to Thee, eternal Lord,
Clothed in a garb of flesh and blood;
Choosing a manger for Thy throne,
While worlds on worlds are Thine alone.

Once did the skies before Thee bow,
A Virgin's arms contain Thee now;
Angels, who did in Thee rejoice,
Now listen for Thine infant voice.

A little child, Thou art our guest,
That weary ones in Thee may rest;
Forlorn and lowly is Thy birth,
That we may rise to heaven from earth.

Thou comest in the darksome night,
To make us children of the light,
To make us in the realms divine,
Like Thine own angels, 'round Thee shine.

All this for us Thy love hath done,
By this to Thee our love is won,
For this we tune our cheerful lays,
And shout our thanks in ceaseless praise.

Martin Luther (1483–1546)

Translator Unknown, 1858

By the time of Martin Luther, most people saw God as shrouded in mystery. Bible study had been relegated to the monastery, theology to the memorization of Latin phrases, and hymn singing to the choir loft. Martin Luther sought to change this, translating the Bible, the catechism, and hymns into German—the language of his people. This allowed everyone to hear God's Word directly and to express praise in their own tongue.

This Christmas hymn appeared originally in Latin and has been attributed to Gregory the Great of the sixth century. Despite Luther's disagreements with the Roman church, he realized that its hymns and traditions contained much of value. Luther's translation of this Latin hymn illustrates his mission to make seeking and worshiping God an activity of the common person.

• • • •

When the right time came, God sent his Son, born of a woman, subject to the law. God sent him to buy freedom for us who were slaves to the law, so that he could adopt us as his very own children. And because we are his children, God has sent the Spirit of his Son into our hearts.

GALATIANS 4:4-6

From Heaven Above to Earth I Come

The coming of Christ at Christmas is in vain unless we allow Him to come and dwell in our hearts as well. This simple and glorious message is captured beautifully in this Christmas hymn by the great reformer Martin Luther. He wrote it for his little son Hans, to be sung at a family Christmas celebration. As God communicated with us by sending His Son that first Christmas night, Luther sought to communicate the life-transforming message of Christ to his son.

What a beautiful reminder that Christ's coming at Christmas is for everyone—old and young, rich and poor, wise and simple. It was such an amazing event: heralded by angels in the heavens, yet witnessed by animals in a pungent stable; beyond the understanding of the wise, yet presented in an event even children can grasp. God became a human being to reveal His loving and gracious character to us.

• • • •

"Don't be afraid!" [the angel] said. "I bring you good news that will bring great joy to all people. The Savior—yes, the Messiah, the Lord—has been born today in Bethlehem, the city of David!"

LUKE 2:10-11

From heaven above to earth I come
To bear good news to every home;
Glad tidings of great joy I bring,
Whereof I now will say and sing.

To you this night is born a child
Of Mary, chosen mother mild;
This little child, of lowly birth,
Shall be the joy of all the earth.

Were earth a thousand times as fair,
Beset with gold and jewels rare,
She yet were far too poor to be
A narrow cradle, Lord, to Thee.

Ah, dearest Jesus, Holy Child,
Make Thee a bed, soft undefiled,
Within my heart, that it may be
A quiet chamber kept for Thee.

"Glory to God in highest heaven,
Who unto man His Son hath given,"
While angels sing with pious mirth
A glad new year to all the earth.

Martin Luther (1483-1546)

Translated by Catherine Winkworth (1827-1878)

Thou Didst Leave Thy Throne

Thou didst leave Thy throne
and Thy kingly crown
When Thou camest to earth for me;
But in Bethlehem's home was there found no room
For Thy holy nativity.

O Come to my heart, Lord Jesus—
There is room in my heart for Thee!

Heaven's arches rang when the angels sang,
Proclaiming Thy royal decree;
But of lowly birth didst Thou come to earth,
And in great humility.

The foxes found rest, and the birds their nest
In the shade of the forest tree;
But Thy couch was the sod, O Thou Son of God,
In the deserts of Galilee.

Thou camest, O Lord, with the living Word
That should set Thy people free;
But with mocking scorn and with crown of thorn
They bore Thee to Calvary.

When the heav'ns shall ring and the angels sing
At Thy coming to victory,
Let Thy voice call me home, saying,
"Yet there is room—
There is room at My side for thee."

My heart shall rejoice, Lord Jesus,
When Thou comest and callest for me!

Emily Elizabeth Steele Elliott (1836–1879)

Emily Elliott had a special concern for those who were sick. She wrote many poems and hymn texts especially for the infirm, publishing forty-eight of them in a little book called *Under the Pillow*. She may have been influenced by her aunt, Charlotte Elliott, who wrote "Just As I Am" (June 22). Charlotte was also a prolific poet and was sickly for much of her life.

This particular hymn was written for children, to teach them about Jesus' birth. It has a simple construction—each of the first four stanzas presents a contrast with the word. *but*. The chorus is a natural response to the predicament, something that even a child could understand.

The last stanza provides a stirring conclusion. The Lord, once rejected and displaced, will soon come in victory—and we should all be waiting.

• • • •

He came into the very world he created, but the world didn't recognize him. He came to his own people, and even they rejected him.
JOHN 1:10-11

Let All Mortal Flesh Keep Silence

Is this hymn about Jesus' first coming or His second? Perhaps both. The first line seems to come from Zechariah 2:13: "Be silent before the Lord, all humanity, for he is springing into action from his holy dwelling." As the Lord comes to be with us on earth, we respond with fear and trembling. Even so, He comes with "blessing in His hand."

It is only right that angels attend Him. They are the bringers of news, and this is news indeed. They are heralds of judgment, and here He acts to judge the earth. Angels are also eternal worshipers, and we can all join them in paying homage to the King of kings.

This hymn may go back to the fifth-century Eastern church and is still used frequently in Orthodox churches.

• • • •

So the Word became human and made his home among us. He was full of unfailing love and faithfulness. And we have seen his glory, the glory of the Father's one and only Son.
JOHN 1:14

Let all mortal flesh keep silence,
And with fear and trembling stand;
Ponder nothing earthly minded,
For with blessing in His hand,
Christ our God to earth descendeth,
Our full homage to demand.

King of kings, yet born of Mary,
As of old on earth He stood,
Lord of lords, in human vesture,
In the body and the blood,
He will give to all the faithful
His own self for heavenly food.

Rank on rank the host of heaven
Spreads its vanguard on the way,
As the Light of light descendeth
From the realms of endless day,
That the powers of hell may vanish
As the darkness clears away.

At His feet the six-winged seraph,
Cherubim, with sleepless eye,
Veil their faces to the presence,
As with ceaseless voice they cry,
Alleluia, Alleluia,
Alleluia, Lord most high!

Liturgy of St. James

Translated by Gerard Moultrie (1829–1885)

In the Bleak Midwinter

In the bleak midwinter,
Frosty wind made moan,
Earth stood hard as iron,
Water like a stone;
Snow had fallen, snow on snow,
Snow on snow,
In the bleak midwinter,
Long ago.

Our God, heaven cannot hold Him,
Nor earth sustain;
Heaven and earth shall flee away
When He comes to reign;
In the bleak midwinter
A stable place sufficed
The Lord God Almighty,
Jesus Christ.

Angels and archangels
May have gathered there,
Cherubim and seraphim
Thronged the air;
But His mother only,
In her maiden bliss,
Worshiped the beloved
With a kiss.

What can I give Him,
Poor as I am?
If I were a shepherd,
I would bring a lamb;
If I were a wise man,
I would do my part;
Yet what I can I give Him:
Give my heart.

Christina G. Rosetti (1830–1894)

Christina Rosetti was the daughter of an Italian immigrant to England. She and her brother were involved in the world of art and literature. She never married, though by all accounts her beauty was quite stunning. A devout Anglican, Christina was engaged once to a Catholic who promised to convert. When he had second thoughts, however, she broke the engagement.

This poem—set to music twelve years after Rosetti's death—is disarming in its simplicity. Powerful notions are presented in the starkest of images. "Snow on snow" shows the bleakness of the earth, which stands "hard as iron." We see the angels "thronged" in the winter sky; we are then immediately transported to the stable, where Mary worships her beloved Son as any new mother would—with a kiss.

• • • •

And while they were there, the time came for her baby to be born. She gave birth to her first child, a son. She wrapped him snugly in strips of cloth and laid him in a manger, because there was no lodging available for them.
LUKE 2:6-7

Earth Has Many a Noble City

Aurelius Clemens Prudentius grew up in Spain, becoming a lawyer and judge. In 379 he was invited to Rome to become part of the emperor's staff. He was fascinated by Rome with its new Christian churches and the tombs of martyrs. Christianity had been legalized earlier that century and was now the official religion of the empire. Perhaps Rome was the "noble city" on which he began this meditation.

Despite his early enthusiasm, Prudentius soon grew weary of public life. He felt he had become too self-centered, so in 395 he forsook his worldly position and entered a monastery. There he wrote several devotional and practical works. A few fragments like this have been translated and set to music.

• • • •

Jesus was born in Bethlehem in Judea, during the reign of King Herod. About that time some wise men from eastern lands arrived in Jerusalem, asking, "Where is the newborn king of the Jews? We saw his star as it rose, and we have come to worship him."

MATTHEW 2:1-2

Earth has many a noble city;
Bethlehem, thou dost all excel;
Out of thee the Lord from heaven
Came to rule His Israel.

Fairer than the sun at morning
Was the star that told His birth,
To the world its God announcing
Seen in fleshly form on earth.

Eastern sages at His cradle
Make oblations rich and rare;
See them give, in deep devotion,
Gold and frankincense and myrrh.

Sacred gifts of mystic meaning:
Incense doth their God disclose;
Gold the King of kings proclaimeth;
Myrrh His sepulcher foreshows.

Jesus, whom the Gentiles worshiped
At Thy glad epiphany,
Unto Thee, with God the Father
And the Spirit, glory be.

Aurelius Clemens Prudentius (348-c. 413)

Translated by Edward Caswall (1814-1878)

Once in Royal David's City

Once in royal David's city
Stood a lowly cattle shed,
Where a mother laid her baby,
In a manger for His bed.
Mary was that mother mild,
Jesus Christ her little Child.

He came down to earth from heaven
Who is God and Lord of all,
And His shelter was a stable,
And His cradle was a stall.
With the poor, and mean, and lowly
Lived on earth, our Savior holy.

And through all His wondrous childhood
He would honor and obey,
Love, and watch the lowly mother
In whose gentle arms He lay.
Christian children all must be
Mild, obedient, good as He.

And our eyes at last shall see Him,
Through His own redeeming love;
For that child so dear and gentle
Is our Lord in heav'n above;
And He leads His children on
To the place where He is gone.

Not in that poor lowly stable,
With the oxen standing round,
We shall see Him, but in heaven,
Set at God's right hand on high,
When, like stars, His children crowned,
All in white shall wait around.

Cecil Frances Alexander (1818–1895)

Cecil Alexander wrote a series of hymns to teach children about the Apostles' Creed. "All Things Bright and Beautiful" (May 5) illustrated the first phrase of the Creed, about God the Father, "maker of heaven and earth." This hymn teaches about the phrase "conceived by the Holy Ghost, born of the Virgin Mary." Later, "There Is a Green Hill Far Away" (March 20) was written for "suffered under Pontius Pilate . . ." Alexander had a knack for taking major biblical themes and boiling them down into four or six easy-to-understand lines.

She also had a heart for the "poor, and mean, and lowly." She regularly visited the sick in the parish where her husband was pastor. She especially tended to the children.

• • • •

"Don't be afraid, Mary," the angel told her, "for you have found favor with God! You will conceive and give birth to a son, and you will name him Jesus. He will be very great and will be called the Son of the Most High. The Lord God will give him the throne of his ancestor David. And he will reign over Israel forever; his Kingdom will never end!" Mary asked the angel, "But how can this happen? I am a virgin." The angel replied, "The Holy Spirit will come upon you, and the power of the Most High will overshadow you. So the baby to be born will be holy, and he will be called the Son of God."
LUKE 1:30-35

The Friendly Beasts

This children's carol may go back as far as the twelfth century. It is a meditation on the animals that may have been present at Jesus' birth. What would each of them have given as a birthday gift to the Christ child?

While we don't know for sure that there were animals present at the birth of Christ, there is a biblical tradition of animals serving God. A donkey challenged Balaam to obey God, and ravens fed Elijah in the wild. A great fish swallowed Jonah whole and delivered him back to shore. The psalms speak freely of all creation joining in the praise of God, and Romans says that all things await their final redemption. The future of donkeys, cattle, sheep, and doves is somehow wrapped up with ours, and so they would have good reason to honor the Messiah's birth.

• • • •

Listen, O heavens! Pay attention, earth! This is what the Lord says: "The children I raised and cared for have rebelled against me. Even an ox knows its owner, and a donkey recognizes its master's care—but Israel doesn't know its master. My people don't recognize my care for them."

ISAIAH 1:2-3

Jesus our brother, strong and good,
Was humbly born in a stable rude;
And the friendly beasts around Him stood,
Jesus our brother, strong and good.

"I," said the donkey, shaggy and brown,
"I carried His mother up hill and down;
I carried her safely to Bethlehem town,
I," said the donkey, shaggy and brown.

"I," said the cow, all white and red,
"I gave Him my manger for His bed;
I gave Him my hay to pillow His head,
I," said the cow, all white and red.

"I," said the sheep with the curly horn,
"I gave Him my wool for His blanket warm.
He wore my coat on Christmas morn,
I," said the sheep with the curly horn.

"I," said the dove from rafters high,
"I cooed Him to sleep so He would not cry,
We cooed Him to sleep, my mate and I;
I," said the dove from rafters high.

And every beast, by some good spell,
In the stable dark was glad to tell,
Of the gift He gave Emmanuel,
The gift He gave Emmanuel.

Traditional English Carol

God Rest Ye Merry, Gentlemen

God rest ye merry, gentlemen,
. Let nothing you dismay,
For Jesus Christ our Savior
Was born upon this day,
To save us all from Satan's power
When we were gone astray.

O tidings of comfort and joy, comfort and joy;
O tidings of comfort and joy!

In Bethlehem in Jewry
This blessed babe was born,
And laid within a manger
Upon this blessed morn:
The which His mother Mary
Did nothing take in scorn.

From God our heavenly Father
A blessed angel came,
And unto certain shepherds
Brought tidings of the same,
How that in Bethlehem was born
The Son of God by name.

The shepherds at those tidings
Rejoiced much in mind,
And left their flocks afeeding
In tempest, storm, and wind,
And went to Bethlehem straightway,
The blessed babe to find.

Now to the Lord sing praises,
All you within this place,
And with true love and brotherhood
Each other now embrace;
This holy tide of Christmas
All other doth deface.

Traditional English Carol (eighteenth century)

This carol was first published in 1827, but even then it was introduced as "an ancient carol, sung in the streets of London." In fact, old London had municipal watchmen who were licensed to perform certain tasks, including the singing of Christmas carols. This was one of their songs.

In *A Christmas Carol* by Charles Dickens, Ebenezer Scrooge hears this song sung joyously in the street and tells the singer he'll hit him with a ruler unless he stops singing. Of course that was not the intended response to this carol. The point is that joy reigns on Christmas Day because of God's great gift of His Son, Jesus Christ. We can "rest merry" in the knowledge that Christ has paid our penalty for going astray and has set us free from the power of evil.

• • • •

This is how Jesus the Messiah was born. His mother, Mary, was engaged to be married to Joseph. But before the marriage took place, while she was still a virgin, she became pregnant through the power of the Holy Spirit. Joseph, her fiancé, was a good man and did not want to disgrace her publicly, so he decided to break the engagement quietly. As he considered this, an angel of the Lord appeared to him in a dream. "Joseph, son of David," the angel said, "do not be afraid to take Mary as your wife. For the child within her was conceived by the Holy Spirit."
MATTHEW 1:18-20

The First Noel

Noel is a French word that may come from the Latin *natalis*, meaning "birth," or from the Latin *novella*, meaning "new." In one sense Noel refers to the whole Christmas season; in another it refers to the good news that Jesus Christ has come. The first Noel, this song says, was sung by an angel to poor shepherds. The chorus rings out like a corner paperboy—"News! News! News! Hear all about it! King of Israel born today!"

Early folk carols such as this one often had a memorable chorus and many stanzas, each presenting some new aspect of the story. An individual or group could sing a stanza, perhaps one newly made up, and the whole crowd would join in the refrain. "The First Noel" was first published in its present form by William Sandys in 1833.

• • • •

Suddenly, an angel of the Lord appeared among them, and the radiance of the Lord's glory surrounded them. They were terrified, but the angel reassured them. "Don't be afraid!" he said. "I bring you good news that will bring great joy to all people."

LUKE 2:9-10

The first Noel, the angel did say,
Was to certain poor shepherds in fields as they lay;
In fields where they lay keeping their sheep,
On a cold winter's night that was so deep.

Noel, Noel, Noel, Noel,
Born is the King of Israel.

They looked up and saw a star
Shining in the east, beyond them far,
And to the earth it gave great light,
And so it continued both day and night.

And by the light of that same star
Three wise men came from country far;
To seek for a king was their intent,
And to follow the star wherever it went.

This star drew nigh to the northwest,
O'er Bethlehem it took its rest,
And there it did both stop and stay,
Right over the place where Jesus lay.

Then entered in those wise men three,
Full rev'rently upon their knee,
And offered there in His presence
Their gold, and myrrh, and frankincense.

Then let us all with one accord
Sing praises to our heav'nly Lord,
That hath made heav'n and earth of naught,
And with His blood mankind hath bought.

Traditional English Carol

Angels, from the Realms of Glory

Angels, from the realms of glory,
Wing your flight o'er all the earth;
Ye who sang creation's story
Now proclaim Messiah's birth:

Come and worship, come and worship,
Worship Christ, the newborn King.

Shepherds, in the field abiding,
Watching o'er your flocks by night,
God with man is now residing;
Yonder shines the infant light:

Sages, leave your contemplations;
Brighter visions beam afar;
Seek the great Desire of nations;
Ye have seen His natal star:

Saints, before the altar bending,
Watching long in hope and fear,
Suddenly the Lord, descending,
In His temple shall appear:

James Montgomery (1771–1854)

Other than Isaac Watts and Charles Wesley, probably no writer has contributed more to the development of Christian hymns than James Montgomery, a London journalist who championed the cause of the poor and downtrodden, as well as foreign missions. It is fitting that the music was composed by a blind organist, Henry Smart, the designer and builder of some of England's finest organs and one of the outstanding musicians of his day.

Montgomery published this poem in his newspaper on Christmas Eve, 1816. In it, he referred not only to the Gospel accounts of Christ's birth, but also to the messianic prophecies of the Old Testament, where the Messiah is called the desired of all nations (Haggai 2:7), who would come suddenly to His Temple (Malachi 3:1).

• • • •

"Don't be afraid!" [the angel] said. "I bring you good news that will bring great joy to all people. The Savior—yes, the Messiah, the Lord—has been born today in Bethlehem, the city of David! And you will recognize him by this sign: You will find a baby wrapped snugly in strips of cloth, lying in a manger."
LUKE 2:10-12

While Shepherds Watched Their Flocks

Along with his friend Nicholas Brady, Nahum Tate was a pioneer in church music. At the end of the seventeenth century, the Church of England still used the Psalter compiled by Sternhold and Hopkins in 1652. Tate and Brady recast the psalms in more "modern" language, publishing the *New Version* of the Psalter in 1696. Even though the old Psalter was often unpoetic and hard to sing, many resisted attempts to change it.

Eventually, though, King William III of England endorsed Tate and Brady's *New Version*, and it became the standard Psalter in both England and America. Ironically, many people later protested when translators tried to improve on Tate and Brady!

In 1700 Tate and Brady published a supplement of sixteen new hymns to go along with their psalms. This Christmas carol, a retelling of the shepherds' story, was in that collection.

• • • •

"And you will recognize him by this sign: You will find a baby wrapped snugly in strips of cloth, lying in a manger." Suddenly, the angel was joined by a vast host of others— the armies of heaven—praising God and saying, "Glory to God in highest heaven, and peace on earth to those with whom God is pleased."

LUKE 2:12-14

While shepherds watched their flocks by night,
All seated on the ground,
The angel of the Lord came down,
And glory shone around,
And glory shone around.

"Fear not!" said he; for mighty dread
Had seized their troubled mind,
"Glad tidings of great joy I bring
To you and all mankind,
To you and all mankind.

"To you, in David's town this day,
Is born of David's line,
The Savior who is Christ the Lord,
And this shall be the sign:
And this shall be the sign:

"The heav'nly Babe you there shall find
To human view displayed,
All meanly wrapped in swathing bands,
And in a manger laid;
And in a manger laid.

"All glory be to God on high,
And to the earth be peace:
Good will henceforth from heav'n to men,
Begin and never cease,
Begin and never cease."

Nahum Tate (1625–1715)

O Come, All Ye Faithful

O come, all ye faithful, joyful and triumphant,
O come ye, O come ye to Bethlehem;
Come and behold Him, born the King of angels;

O come, let us adore Him,
O come, let us adore Him,
O come, let us adore Him,
Christ, the Lord!

Sing, choirs of angels, sing in exultation,
O sing, all ye citizens of heaven above!
Glory to God, all glory in the highest;

Yea, Lord, we greet Thee, born this happy morning,
Jesus, to Thee be all glory given;
Word of the Father, now in flesh appearing;

Latin Hymn (eighteenth century)

Attributed to John Francis Wade (1711–1786)
Translated by Frederick Oakeley (1802–1880) and others

John Francis Wade made his living copying manuscripts by hand. Wade became famous for his artistic calligraphy, and he had a knack for copying music as well. Scholars have debated whether Wade merely copied this Christmas hymn, or whether he actually wrote it. But recent scholarship indicates that he did, in fact, write the hymn.

It was originally written in Latin as "Adeste Fidelis." Wade was a Roman Catholic, and all services in the church were conducted in Latin. In 1750 he slipped this hymn into a manuscript he was copying for the English Roman Catholic College in Lisbon, Portugal. Over thirty years later, in 1785, it was sent to the Portuguese chapel in London. The Duke of Leeds heard it sung there and included it in the repertoire of his own singing group. It soon became known around the world.

• • • •

When the angels had returned to heaven, the shepherds said to each other, "Let's go to Bethlehem! Let's see this thing that has happened, which the Lord has told us about." They hurried to the village and found Mary and Joseph. And there was the baby, lying in the manger.
LUKE 2:15-16

It Came upon the Midnight Clear

Edmund Sears was a Unitarian minister. Unlike many of his colleagues, he did believe in the deity of Christ. He also believed in the angels' message of "peace on earth."

This hymn, written in Massachusetts in 1849, focuses on the angels' song of "peace on earth." Like many other hymns written in America during the mid-1800s, it might be called a "horizontal hymn." Such hymns called people to live well, to be at peace, and to honor God, but God was neither the recipient of praise nor the central focus of the song. The focus was on the human struggle in this world.

Peace was a timely topic when Sears penned these words. Tensions were rising in America, leading toward the Civil War. But the peace promised by the angel is not only national; it is personal as well. Sears's third stanza encourages the weary traveler to draw hope from the angels' song.

• • • •

For a child is born to us, a son is given to us. The government will rest on his shoulders. And he will be called: Wonderful Counselor, Mighty God, Everlasting Father, Prince of Peace.

ISAIAH 9:6

It came upon the midnight clear,
That glorious song of old,
From angels bending near the earth
To touch their harps of gold:
"Peace on the earth, goodwill to men,
From heav'n's all-gracious King!"
The world in solemn stillness lay
To hear the angels sing.

Still through the cloven skies they come
With peaceful wings unfurled,
And still their heav'nly music floats
O'er all the weary world:
Above its sad and lowly plains
They bend on hov'ring wing,
And ever o'er its Babel sounds
The blessed angels sing.

And ye, beneath life's crushing load,
Whose forms are bending low,
Who toil along the climbing way
With painful steps and slow,
Look now! for glad and golden hours
Come swiftly on the wing:
O rest beside the weary road
And hear the angels sing.

For lo, the days are hast'ning on,
By prophets seen of old,
When with the ever-circling years
Shall come the time foretold,
When the new heav'n and earth shall own
The Prince of Peace their King,
And the whole world send back the song
Which now the angels sing.

Edmund Hamilton Sears (1810–1876)

Angels We Have Heard on High

Angels we have heard on high
Sweetly singing o'er the plains,
And the mountains in reply
Echoing their joyous strains.

**Gloria in excelsis Deo,
Gloria in excelsis Deo.**

Shepherds, why this jubilee?
Why your joyous strains prolong?
What the gladsome tidings be
Which inspire your heavenly song?

Come to Bethlehem and see
Him whose birth the angels sing;
Come, adore on bended knee
Christ the Lord, the newborn King.

See Him in a manger laid,
Whom the choirs of angels praise;
Mary, Joseph, lend your aid,
While our hearts in love we raise.

James Chadwick (1813-1882)

This traditional French carol tells the shepherds' story as recorded in the Gospel of Luke. It tells about the angelic chorus, the trip to Bethlehem, the meeting with Mary and Joseph, and the adoration of the baby Jesus.

Luke 2:17-20 tells of the reaction of the shepherds after they had been to Bethlehem's manger. They spread the word, and all who heard were amazed at what the shepherds said. Then the shepherds "returned, glorifying and praising God for all the things they had heard and seen" (NIV).

Sometimes our Christmas season ends with the viewing of the manger scene. We never get to the glorifying and praising, joining the angel chorus in the fullness of *Gloria in excelsis Deo*—"Glory to God in the highest." Make Christmas complete this year by following the shepherds' example, giving the highest glory to our Redeemer God.

• • • •

The shepherds went back to their flocks, glorifying and praising God for all they had heard and seen. It was just as the angel had told them.

LUKE 2:20

O Little Town of Bethlehem

Phillips Brooks was a giant of a man and a prince of a preacher. When his six-foot-six frame filled the pulpit, the people of his churches learned and responded. He served Episcopal congregations in Philadelphia and Massachusetts.

In 1865 Brooks went to the Holy Land and was especially impressed by a Christmas Eve service at Bethlehem's Church of the Nativity. Three years later he wanted to write a Christmas song for the children's service at his church in Philadelphia. For inspiration, he thought back to his experience in Bethlehem.

It is said that after Brooks died, one five-year-old girl of the church was upset because she hadn't seen him recently. Her mother told her gently that Bishop Brooks had gone to heaven. The girl's face brightened as she said, "Oh, Mama, how happy the angels will be!"

• • • •

But you, O Bethlehem Ephrathah, are only a small village among all the people of Judah. Yet a ruler of Israel will come from you, one whose origins are from the distant past.

MICAH 5:2

O little town of Bethlehem,
How still we see thee lie!
Above thy deep and dreamless sleep
The silent stars go by.
Yet in thy dark streets shineth
The everlasting light;
The hopes and fears of all the years
Are met in thee tonight.

For Christ is born of Mary,
And gathered all above,
While mortals sleep, the angels keep
Their watch of wond'ring love.
O morning stars, together
Proclaim the holy birth!
And praises sing to God the King,
And peace to men on earth.

How silently, how silently
The wondrous gift is giv'n!
So God imparts to human hearts
The blessings of His heav'n.
No ear may hear His coming,
But in this world of sin,
Where meek souls will receive Him still
The dear Christ enters in.

O holy Child of Bethlehem!
Descend to us, we pray;
Cast out our sin, and enter in;
Be born in us today.
We hear the Christmas angels
The great glad tidings tell;
O come to us, abide with us,
Our Lord Emmanuel.

Phillips Brooks (1835–1893)

Hark! the Herald Angels Sing

Hark! the herald angels sing,
"Glory to the newborn King;
Peace on earth, and mercy mild,
God and sinners reconciled!"
Joyful, all ye nations, rise,
Join the triumph of the skies;
With th' angelic host proclaim,
"Christ is born in Bethlehem!"

**Hark! the herald angels sing,
"Glory to the newborn King!"**

Christ, by highest heaven adored;
Christ, the everlasting Lord!
Late in time behold Him come,
Offspring of the virgin's womb.
Veiled in flesh the Godhead see;
Hail th' incarnate Deity,
Pleased as man with men to dwell,
Jesus, our Emmanuel.

Hail the heaven-born Prince of Peace!
Hail the Sun of Righteousness!
Light and life to all He brings,
Risen with healing in His wings,
Mild He lays His glory by,
Born that man no more may die,
Born to raise the sons of earth,
Born to give them second birth.

Charles Wesley (1707–1788)

Altered by George Whitefield (1714–1770)

Charles Wesley wrote over six thousand hymn texts, but this may be his best. In singing this hymn we not only join the shepherds under a canopy of singing angels, we also learn about the Jesus they proclaimed. We discover who He is and what His coming means.

Wesley's carol is filled with powerful scriptural ideas; a month could be spent exploring these stanzas. But let's focus now on the last three lines. This is why Jesus came: so we would not have to face eternal death; so He could raise us with Him; so He could regenerate us into children of God. For this and so much more, He deserves our praise. "Glory to the newborn King!"

• • • •

Suddenly, an angel of the Lord appeared among them, and the radiance of the Lord's glory surrounded them. They were terrified, but the angel reassured them. "Don't be afraid!" he said. "I bring you good news that will bring great joy to all people. The Savior— yes, the Messiah, the Lord—has been born today in Bethlehem, the city of David! . . . Suddenly, the angel was joined by a vast host of others—the armies of heaven—praising God and saying, "Glory to God in highest heaven, and peace on earth to those with whom God is pleased."

LUKE 2:9-11, 13-14

What Child Is This?

The tune for this Christmas hymn was sung long before its words were written. "Greensleeves" is an English folk song that can be traced back as far as the 1500s. Shakespeare even mentioned it in one of his plays.

William Dix was an Anglican layman, born in Bristol, England. He settled in Glasgow, Scotland, where he became a successful insurance salesman. As a young man of twenty-nine, Dix was stricken by a serious illness and was confined to bed for some time. He suffered deep depression during this time, but through it all he met God in a very personal way. His spiritual experience led to the composition of this hymn and many others, including "Alleluia! Sing to Jesus" (May 7).

This lovely text was originally part of a longer Christmas poem called "The Manger Throne."

• • • •

When [the wise men] saw the star, they were filled with joy! They entered the house and saw the child with his mother, Mary, and they bowed down and worshiped him. Then they opened their treasure chests and gave him gifts of gold, frankincense, and myrrh.

MATTHEW 2:10-11

What child is this, who, laid to rest,
On Mary's lap is sleeping?
Whom angels greet with anthems sweet,
While shepherds watch are keeping?

This, this is Christ the King,
Whom shepherds guard and angels sing;
Haste, haste to bring Him laud,
The babe, the son of Mary.

Why lies He in such mean estate
Where ox and ass are feeding?
Good Christian, fear, for sinners here
The silent Word is pleading.

So bring Him incense, gold, and myrrh,
Come, peasant, king, to own Him;
The King of kings salvation brings,
Let loving hearts enthrone Him.

William Chatterton Dix (1837–1898)

Silent Night, Holy Night

Silent night, holy night,
All is calm, all is bright
Round yon virgin mother and Child.
Holy Infant so tender and mild,
Sleep in heavenly peace,
Sleep in heavenly peace.

Silent night, holy night,
Shepherds quake at the sight.
Glories stream from heaven afar,
Heavenly hosts sing alleluia;
Christ the Savior is born!
Christ the Savior is born!

Silent night, holy night,
Son of God, love's pure light
Radiant beams from Thy holy face,
With the dawn of redeeming grace,
Jesus, Lord, at Thy birth,
Jesus, Lord, at Thy birth.

Joseph Mohr (1792–1848)

Translated by John Freeman Young (1820–1885)

In their village high in the Austrian Alps in 1818, a Catholic priest and his organist faced a dilemma just before Christmas when the church organ broke down. They needed a hymn that could be easily sung by the congregation, even without a booming organ to lead the way.

Joseph Mohr, the priest, took up the challenge and quickly wrote the words for "Silent Night." He handed them to Franz Grüber, the organist, who said, "You have found it—the right song—God be praised!" Then Grüber wrote a tune that could be effective with guitar accompaniment.

The hymn might have remained an obscure Alpine folk song if it weren't for the organ repairman. A few days after Christmas, he got a copy of the song and began sharing it with others. Today it is one of the most beloved of all Christmas songs.

• • • •

[The shepherds] hurried to the village and found Mary and Joseph. And there was the baby, lying in the manger. After seeing him, the shepherds told everyone what had happened and what the angel had said to them about this child. All who heard the shepherds' story were astonished.

LUKE 2:16-18

Joy to the World!

When is a Christmas carol not a Christmas carol? When it doesn't focus on the birth of Christ, perhaps?

Take this one, for instance. Isaac Watts based this text on the last half of Psalm 98, which celebrates the coming of the Lord to judge the world in righteousness. The psalmist calls on all creation to sing and shout for joy at His coming. There is nothing in the psalm or in Watts's paraphrase that specifically mentions the *birth* of Christ, just the Lord's return in judgment.

So should we stop singing this at Christmas? Not at all! This hymn celebrates God's involvement with His people—and this work of God began at the stable in Bethlehem.

• • • •

Shout to the Lord, all the earth; break out in praise and sing for joy! . . . Let the sea and everything in it shout his praise! Let the earth and all living things join in. Let the rivers clap their hands in glee! Let the hills sing out their songs of joy before the Lord. For the Lord is coming to judge the earth. He will judge the world with justice, and the nations with fairness.

PSALM 98:4, 7-9

Joy to the world! the Lord is come;
Let earth receive her King;
Let ev'ry heart prepare Him room,
And heav'n and nature sing,
And heav'n and nature sing,
And heav'n, and heav'n and nature sing.

Joy to the earth! the Savior reigns;
Let men their songs employ;
While fields and floods, rocks, hills, and plains
Repeat the sounding joy,
Repeat the sounding joy,
Repeat, repeat the sounding joy.

No more let sins and sorrows grow,
Nor thorns infest the ground;
He comes to make His blessings flow
Far as the curse is found,
Far as the curse is found,
Far as, far as the curse is found.

He rules the world with truth and grace,
And makes the nations prove
The glories of His righteousness,
And wonders of His love,
And wonders of His love,
And wonders, wonders of His love.

Isaac Watts (1674-1748)

Away in a Manger

Away in a manger, no crib for a bed,
The little Lord Jesus laid down His sweet head;
The stars in the sky looked down where He lay,
The little Lord Jesus, asleep on the hay.

The cattle are lowing, the Baby awakes,
But little Lord Jesus no crying He makes,
I love Thee, Lord Jesus, look down from the sky,
And stay by my cradle till morning is nigh.

Be near me, Lord Jesus, I ask Thee to stay
Close by me forever, and love me, I pray.
Bless all the dear children in Thy tender care,
And fit us for heaven, to live with Thee there.

Stanzas 1 and 2, Unknown

Stanza 3, John Thomas McFarland (1851–1913)

"Away in a Manger" is usually considered a children's carol, yet its beauty and power is loved equally by people of all ages. All of us can pray, "I love you, Lord Jesus! Stay close to me tonight."

For many years this hymn was attributed to Martin Luther. The song first appeared in a Lutheran hymnal in the mid-1800s. The next publisher to pick it up called it "Luther's Cradle Hymn," assuming that since it was anonymous and in a Lutheran hymnal, it must be Luther's.

But regardless of its author, the beauty of this carol is the beauty of Christmas. It is simple. Christmas is not the gold or glitter, the wrappings or trappings. It is the story of God humbling Himself to become a baby, born in crude circumstances to a young woman in ancient Palestine. Sing this carol softly. It is what Christmas is all about.

• • • •

My servant grew up in the Lord's presence like a tender green shoot, like a root in dry ground. There was nothing beautiful or majestic about his appearance, nothing to attract us to him.

ISAIAH 53:2

Who Is He in Yonder Stall?

As we trace the life of Jesus on earth in the Gospel accounts we see a baby in a stable, whisked off to Egypt to avoid danger. We see a man fasting in the desert; then he moves on after overcoming temptation. We see Him weeping at the tomb of Lazarus and then praying in Gethsemane as His friends sleep. We see Him die, rise, and ascend to heaven. In the vast sweep of history we catch only a short, though unforgettable, glimpse of Jesus. We may ask, "Who is He?"

This song answers the question in its strong refrain. Jesus is the King of glory, Lord of all. He was born, He served and taught, and He died and rose again "to heal and help and save" us.

• • • •

Now all glory to God, who is able, through his mighty power at work within us, to accomplish infinitely more than we might ask or think. Glory to him in the church and in Christ Jesus through all generations forever and ever! Amen.

EPHESIANS 3:20-21

Who is He in yonder stall,
At whose feet the shepherds fall?
Who is He in deep distress,
Fasting in the wilderness?

'Tis the Lord! O wondrous story!
'Tis the Lord! the King of glory!
At His feet we humbly fall,
Crown Him! Crown Him, Lord of all!

Who is He the people bless
For His words of gentleness?
Who is He to whom they bring
All the sick and sorrowing?

Who is He that stands and weeps
At the grave where Lazarus sleeps?
Who is He the gath'ring throng
Greet with loud triumphant song?

Lo! at midnight, who is He
Prays in dark Gethsemane?
Who is He on yonder tree
Dies in grief and agony?

Who is He that from the grave
Comes to heal and help and save?
Who is He that from His throne
Rules through all the world alone?

Benjamin Russell Hanby (1833-1867)

All Glory Be to God on High

All glory be to God on high,
Who hath our race befriended;
To us no harm shall now come nigh,
The strife at last is ended;
God showeth His good will to men,
And peace shall reign on earth again;
O thank Him for His goodness.

We praise, we worship Thee, we trust,
And give Thee thanks for ever,
O Father, that Thy rule is just
And wise, and changes never;
Thy boundless power o'er all things reigns,
Thou dost whate'er Thy will ordains:
'Tis well Thou art our Ruler!

O Jesus Christ, our God and Lord,
Begotten of the Father,
Who hast our fallen race restored
And straying sheep dost gather,
Thou Lamb of God, enthroned on high,
Behold our need, and hear our cry:
Have mercy on us, Jesus!

O Holy Spirit, precious Gift,
Thou Comforter unfailing,
Do Thou our troubled souls uplift,
Against the foe prevailing;
Since Christ for us His Blood hath shed,
Avert our woes and calm our dread;
We trust in Thee to help us!

Nikolaus Decius (1490-1541)

Translated by Catherine Winkworth (1827-1878)

It is said that the Reformers taught the church how to sing hymns. But a year before Martin Luther wrote his first hymn, one of his students, Nikolaus Decius, began writing hymns in low German for the common people to sing. Decius was not a major figure in the Lutheran movement. In fact, he fell out of favor with Martin Luther because he leaned toward the teachings of John Calvin. Yet Decius's hymns have appeared in virtually all Lutheran hymnals.

Like many hymns of praise, this one extols in turn the Father, Son, and Holy Spirit. It is a good exercise to follow the example of this great classic hymn and to be specific in our praise to each person of the Trinity. Then we, too, will sing, "All glory be to God on high!"

• • • •

I am overwhelmed with joy in the Lord my God! For he has dressed me with the clothing of salvation and draped me in a robe of righteousness. I am like a bridegroom in his wedding suit or a bride with her jewels. The Sovereign Lord will show his justice to the nations of the world. Everyone will praise him! His righteousness will be like a garden in early spring, with plants springing up everywhere.
ISAIAH 61:10-11

Go Tell It on the Mountain

Around the turn of the twentieth century every Christmas at Fisk University began with song. The Jubilee Singers, a nationally known choir based at the Nashville school, got up at five o'clock in the morning to stroll the campus singing Christmas songs. Among their favorites was this old spiritual.

The chorus had been around for generations, but John Work added the stanzas. Work had graduated from Fisk and returned to teach Latin and Greek there and to arrange music for the Jubilee Singers. Along with his brother Frederick, he was a major force in the collecting and arranging of American spirituals.

• • • •

O Zion, messenger of good news, shout
from the mountaintops! Shout it louder,
O Jerusalem. Shout, and do not be afraid.
Tell the towns of Judah, "Your God is coming!"
ISAIAH 40:9

Go tell it on the mountain,
Over the hills and ev'rywhere;
Go tell it on the mountain,
That Jesus Christ is born.

While shepherds kept their watching
O'er silent flocks by night,
Behold, throughout the heavens
There shone a holy light.

The shepherds feared and trembled
When, lo! above the earth
Rang out the angel chorus
That hailed our Savior's birth.

Down in a lowly manger
The humble Christ was born,
And brought us God's salvation
That blessed Christmas morn.

Traditional spiritual

Stanzas by John W. Work II (1872-1925)

For All the Blessings of the Year

For all the blessings of the year,
For all the friends we hold so dear,
For peace on earth, both far and near,
We thank Thee, O Lord.

For life and health, those common things,
Which every day and hour brings,
For home, where our affection clings,
We thank Thee, O Lord.

For love of Thine, which never tires,
Which all our better thought inspires,
And warms our lives with heavenly fires,
We thank Thee, O Lord.

Albert H. Hutchinson (n.d.)

Each week across the country, small groups of Christians meet together for Bible study and prayer. As they share prayer requests, one member faithfully jots down the various needs and concerns. One person might need a job; another is having financial troubles; still another is about to enter the hospital. Week after week they pray for these personal needs.

At the end of the year, if the group takes the time to go back through the year's prayer requests, they may be stunned to see how God has been working throughout the year. Not every request will have been answered the way they wanted or expected, but it will be amazing how many were. Some situations probably turned out even better than anyone had hoped.

After looking back at the events of the previous year, we need to make a point of thanking God "for all the blessings of the year."

• • • •

My heart is confident in you, O God; no wonder I can sing your praises with all my heart! Wake up, lyre and harp! I will wake the dawn with my song. I will thank you, Lord, among all the people. I will sing your praises among the nations.
PSALM 108:1-3

For Thy Mercy and Thy Grace

As we come to the end of one year and the beginning of a new one, look at what God has done in the past year. Have there been challenges He has helped you through? Joys He has brought you? Sorrows in which He has comforted you? Thank God for the year past with all its ups and downs.

Look also at the future. What does the next year hold? Try to discover what sort of excitement God might have in mind for you. Think about how you might grow in Him and serve Him in the coming year.

The Bible says that "Jesus Christ is the same yesterday, today, and forever" (Hebrews 13:8). The strength He provided for you this year can be counted on again in the next. He will "be our true and living way" in the year ahead.

• • • •

Those who trust in the Lord are as secure as Mount Zion; they will not be defeated but will endure forever. Just as the mountains surround Jerusalem, so the Lord surrounds his people, both now and forever.

PSALM 125:1-2

For Thy mercy and Thy grace,
Constant through another year,
Hear our song of thankfulness,
Father and Redeemer, hear!

Dark the future; let Thy light
Guide us, bright and morning star:
Fierce our foes and hard the fight;
Arm us, Savior, for the war.

In our weakness and distress,
Rock of strength, be Thou our stay;
In the pathless wilderness,
Be our true and living way.

Keep us faithful, keep us pure,
Keep us evermore Thine own;
Help, O help us to endure;
Fit us for the promised crown.

Henry Downton (1818–1885)

INDEX OF HYMN TITLES

INDEX OF AUTHORS, TRANSLATORS, ARRANGERS, AND SOURCES

TOPICAL INDEX
OF HYMN TITLES

ADVENT (see Christmas/Advent)

ATONEMENT FOR SIN

There Is a Green Hill Far Away . . . *March 20*
The Old Rugged Cross . . . *March 24*
Cross of Jesus, Cross of Sorrow . . . *April 6*
Alas! And Did My Savior Bleed? . . . *April 14*
Hallelujah, What a Savior! . . . *April 19*
There Is a Fountain Filled with Blood . . . *April 20*
I Will Sing of My Redeemer . . . *April 23*
Redeemed . . . *April 25*
Rock of Ages . . . *July 19*
Jesus, Thy Blood and Righteousness . . . *July 21*
To God Be the Glory . . . *October 17*
Thy Works, Not Mine, O Christ . . . *October 30*

BIBLE (see Word of God)

CHILDREN'S HYMNS

The Wise May Bring Their Learning . . . *September 7*
Now the Day Is Over . . . *September 8*
Jesus Loves Me . . . *October 10*
Shepherd of Eager Youth . . . *October 18*
The Friendly Beasts . . . *December 13*

CHRISTIAN LIVING

May the Mind of Christ, My Savior . . . *January 2*
Awake, My Soul, and with the Sun . . . *March 9*
Go to Dark Gethsemane . . . *April 1*
Come, Let Us Rise with Christ . . . *May 12*
Spirit of God, Descend upon My Heart . . . *May 17*
Come, Gracious Spirit, Heavenly Dove . . . *May 19*
Take Time to Be Holy . . . *May 31*
Be Thou My Vision . . . *June 10*
O God of Earth and Altar . . . *July 3*
When Morning Gilds the Skies . . . *July 31*
Before Thy Throne, O God, We Kneel . . . *August 4*
We Give Thee but Thine Own . . . *August 21*
O to Be like Thee! . . . *August 22*
More about Jesus . . . *August 24*
O for a Heart to Praise My God . . . *August 26*
Open My Eyes, That I May See . . . *October 25*

CHRISTMAS/ADVENT

Hark! A Thrilling Voice Is Sounding . . . *November 20*
Immanuel, to Thee We Sing . . . *November 26*
Lo! How a Rose E'er Blooming . . . *November 28*
The People That in Darkness Sat . . . *November 29*

Lift Up Your Heads, Ye Mighty Gates . . . *November 30*
Watchman, Tell Us of the Night . . . *December 1*
Come, Thou Long-Expected Jesus . . . *December 2*
O Come, O Come, Emmanuel . . . *December 4*
Good Christian Men, Rejoice . . . *December 5*
All Praise to Thee, Eternal Lord . . . *December 6*
From Heaven Above to Earth I Come . . . *December 7*
Thou Didst Leave Thy Throne . . . *December 8*
In the Bleak Midwinter . . . *December 10*
Earth Has Many a Noble City . . . *December 11*
The Friendly Beasts . . . *December 13*
God Rest Ye Merry, Gentlemen . . . *December 14*
The First Noel . . . *December 15*
Angels, from the Realms of Glory . . . *December 16*
While Shepherds Watched Their Flocks . . . *December 17*
O Come, All Ye Faithful . . . *December 18*
It Came upon the Midnight Clear . . . *December 19*
Angels We Have Heard on High . . . *December 20*
O Little Town of Bethlehem . . . *December 21*
Hark! the Herald Angels Sing . . . *December 22*
What Child Is This? . . . *December 23*
Silent Night, Holy Night . . . *December 24*
Joy to the World! . . . *December 25*
Away in a Manger . . . *December 26*
Who Is He in Yonder Stall? . . . *December 27*
Go Tell It on the Mountain . . . *December 29*

CHURCH (see also Fellowship)

Let Us Break Bread Together . . . *April 13*
Lord Jesus Christ, Be Present Now . . . *May 24*
Onward, Christian Soldiers . . . *June 6*
Blessed Jesus, at Thy Word . . . *June 15*
The Church's One Foundation . . . *August 15*
I Love Thy Kingdom, Lord . . . *August 16*
Christ Is Made the Sure Foundation . . . *August 19*
Brethren, We Have Met to Worship . . . *October 8*

COMFORT AND ENCOURAGEMENT

There Is a Balm in Gilead . . . *March 6*
Arise, My Soul, Arise . . . *July 14*
Come, Ye Disconsolate . . . *August 30*
Under His Wings I Am Safely Abiding . . . *October 19*
Comfort, Comfort Ye My People . . . *November 27*

COMMUNION

Here, O My Lord, I See Thee . . . *February 18*
According to Thy Gracious Word . . . *March 3*

373

Do-able. Daily. Devotions.

START ANY DAY THE ONE YEAR WAY.

For Women

The One Year®
Home and
Garden
Devotions

The One Year®
Devotions for
Women

The One Year®
Daily Acts of
Friendship

The One Year®
Women of the
Bible

The One Year®
Coffee with God

The One Year®
Devotional of Joy
and Laughter

The One Year®
Women's
Friendship
Devotional

The One Year®
Wisdom
for Women
Devotional

The One Year®
Daily Moments
of Peace

The One Year®
Women in
Christian History
Devotional

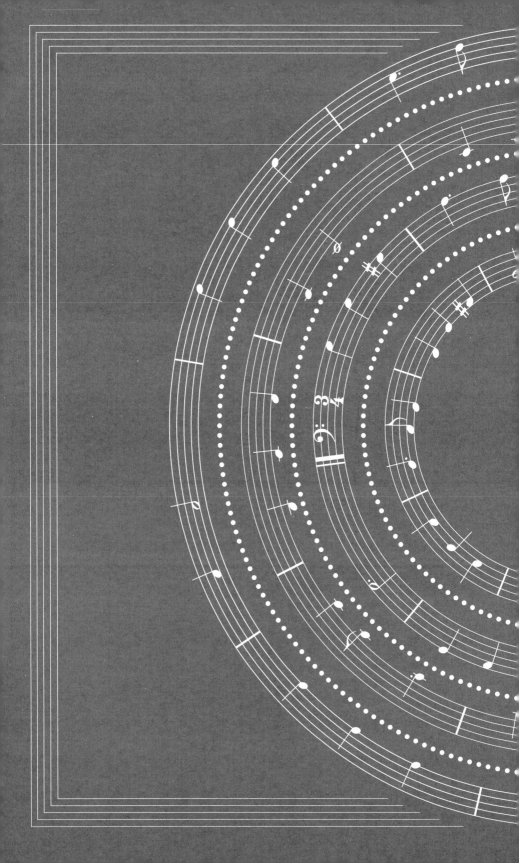